Seraph of the End
VAMPIRE REIGN

22

STORY BY **Takaya Kagami**
ART BY **Yamato Yamamoto**
STORYBOARDS BY **Daisuke Furuya**

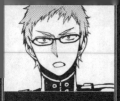

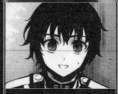

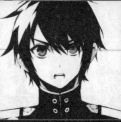

YUICHIRO HYAKUYA

A boy who escaped from the vampire capital, he has both great kindness and a great desire for revenge. Lone wolf. His Cursed Gear is Asuramaru, a katana.

YOICHI SAOTOME

Yuichiro's friend. His sister was killed by a vampire. His Cursed Gear is Gekkouin, a bow.

SHIHO KIMIZUKI

Yuichiro's friend. Smart but abrasive. His Cursed Gear is Kiseki-o, twin blades.

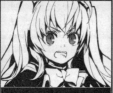

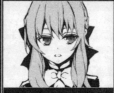

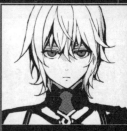

MIKAELA HYAKUYA

Yuichiro's best friend. He was supposedly killed but has come back to life as a vampire. Currently working with Shinoa Squad.

SHINOA HIRAGI

Guren's subordinate and Yuichiro's surveillance officer. Member of the illustrious Hiragi family. Her Cursed Gear is Shikama Doji, a scythe.

MITSUBA SANGU

An elite soldier who has been part of the Moon Demon Company since age 13. Bossy. Her Cursed Gear is Tenjiryu, a giant axe.

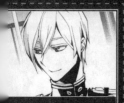

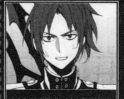

MAKOTO NARUMI

Former leader of Narumi Squad. After his entire squad died during the battle of Nagoya, he deserted the Demon Army with Shinoa Squad.

SHINYA HIRAGI

A Major General and adoptee into the Hiragi Family. He was Mahiru Hiragi's fiancé.

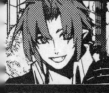

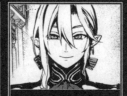

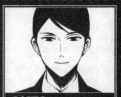

SAITO

A mysterious man somehow connected with the Hyakuya Sect. He was once a Second Progenitor vampire.

FERID BATHORY

A Seventh Progenitor vampire, he killed Mikaela.

CROWLEY EUSFORD

A Thirteenth Progenitor vampire. Part of Ferid's faction.

KRUL TEPES
Third Progenitor and Queen of the Vampires. She was held prisoner by Urd Geales, but what is her goal now?

MAHIRU HIRAGI
Shinoa's older sister. Most believe her dead, but she currently inhabits Guren's sword.

GUREN ICHINOSE
Lt. Colonel of the Moon Demon Company. He recruited Yuichiro into the Demon Army, but recently has started acting on some secret plot... His Cursed Gear is Mahiru-no-yo, a katana.

SHIKAMA DOJI
The being that inhabits Shinoa's scythe. He's actually the long-missing First Progenitor of the vampires.

ASURAMARU
The demon that possesses Yuichiro's sword. A long time ago, he was a human boy named Ashera.

NOYA
The demon sealed inside Guren's sword.

STORY

A mysterious virus decimates the human population, and vampires claim dominion over the world. Yuichiro and his adopted family of orphans are kept as vampire fodder in an underground city until the day Mikaela, Yuichiro's best friend, plots an ill-fated escape for the orphans. Only Yuichiro survives and reaches the surface.

Four years later, Yuichiro enters the Moon Demon Company, a Vampire Extermination Unit in the Japanese Imperial Demon Army, to enact his revenge. There he gains Asuramaru, a demon-possessed weapon capable of killing vampires, and a squad of trusted friends—Shinoa, Yoichi, Kimizuki and Mitsuba.

In his battles against the vampires, Yuichiro discovers that not only is Mikaela alive, but he also has been turned into a vampire. After misunderstandings and near-misses, Yuichiro and Mikaela finally rejoin each other in Nagoya.

After much chaos and confusion, the Shinoa Squad deserts the Demon Army to follow Ferid and Crowley. Navigating through both human and vampire plots, the group returns to Shibuya.

From there, it's been disaster after disaster. Shinoa is possessed by the First Progenitor. Saito's Hyakuya Sect attack the city. And Guren and Mahiru proclaim they'll betray everyone?!

Guren and Mahiru succeed in sealing The First and driving off the Hyakuya Sect, but Yu and Mika sense something is off with him. They try to run, but at the end of an intense battle Mika is chopped in half! Then Krul arrives...

Seraph of the End

—VAMPIRE REIGN—

CONTENTS

22

Chapter 90
Because of Mikaela

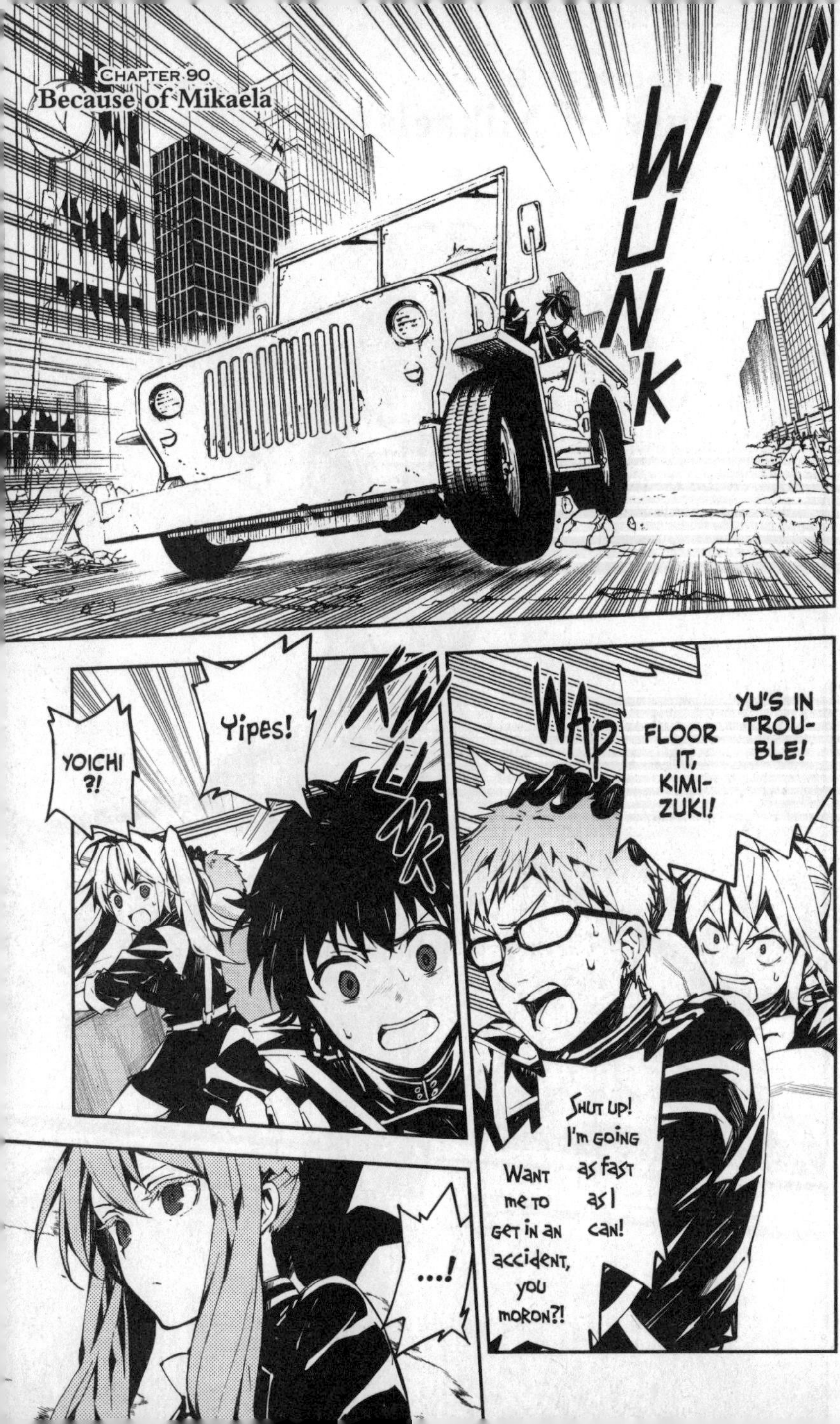
WUNK
YU'S IN TROUBLE!
FLOOR IT, KIMIZUKI!
WAP
Shut up! I'm going as fast as I can!
Want me to get in an accident, you moron?!
KWUNK
Yipes!
YOICHI?!
...!

CHAPTER 90

Because of Mikaela

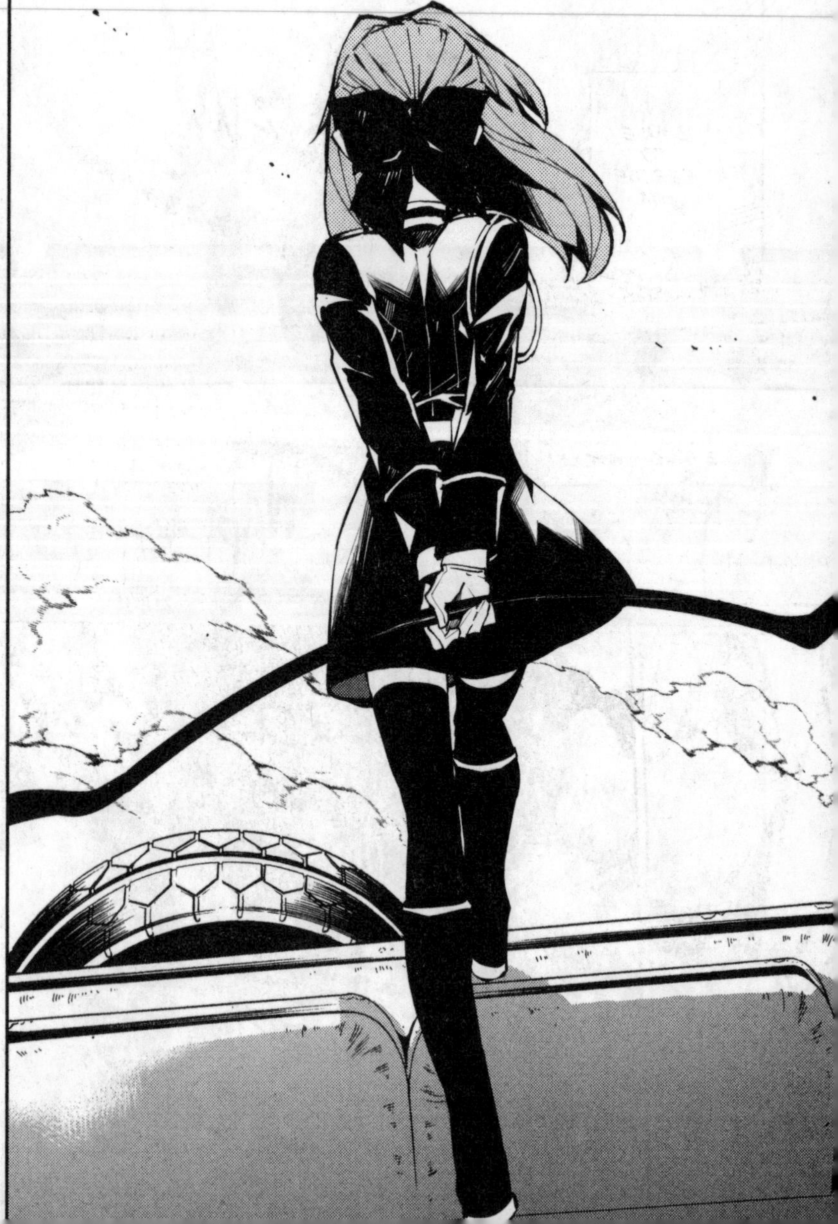

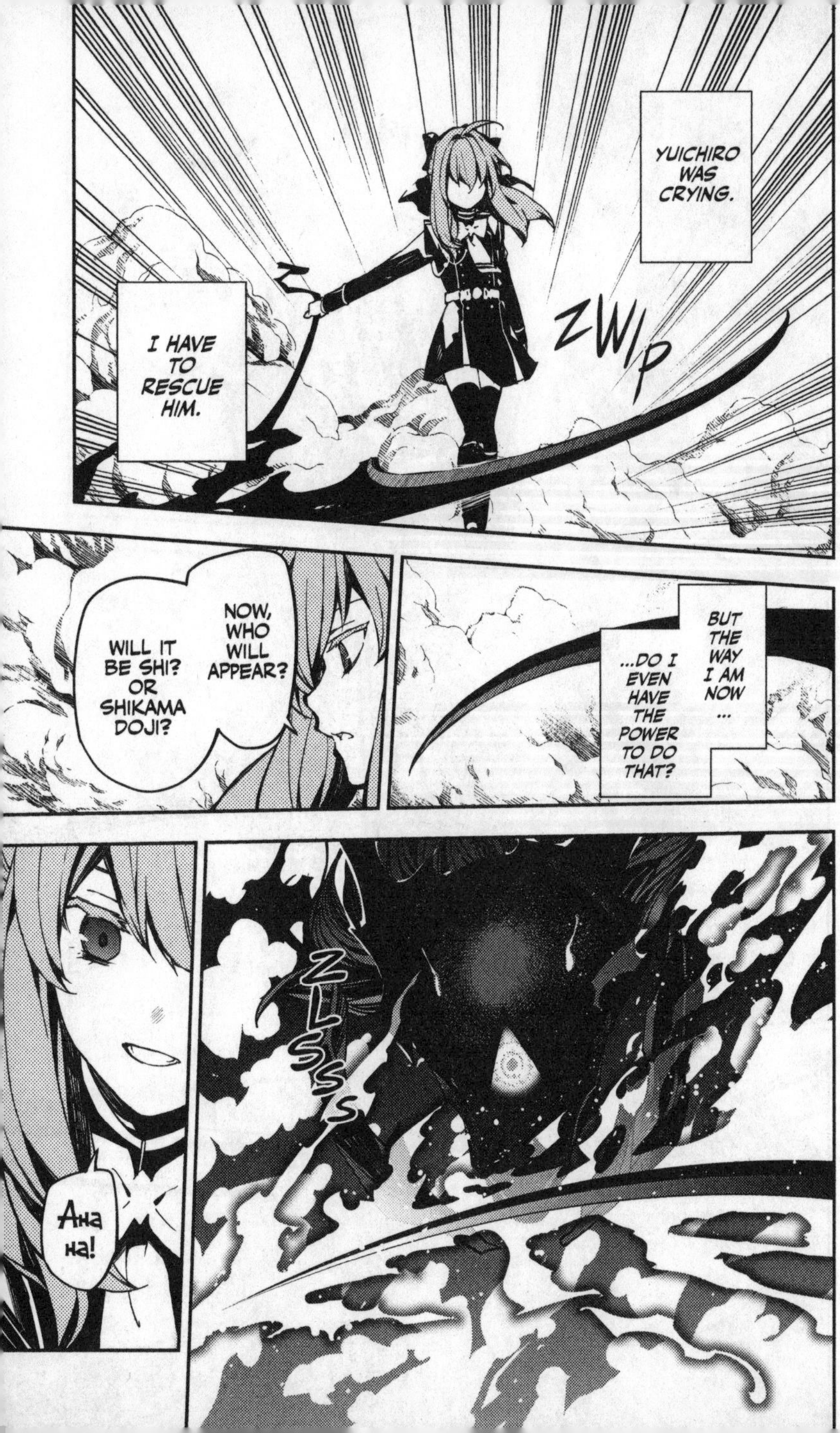
YUICHIRO WAS CRYING.
ZWIP
I HAVE TO RESCUE HIM.
BUT THE WAY I AM NOW ...
...DO I EVEN HAVE THE POWER TO DO THAT?
NOW, WHO WILL APPEAR?
WILL IT BE SHI? OR SHIKAMA DOJI?
ZZLLSSSS
AHA HA!

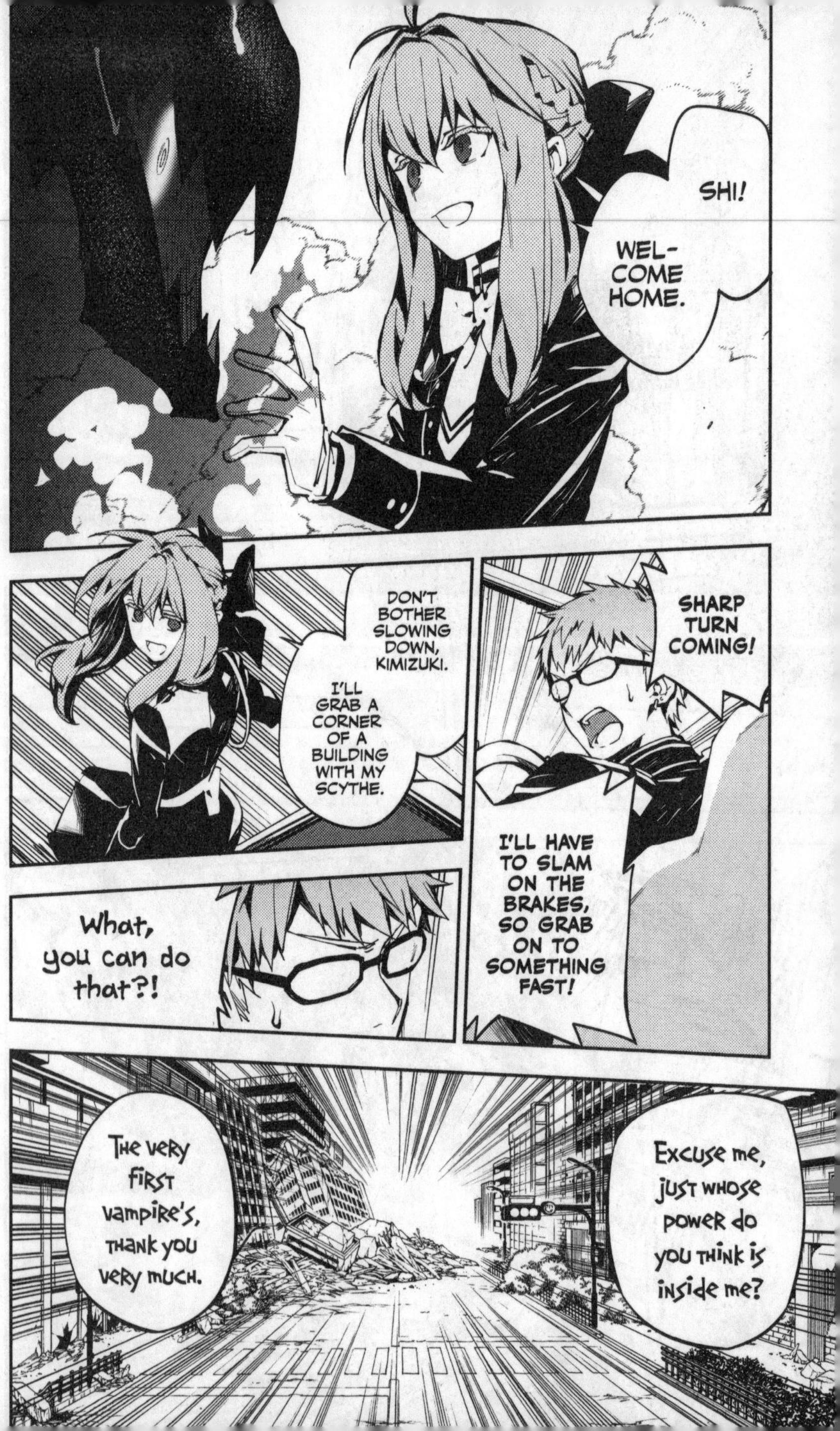
SHI!
WEL-COME HOME.
SHARP TURN COMING!
I'LL HAVE TO SLAM ON THE BRAKES, SO GRAB ON TO SOMETHING FAST!
DON'T BOTHER SLOWING DOWN, KIMIZUKI.
I'LL GRAB A CORNER OF A BUILDING WITH MY SCYTHE.
What, you can do that?!
Excuse me, just whose power do you think is inside me?
The very first vampire's, thank you very much.

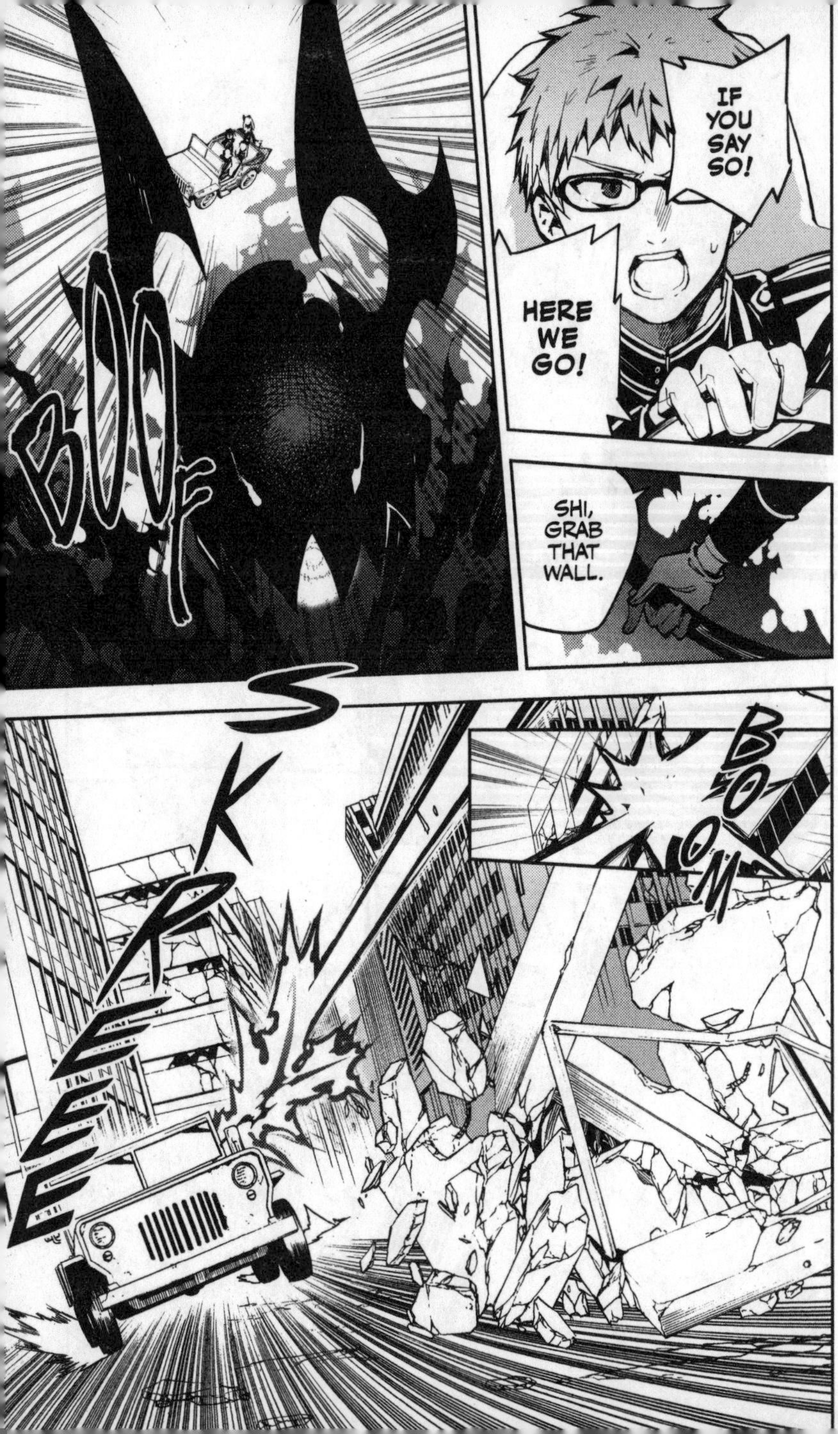
IF YOU SAY SO!
HERE WE GO!
SHI, GRAB THAT WALL.
BOOF
BOOM
SKREEEEE

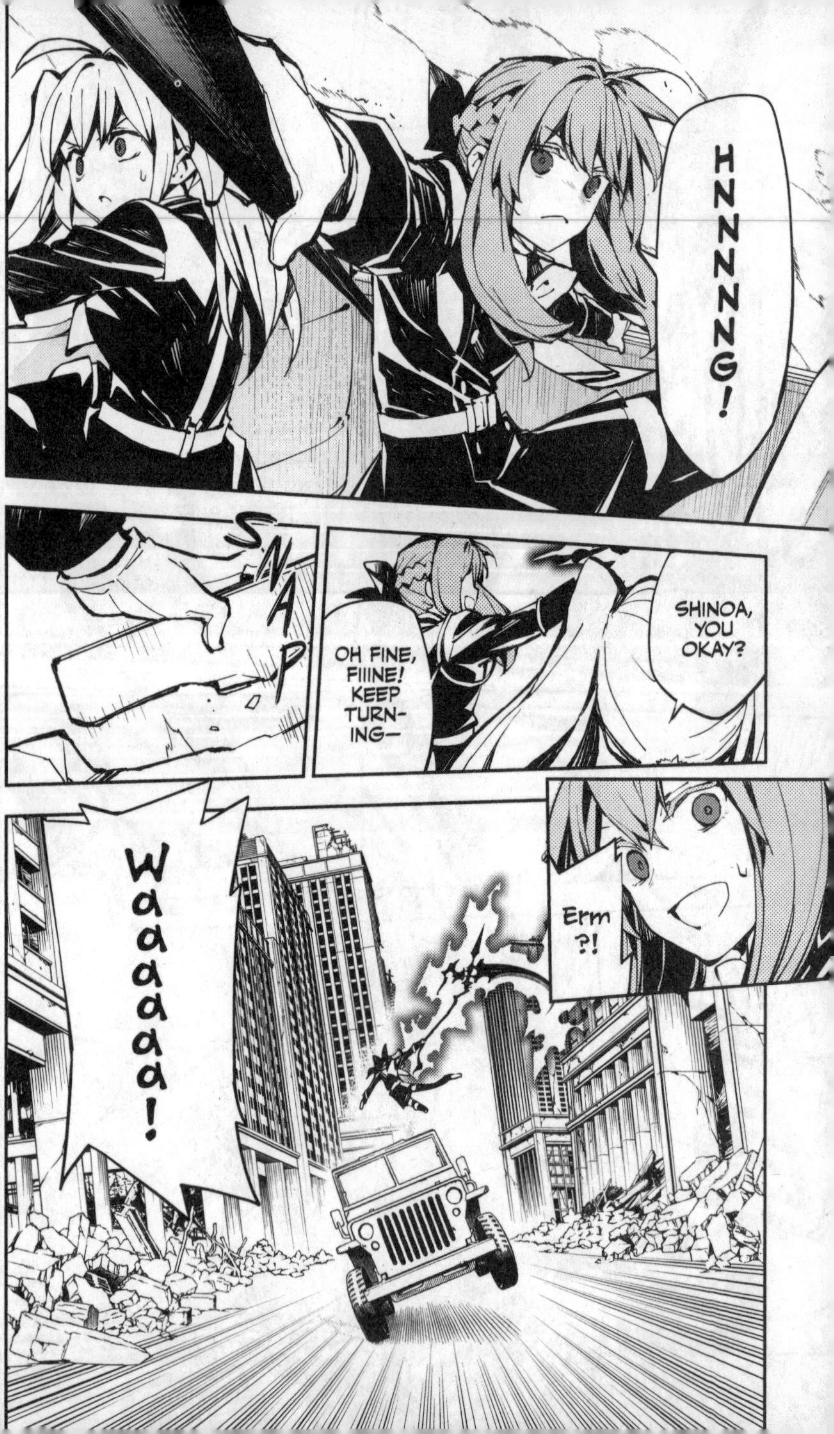
HNNNNNG!
SNAP
SHINOA, YOU OKAY?
OH FINE, FIIINE! KEEP TURNING—
Erm ?!
Waaaaaa!

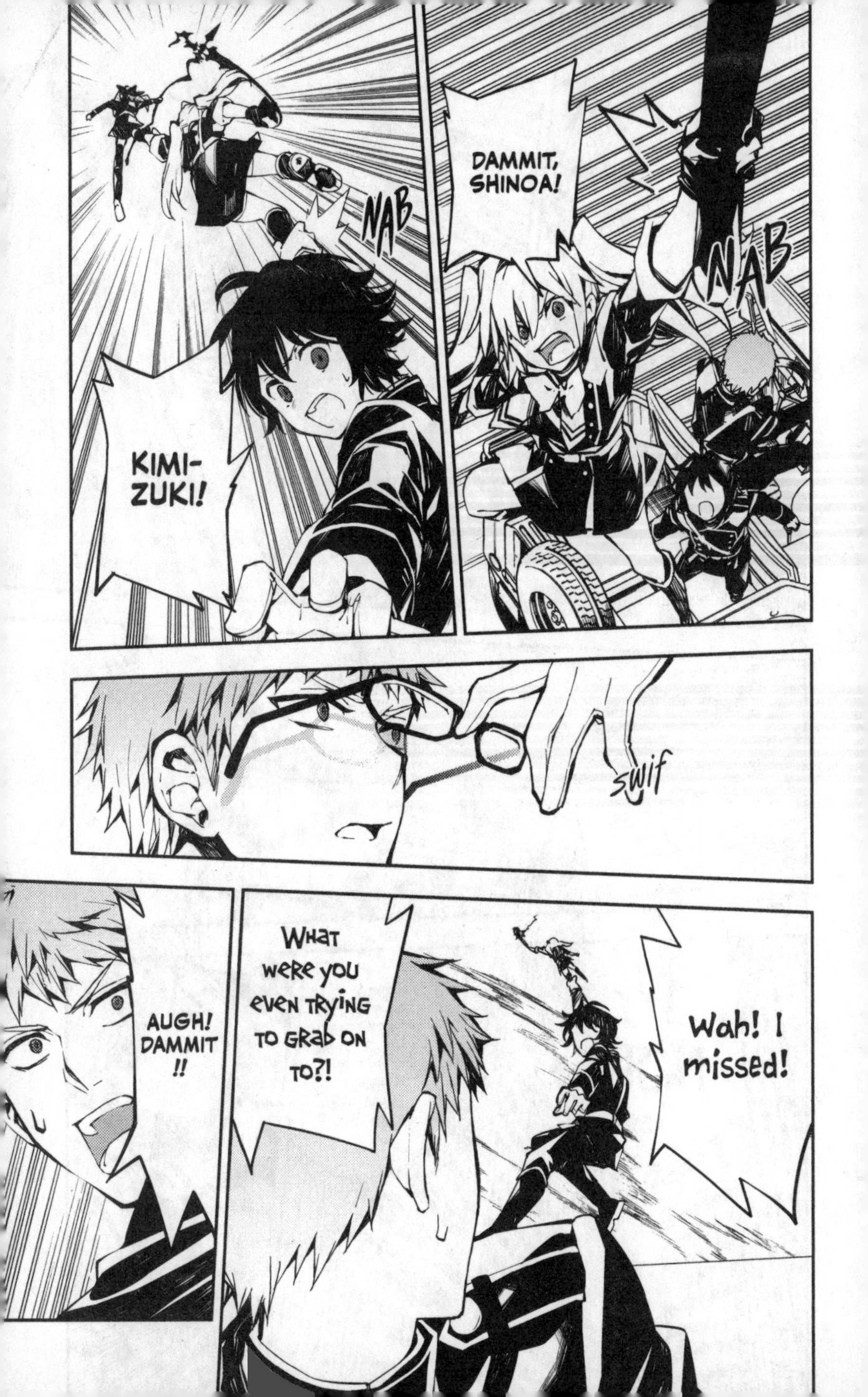
DAMMIT, SHINOA!
NAB
NAB
KIMI-ZUKI!
swif
Wah! I missed!
WHAT were you even trying to grab on to?!
AUGH! DAMMIT !!

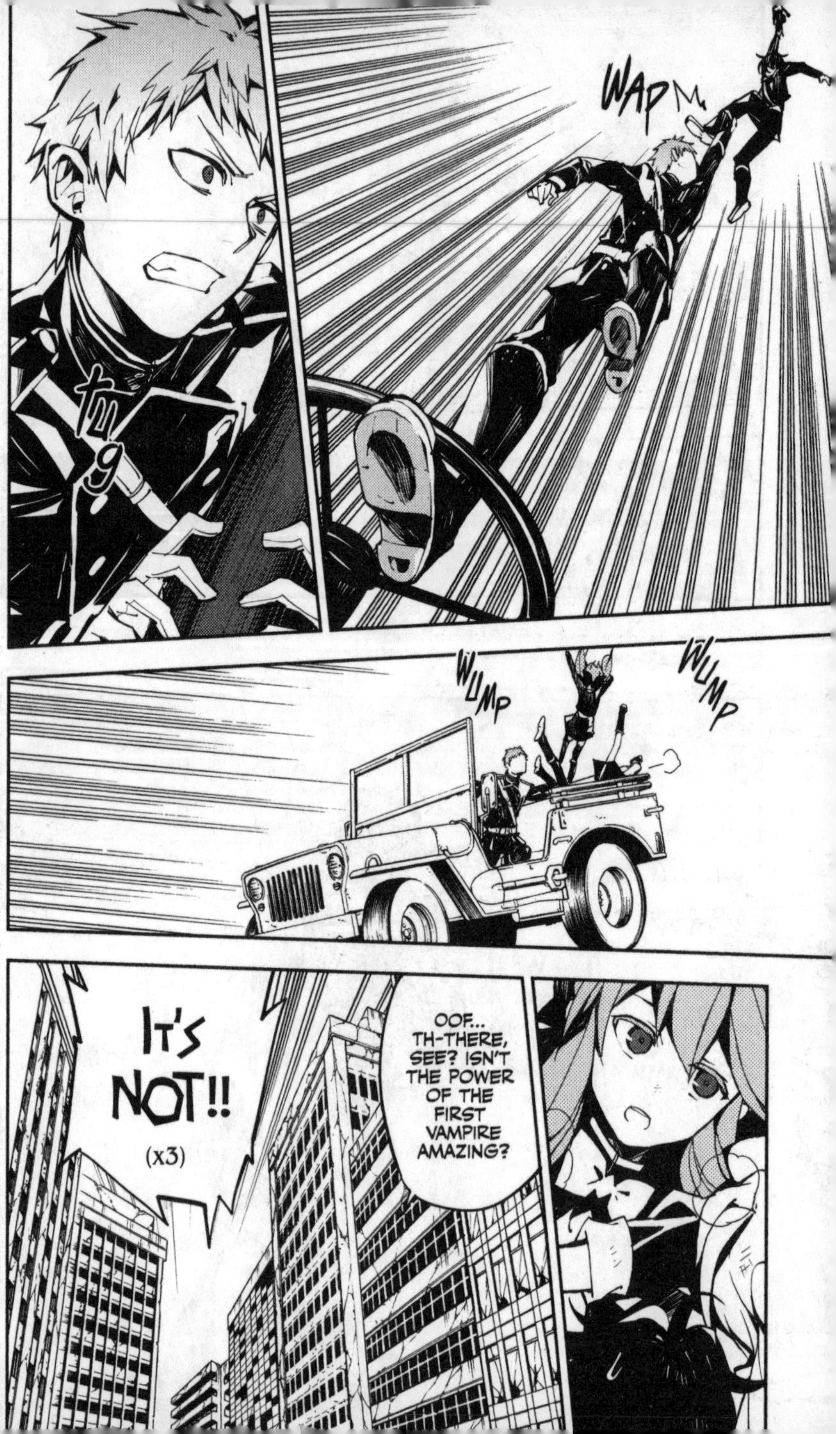
WAP
tug
WUMP
WUMP
OOF... TH-THERE, SEE? ISN'T THE POWER OF THE FIRST VAMPIRE AMAZING?
IT'S NOT!!
(x3)

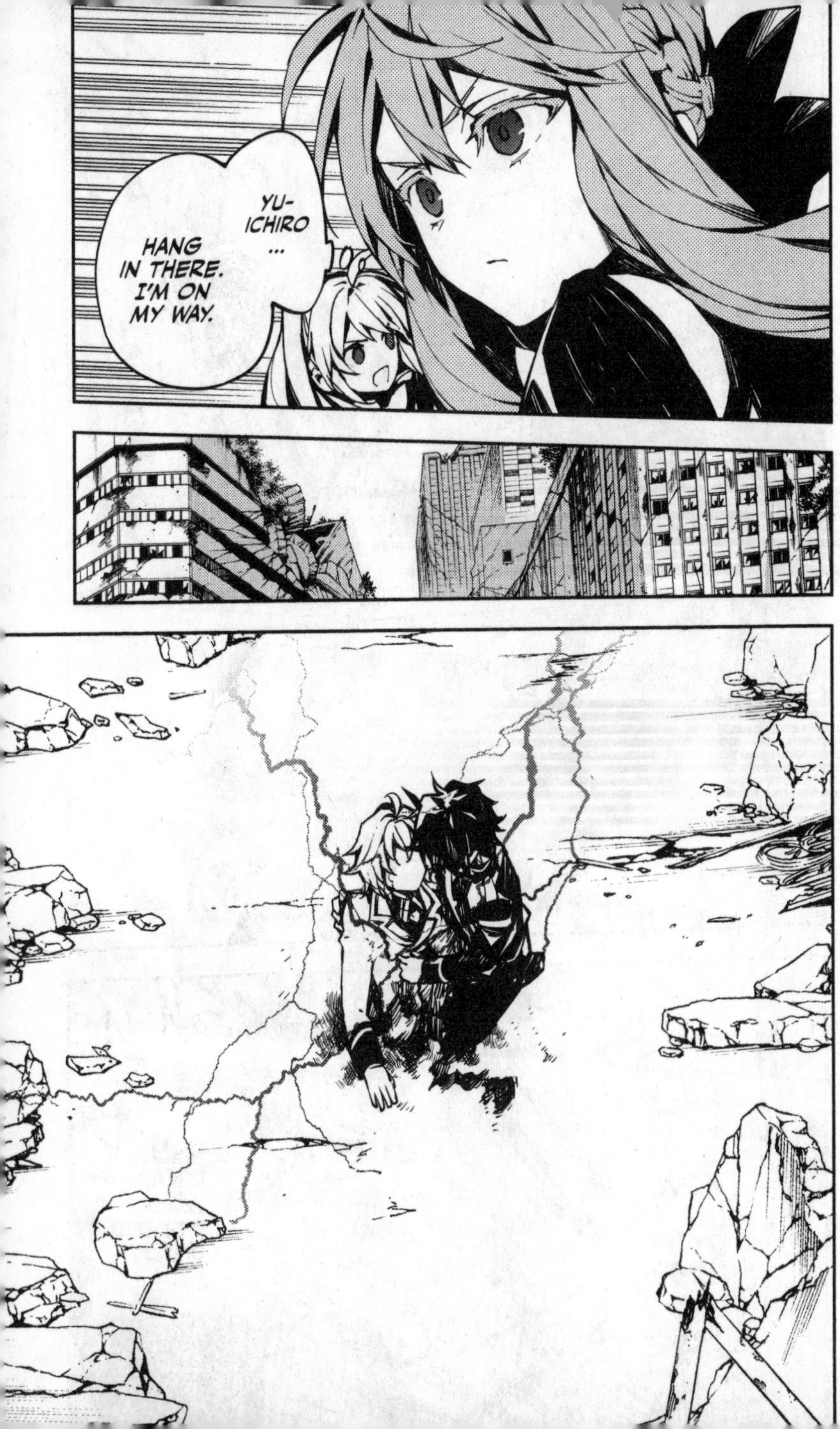
YU-ICHIRO ...
HANG IN THERE. I'M ON MY WAY.

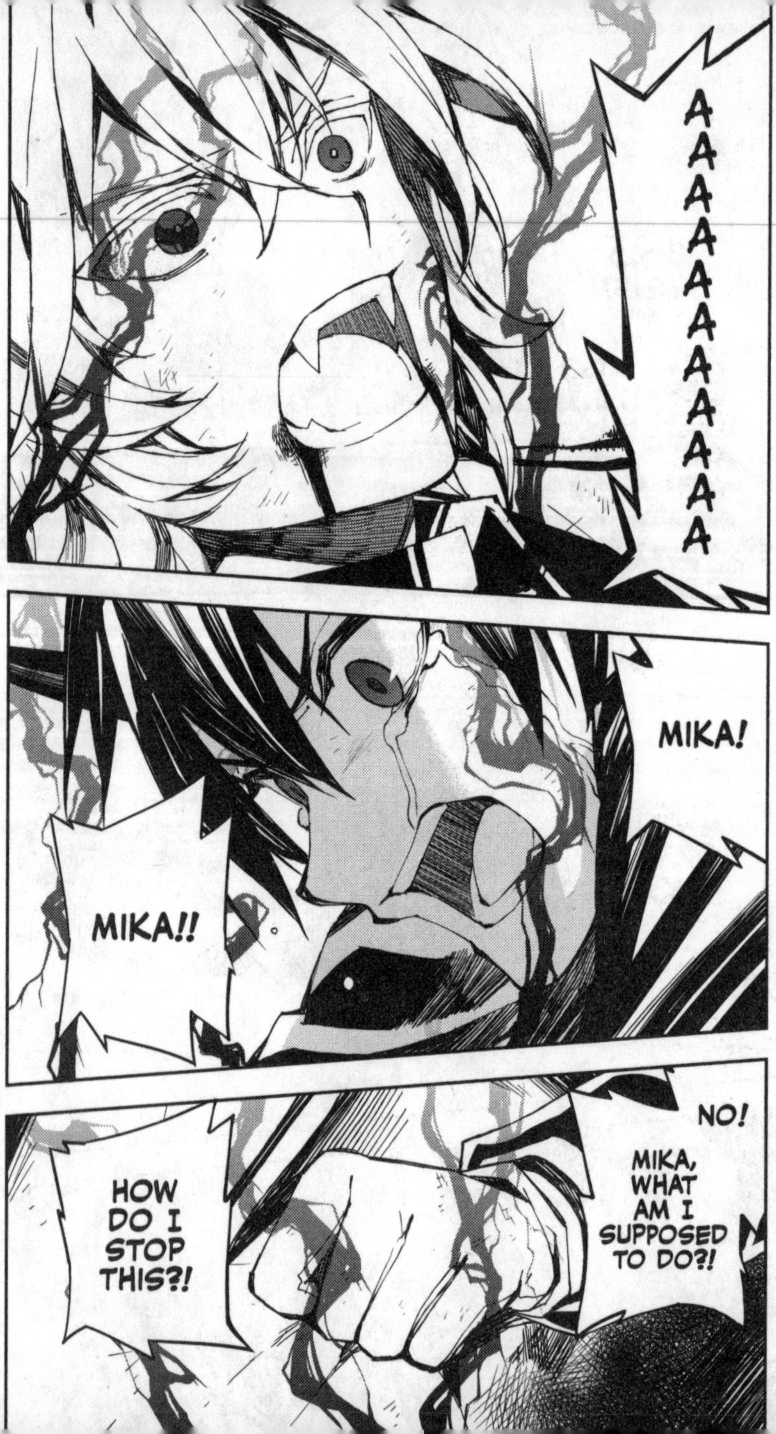
AAAAAAAAAAAAA
MIKA!
MIKA!!
NO!
MIKA, WHAT AM I SUPPOSED TO DO?!
HOW DO I STOP THIS?!

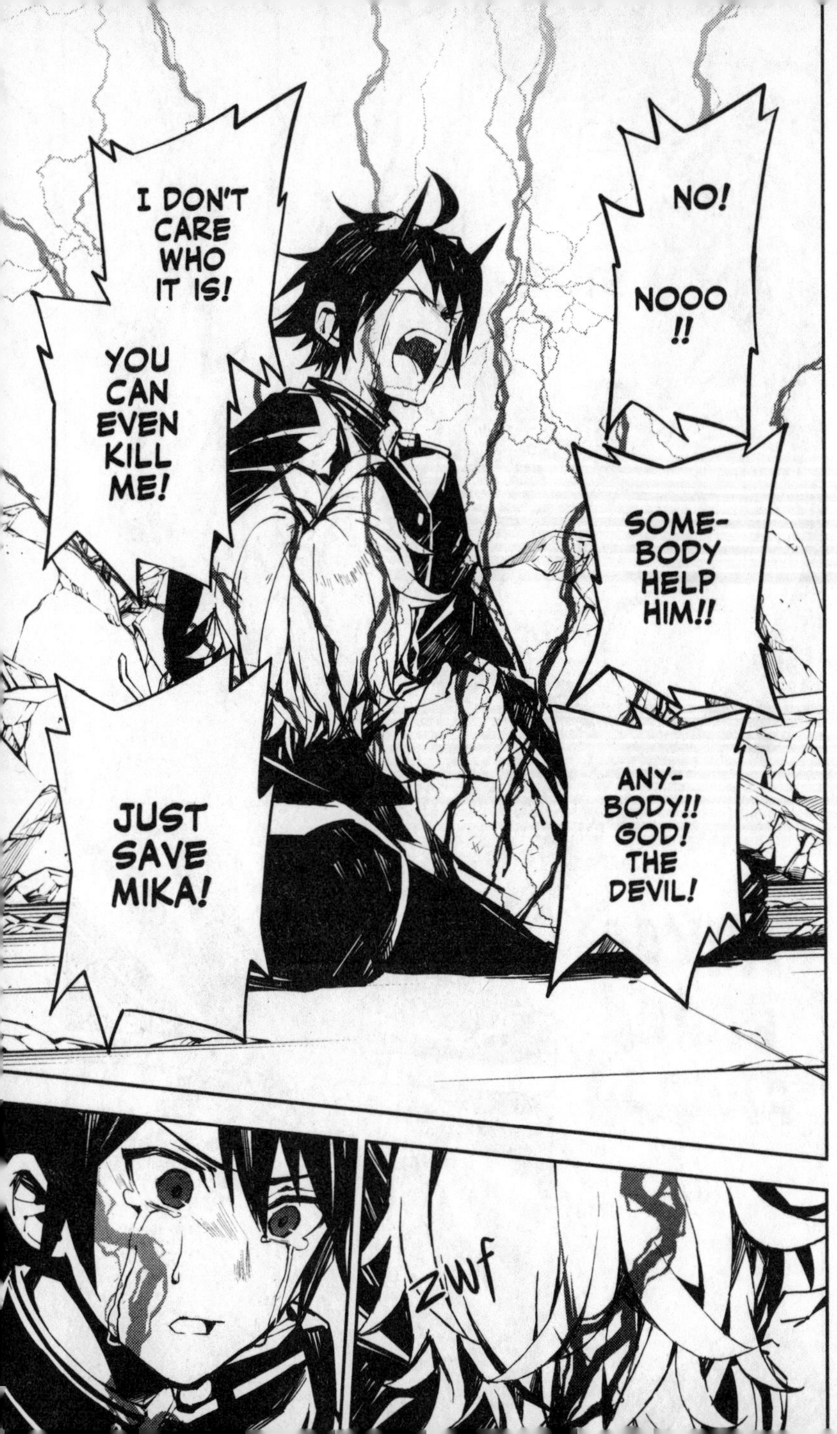
NO!
NOOO!!
SOME-BODY HELP HIM!!
ANY-BODY!! GOD! THE DEVIL!
I DON'T CARE WHO IT IS!
YOU CAN EVEN KILL ME!
JUST SAVE MIKA!
ZWF

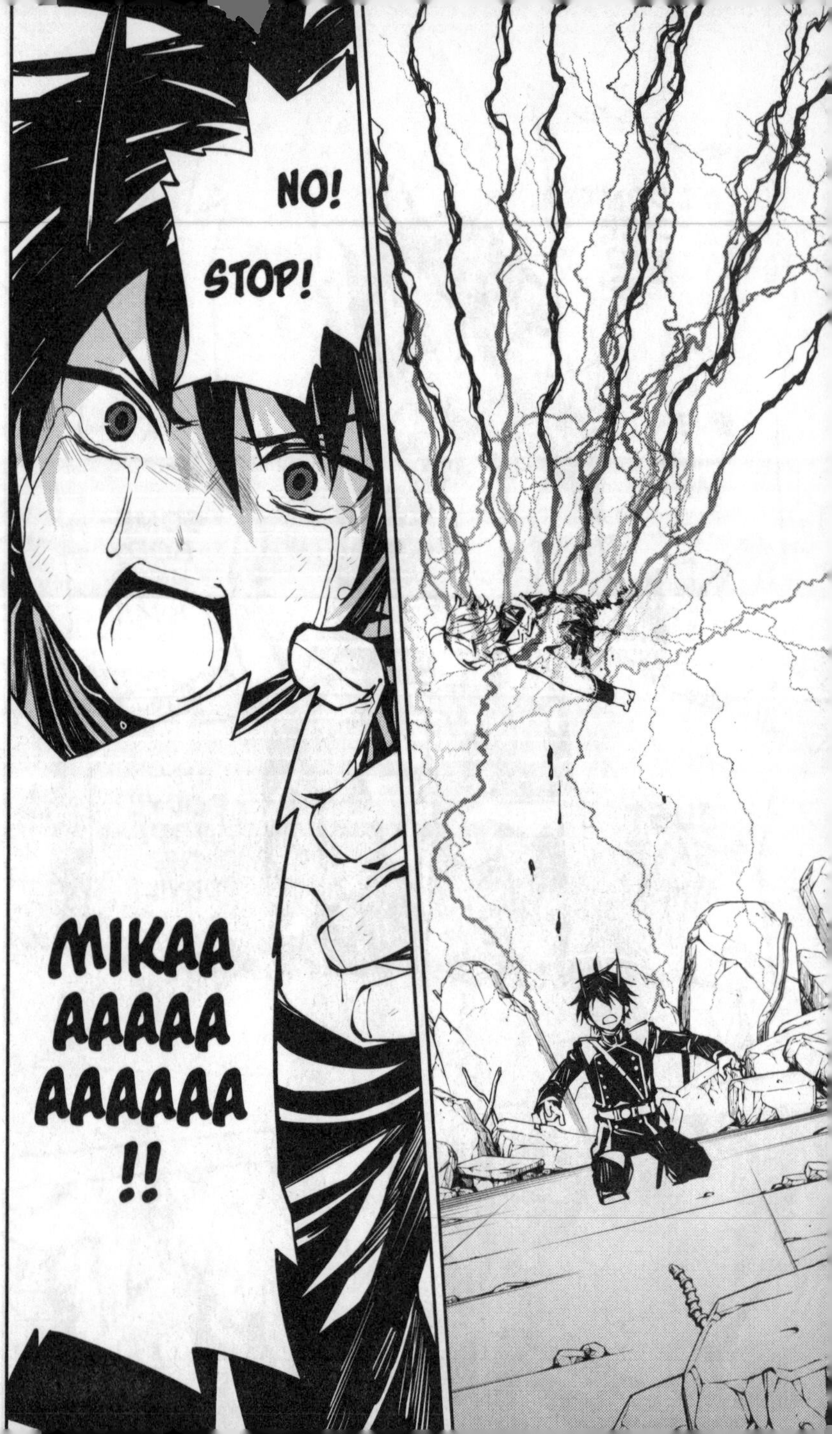
NO!
STOP!
MIKAA AAAAA AAAAAA!!

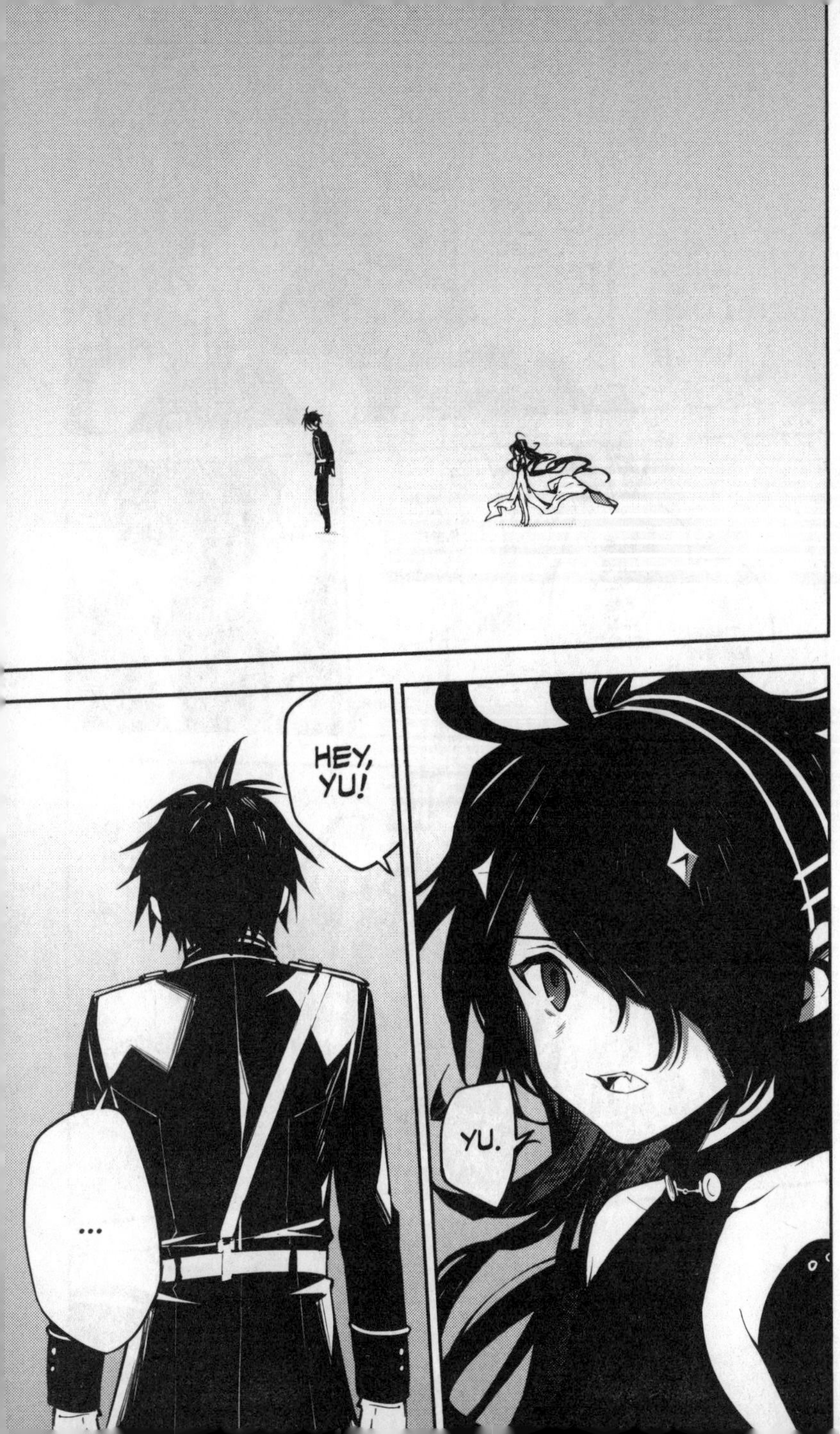
YU.
HEY, YU!
...

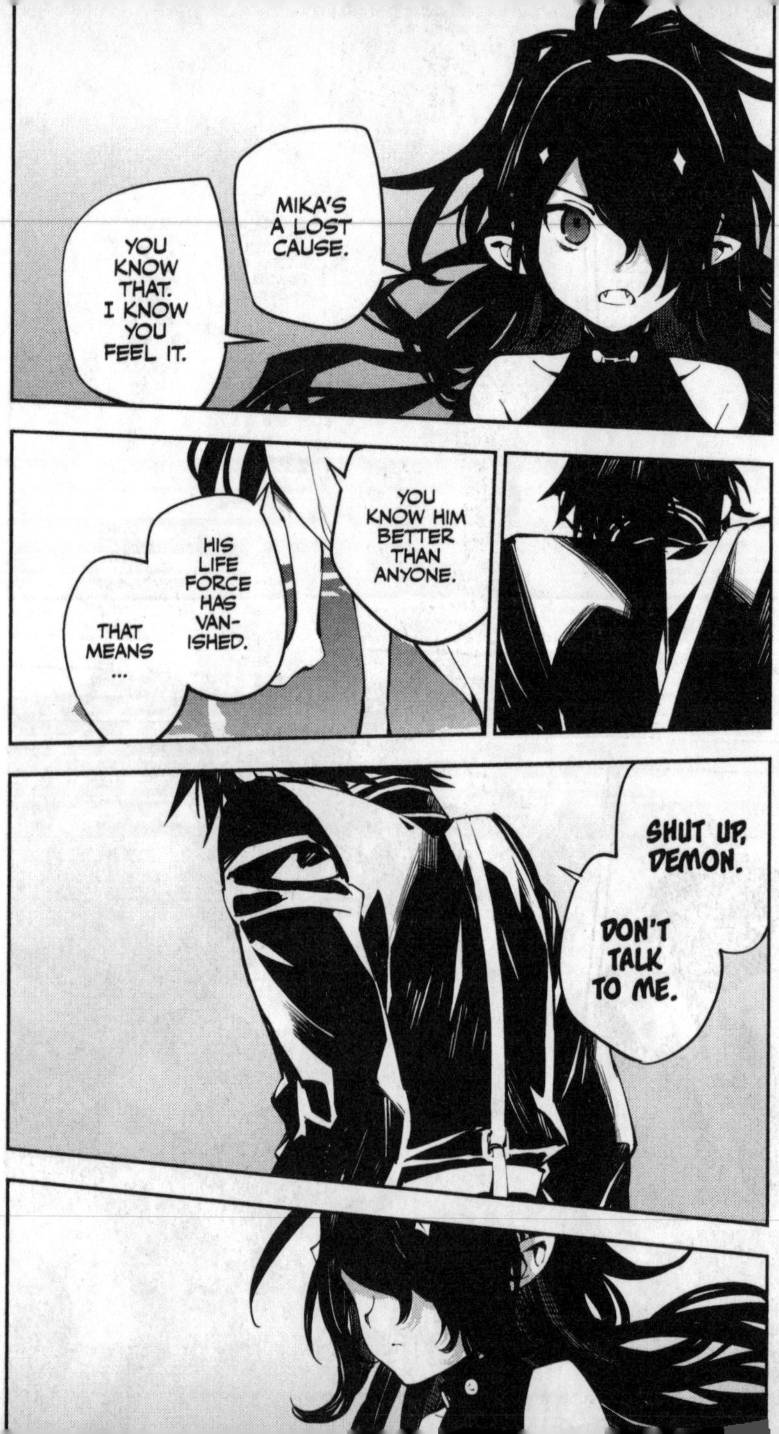
MIKA'S A LOST CAUSE.
YOU KNOW THAT. I KNOW YOU FEEL IT.
YOU KNOW HIM BETTER THAN ANYONE.
HIS LIFE FORCE HAS VAN-ISHED.
THAT MEANS ...
SHUT UP, DEMON.
DON'T TALK TO ME.

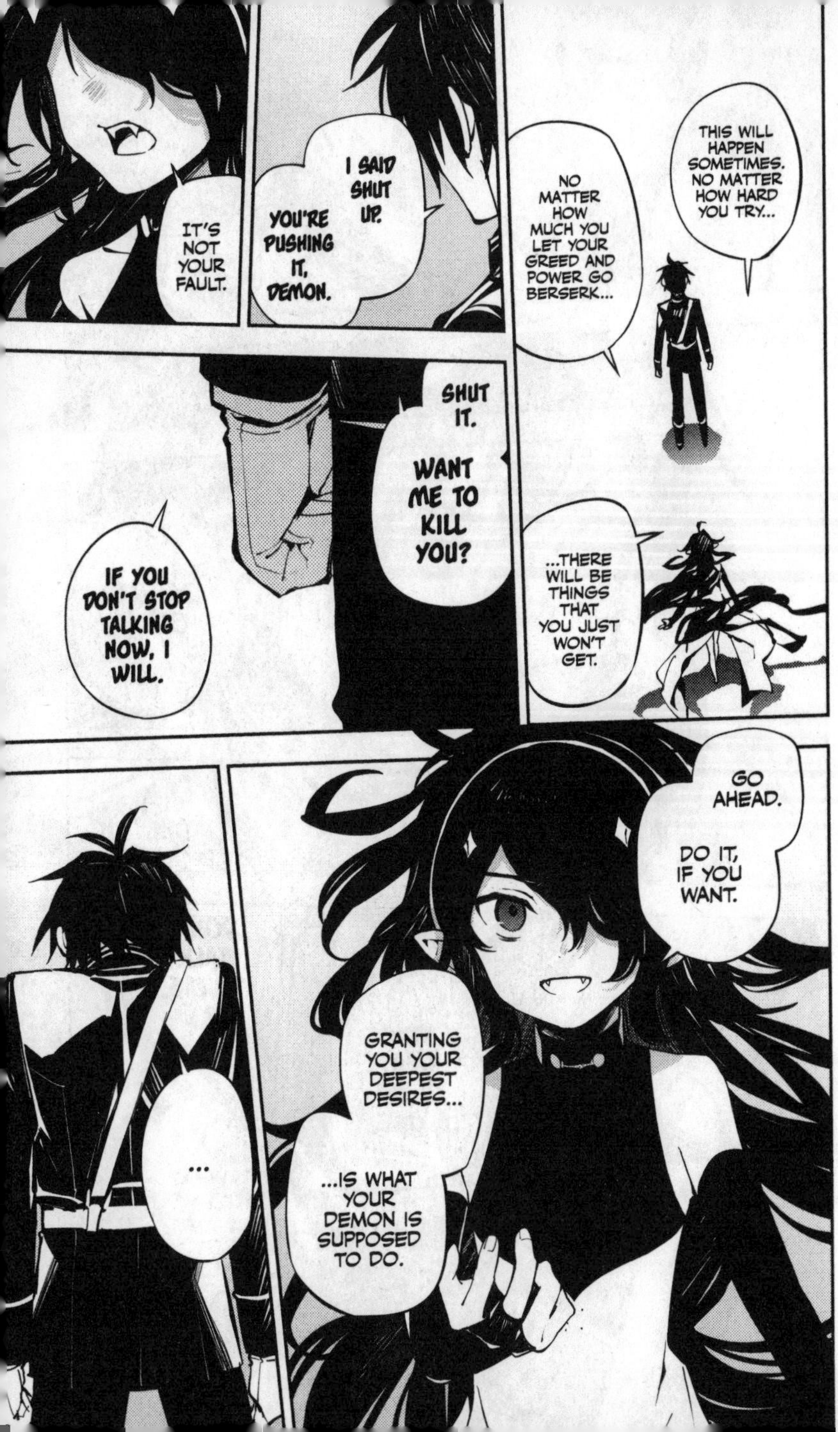
THIS WILL HAPPEN SOMETIMES. NO MATTER HOW HARD YOU TRY...
NO MATTER HOW MUCH YOU LET YOUR GREED AND POWER GO BERSERK...
...THERE WILL BE THINGS THAT YOU JUST WON'T GET.
I SAID SHUT UP.
YOU'RE PUSHING IT, DEMON.
IT'S NOT YOUR FAULT.
SHUT IT.
WANT ME TO KILL YOU?
IF YOU DON'T STOP TALKING NOW, I WILL.
GO AHEAD.
DO IT, IF YOU WANT.
GRANTING YOU YOUR DEEPEST DESIRES...
...IS WHAT YOUR DEMON IS SUPPOSED TO DO.
...

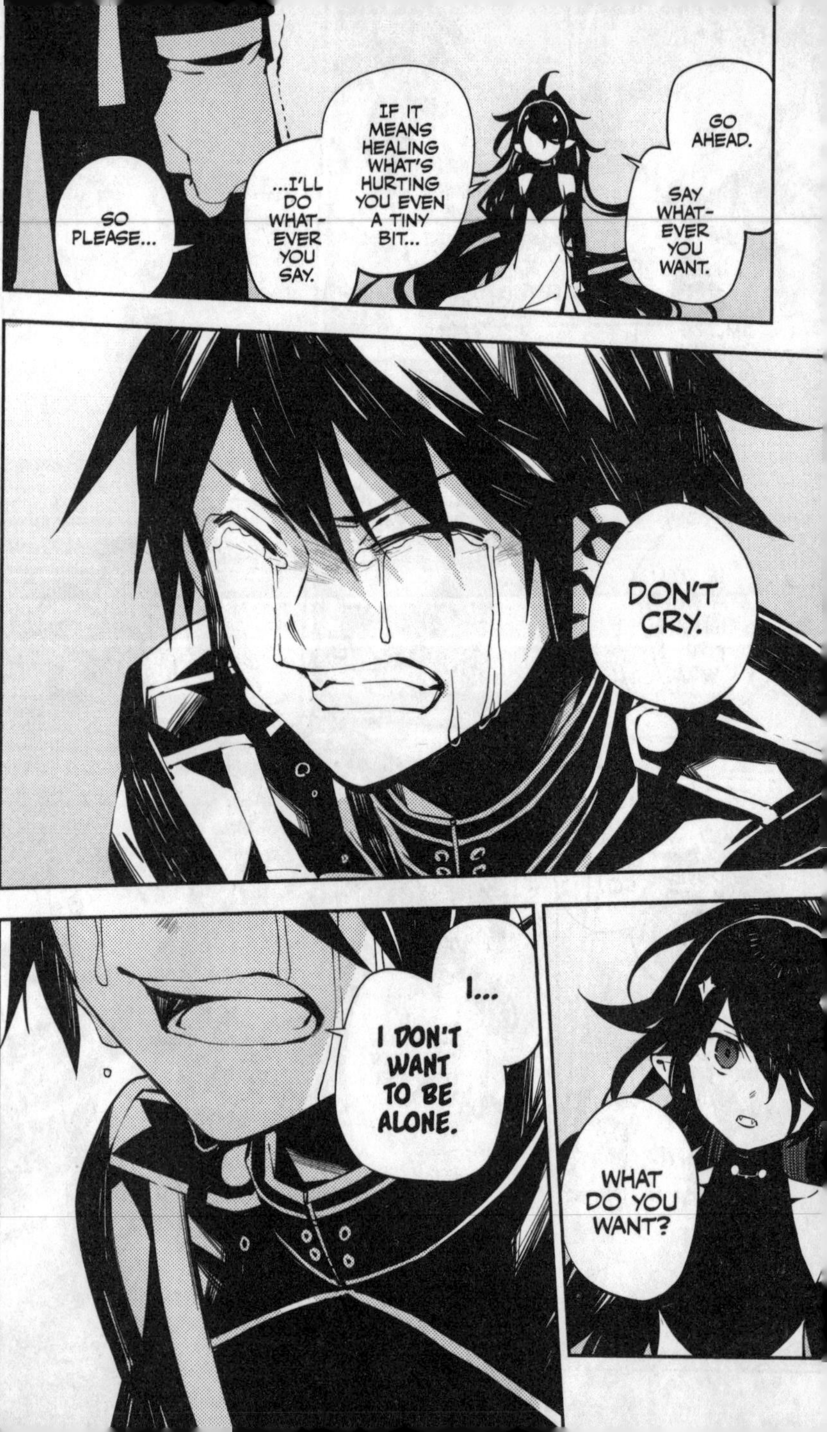
GO AHEAD.
SAY WHATEVER YOU WANT.
IF IT MEANS HEALING WHAT'S HURTING YOU EVEN A TINY BIT...
...I'LL DO WHATEVER YOU SAY.
SO PLEASE...
DON'T CRY.
WHAT DO YOU WANT?
I...
I DON'T WANT TO BE ALONE.

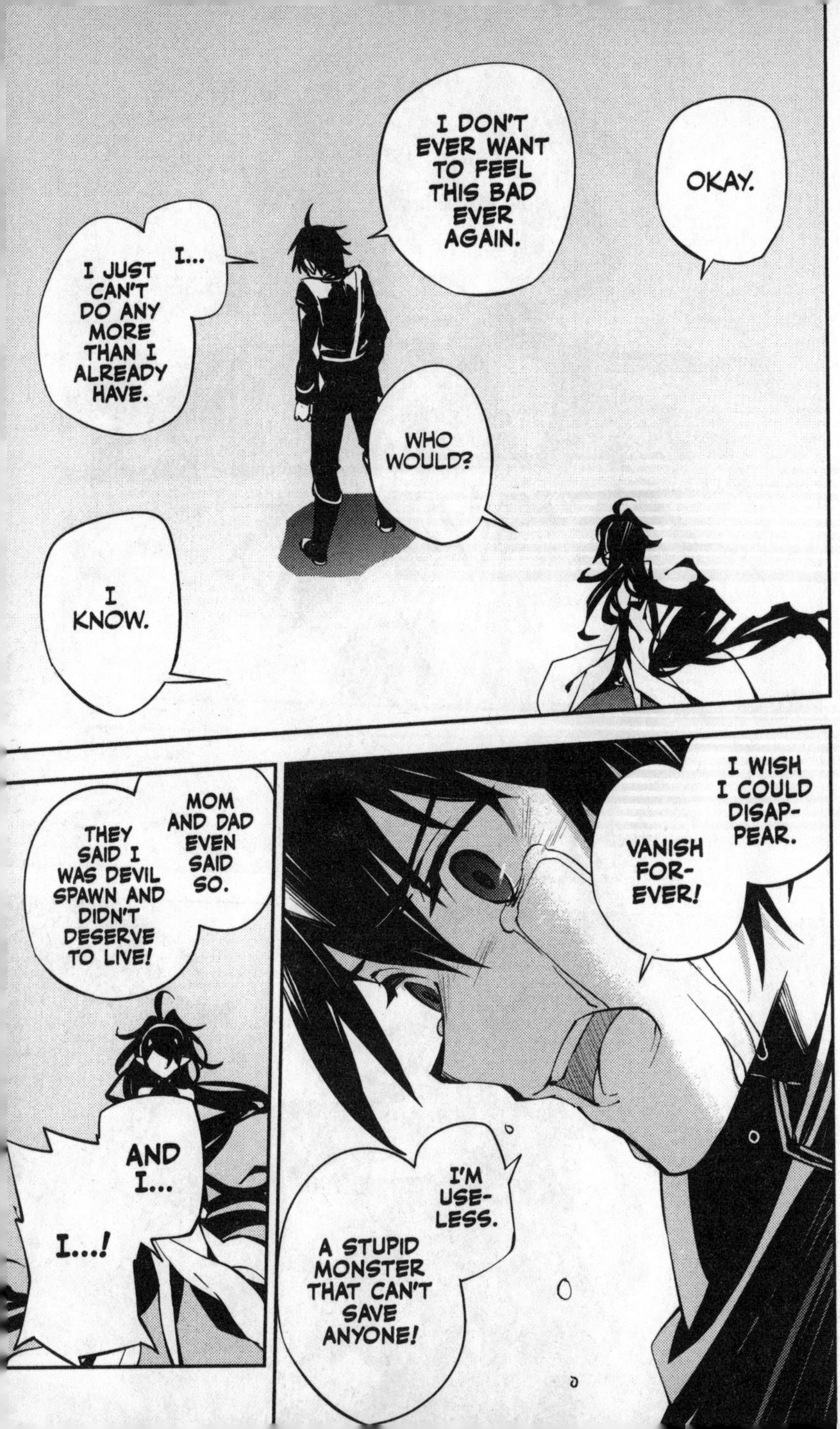
OKAY.
I DON'T EVER WANT TO FEEL THIS BAD EVER AGAIN.
I...
I JUST CAN'T DO ANY MORE THAN I ALREADY HAVE.
WHO WOULD?
I KNOW.
I WISH I COULD DISAPPEAR.
VANISH FOREVER!
I'M USELESS.
A STUPID MONSTER THAT CAN'T SAVE ANYONE!
MOM AND DAD EVEN SAID SO.
THEY SAID I WAS DEVIL SPAWN AND DIDN'T DESERVE TO LIVE!
AND I...
I...!

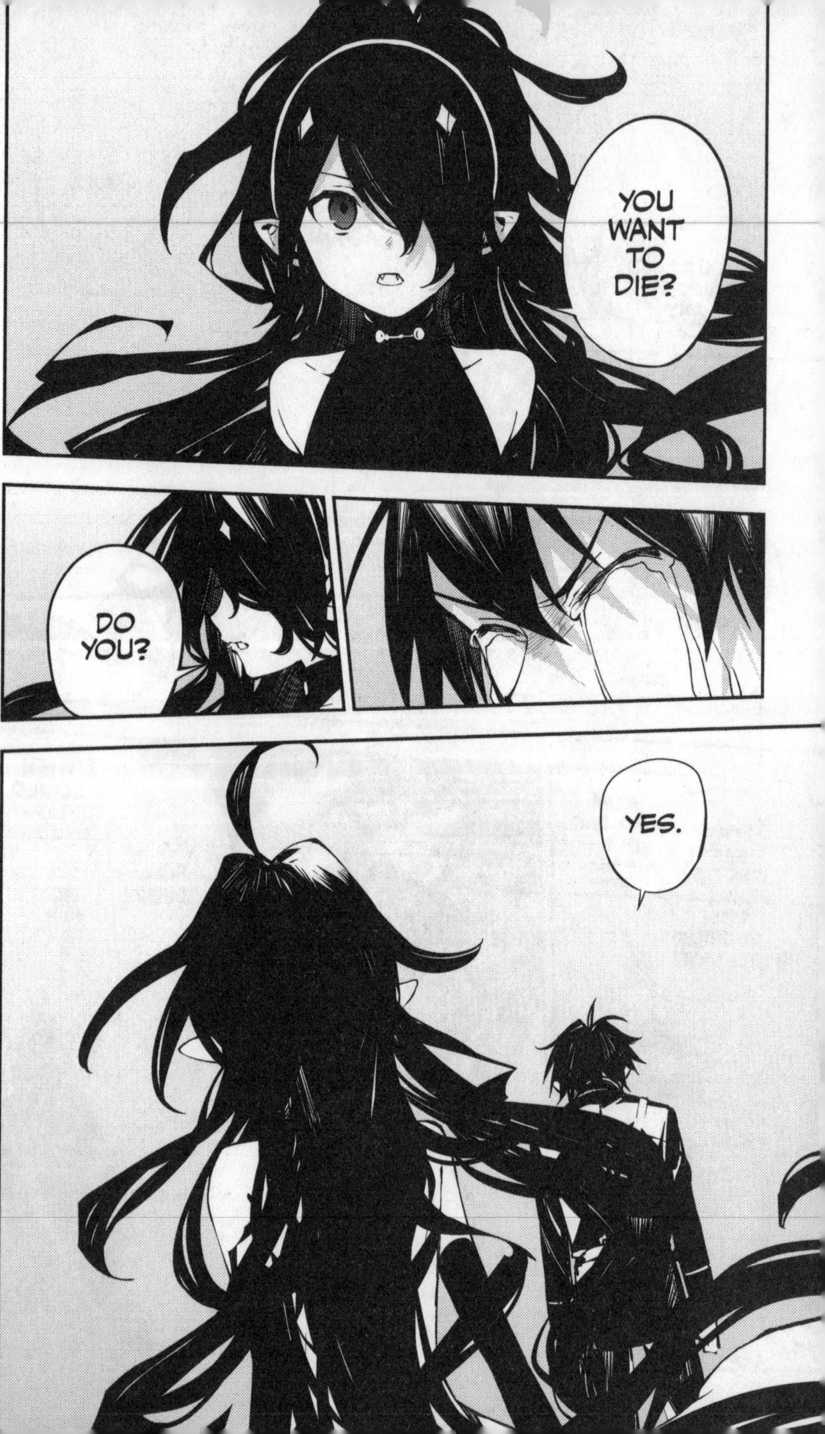
YOU WANT TO DIE?
DO YOU?
YES.

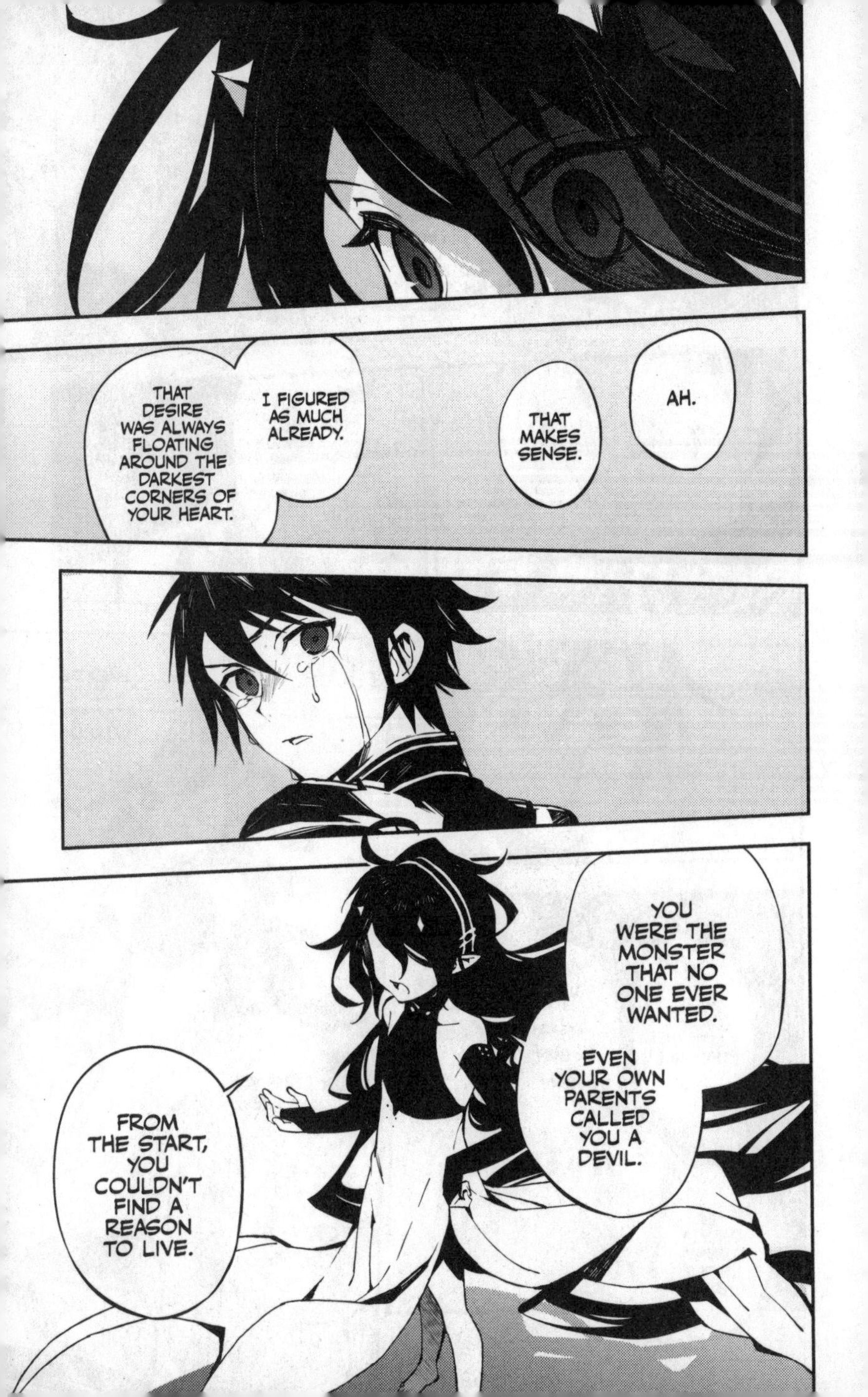
AH.
THAT MAKES SENSE.
I FIGURED AS MUCH ALREADY.
THAT DESIRE WAS ALWAYS FLOATING AROUND THE DARKEST CORNERS OF YOUR HEART.
YOU WERE THE MONSTER THAT NO ONE EVER WANTED.
EVEN YOUR OWN PARENTS CALLED YOU A DEVIL.
FROM THE START, YOU COULDN'T FIND A REASON TO LIVE.

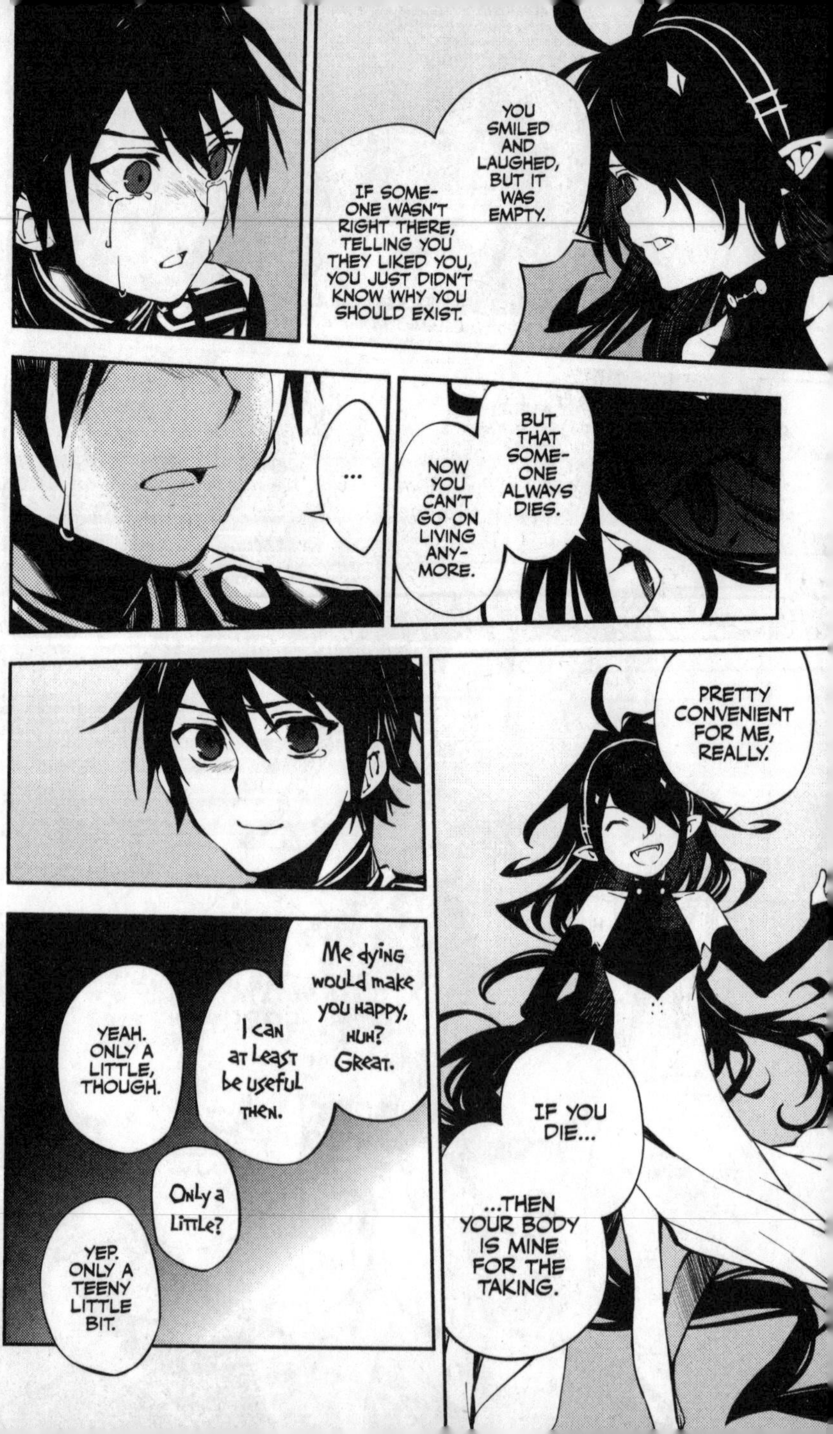
YOU SMILED AND LAUGHED, BUT IT WAS EMPTY.
IF SOME-ONE WASN'T RIGHT THERE, TELLING YOU THEY LIKED YOU, YOU JUST DIDN'T KNOW WHY YOU SHOULD EXIST.
BUT THAT SOME-ONE ALWAYS DIES.
NOW YOU CAN'T GO ON LIVING ANY-MORE.
...
PRETTY CONVENIENT FOR ME, REALLY.
IF YOU DIE...
...THEN YOUR BODY IS MINE FOR THE TAKING.
Me dying would make you happy, huh? Great.
I can at least be useful then.
YEAH. ONLY A LITTLE, THOUGH.
Only a little?
YEP. ONLY A TEENY LITTLE BIT.

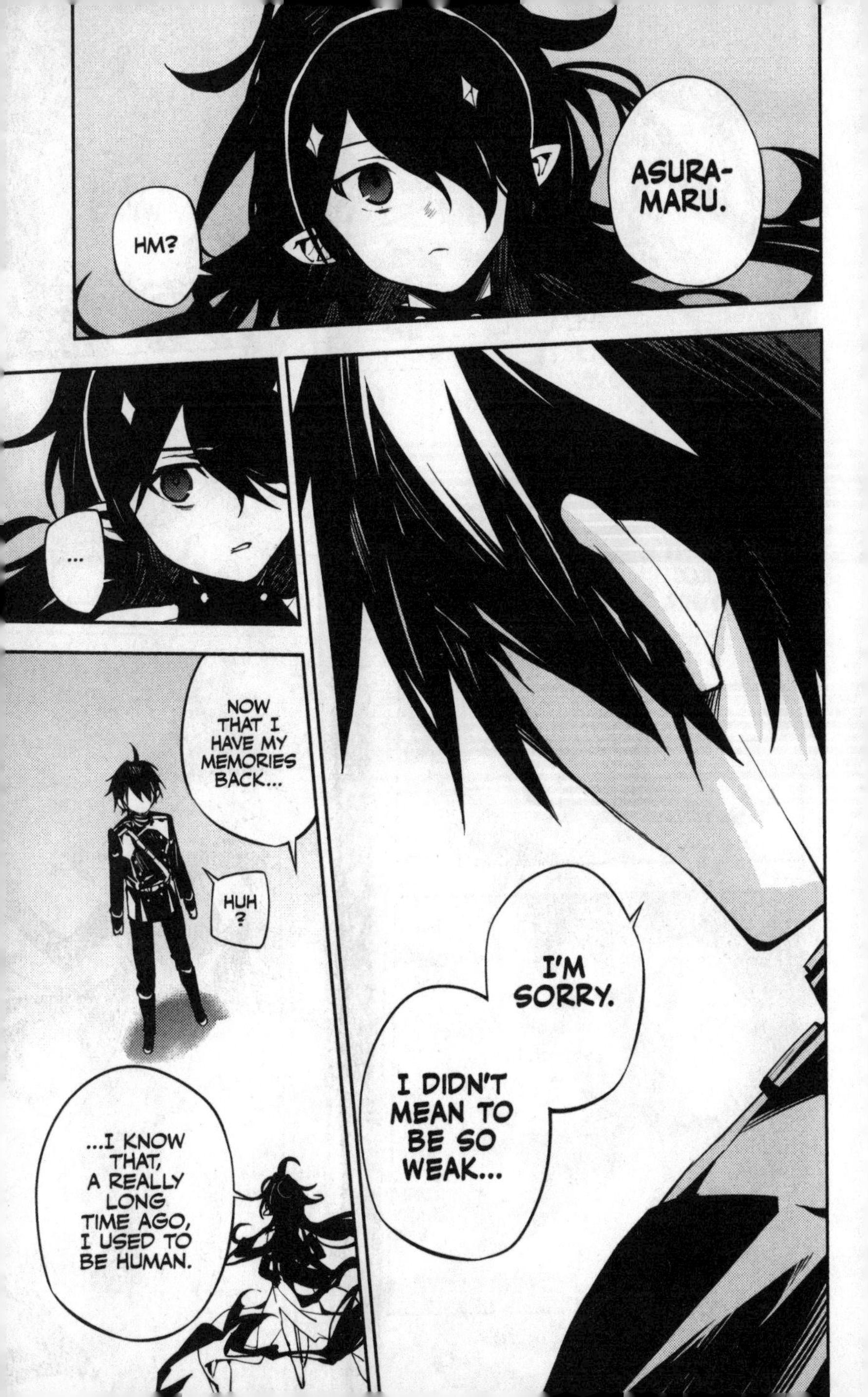
ASURA-MARU.
HM?
I'M SORRY.
I DIDN'T MEAN TO BE SO WEAK...
...
NOW THAT I HAVE MY MEMORIES BACK...
HUH?
...I KNOW THAT, A REALLY LONG TIME AGO, I USED TO BE HUMAN.

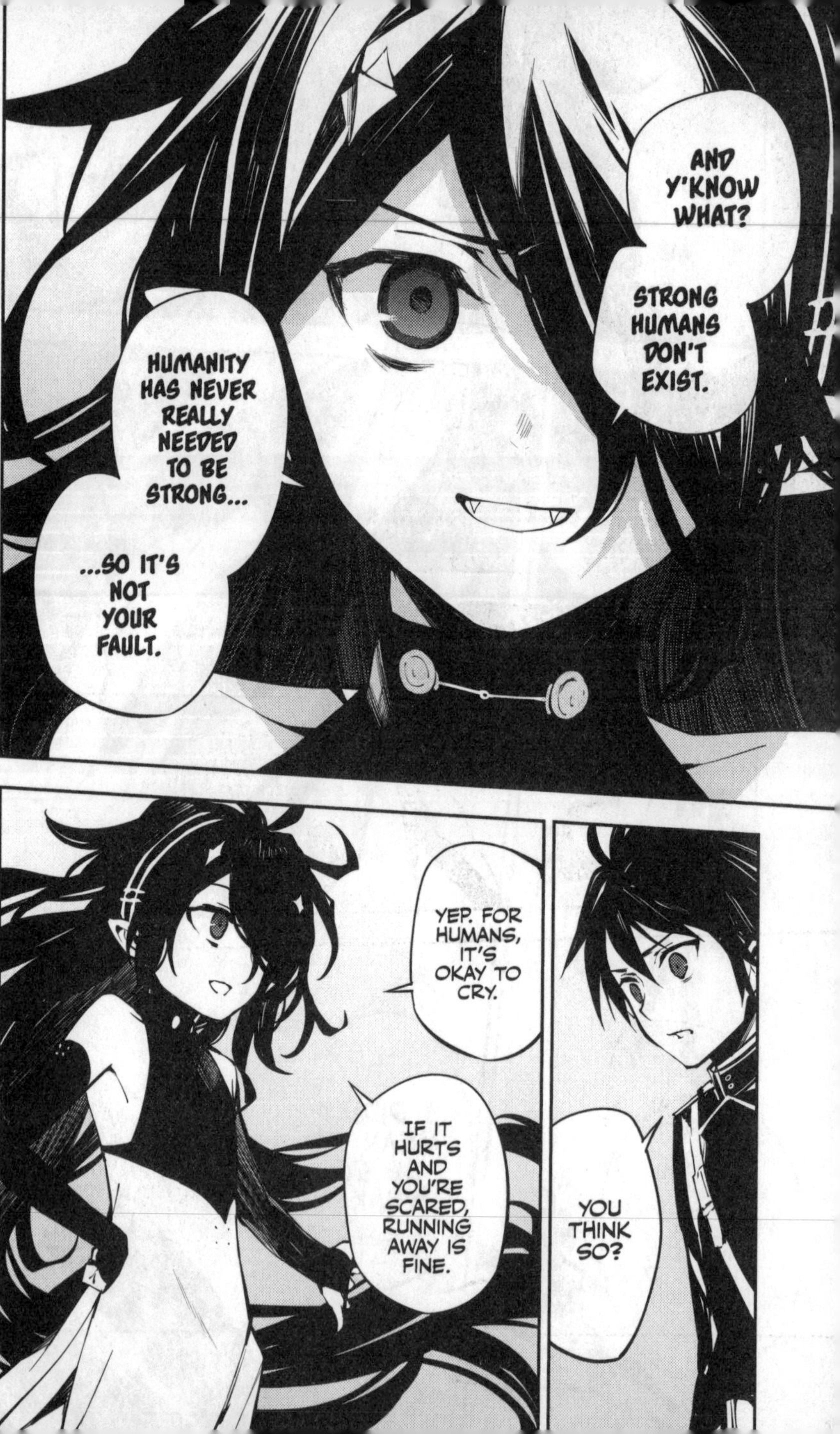
AND Y'KNOW WHAT?
STRONG HUMANS DON'T EXIST.
HUMANITY HAS NEVER REALLY NEEDED TO BE STRONG...
...SO IT'S NOT YOUR FAULT.
YEP. FOR HUMANS, IT'S OKAY TO CRY.
IF IT HURTS AND YOU'RE SCARED, RUNNING AWAY IS FINE.
YOU THINK SO?

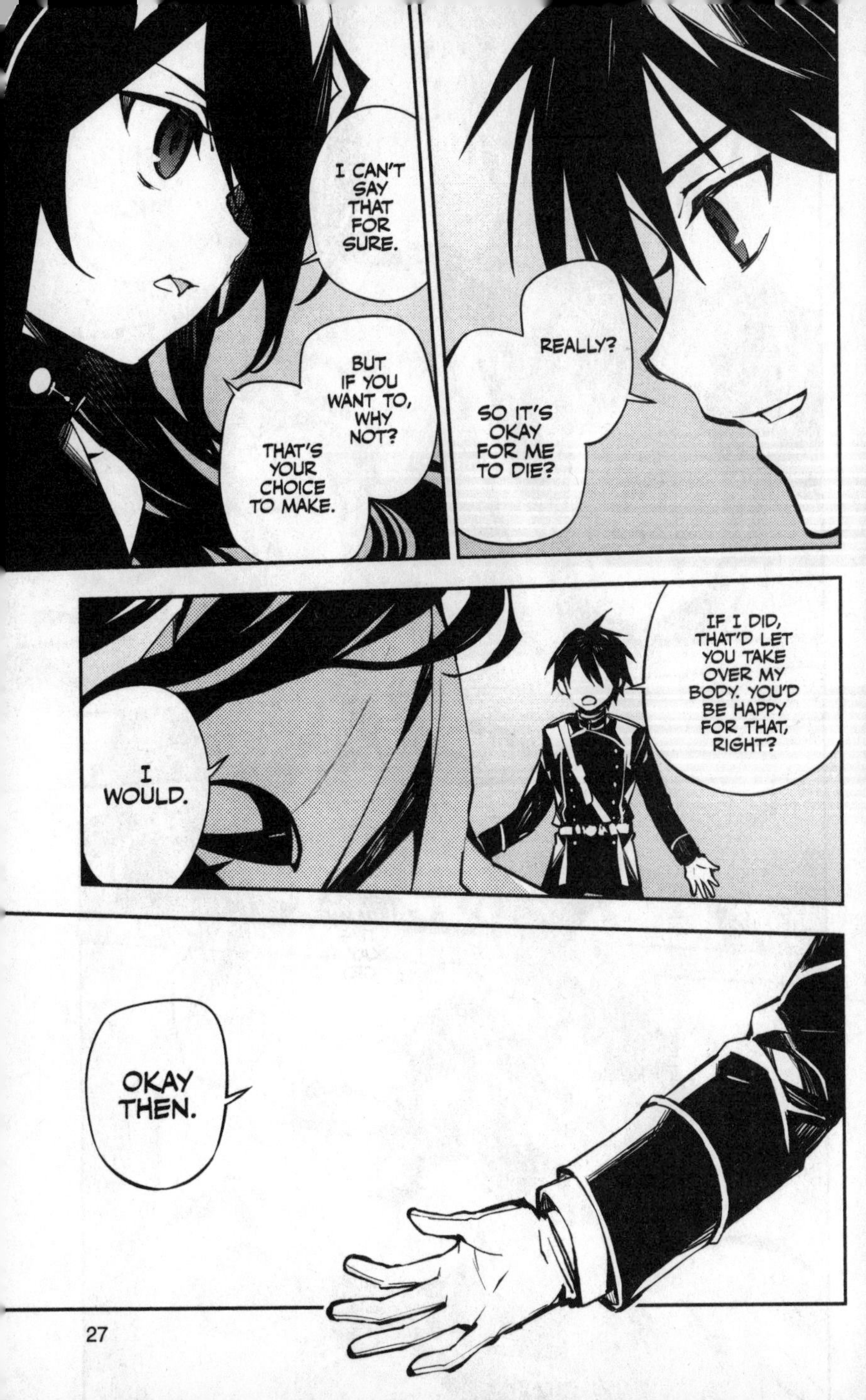
REALLY?
SO IT'S OKAY FOR ME TO DIE?
I CAN'T SAY THAT FOR SURE.
BUT IF YOU WANT TO, WHY NOT?
THAT'S YOUR CHOICE TO MAKE.
IF I DID, THAT'D LET YOU TAKE OVER MY BODY. YOU'D BE HAPPY FOR THAT, RIGHT?
I WOULD.
OKAY THEN.

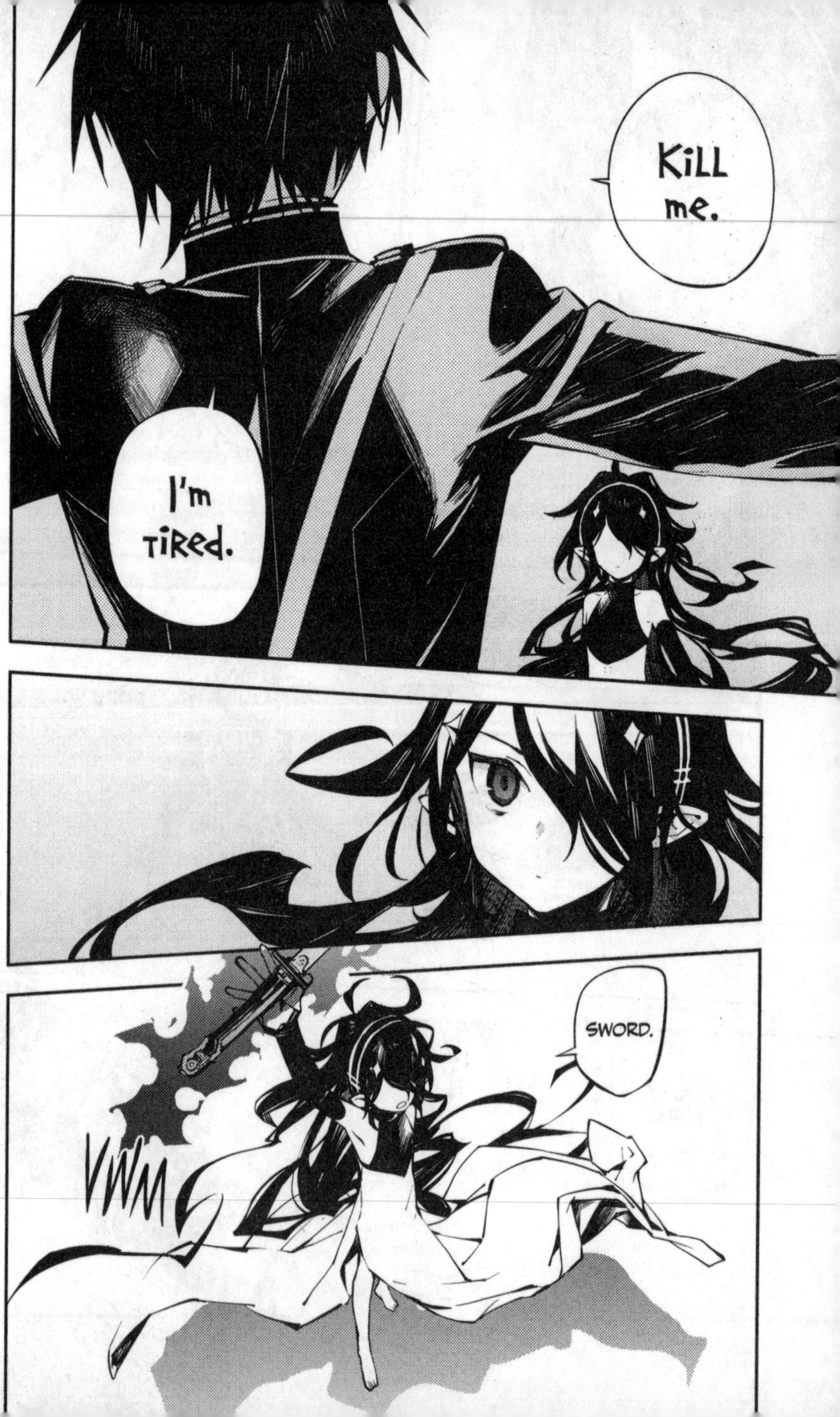
Kill me.
I'm tired.
SWORD.
VWM

chk

I'M SORRY.

HM?

ASURA-MARU.

HMPH.

GOOD-BYE.

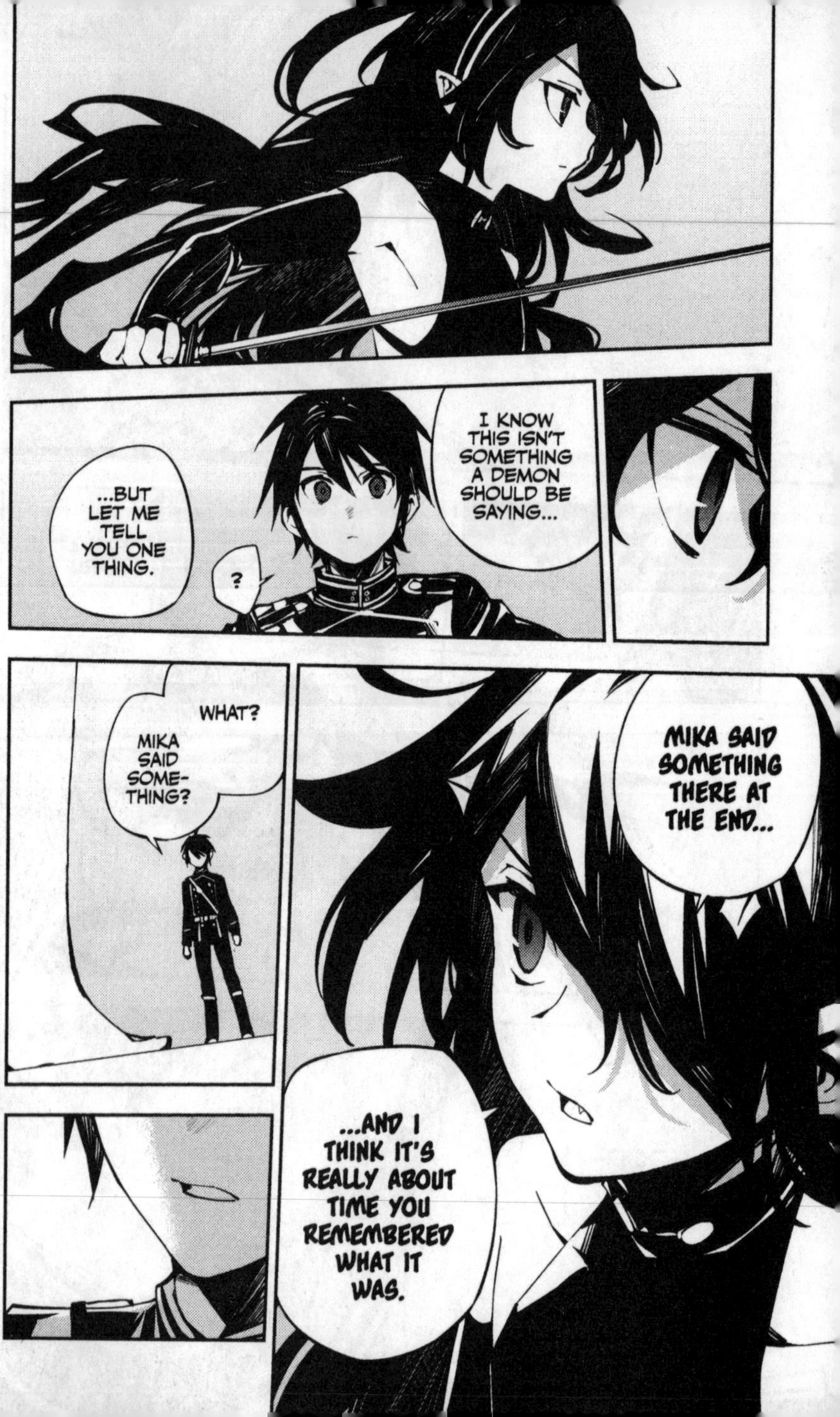
I KNOW THIS ISN'T SOMETHING A DEMON SHOULD BE SAYING...
...BUT LET ME TELL YOU ONE THING.
?
MIKA SAID SOMETHING THERE AT THE END...
...AND I THINK IT'S REALLY ABOUT TIME YOU REMEMBERED WHAT IT WAS.
WHAT?
MIKA SAID SOME-THING?

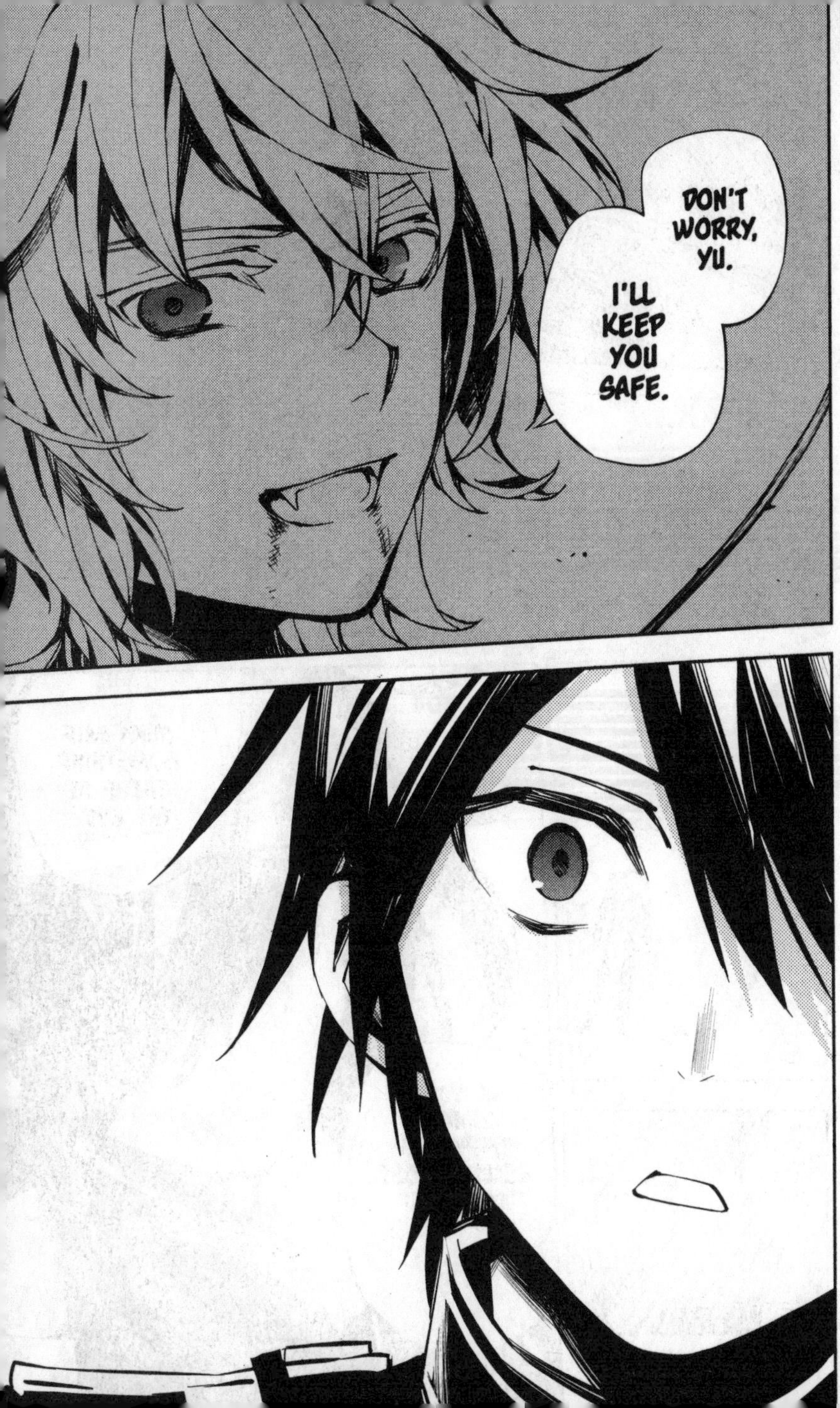
DON'T WORRY, YU.
I'LL KEEP YOU SAFE.

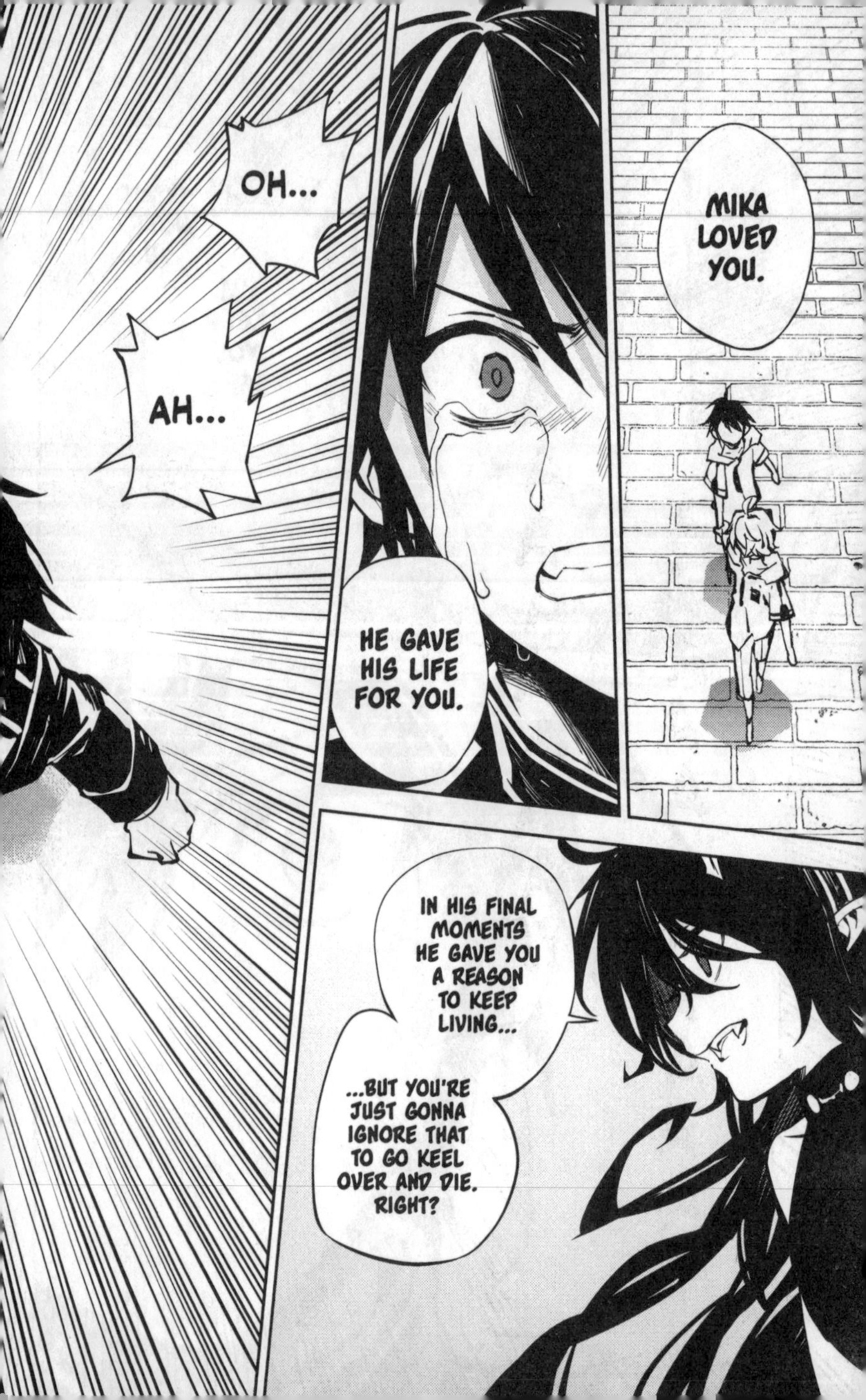
MIKA LOVED YOU.
HE GAVE HIS LIFE FOR YOU.
IN HIS FINAL MOMENTS HE GAVE YOU A REASON TO KEEP LIVING...
...BUT YOU'RE JUST GONNA IGNORE THAT TO GO KEEL OVER AND DIE. RIGHT?
OH...
AH...

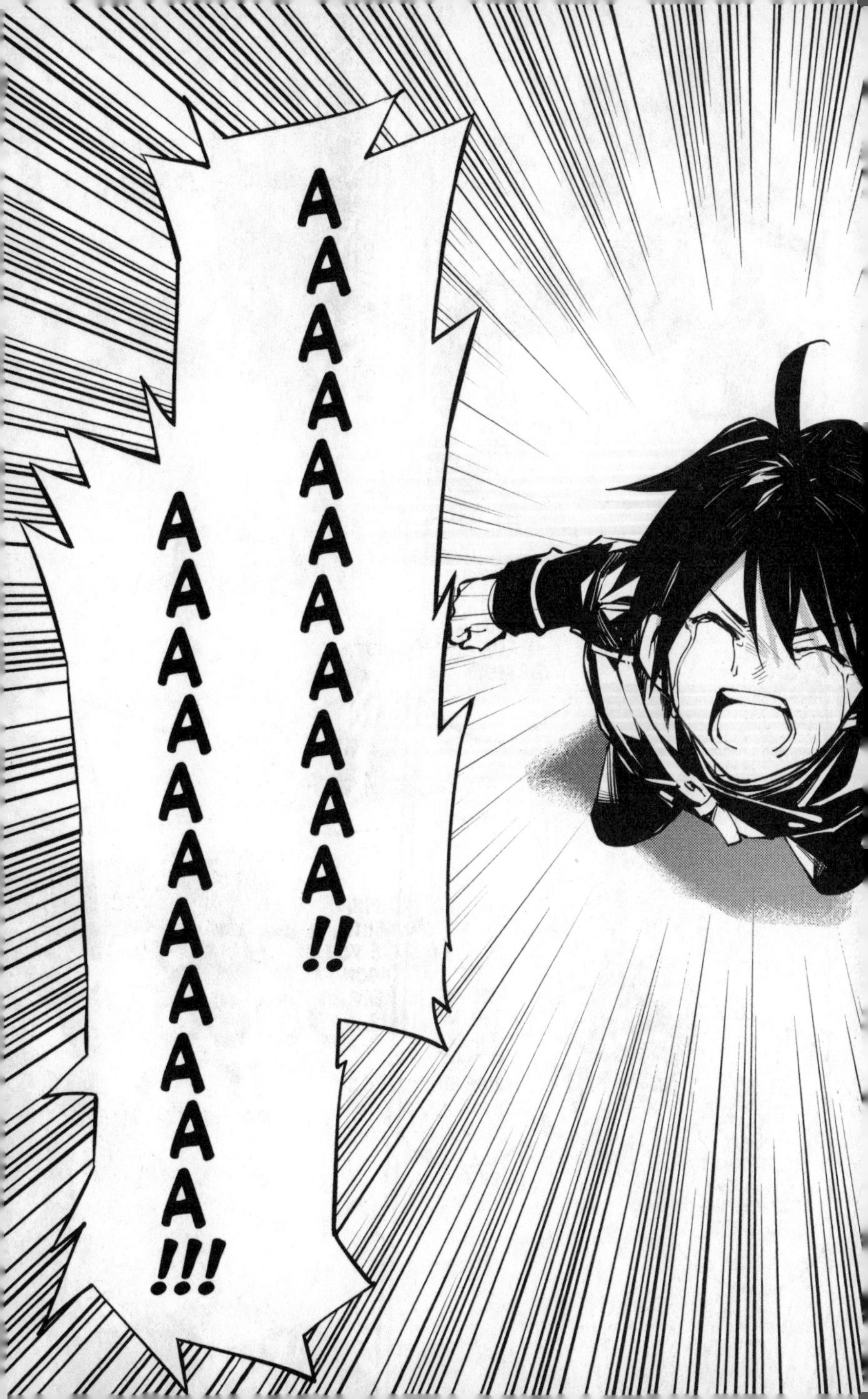
AAAAAAAAAAA!!
AAAAAAAAAAA!!!

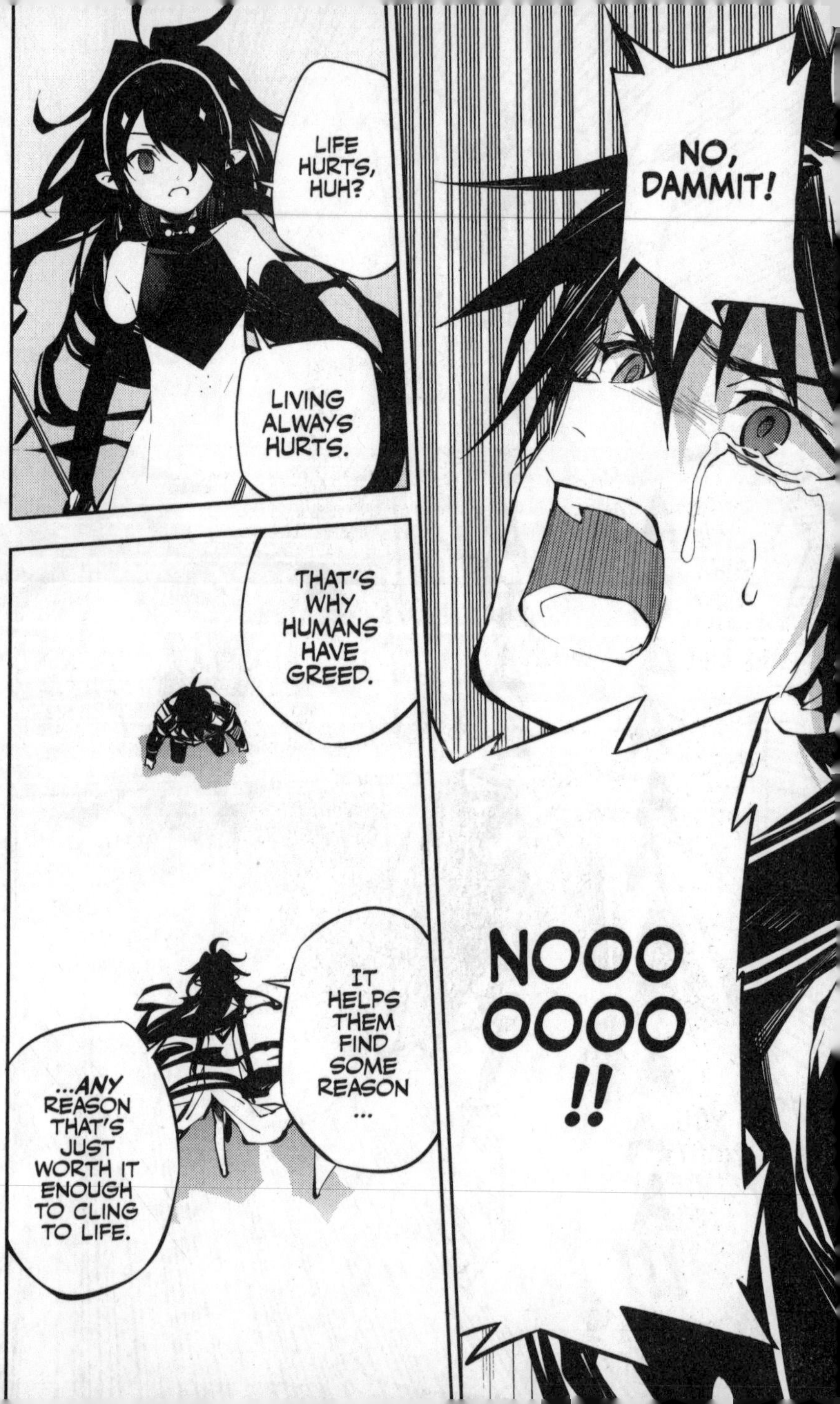
NO, DAMMIT!
NOOOOOOO!!
LIFE HURTS, HUH?
LIVING ALWAYS HURTS.
THAT'S WHY HUMANS HAVE GREED.
IT HELPS THEM FIND SOME REASON...
...ANY REASON THAT'S JUST WORTH IT ENOUGH TO CLING TO LIFE.

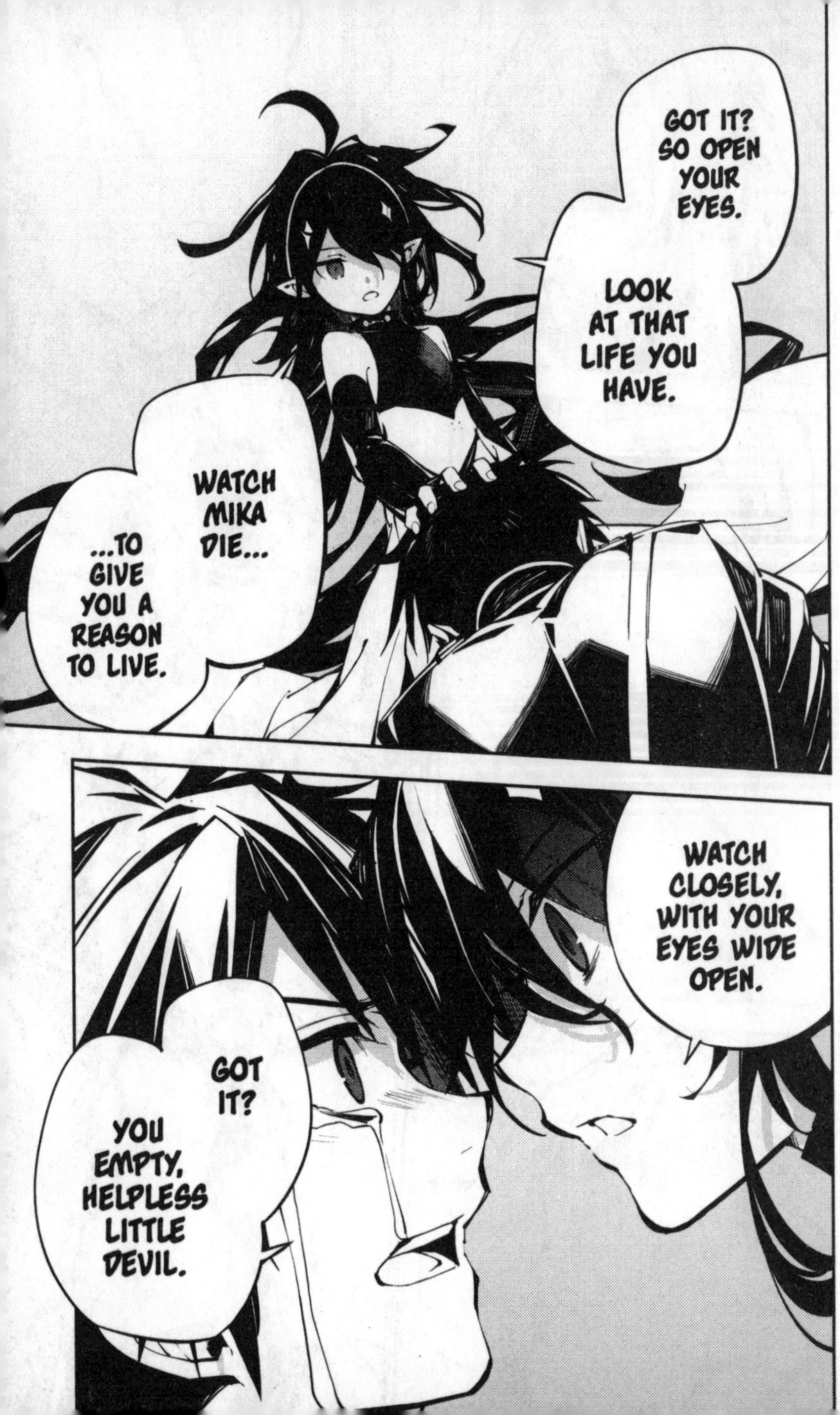
GOT IT? SO OPEN YOUR EYES.
LOOK AT THAT LIFE YOU HAVE.
WATCH MIKA DIE...
...TO GIVE YOU A REASON TO LIVE.
WATCH CLOSELY, WITH YOUR EYES WIDE OPEN.
GOT IT?
YOU EMPTY, HELPLESS LITTLE DEVIL.

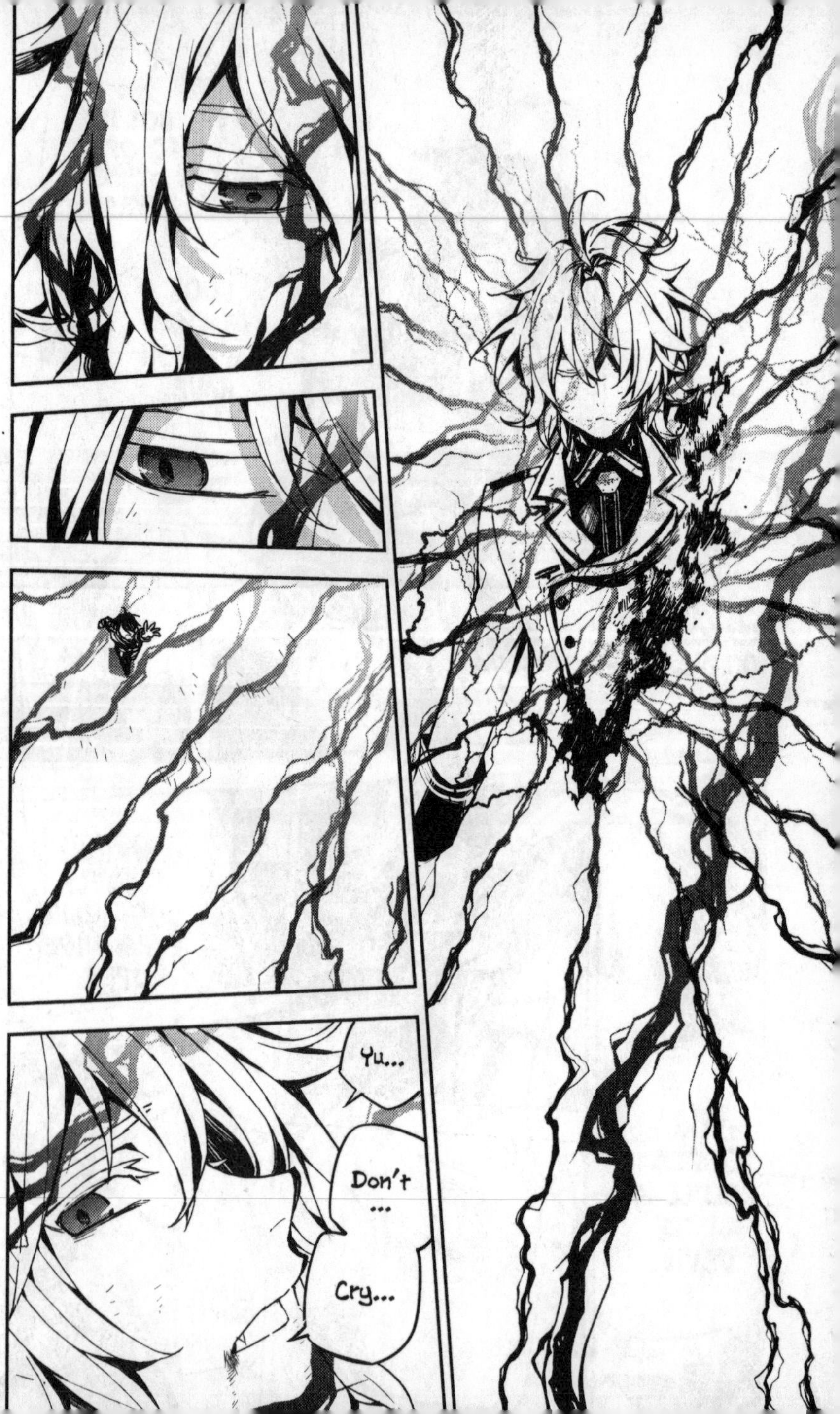
Yu...
Don't ...
Cry...

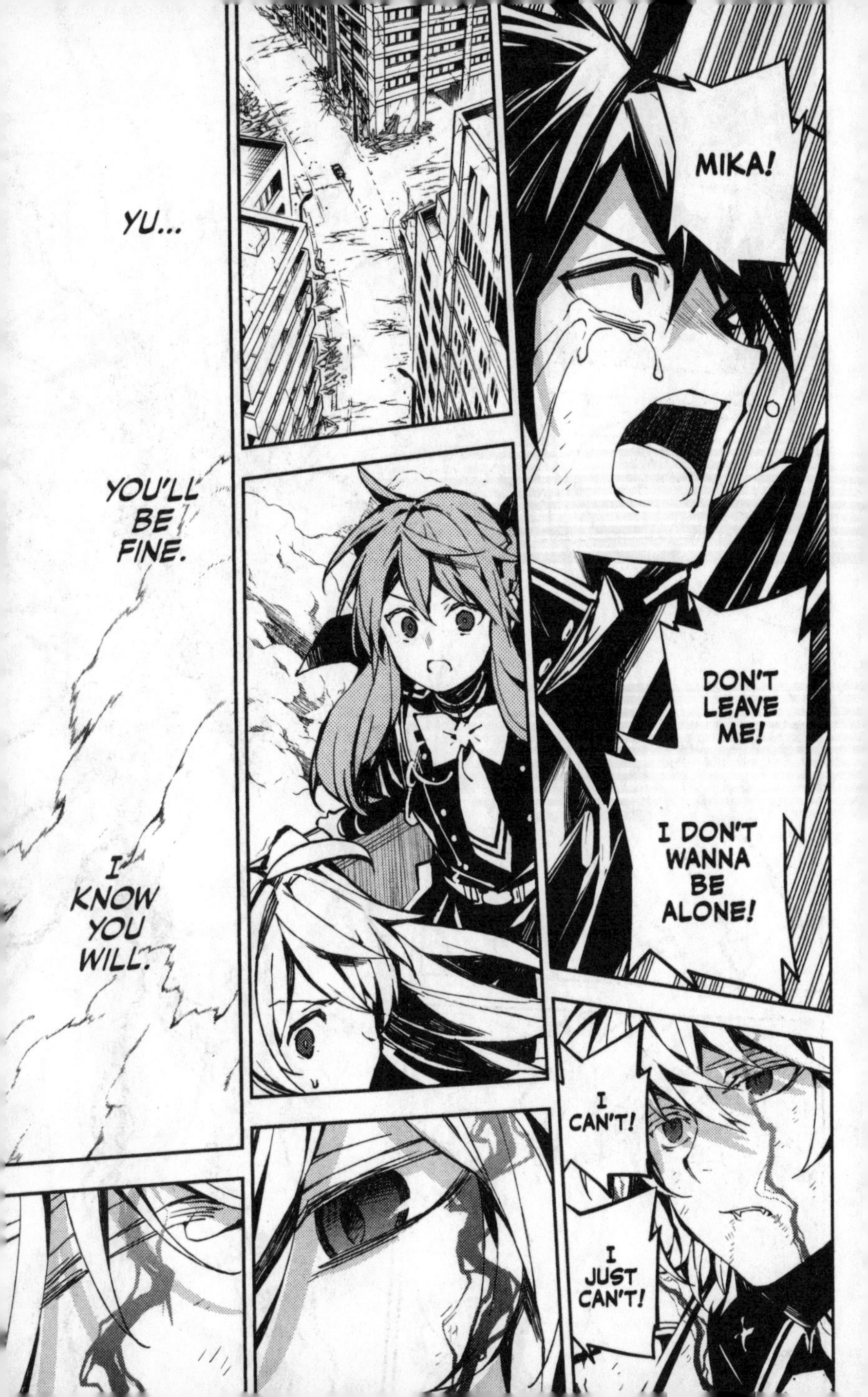
MIKA!
DON'T LEAVE ME!
I DON'T WANNA BE ALONE!
YU...
YOU'LL BE FINE.
I KNOW YOU WILL.
I CAN'T!
I JUST CAN'T!

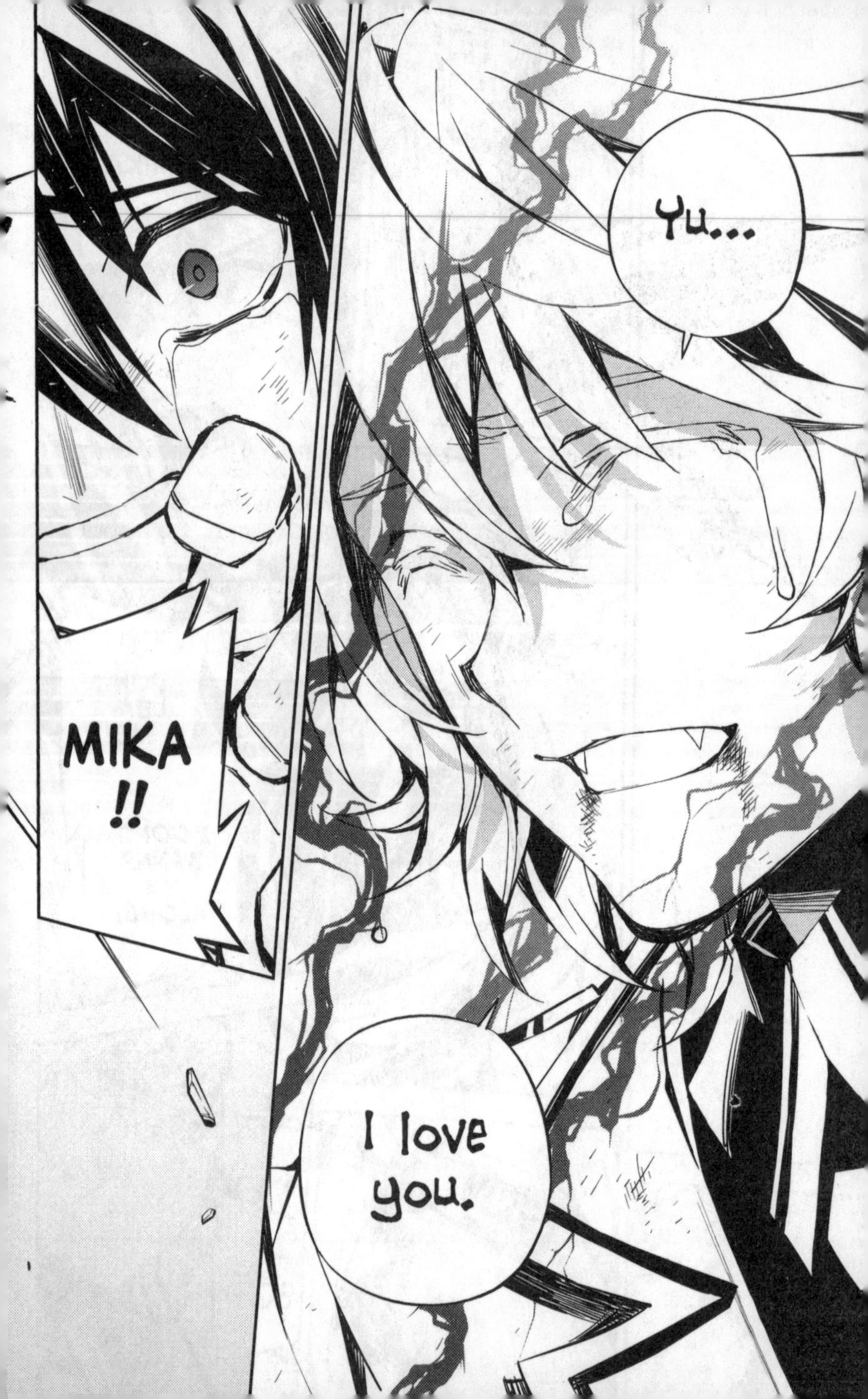
YU...
I love you.
MIKA !!

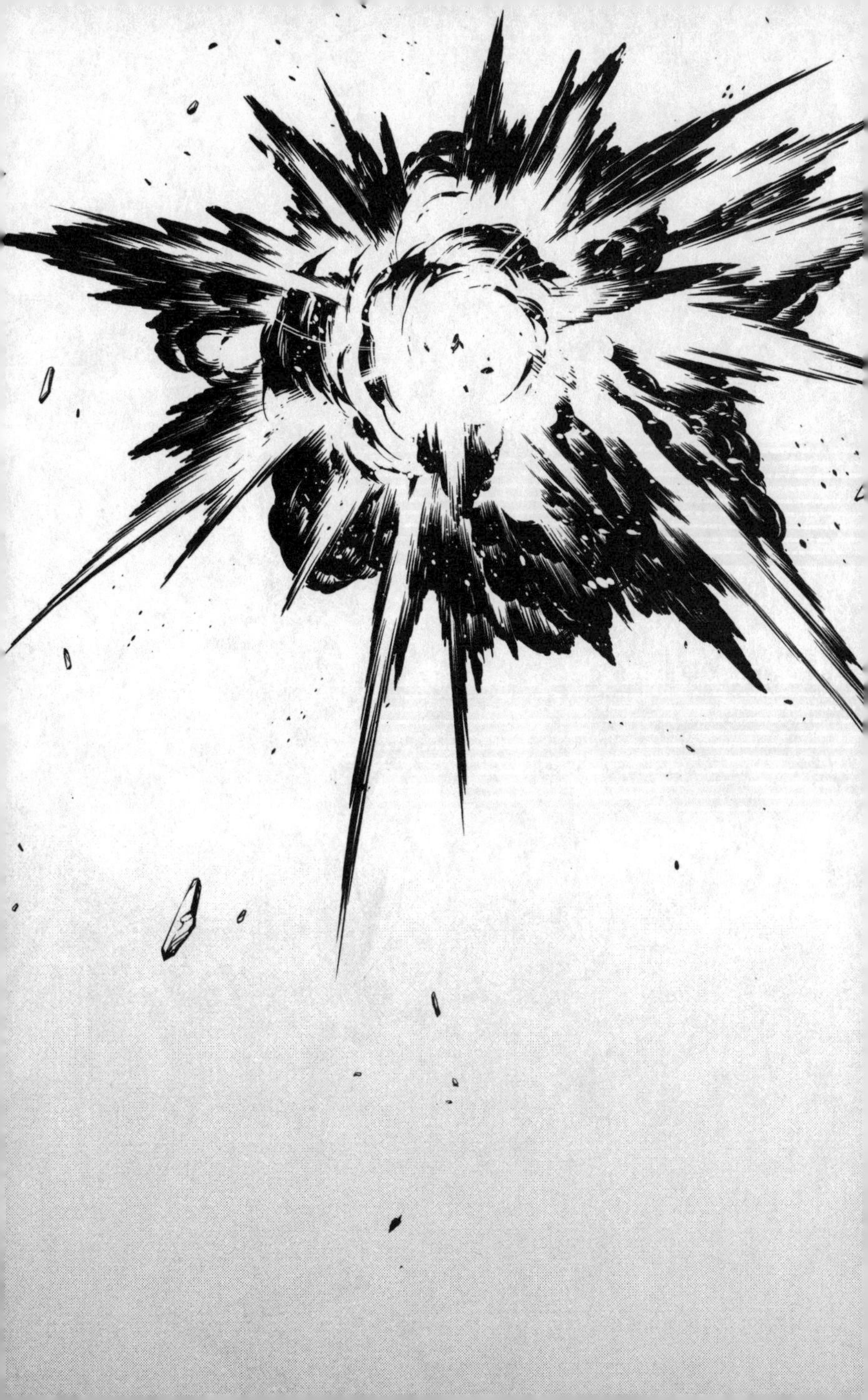

Seraph of the End
—VAMPIRE REIGN—

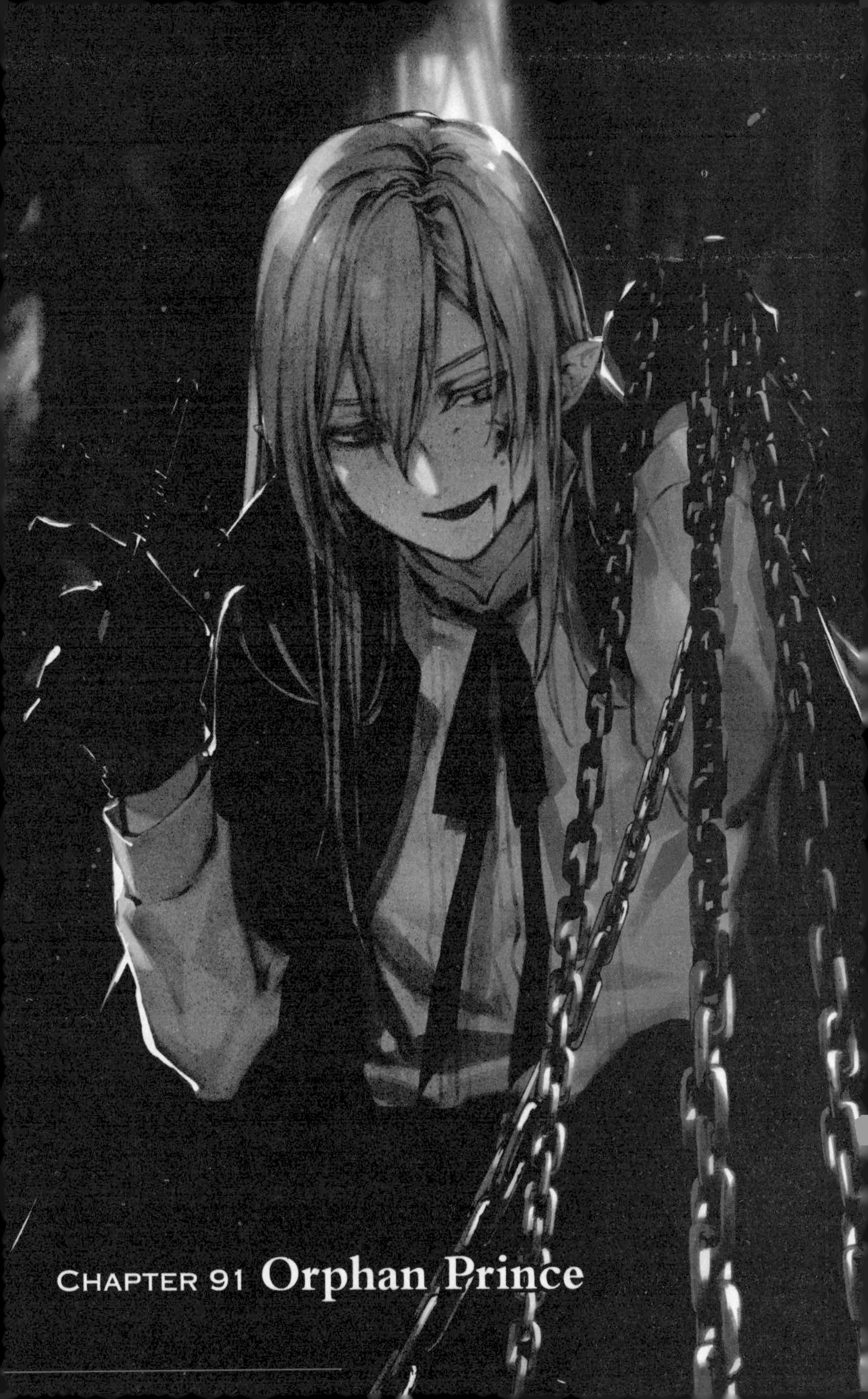

CHAPTER 91 Orphan Prince

Seraph of the End
VAMPIRE REIGN

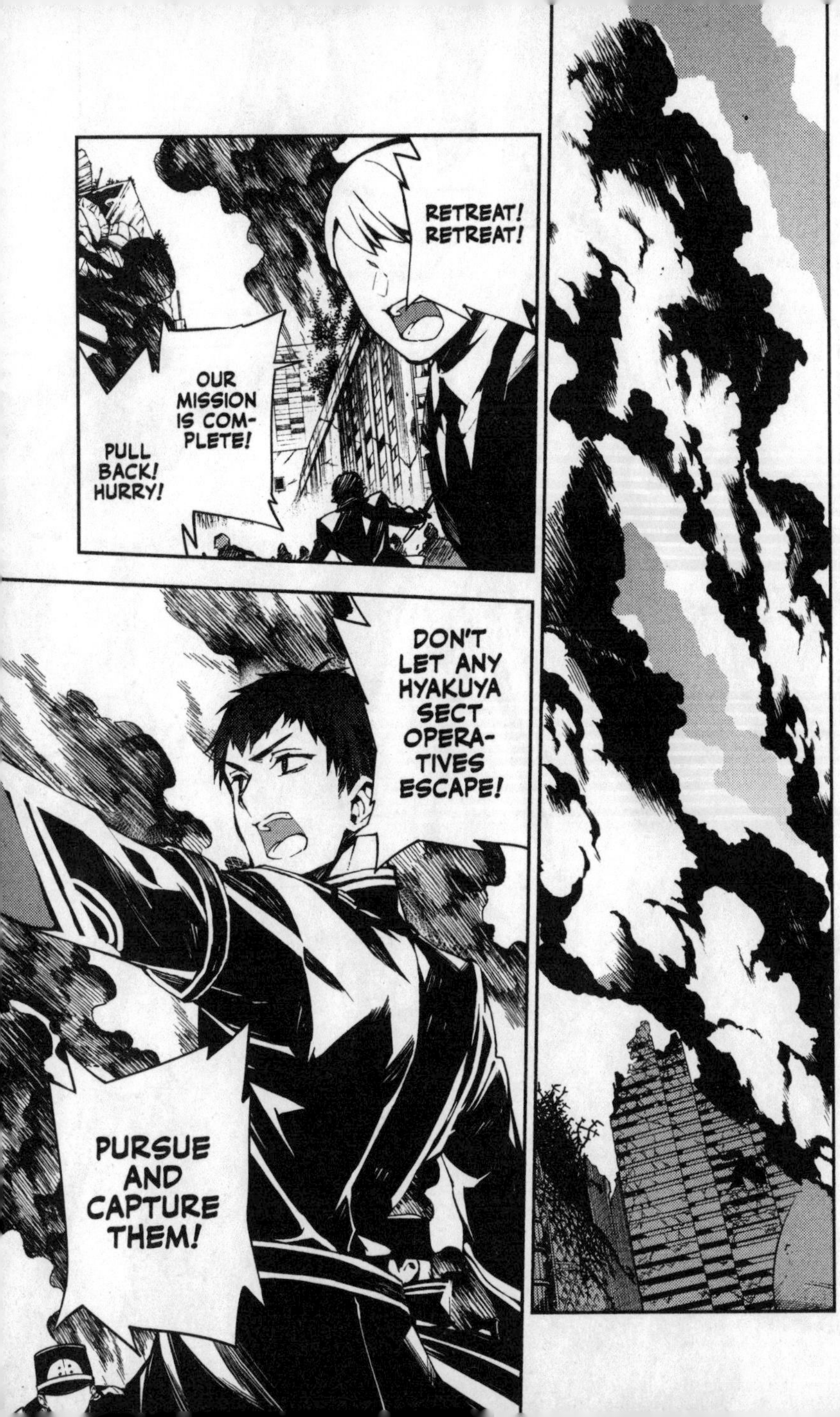
RETREAT! RETREAT!
OUR MISSION IS COMPLETE!
PULL BACK! HURRY!
DON'T LET ANY HYAKUYA SECT OPERATIVES ESCAPE!
PURSUE AND CAPTURE THEM!

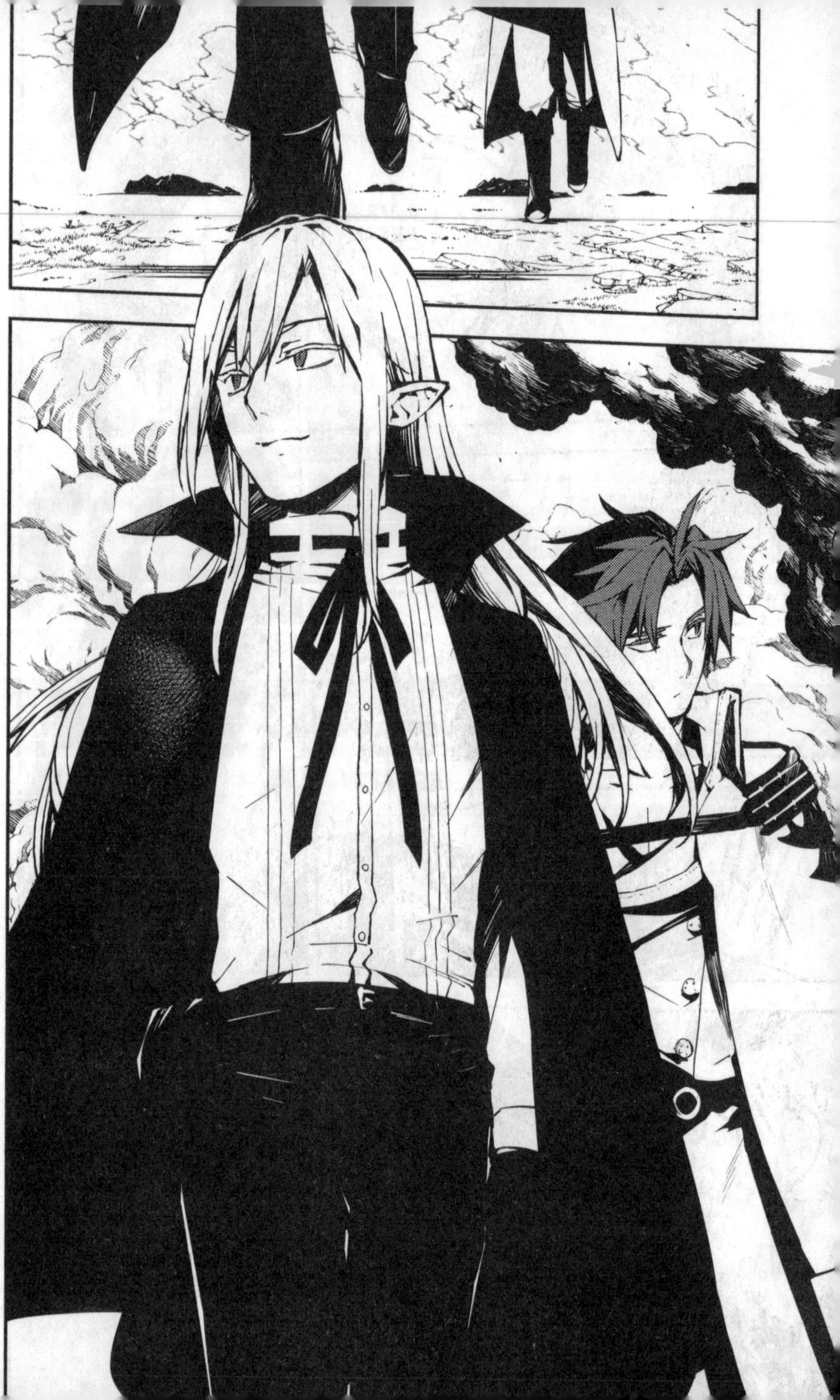

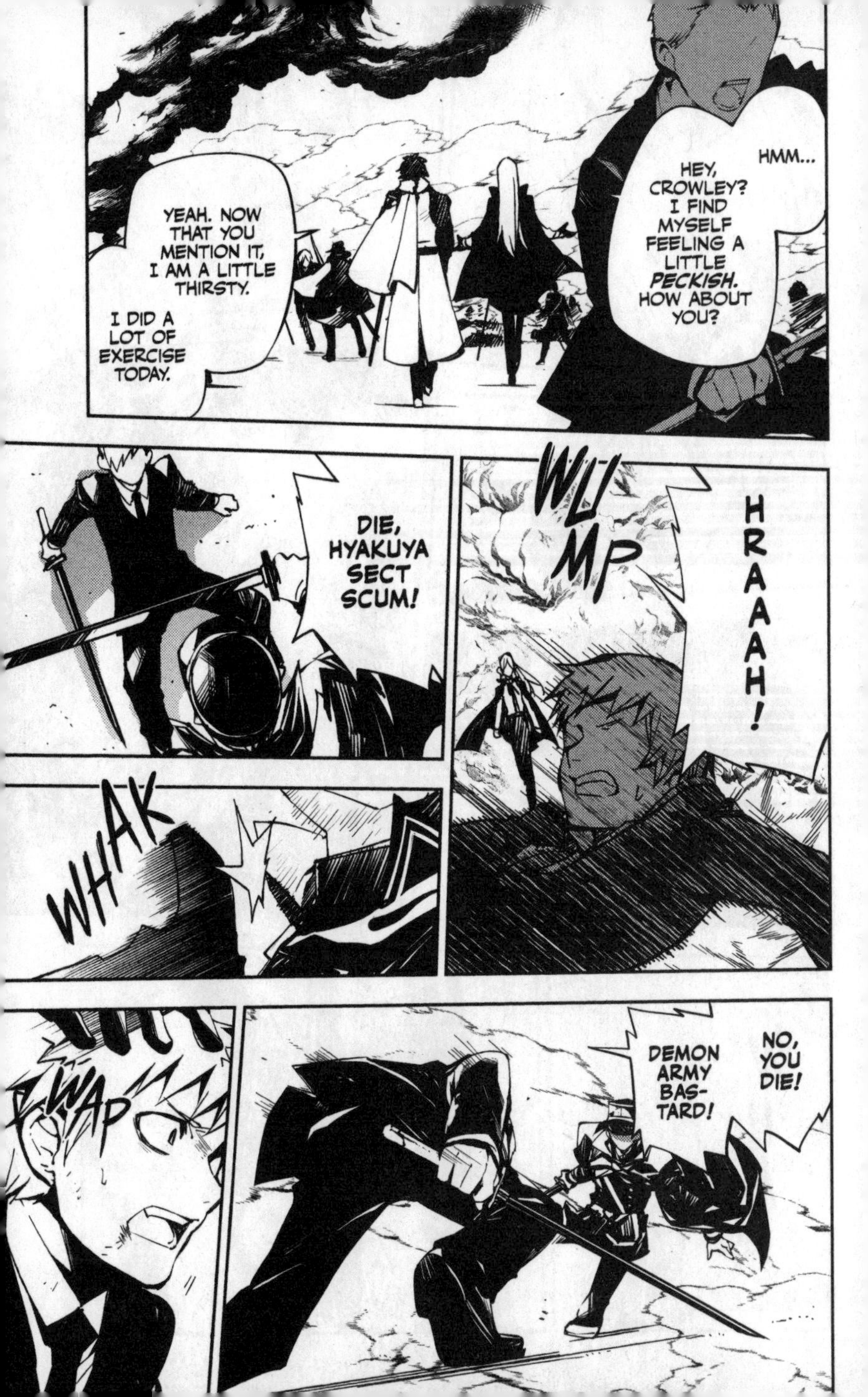
HMM...
HEY, CROWLEY? I FIND MYSELF FEELING A LITTLE *PECKISH.* HOW ABOUT YOU?
YEAH. NOW THAT YOU MENTION IT, I AM A LITTLE THIRSTY.
I DID A LOT OF EXERCISE TODAY.
WUMP
HRAAAH!
DIE, HYAKUYA SECT SCUM!
WHAK
NO, YOU DIE!
DEMON ARMY BASTARD!
WAP

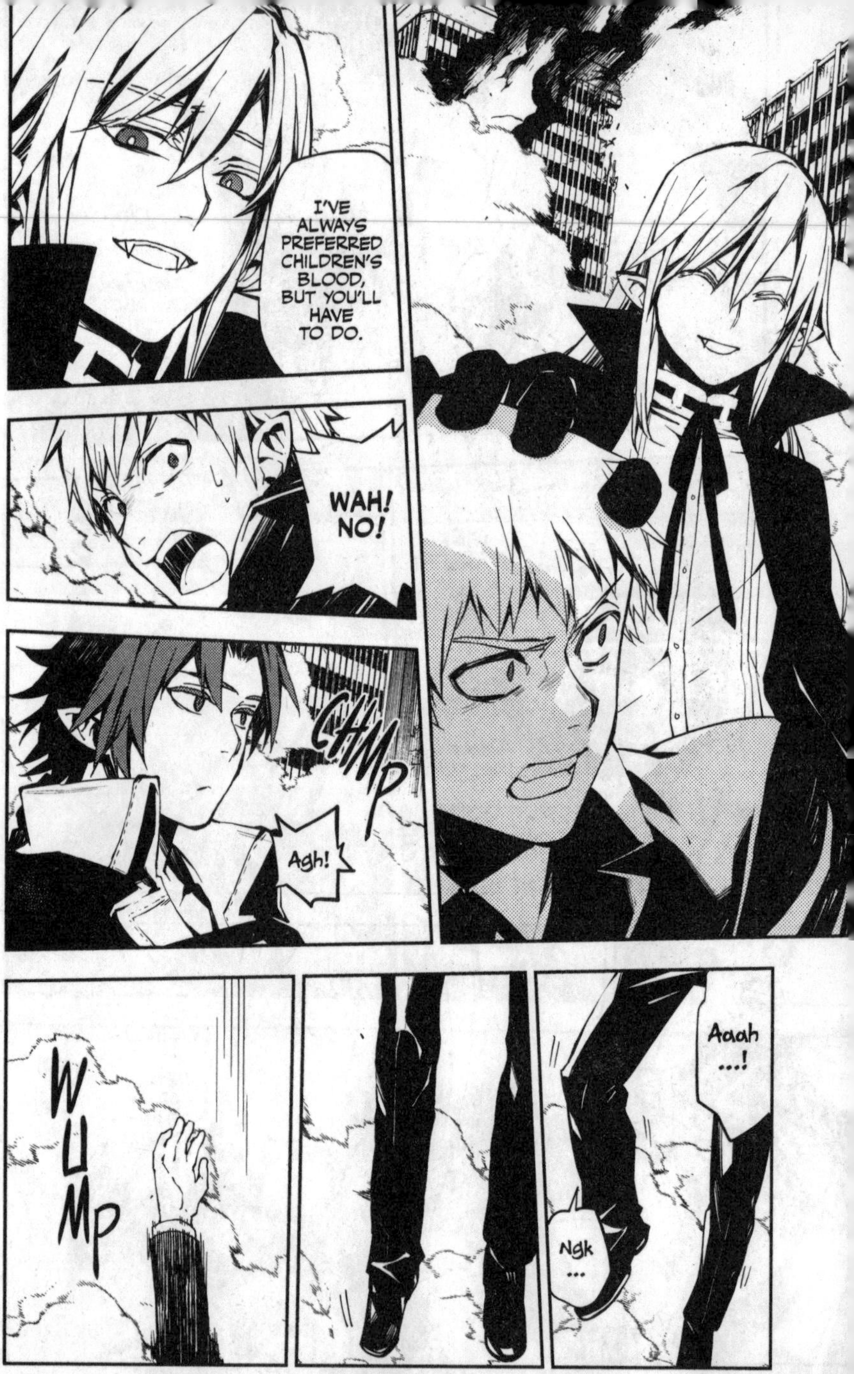
I'VE ALWAYS PREFERRED CHILDREN'S BLOOD, BUT YOU'LL HAVE TO DO.
WAH! NO!
CHMP
Agh!
Aaah ...!
Ngk ...
WUMP

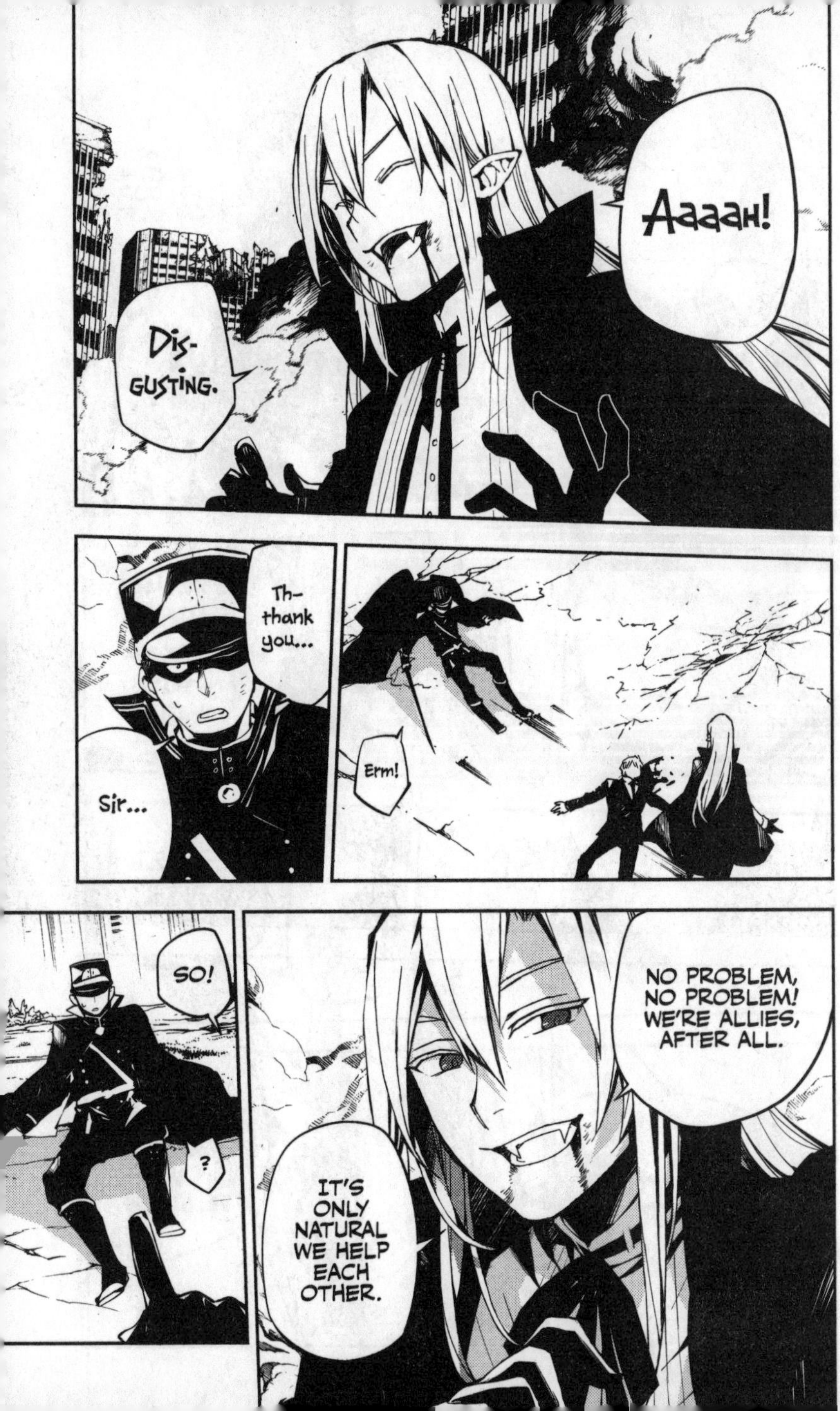
Aaaah!
Dis-GUSTING.
Erm!
Th-thank you...
Sir...
NO PROBLEM, NO PROBLEM! WE'RE ALLIES, AFTER ALL.
IT'S ONLY NATURAL WE HELP EACH OTHER.
SO!
?

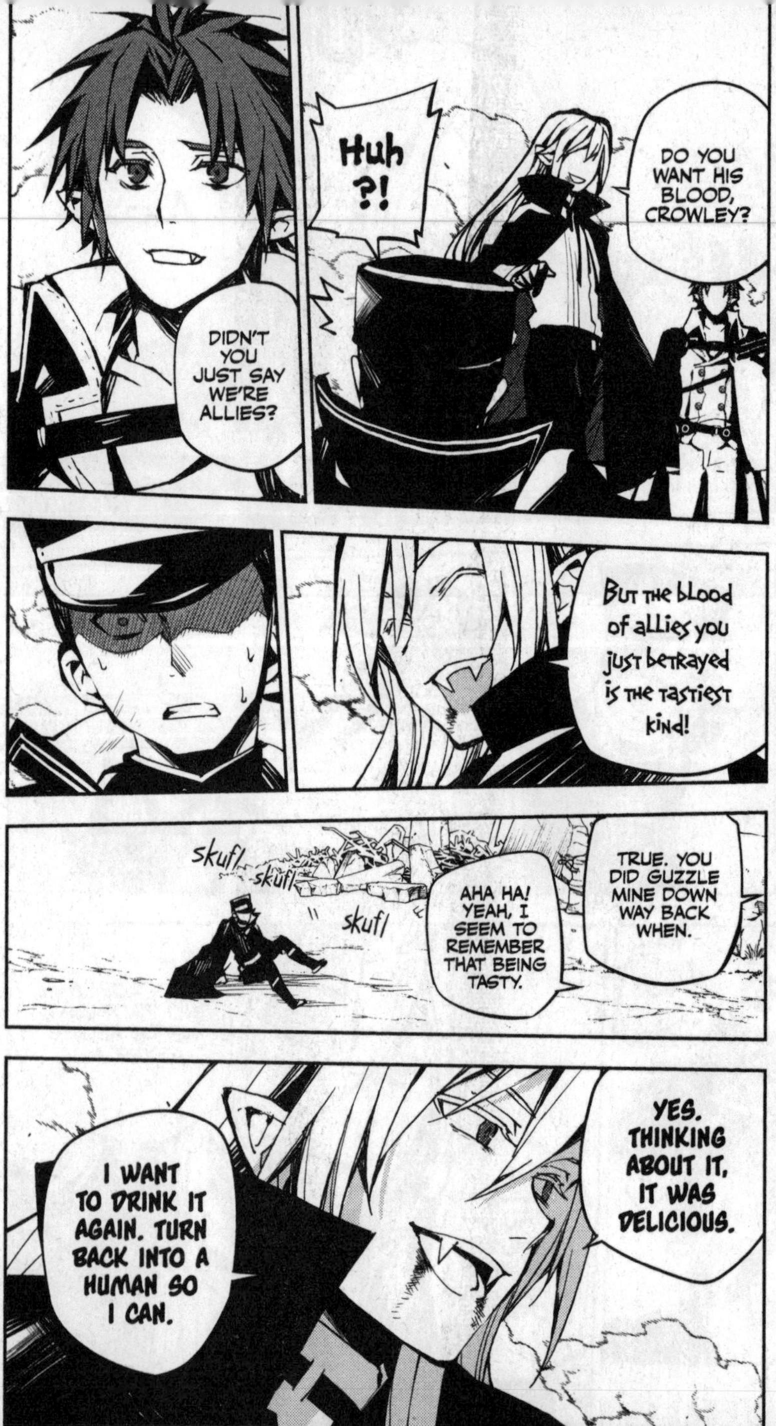
DO YOU WANT HIS BLOOD, CROWLEY?
Huh ?!
DIDN'T YOU JUST SAY WE'RE ALLIES?
But the blood of allies you just betrayed is the tastiest kind!
TRUE. YOU DID GUZZLE MINE DOWN WAY BACK WHEN.
AHA HA! YEAH, I SEEM TO REMEMBER THAT BEING TASTY.
skufl
skufl
skufl
YES. THINKING ABOUT IT, IT WAS DELICIOUS.
I WANT TO DRINK IT AGAIN. TURN BACK INTO A HUMAN SO I CAN.

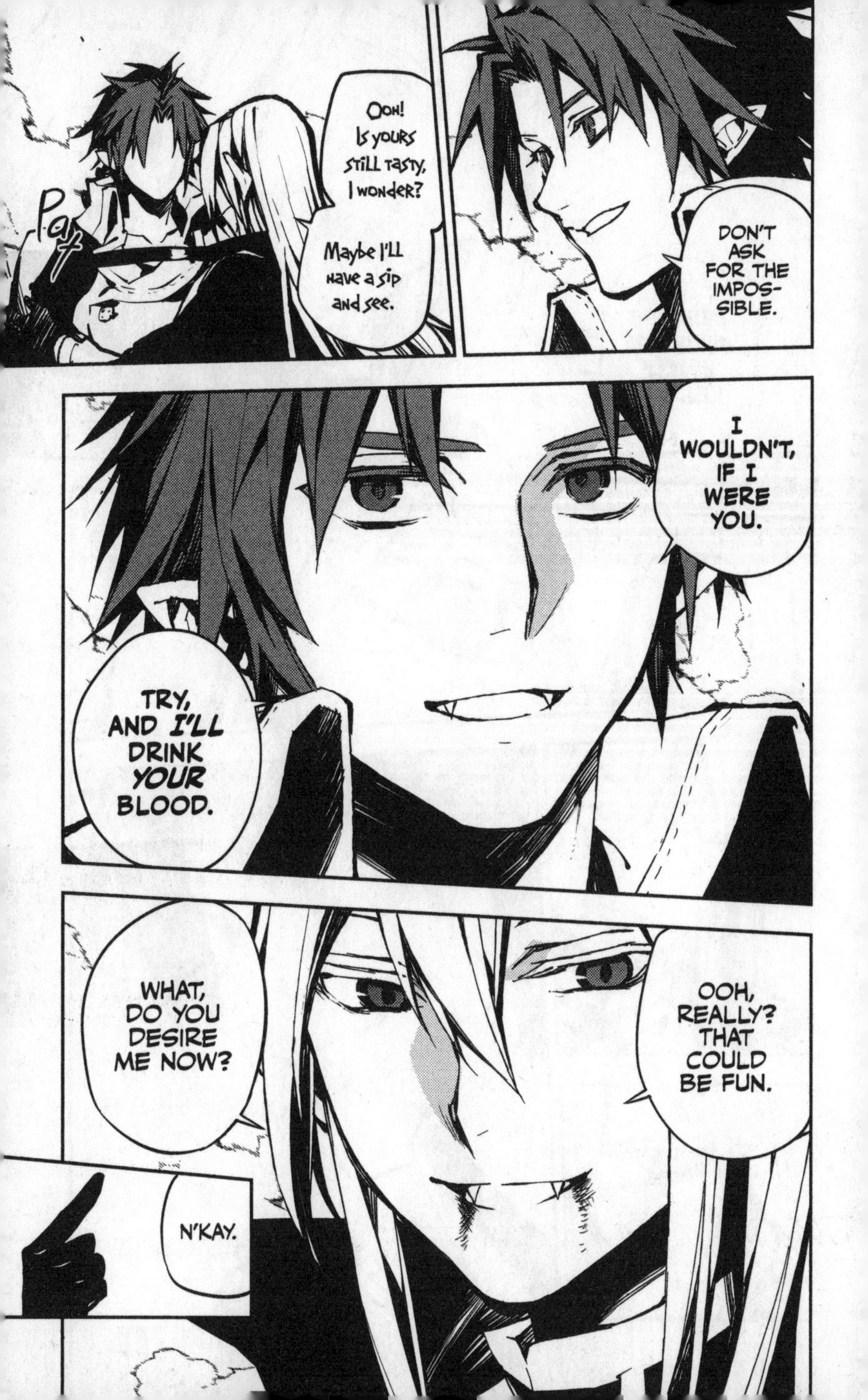
DON'T ASK FOR THE IMPOS-SIBLE.
Ooh! Is yours still tasty, I wonder?
Maybe I'll have a sip and see.
Pat
I WOULDN'T, IF I WERE YOU.
TRY, AND *I'LL* DRINK *YOUR* BLOOD.
OOH, REALLY? THAT COULD BE FUN.
WHAT, DO YOU DESIRE ME NOW?
N'KAY.

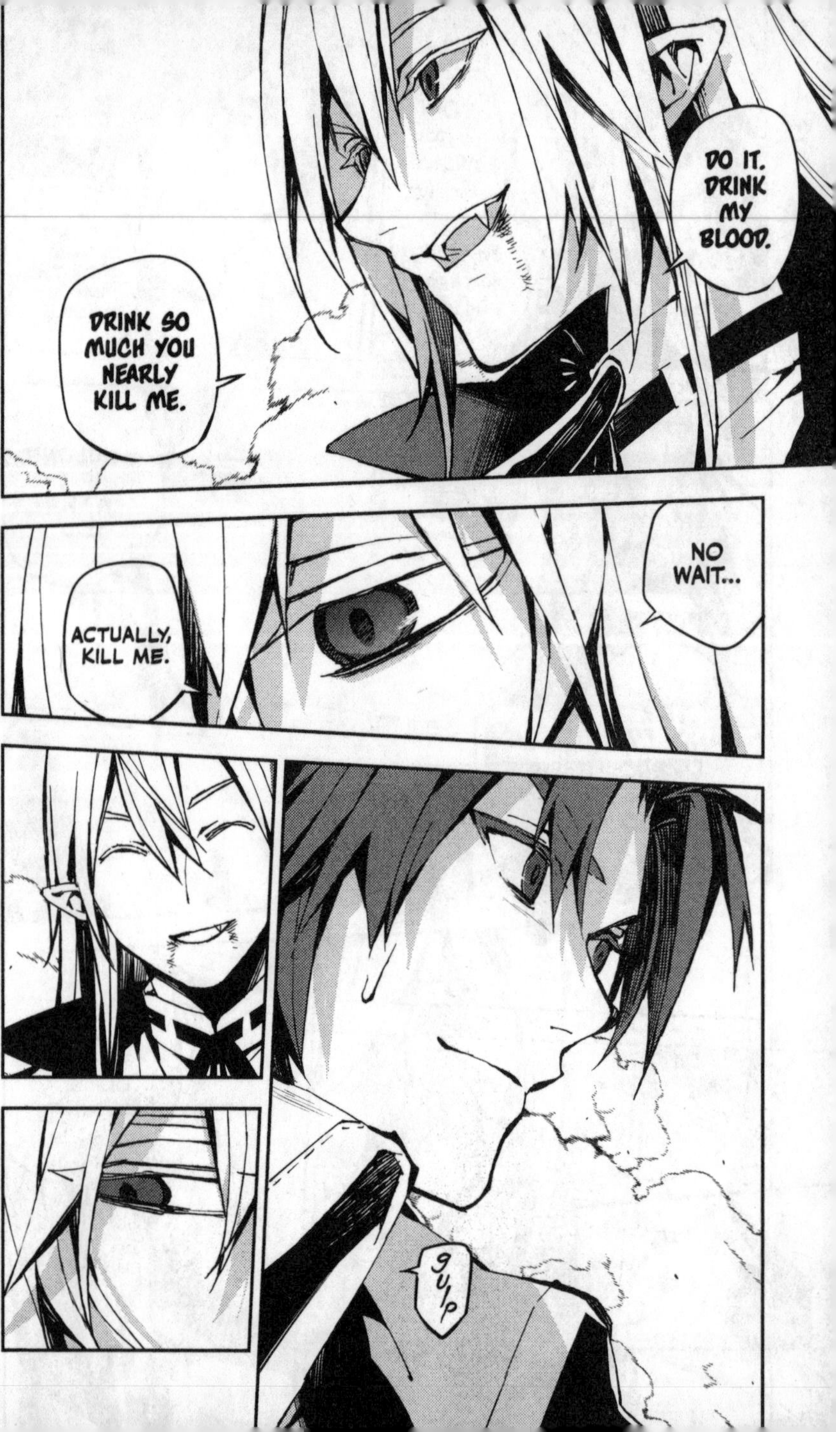
DO IT. DRINK MY BLOOD.
DRINK SO MUCH YOU NEARLY KILL ME.
NO WAIT...
ACTUALLY, KILL ME.
gulp

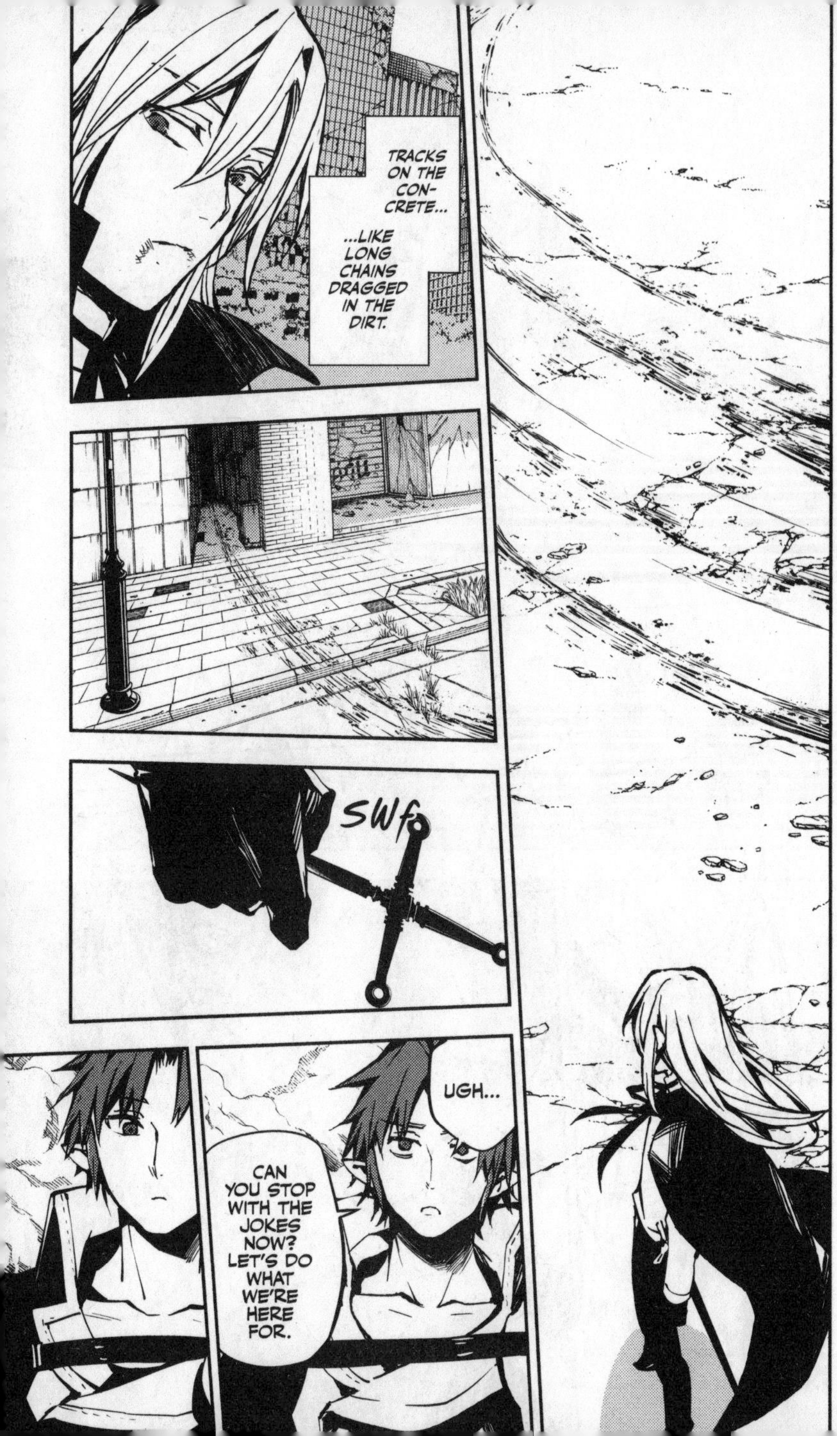
TRACKS ON THE CON-CRETE...
...LIKE LONG CHAINS DRAGGED IN THE DIRT.
SWf
UGH...
CAN YOU STOP WITH THE JOKES NOW? LET'S DO WHAT WE'RE HERE FOR.

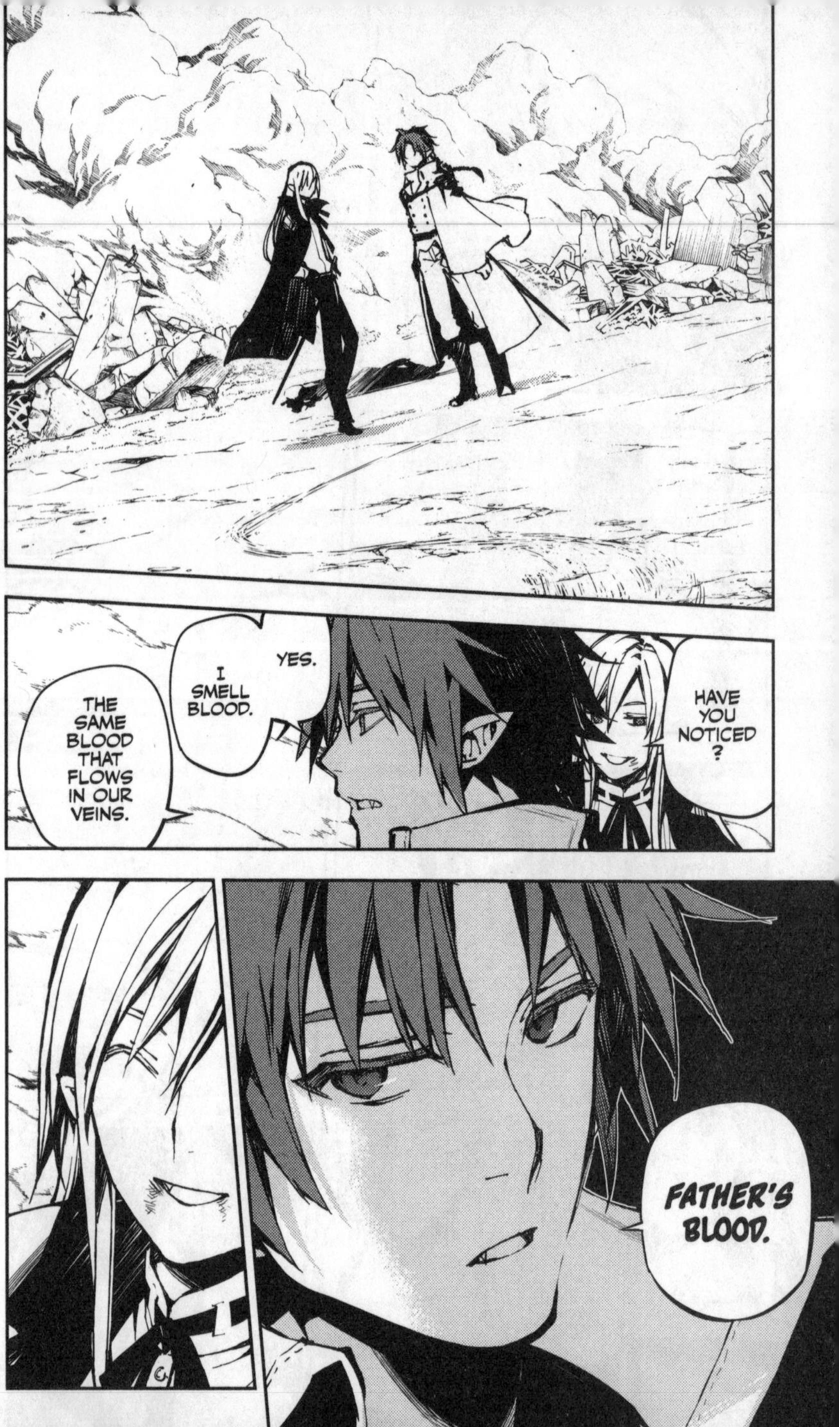
HAVE YOU NOTICED?
YES.
I SMELL BLOOD.
THE SAME BLOOD THAT FLOWS IN OUR VEINS.
FATHER'S BLOOD.

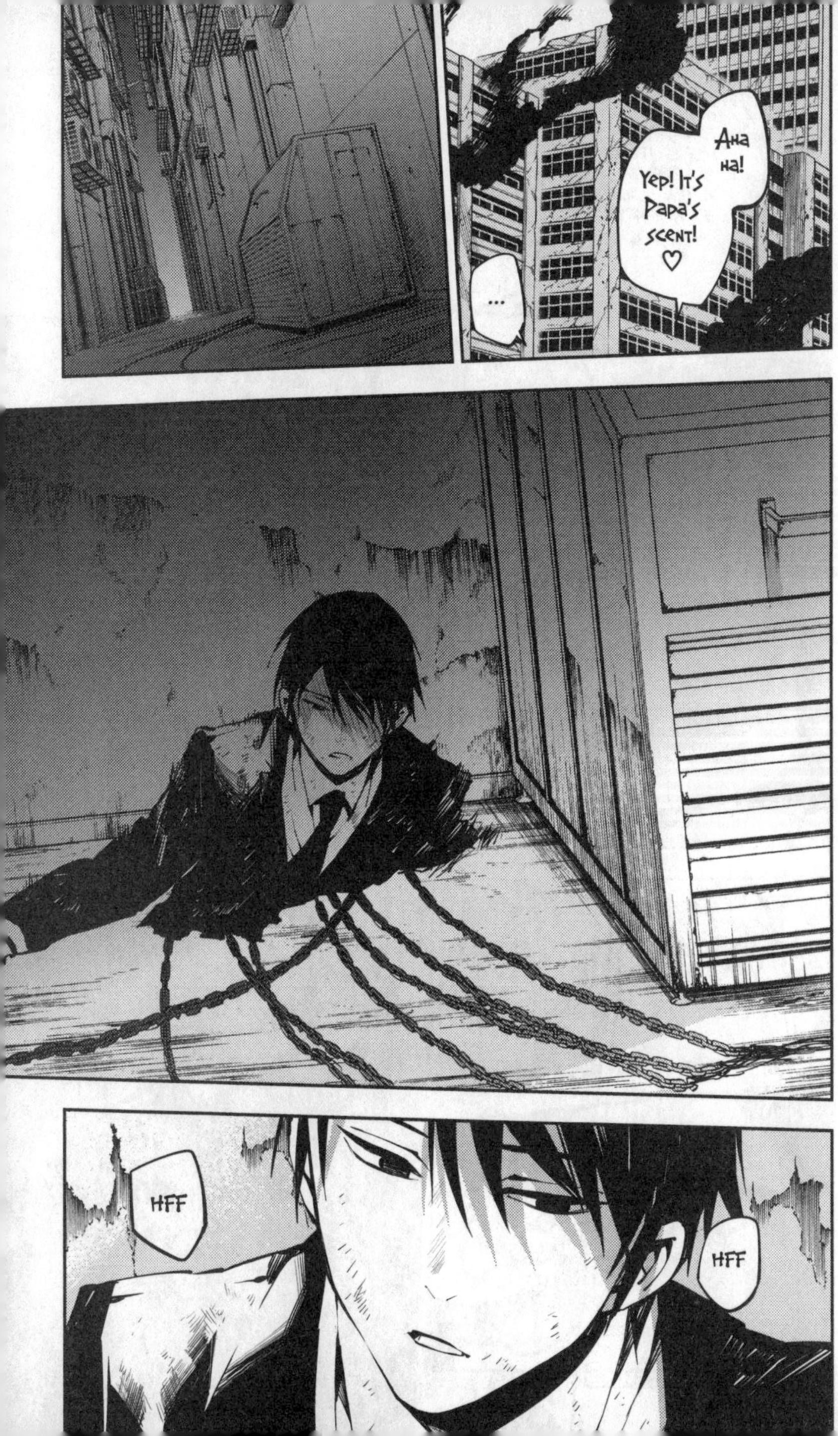
Aha ha!
Yep! It's Papa's scent! ♡
...
HFF
HFF

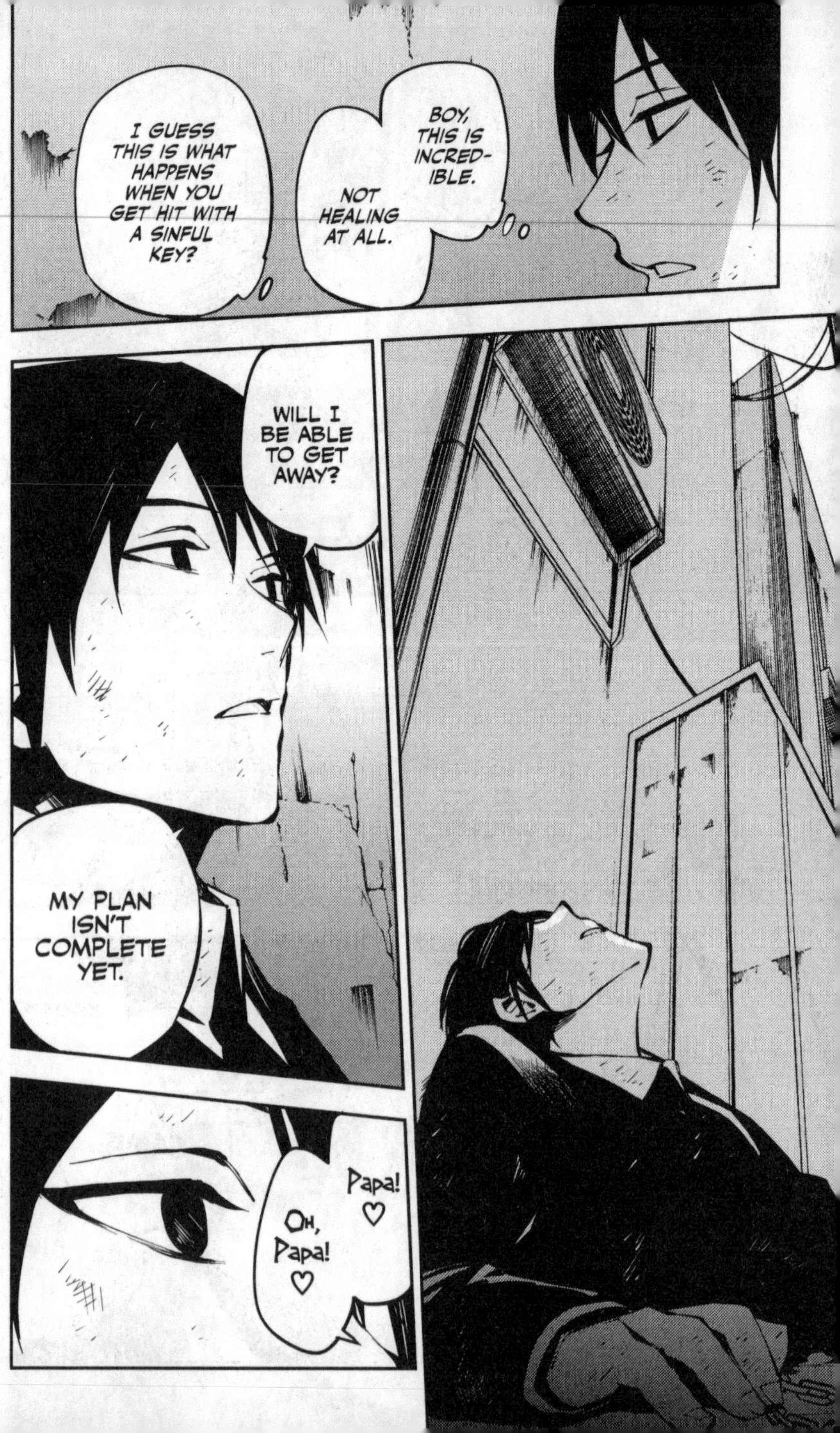
BOY, THIS IS INCREDIBLE.
NOT HEALING AT ALL.
I GUESS THIS IS WHAT HAPPENS WHEN YOU GET HIT WITH A SINFUL KEY?
WILL I BE ABLE TO GET AWAY?
MY PLAN ISN'T COMPLETE YET.
Papa! ♡
Oh, Papa! ♡

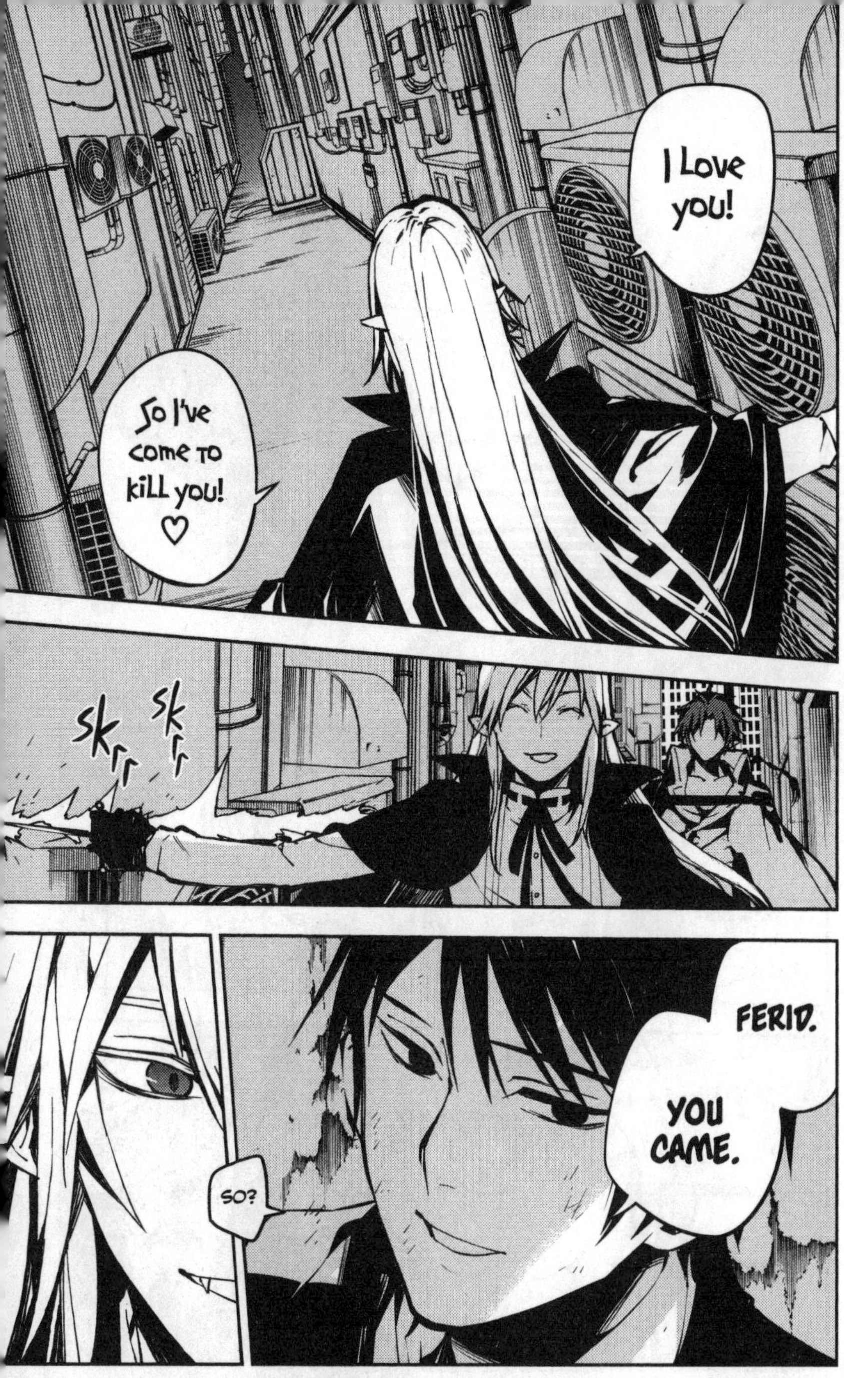
I Love you!
So I've come to kill you! ♡
Skrr
Skrr
FERID.
YOU CAME.
SO?

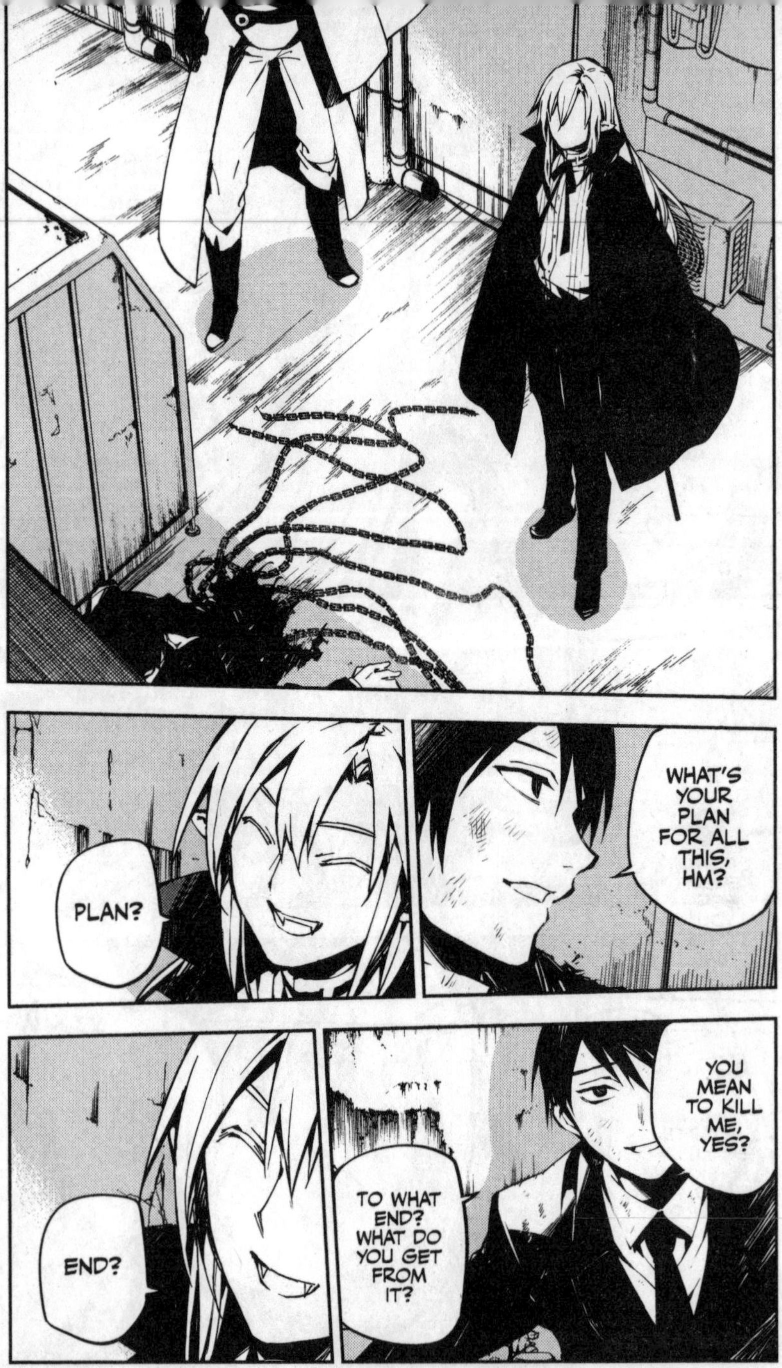
WHAT'S YOUR PLAN FOR ALL THIS, HM?
PLAN?
YOU MEAN TO KILL ME, YES?
TO WHAT END? WHAT DO YOU GET FROM IT?
END?

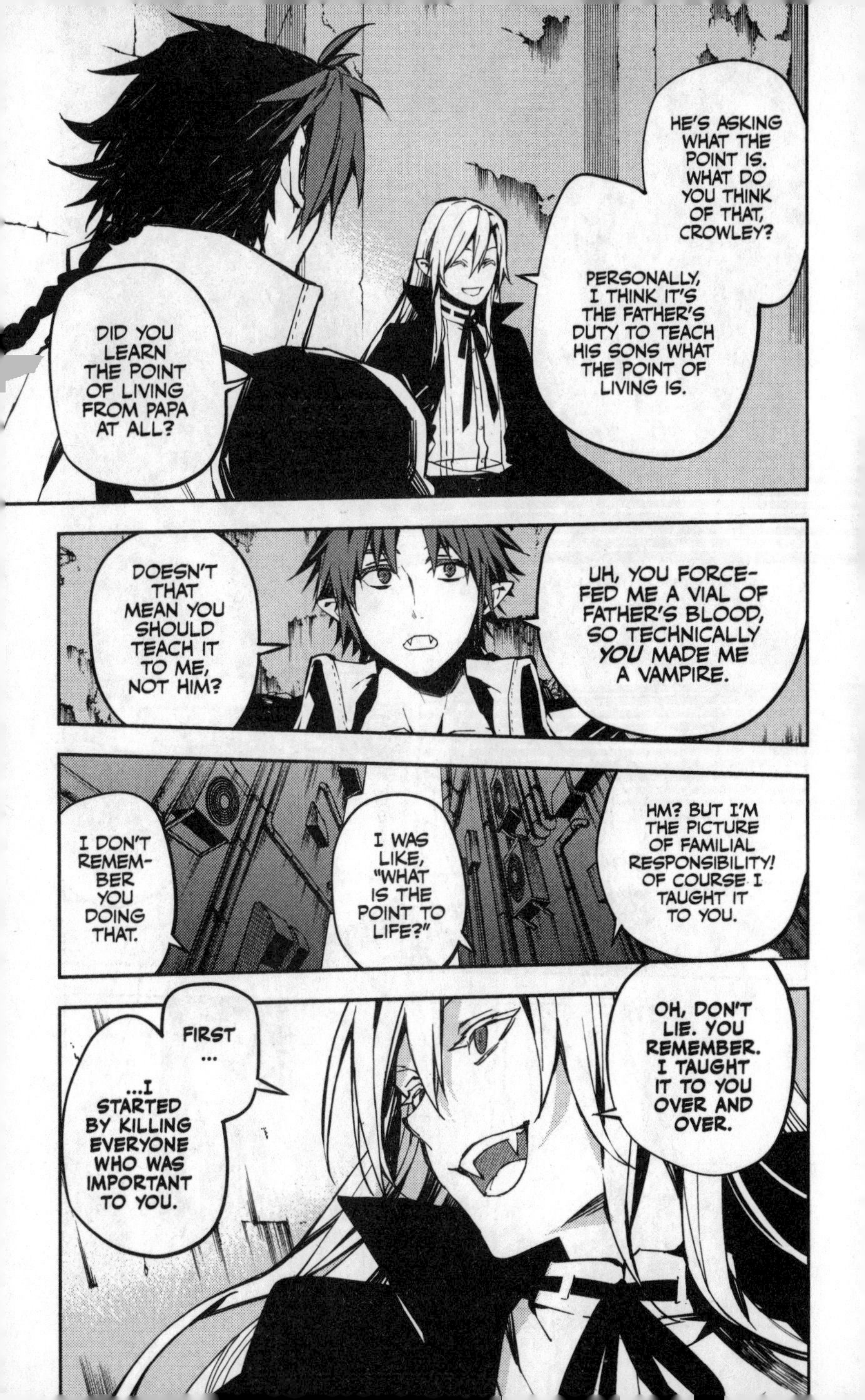
HE'S ASKING WHAT THE POINT IS. WHAT DO YOU THINK OF THAT, CROWLEY?
PERSONALLY, I THINK IT'S THE FATHER'S DUTY TO TEACH HIS SONS WHAT THE POINT OF LIVING IS.
DID YOU LEARN THE POINT OF LIVING FROM PAPA AT ALL?
UH, YOU FORCE-FED ME A VIAL OF FATHER'S BLOOD, SO TECHNICALLY *YOU* MADE ME A VAMPIRE.
DOESN'T THAT MEAN YOU SHOULD TEACH IT TO ME, NOT HIM?
HM? BUT I'M THE PICTURE OF FAMILIAL RESPONSIBILITY! OF COURSE I TAUGHT IT TO YOU.
I WAS LIKE, "WHAT IS THE POINT TO LIFE?"
I DON'T REMEM-BER YOU DOING THAT.
OH, DON'T LIE. YOU REMEMBER. I TAUGHT IT TO YOU OVER AND OVER.
FIRST ...
...I STARTED BY KILLING EVERYONE WHO WAS IMPORTANT TO YOU.

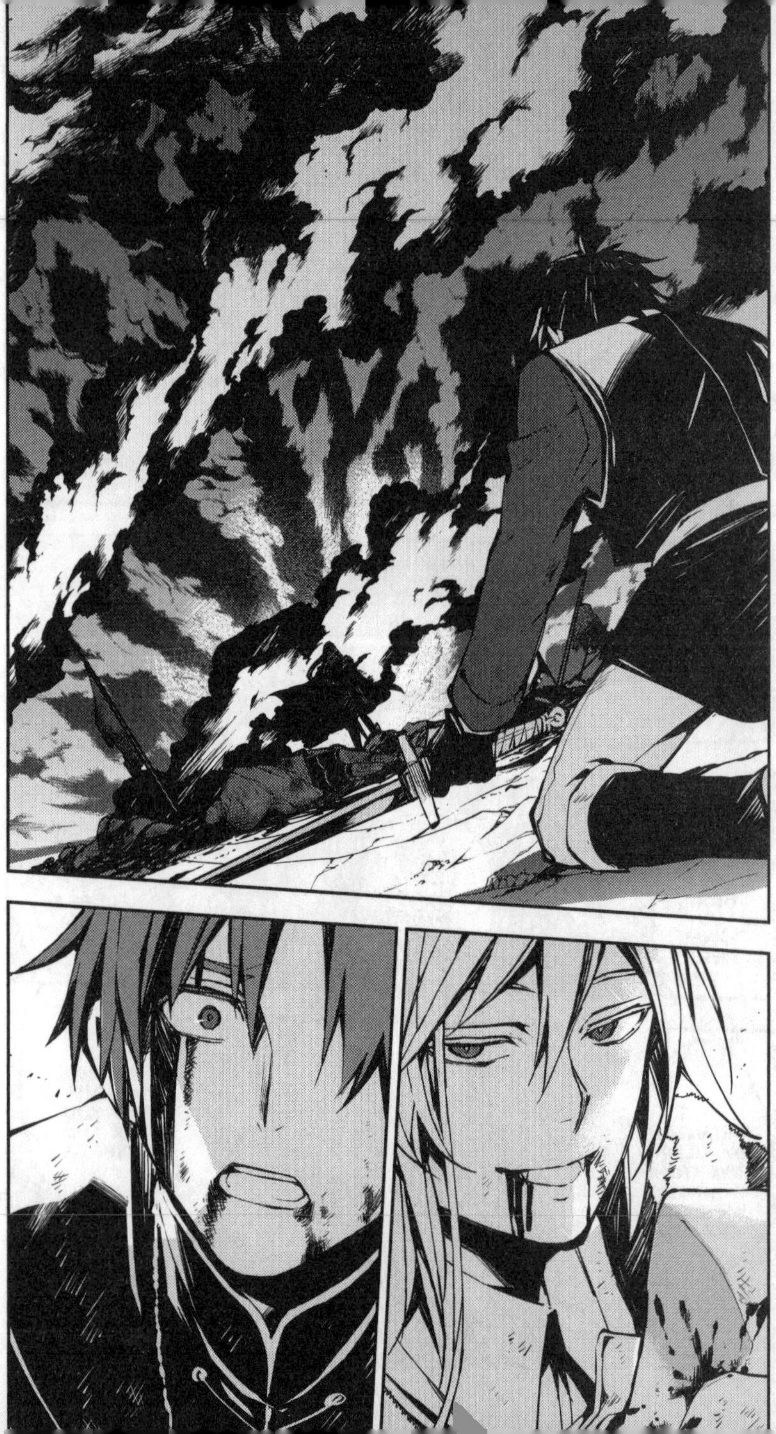

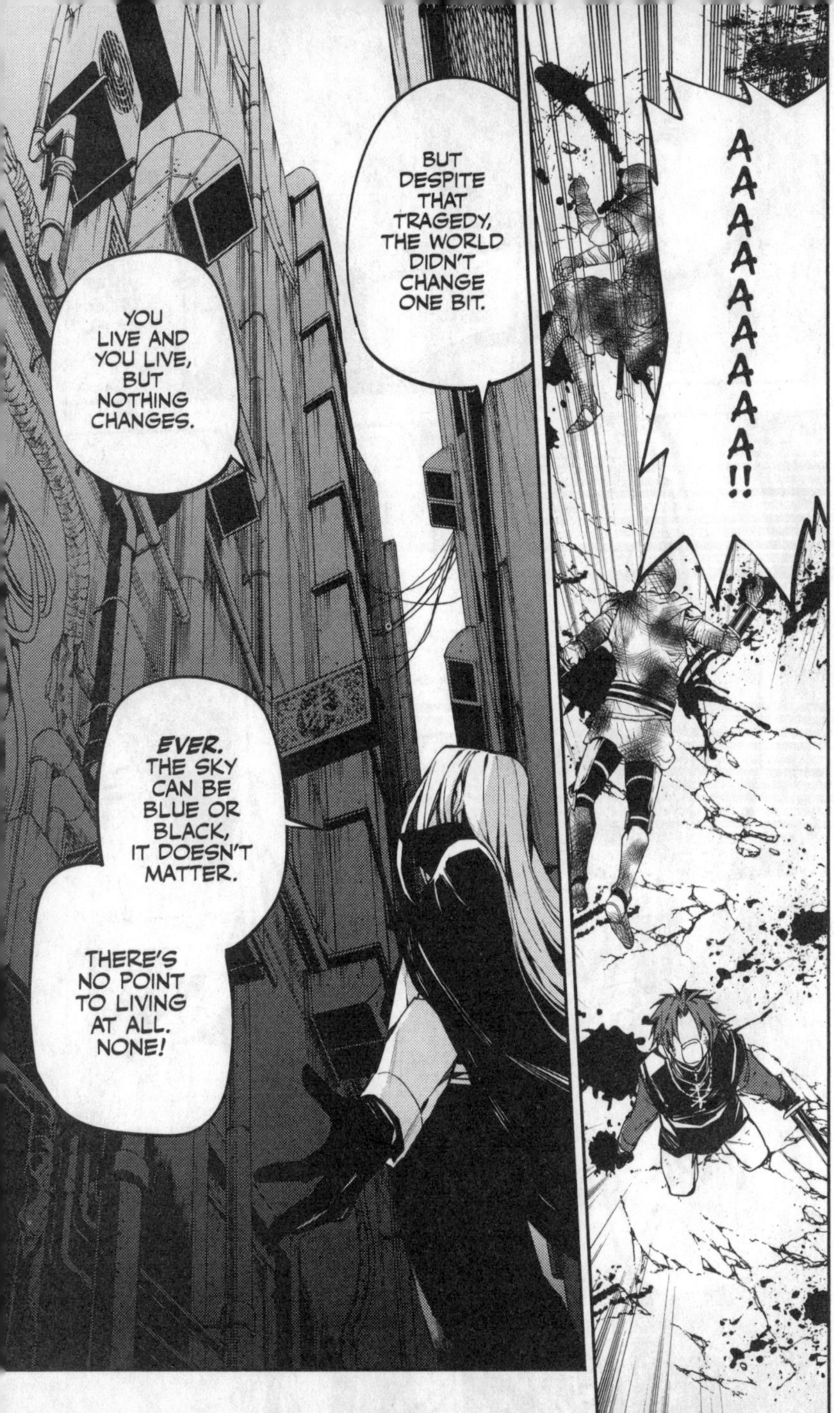
AAAAAAAAA!!
BUT DESPITE THAT TRAGEDY, THE WORLD DIDN'T CHANGE ONE BIT.
YOU LIVE AND YOU LIVE, BUT NOTHING CHANGES.
EVER. THE SKY CAN BE BLUE OR BLACK, IT DOESN'T MATTER.
THERE'S NO POINT TO LIVING AT ALL. NONE!

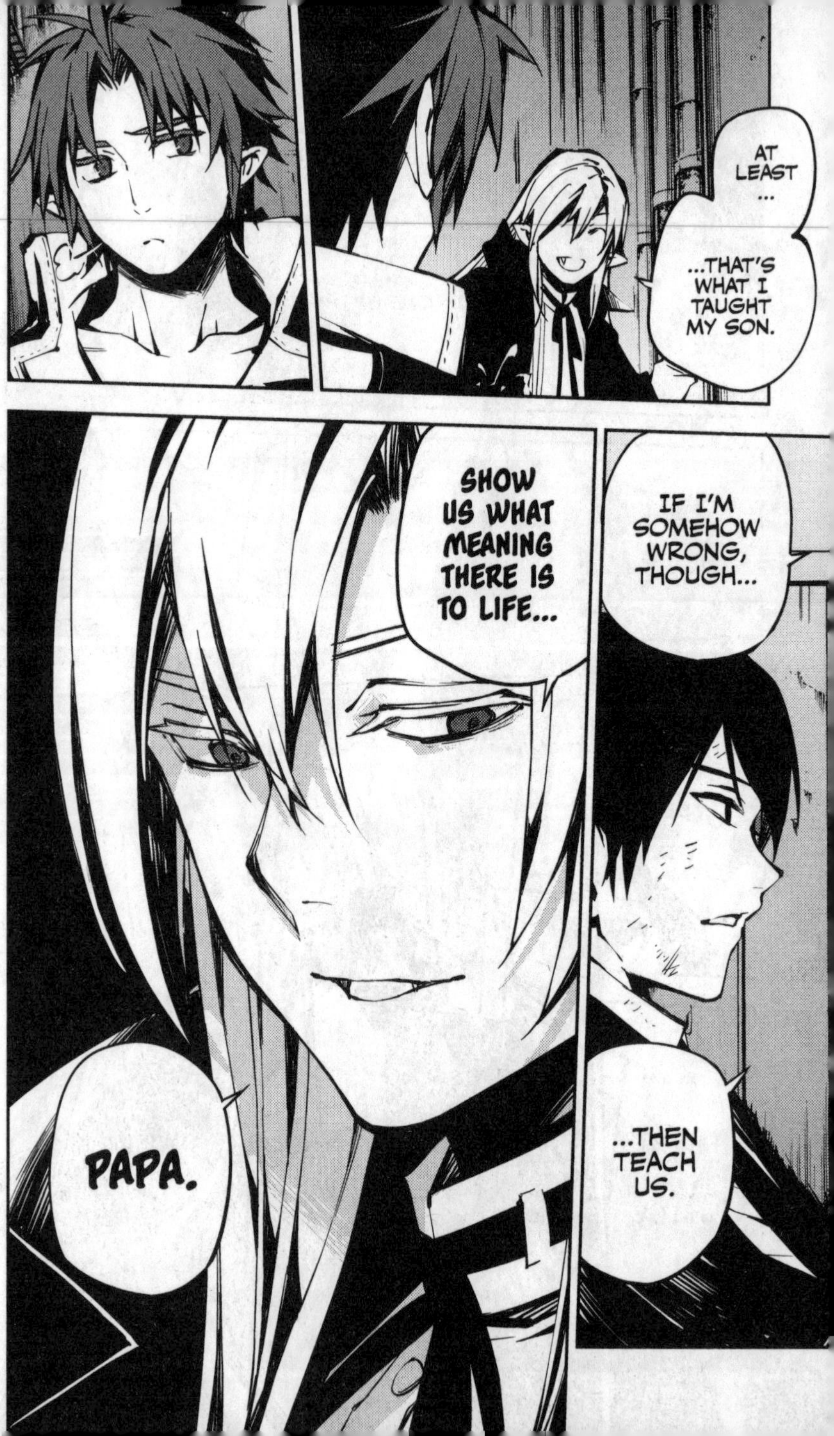
AT LEAST ...
...THAT'S WHAT I TAUGHT MY SON.
IF I'M SOMEHOW WRONG, THOUGH...
...THEN TEACH US.
SHOW US WHAT MEANING THERE IS TO LIFE...
PAPA.

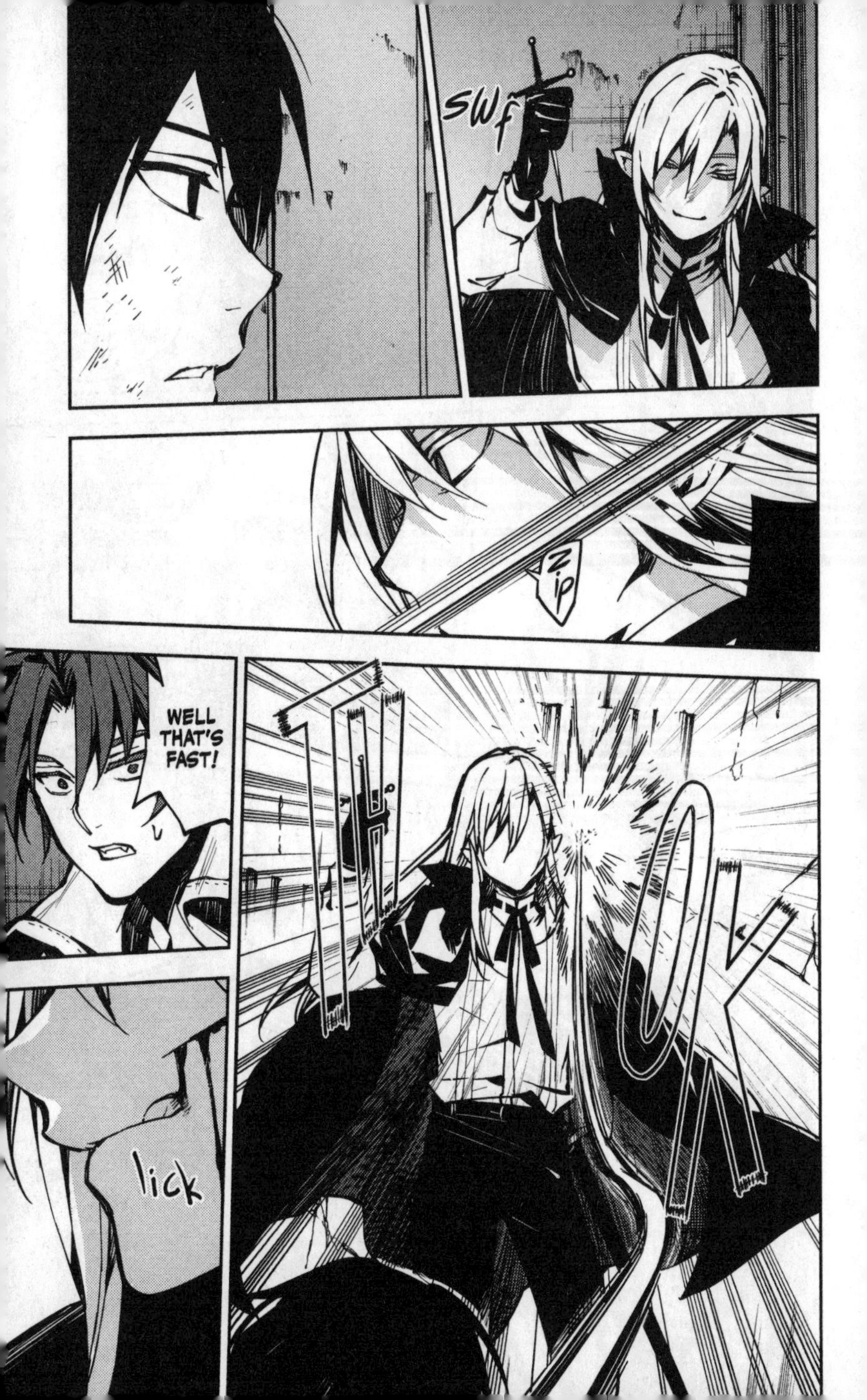
SWf
ZIP
THONK
WELL THAT'S FAST!
lick

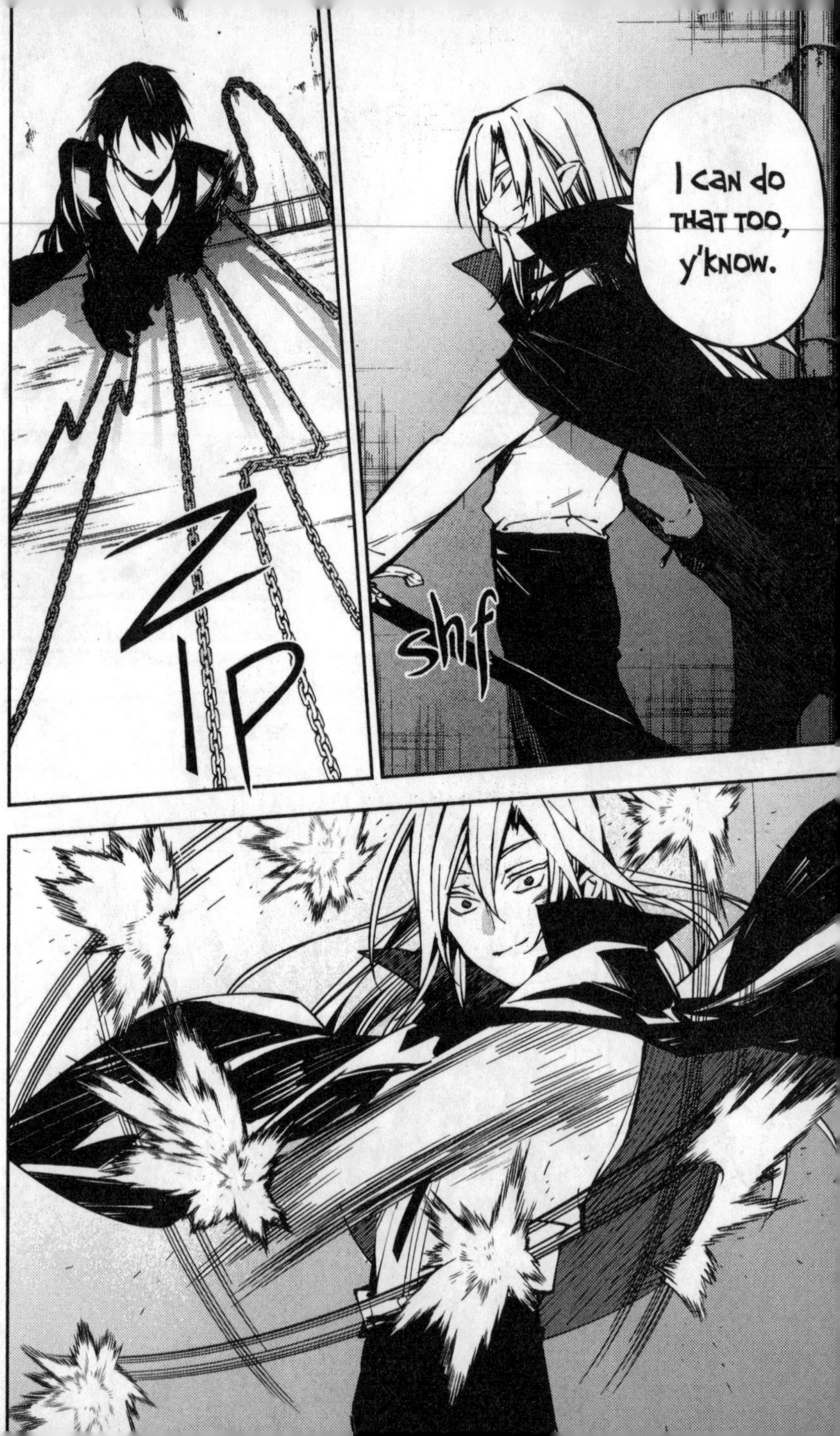
I can do that too, y'know.
shf
ZIP

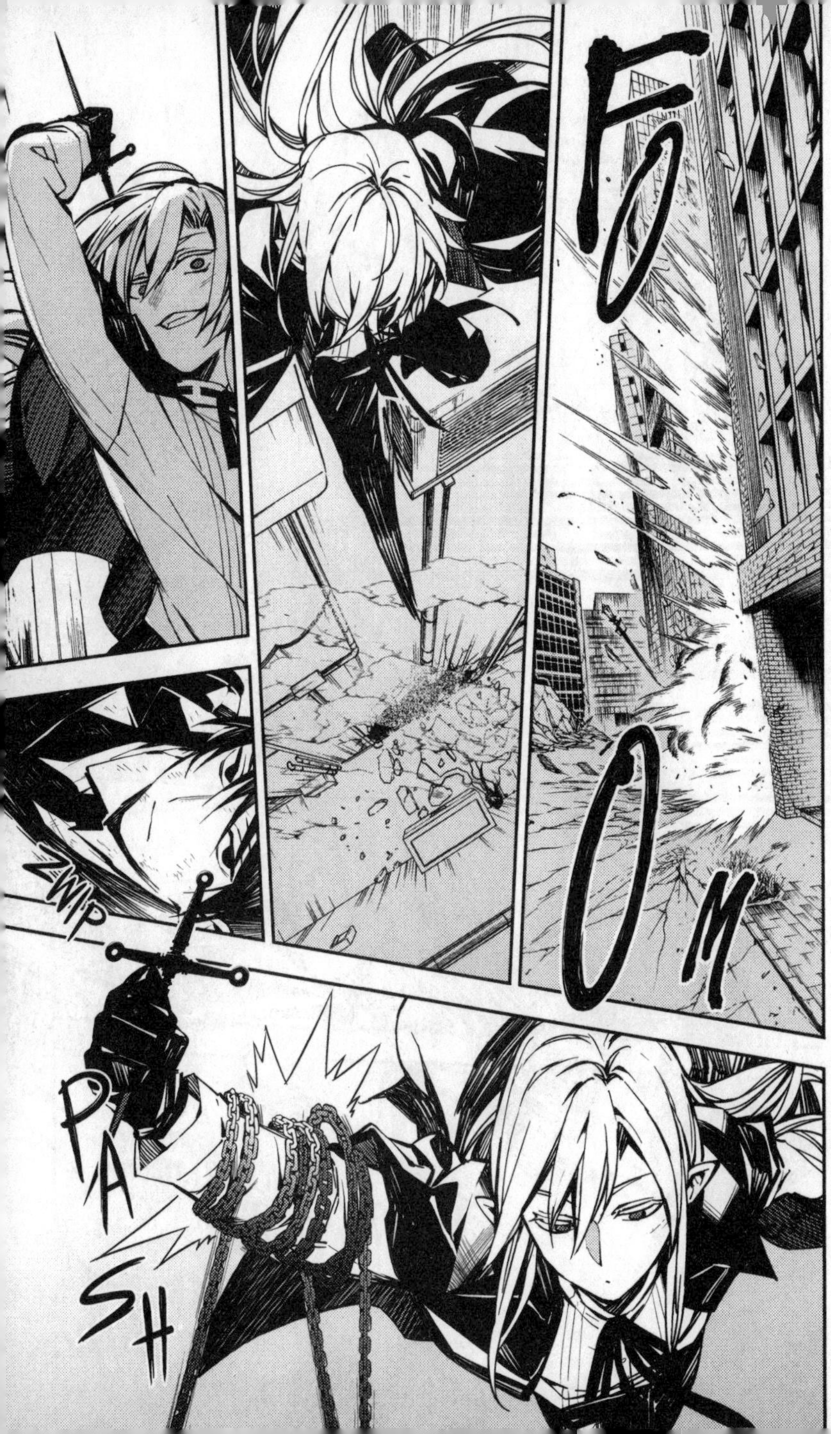
FOOM
ZWIP
PASH

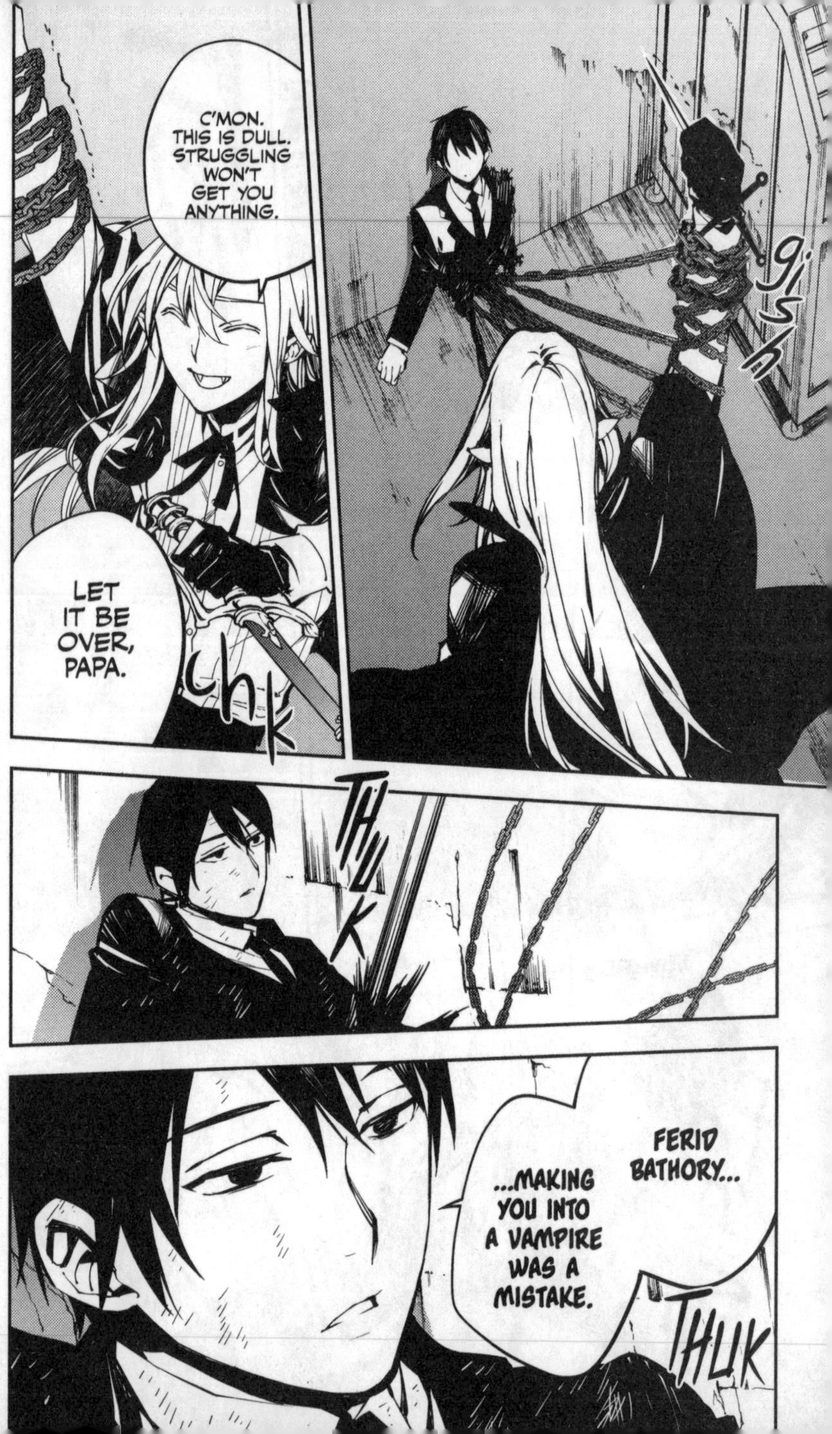
gishh
C'MON. THIS IS DULL. STRUGGLING WON'T GET YOU ANYTHING.
LET IT BE OVER, PAPA.
chk
THUNK
FERID BATHORY...
...MAKING YOU INTO A VAMPIRE WAS A MISTAKE.
THUK

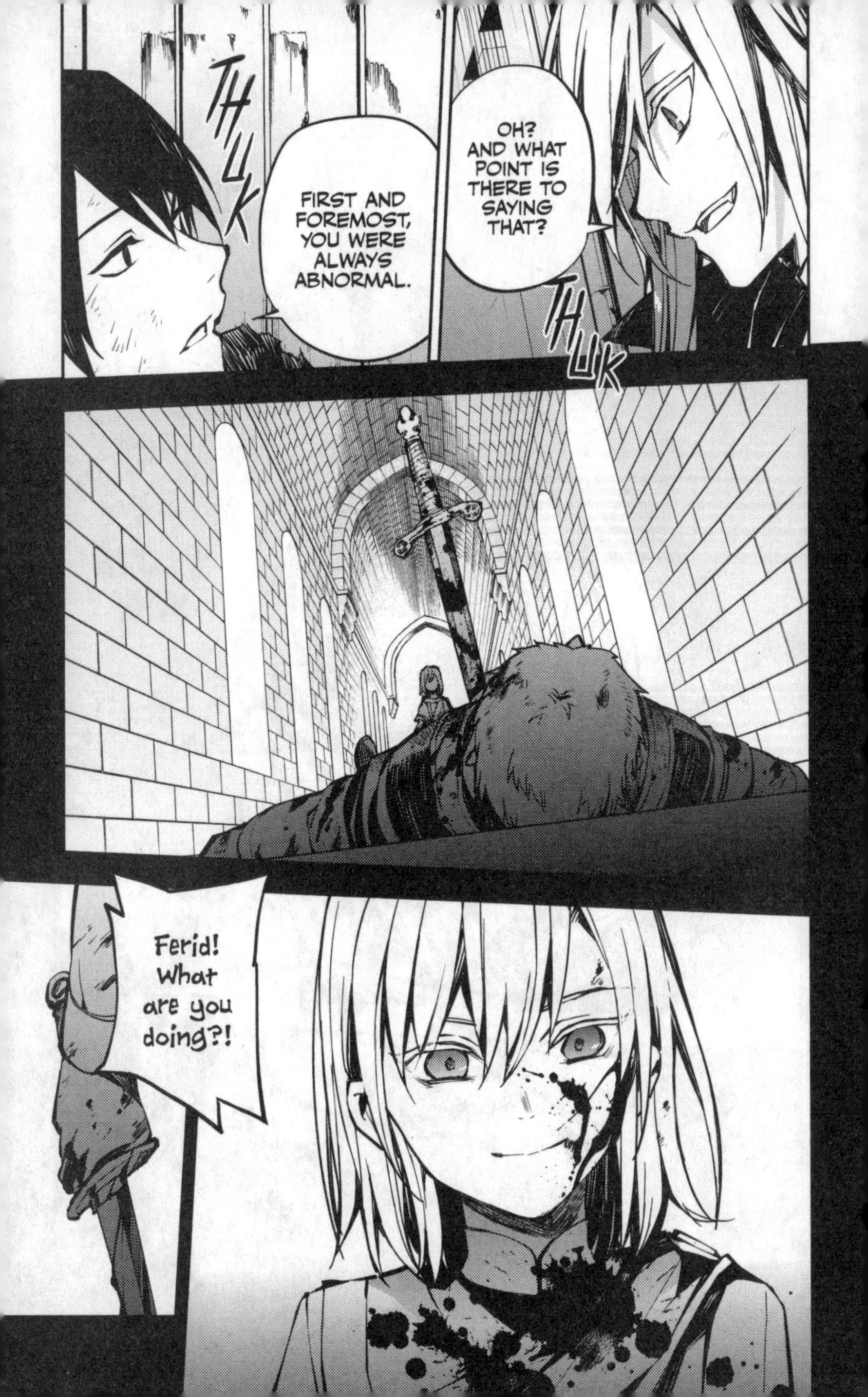
OH? AND WHAT POINT IS THERE TO SAYING THAT?
THUK
FIRST AND FOREMOST, YOU WERE ALWAYS ABNORMAL.
THUK
Ferid! What are you doing?!

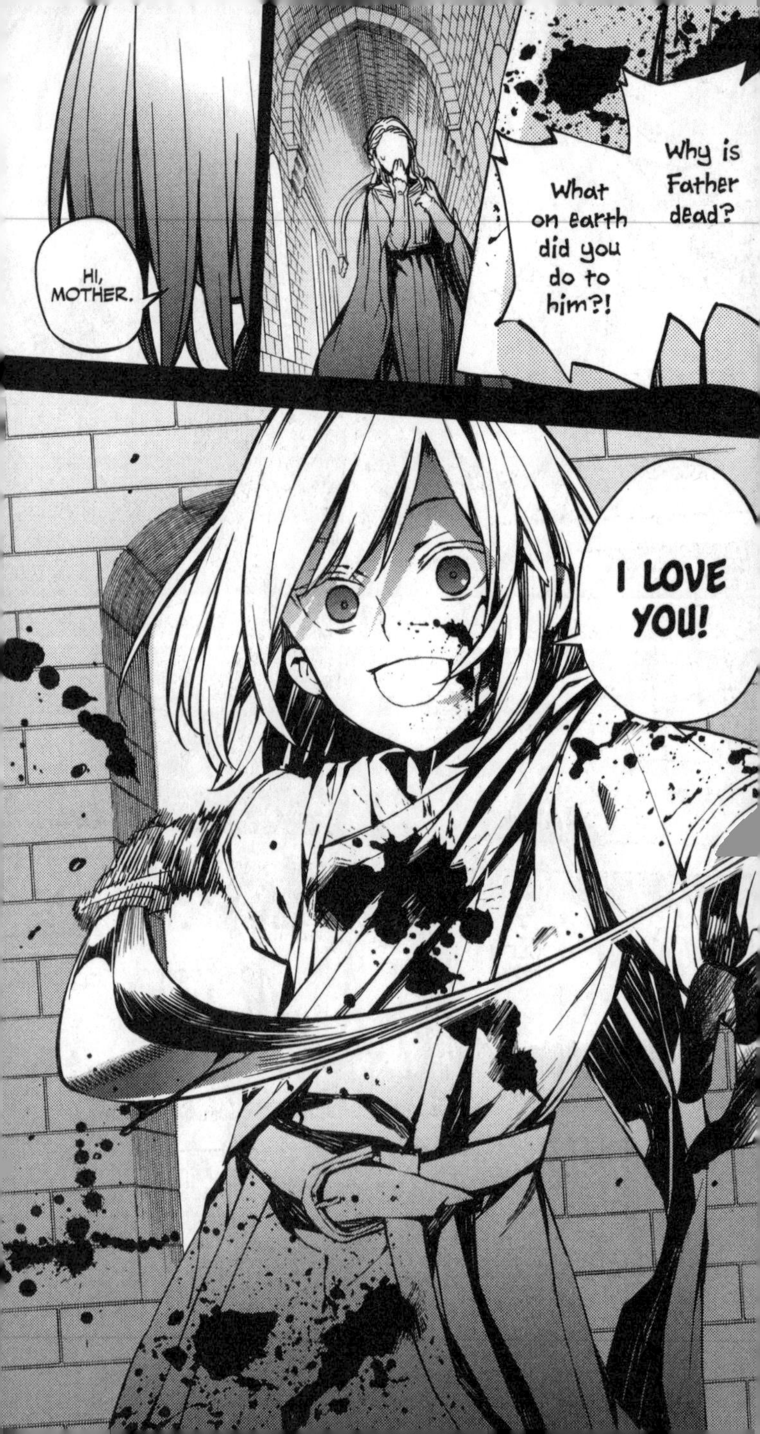
Why is Father dead?
What on earth did you do to him?!
HI, MOTHER.
I LOVE YOU!

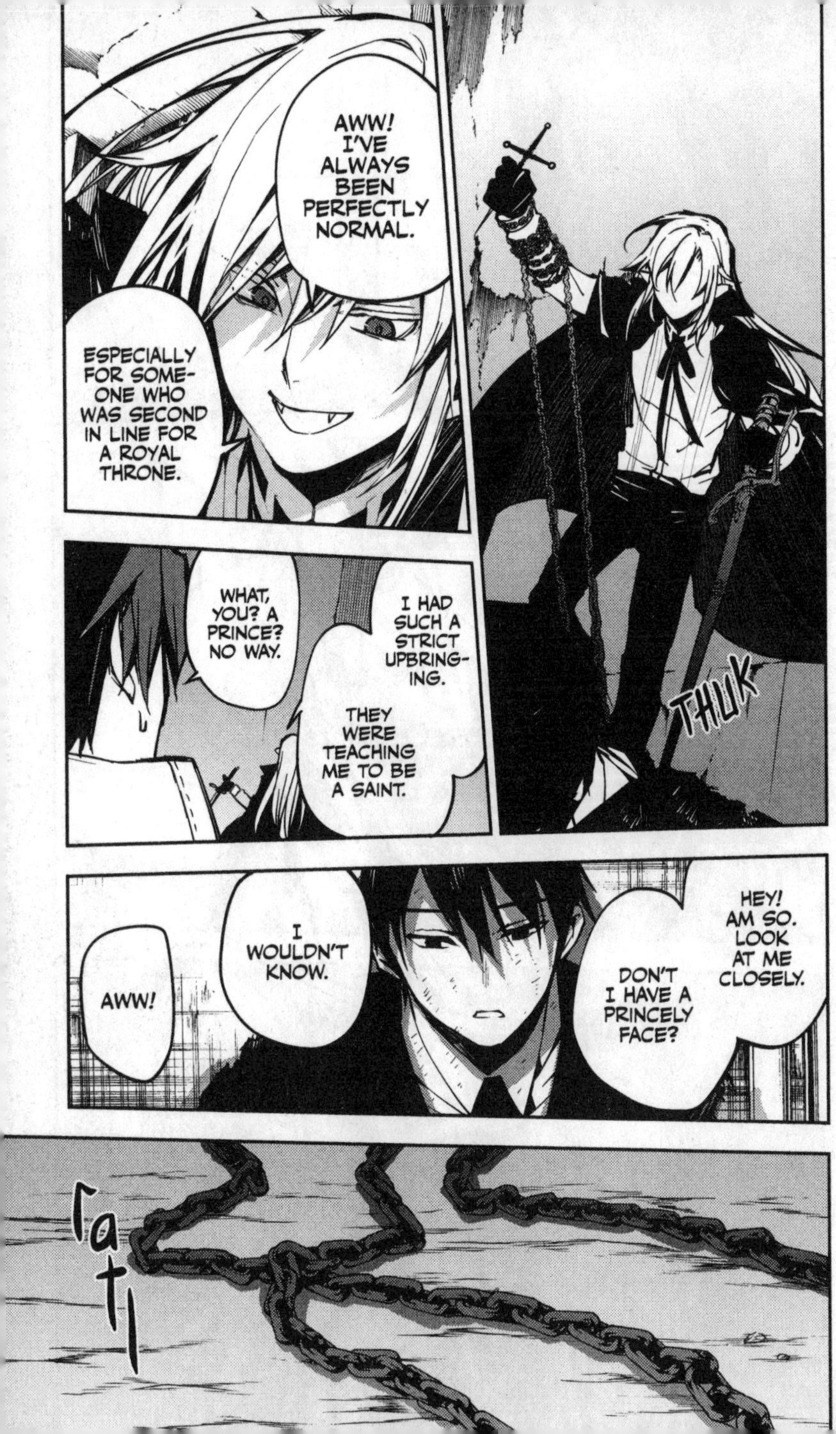
THUK
AWW! I'VE ALWAYS BEEN PERFECTLY NORMAL.
ESPECIALLY FOR SOME-ONE WHO WAS SECOND IN LINE FOR A ROYAL THRONE.
WHAT, YOU? A PRINCE? NO WAY.
I HAD SUCH A STRICT UPBRING-ING.
THEY WERE TEACHING ME TO BE A SAINT.
HEY! AM SO. LOOK AT ME CLOSELY.
DON'T I HAVE A PRINCELY FACE?
I WOULDN'T KNOW.
AWW!
ratl

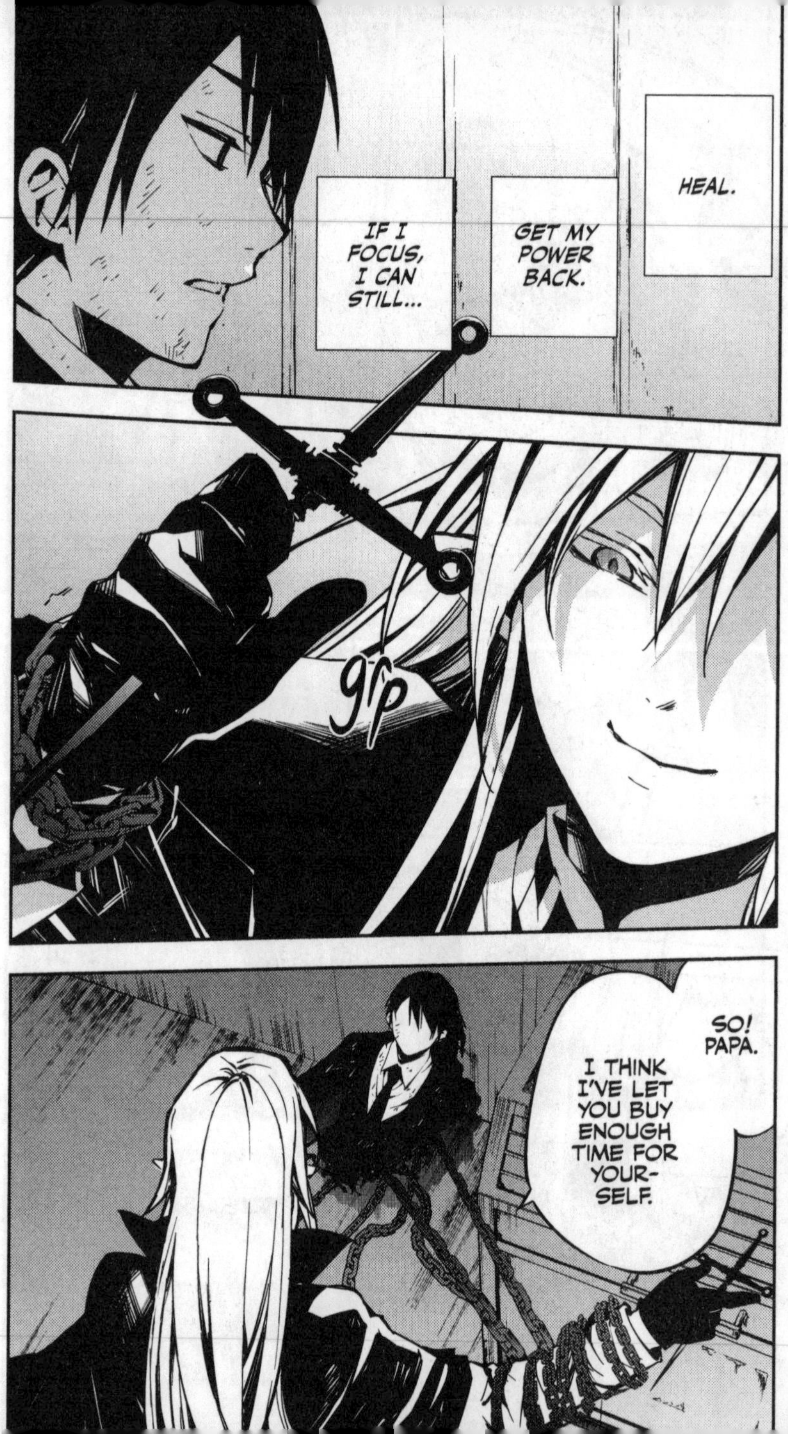
HEAL.
GET MY POWER BACK.
IF I FOCUS, I CAN STILL...
grip
SO! PAPA.
I THINK I'VE LET YOU BUY ENOUGH TIME FOR YOUR-SELF.

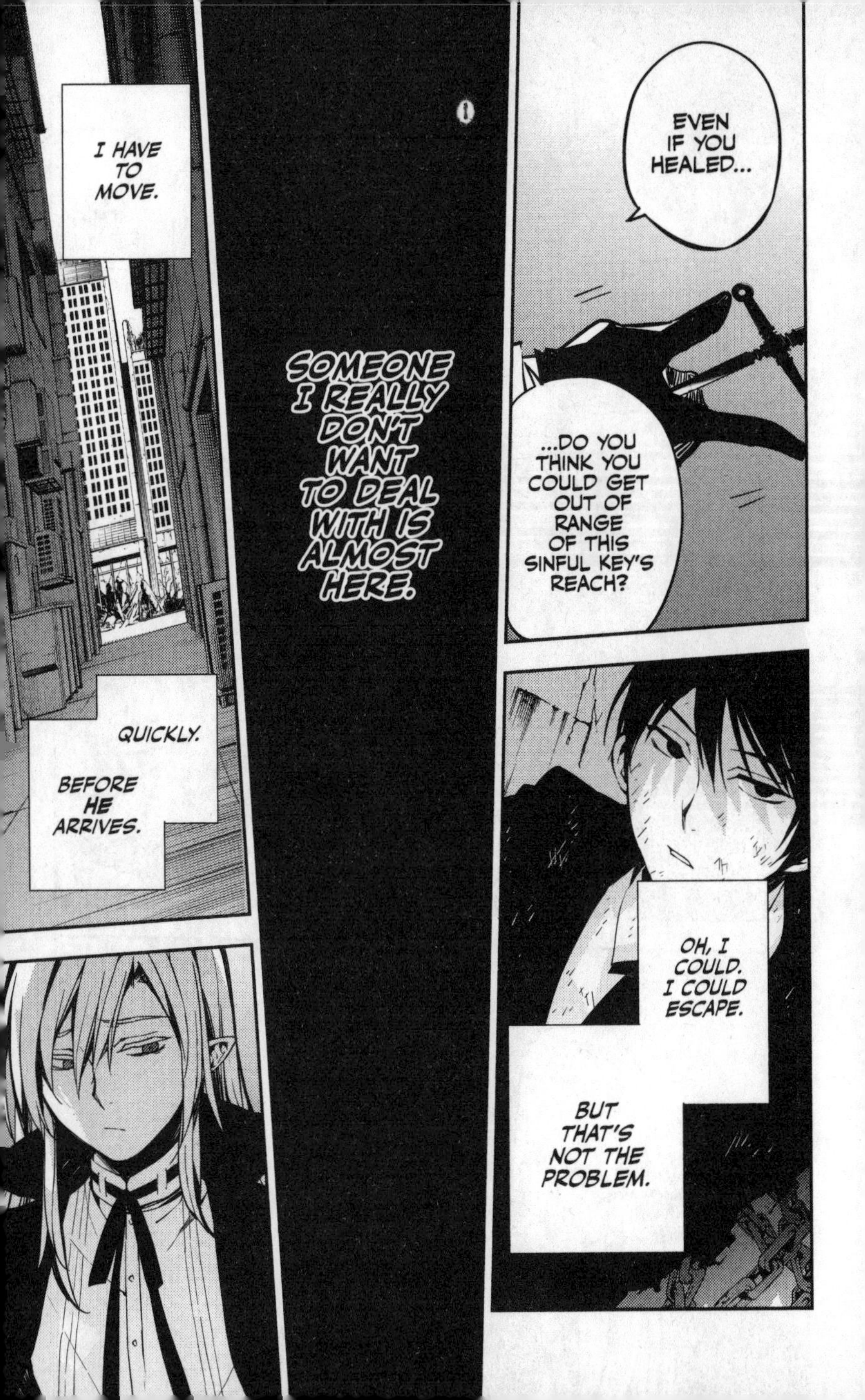
EVEN IF YOU HEALED...
...DO YOU THINK YOU COULD GET OUT OF RANGE OF THIS SINFUL KEY'S REACH?
OH, I COULD. I COULD ESCAPE.
BUT THAT'S NOT THE PROBLEM.
SOMEONE I REALLY DON'T WANT TO DEAL WITH IS ALMOST HERE.
I HAVE TO MOVE.
QUICKLY.
BEFORE HE ARRIVES.

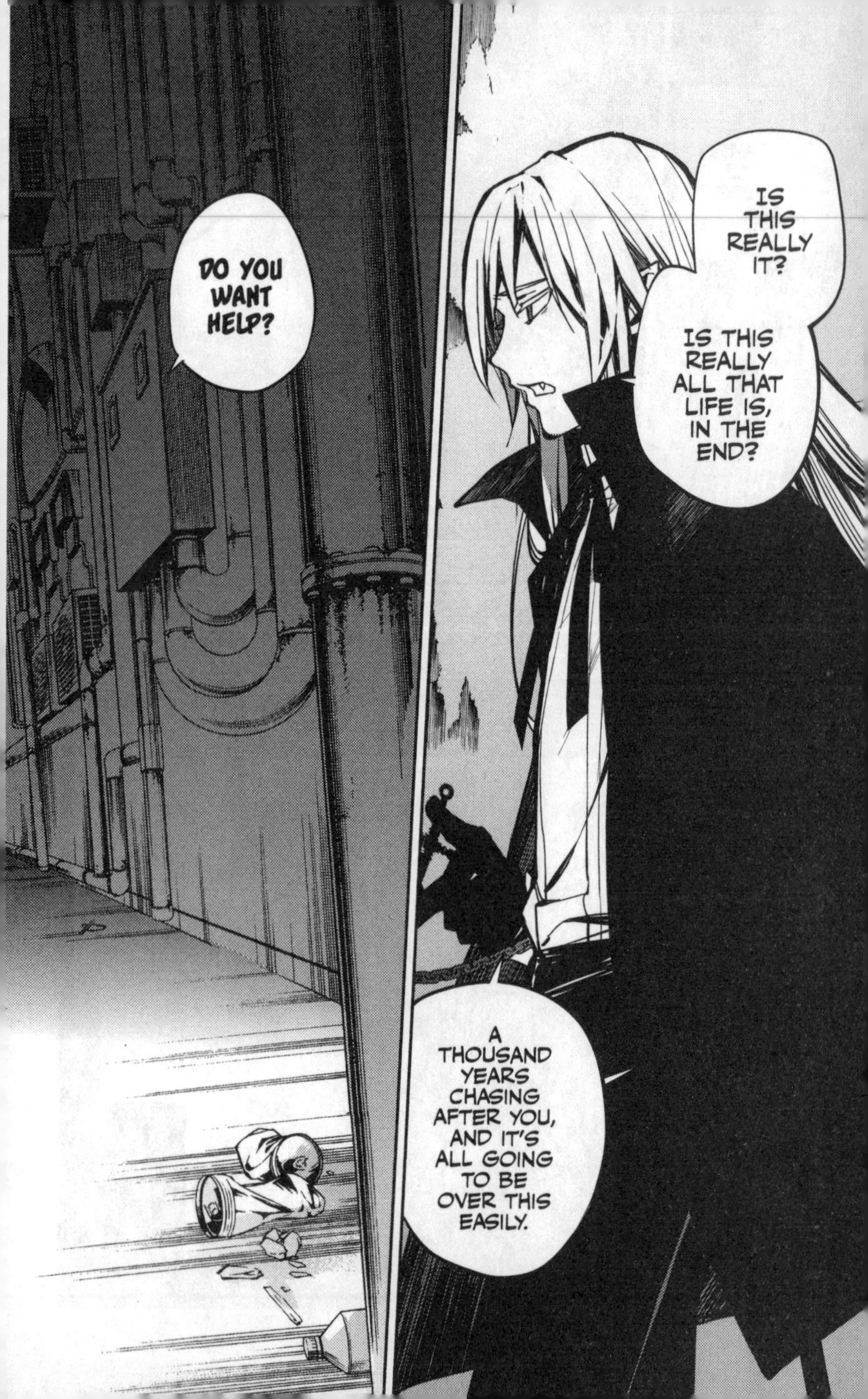
IS THIS REALLY IT?
IS THIS REALLY ALL THAT LIFE IS, IN THE END?
A THOUSAND YEARS CHASING AFTER YOU, AND IT'S ALL GOING TO BE OVER THIS EASILY.
DO YOU WANT HELP?

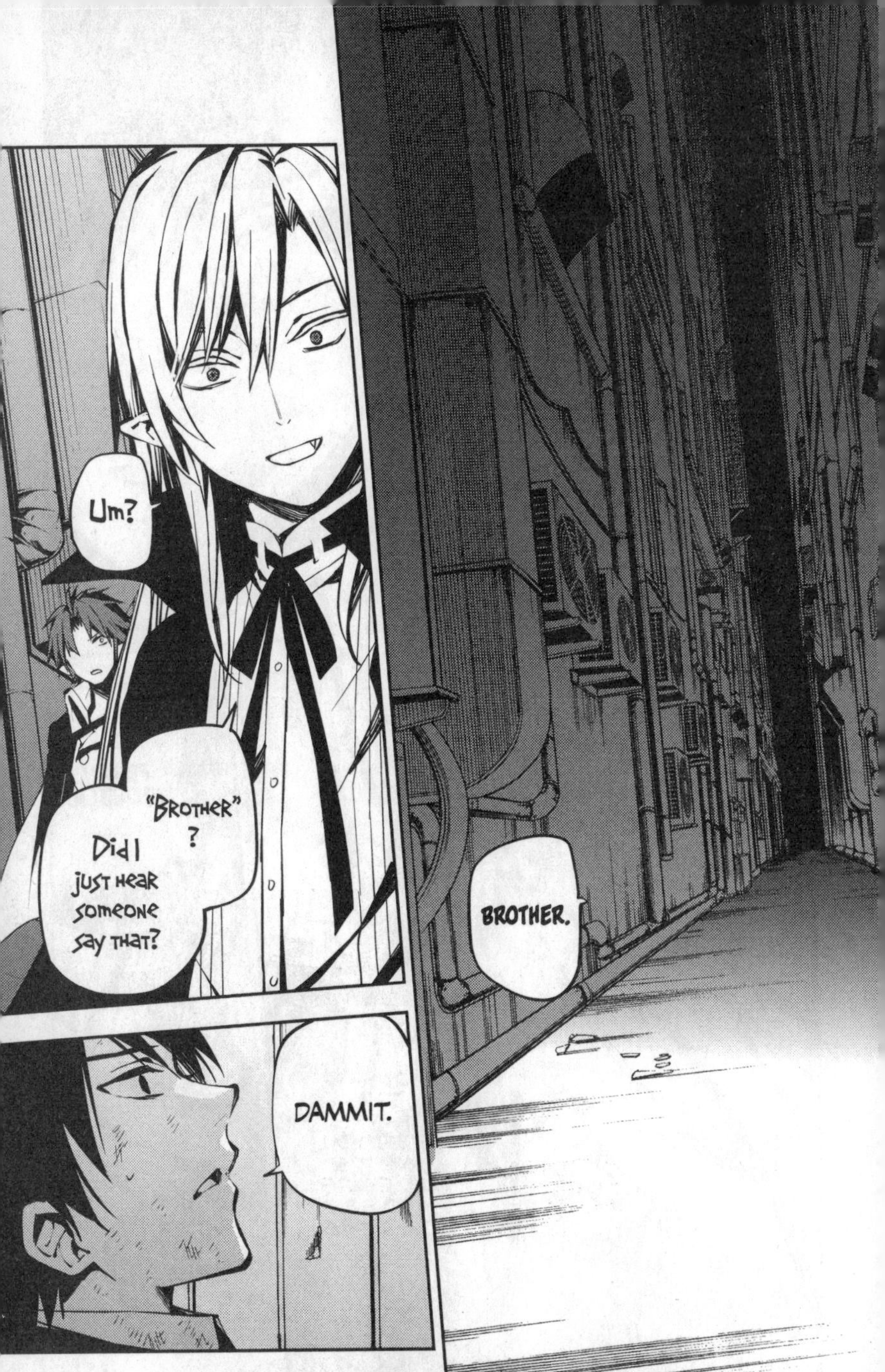
BROTHER.
Um?
"BROTHER"?
Did I just hear someone say that?
DAMMIT.

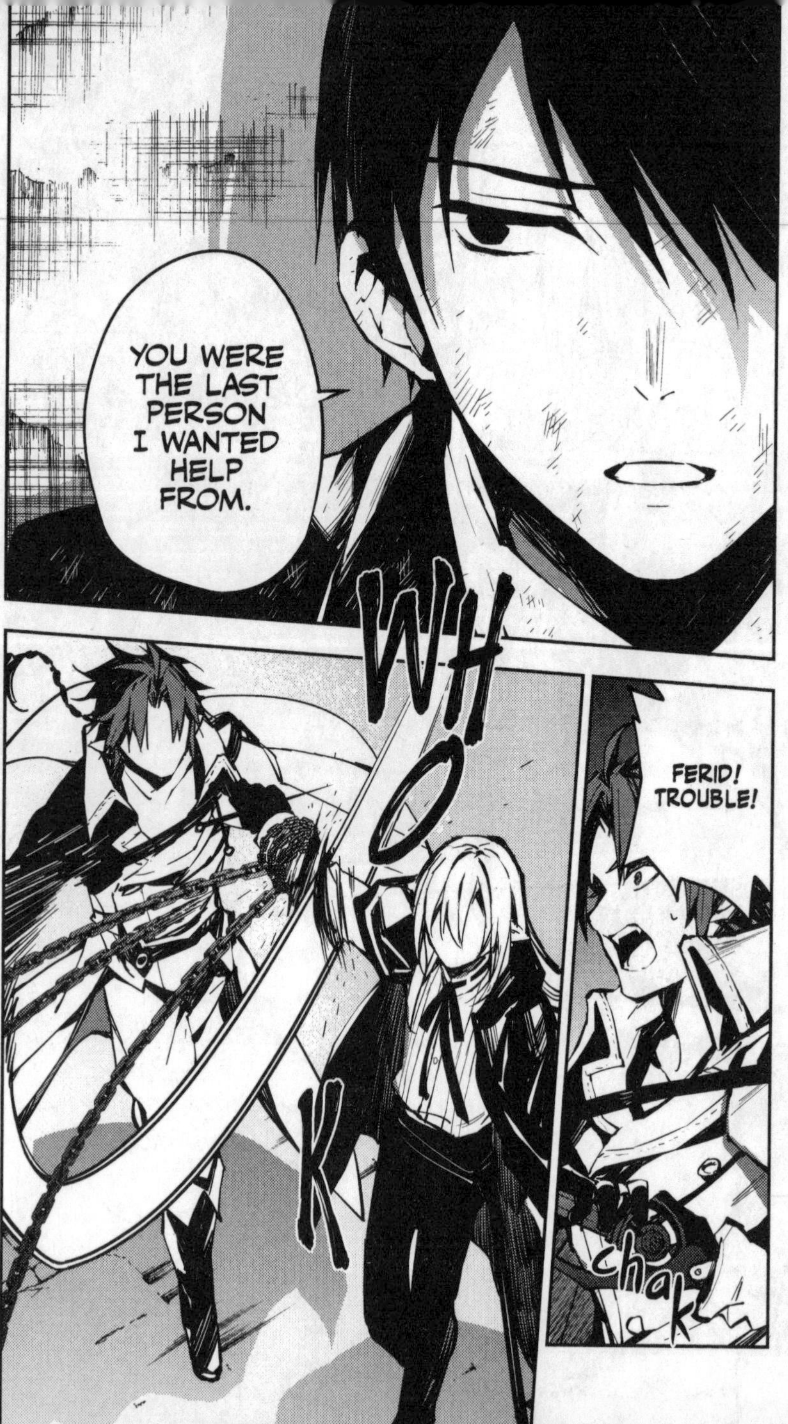
YOU WERE THE LAST PERSON I WANTED HELP FROM.
WHOOK
FERID! TROUBLE!
chak

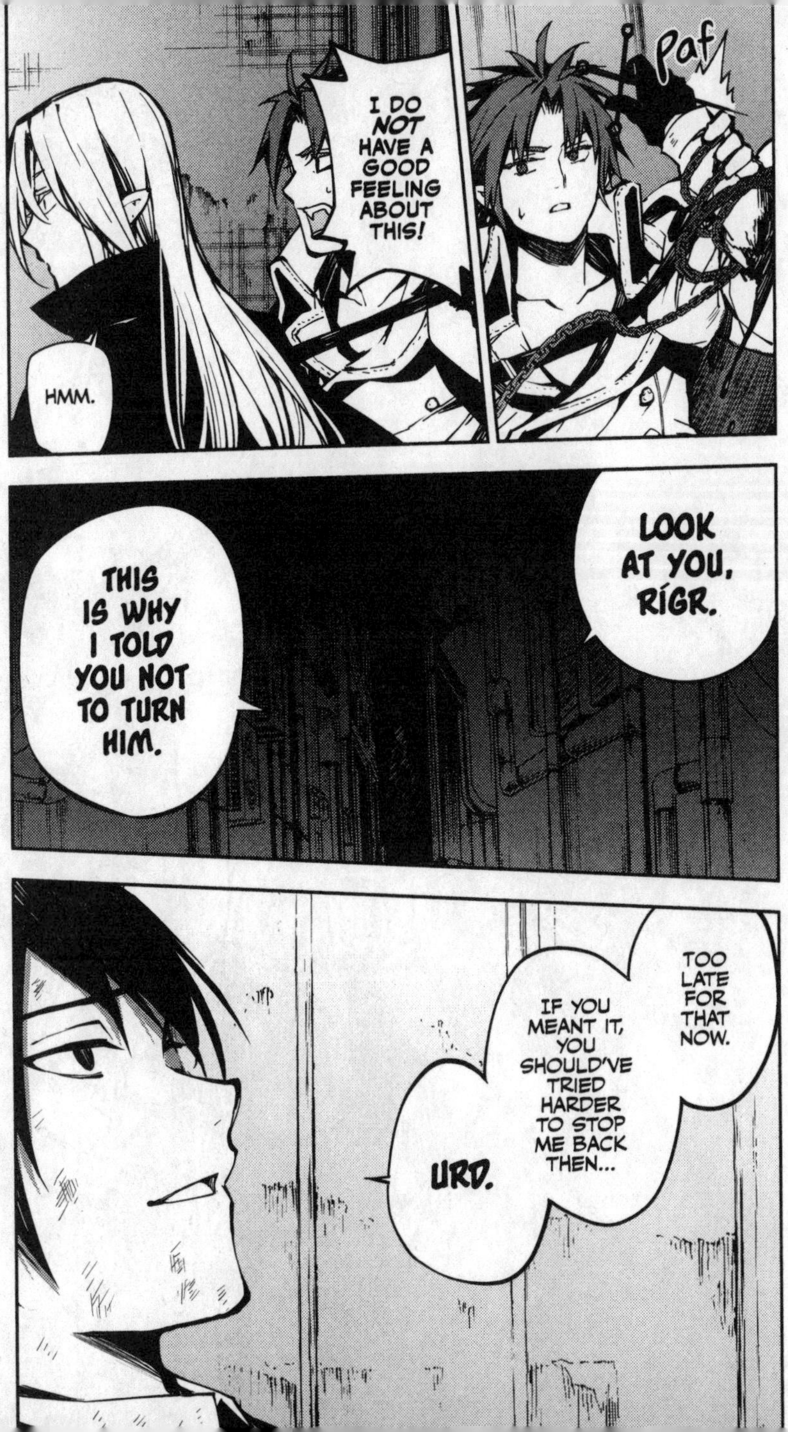
Paf
I DO NOT HAVE A GOOD FEELING ABOUT THIS!
HMM.
LOOK AT YOU, RÍGR.
THIS IS WHY I TOLD YOU NOT TO TURN HIM.
TOO LATE FOR THAT NOW.
IF YOU MEANT IT, YOU SHOULD'VE TRIED HARDER TO STOP ME BACK THEN...
URD.

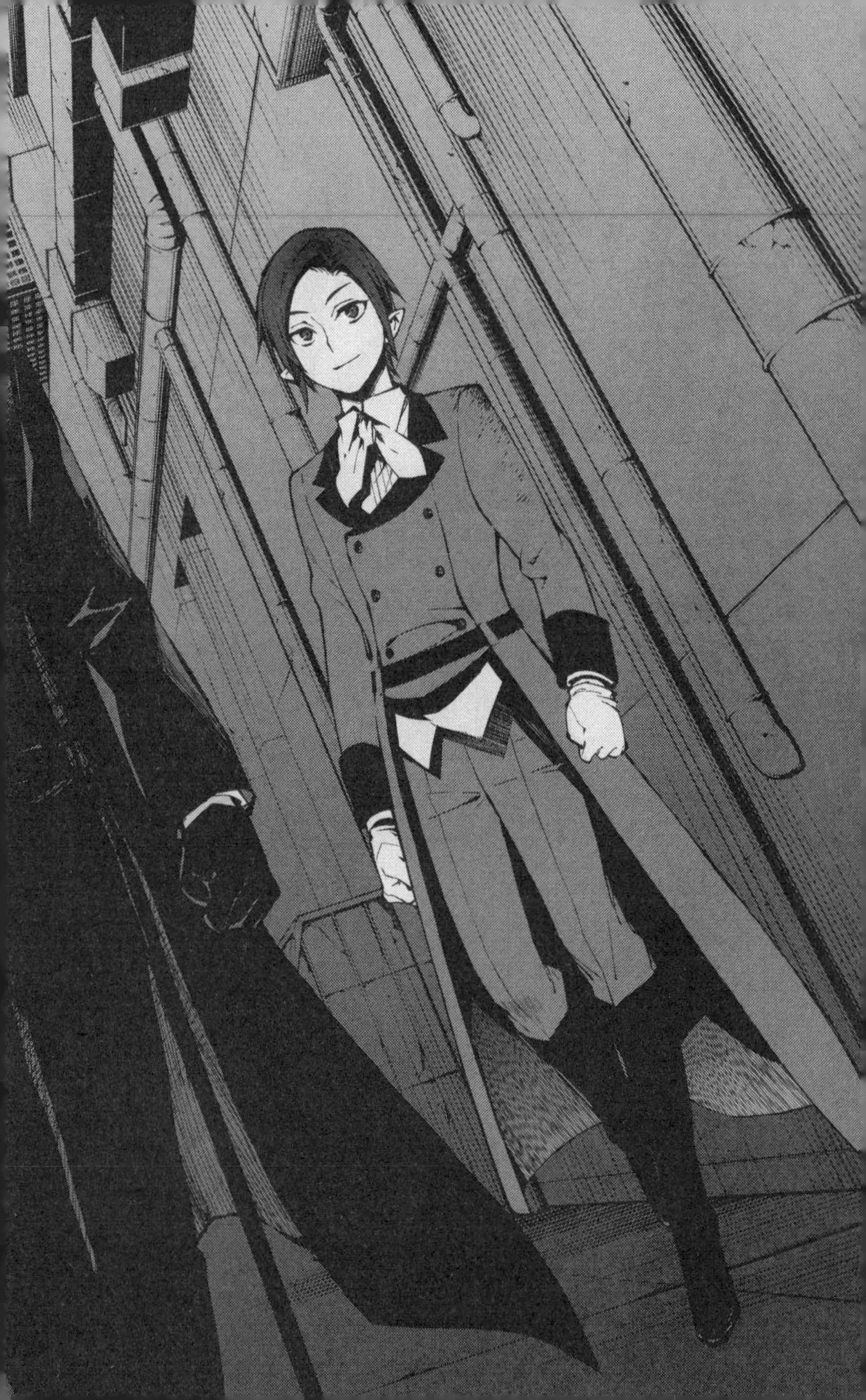

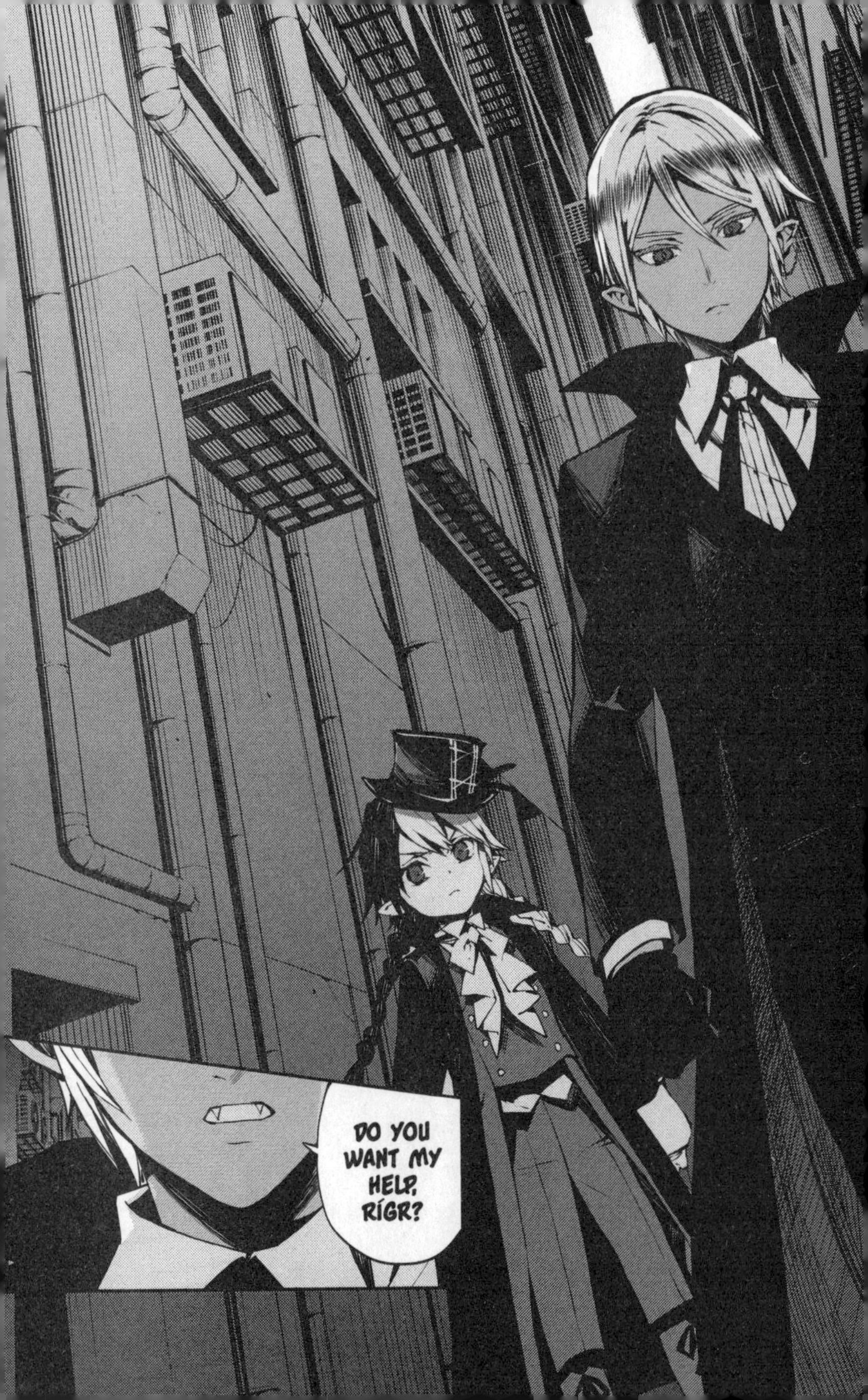
DO YOU WANT MY HELP, RIGR?

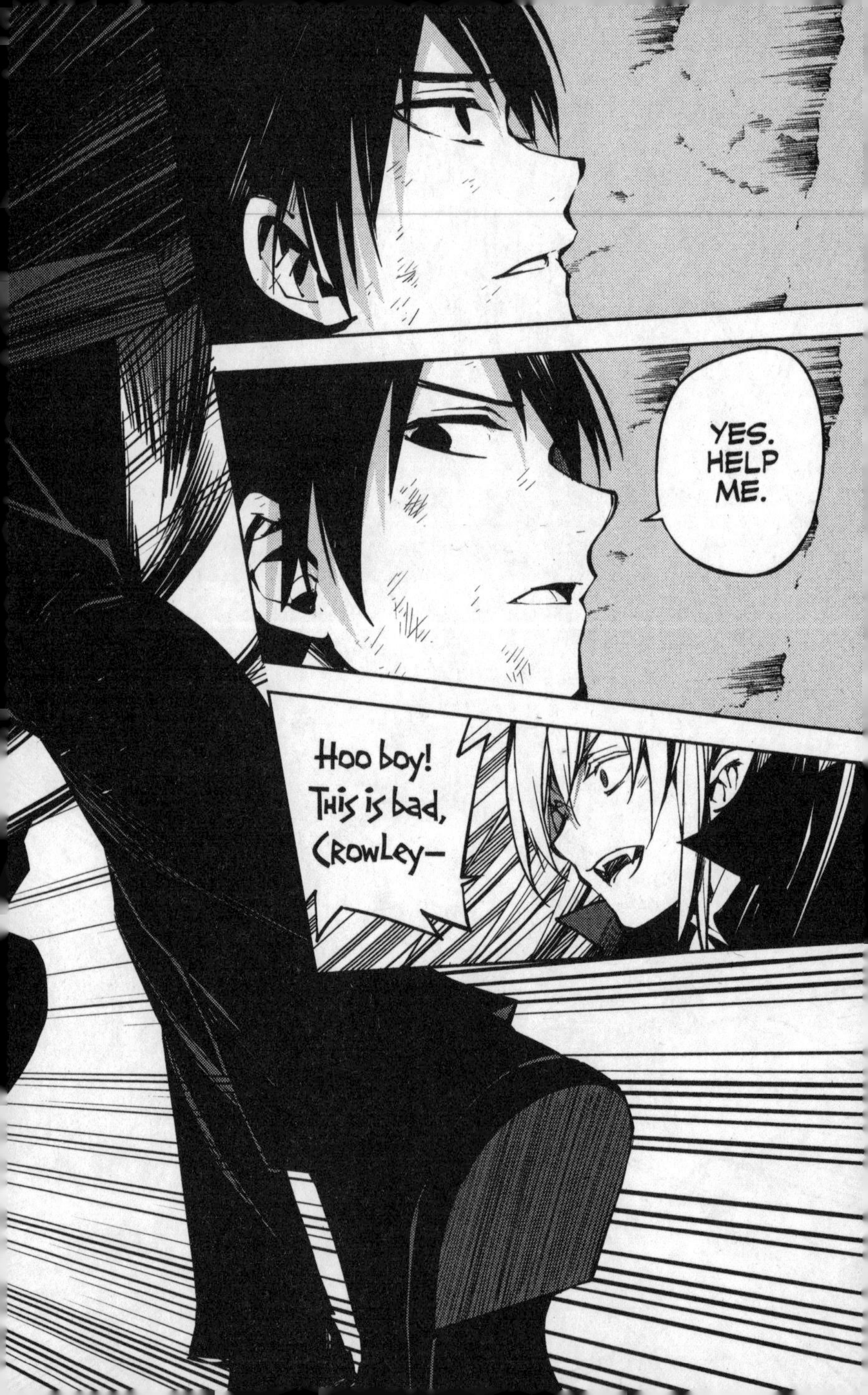
YES. HELP ME.
Hoo boy! This is bad, Crowley-

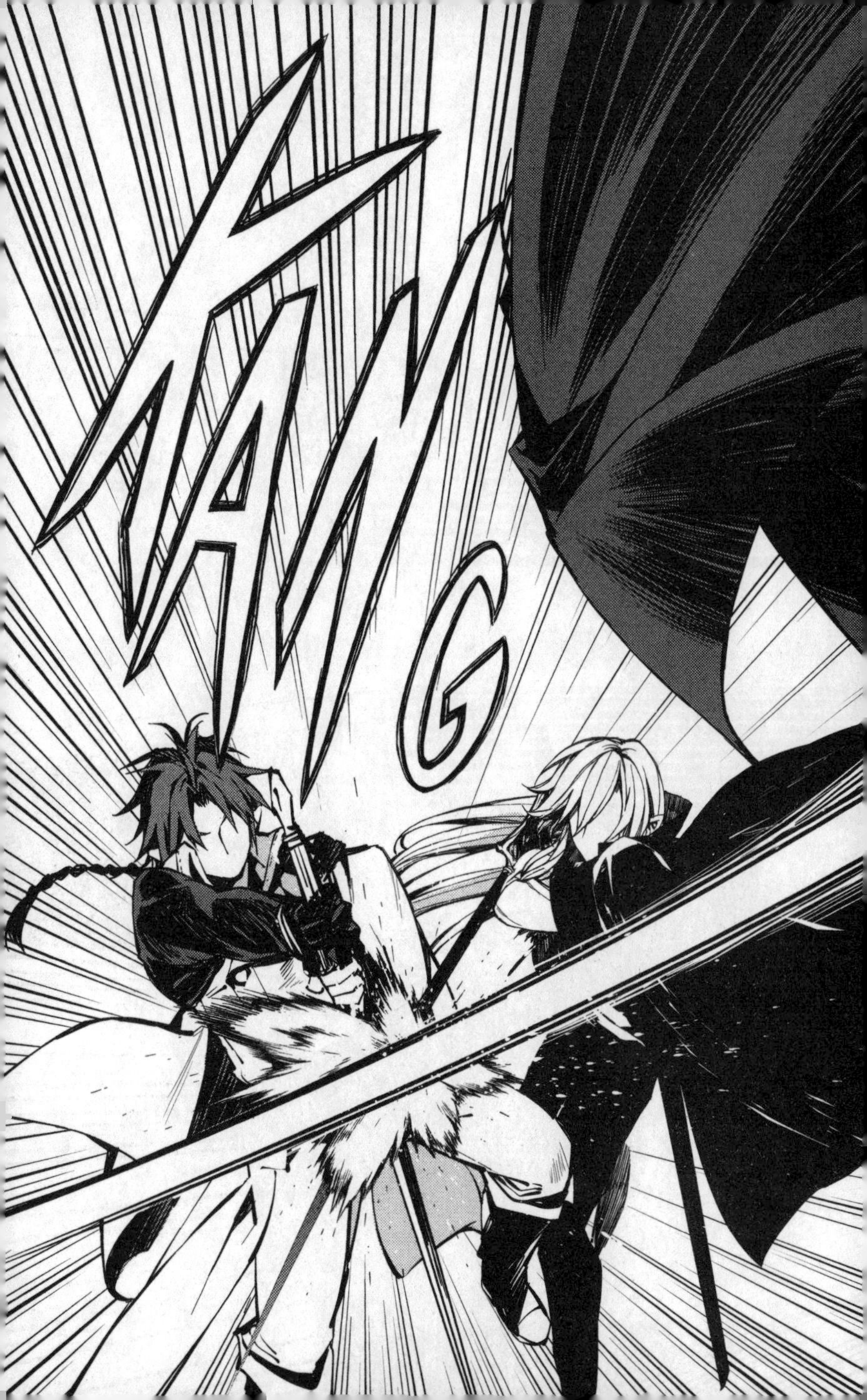
KANG

Seraph of the End
—VAMPIRE REIGN—

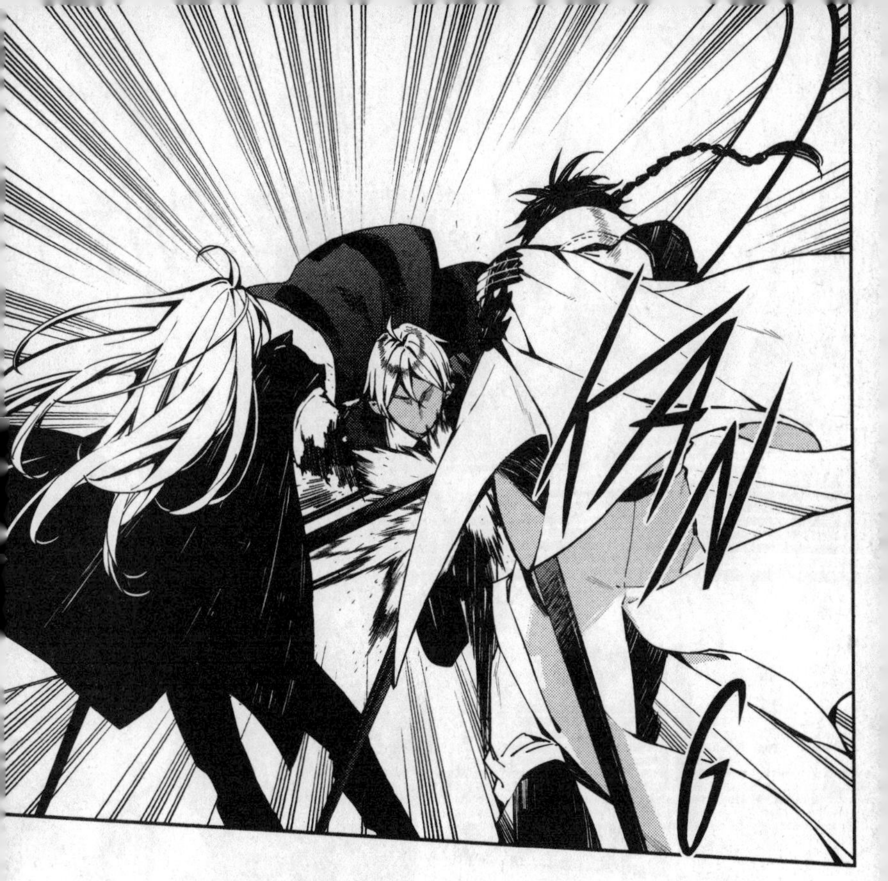

CHAPTER 92
Black Demon Scenario

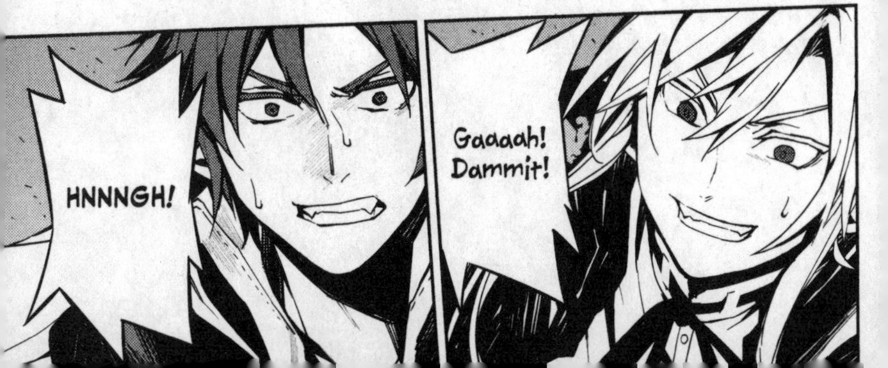

Gaaaah! Dammit!
HNNNGH!

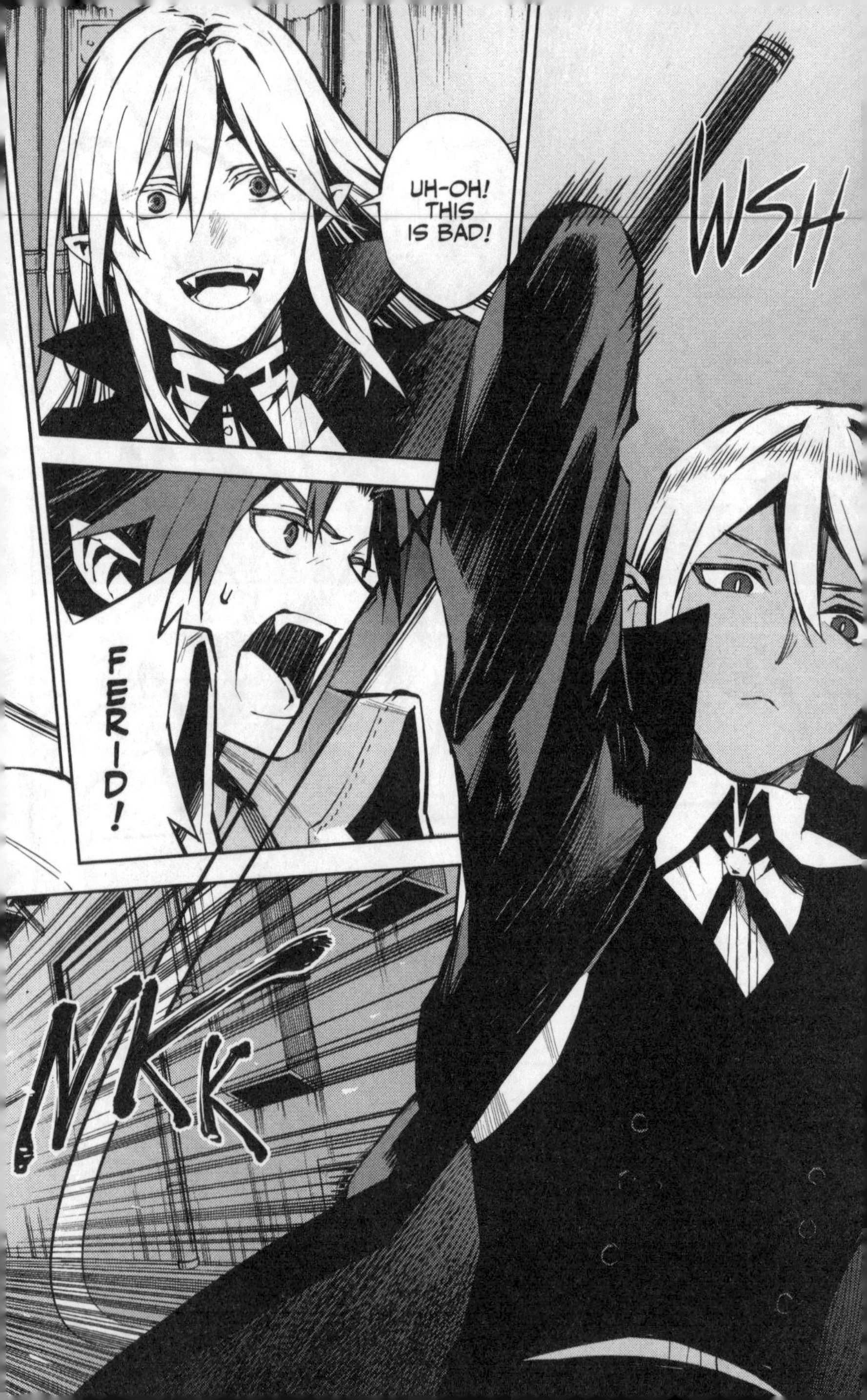
WSH
UH-OH! THIS IS BAD!
FERID!
NKK

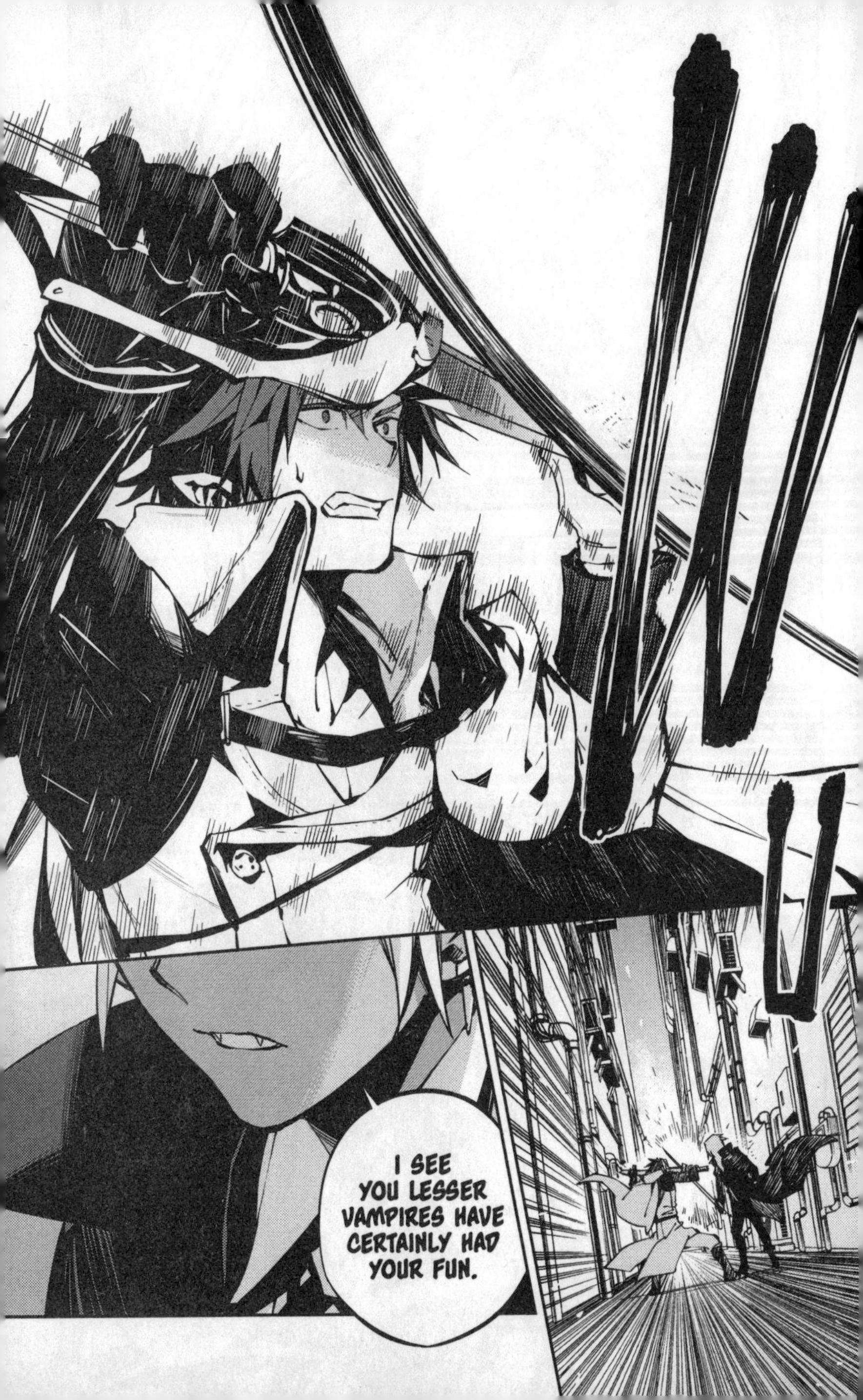
I SEE YOU LESSER VAMPIRES HAVE CERTAINLY HAD YOUR FUN.

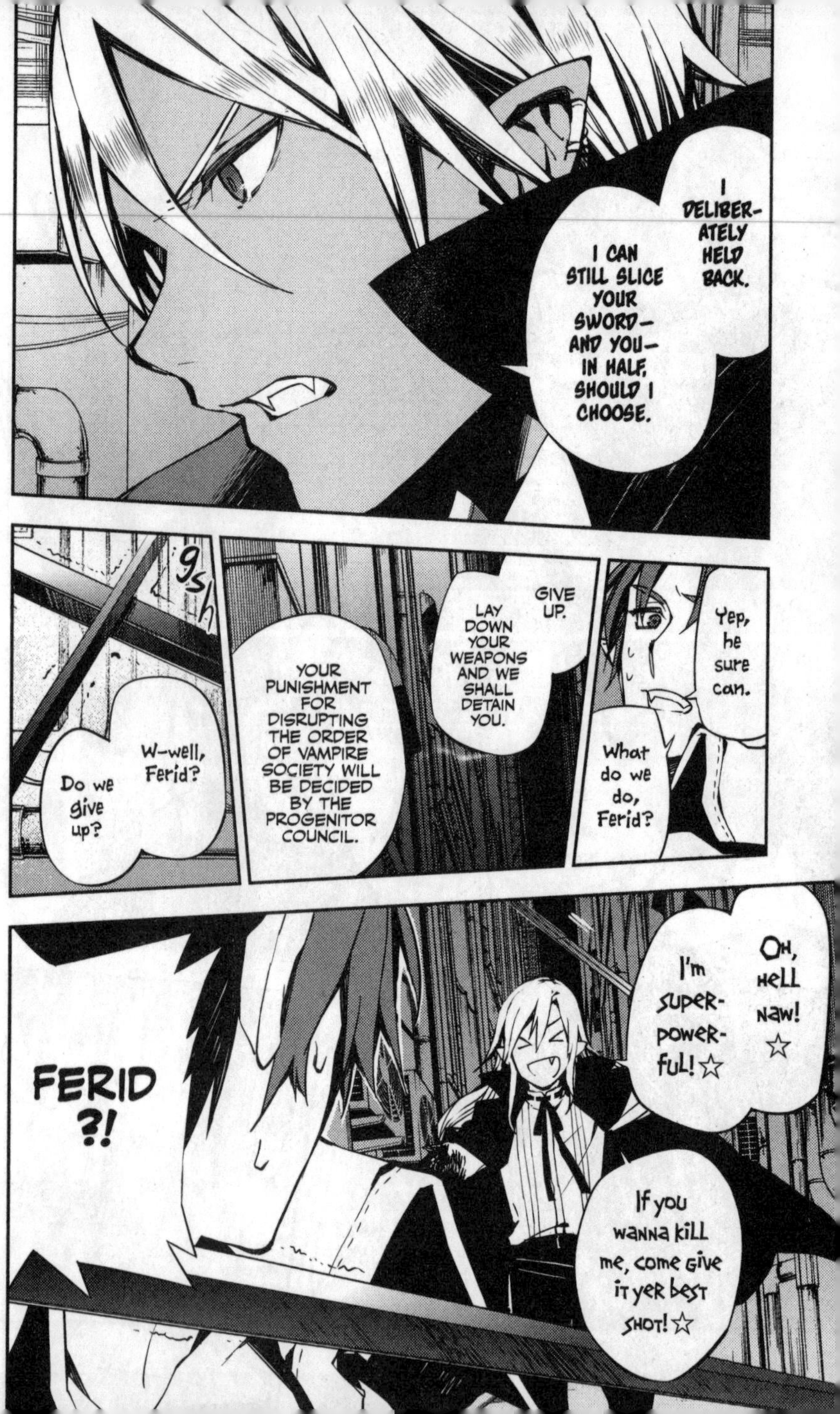
I DELIBERATELY HELD BACK.
I CAN STILL SLICE YOUR SWORD—AND YOU—IN HALF, SHOULD I CHOOSE.
Yep, he sure can.
What do we do, Ferid?
GIVE UP.
LAY DOWN YOUR WEAPONS AND WE SHALL DETAIN YOU.
YOUR PUNISHMENT FOR DISRUPTING THE ORDER OF VAMPIRE SOCIETY WILL BE DECIDED BY THE PROGENITOR COUNCIL.
gsh
W-well, Ferid?
Do we give up?
Oh, hell naw! ☆
I'm super-powerful! ☆
If you wanna kill me, come give it yer best shot! ☆
FERID ?!

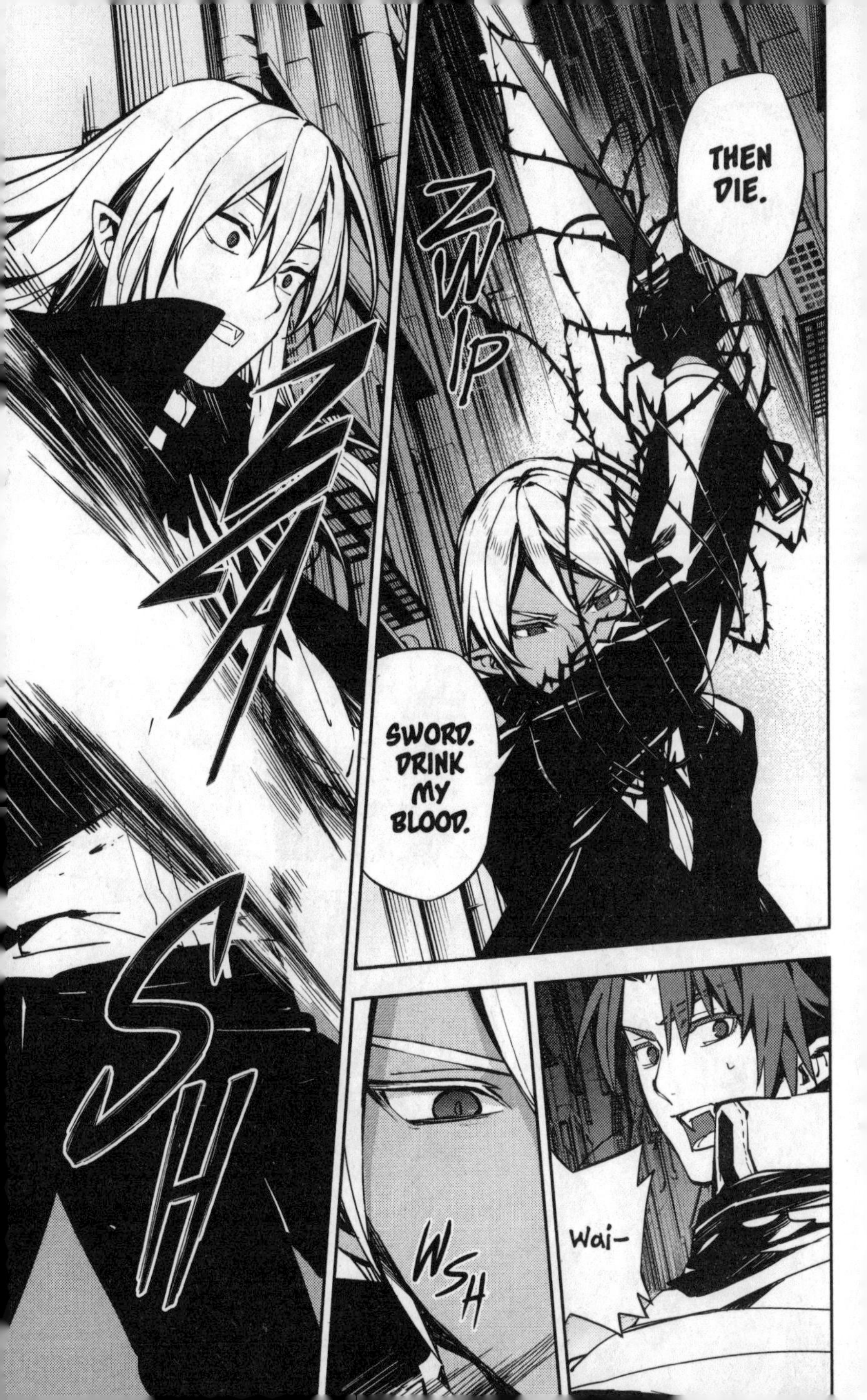
THEN DIE.
ZWIP
SWORD. DRINK MY BLOOD.
Wai-
WSH
SH

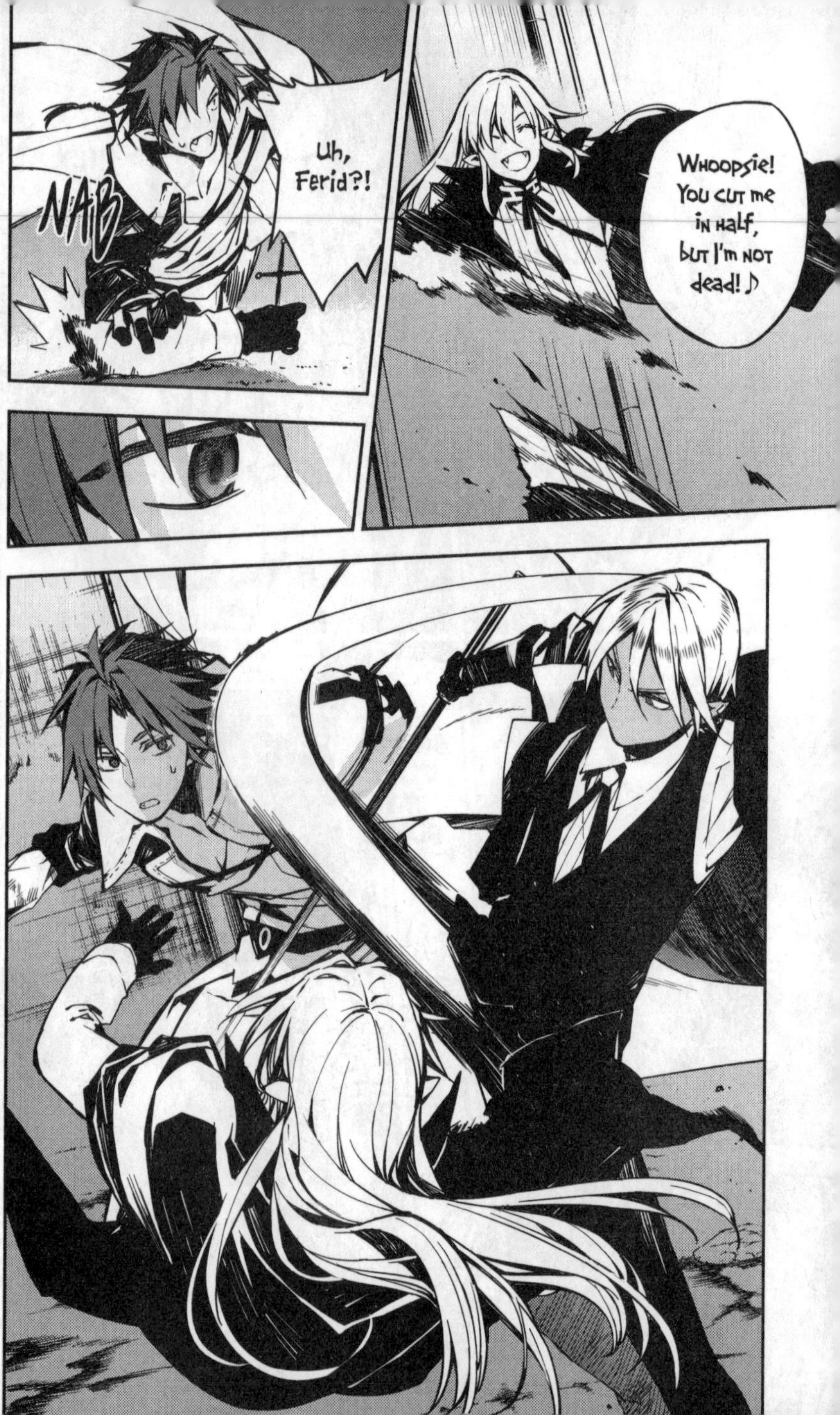
Whoopsie! You cut me in half, but I'm not dead! ♪
Uh, Ferid?!
NAB

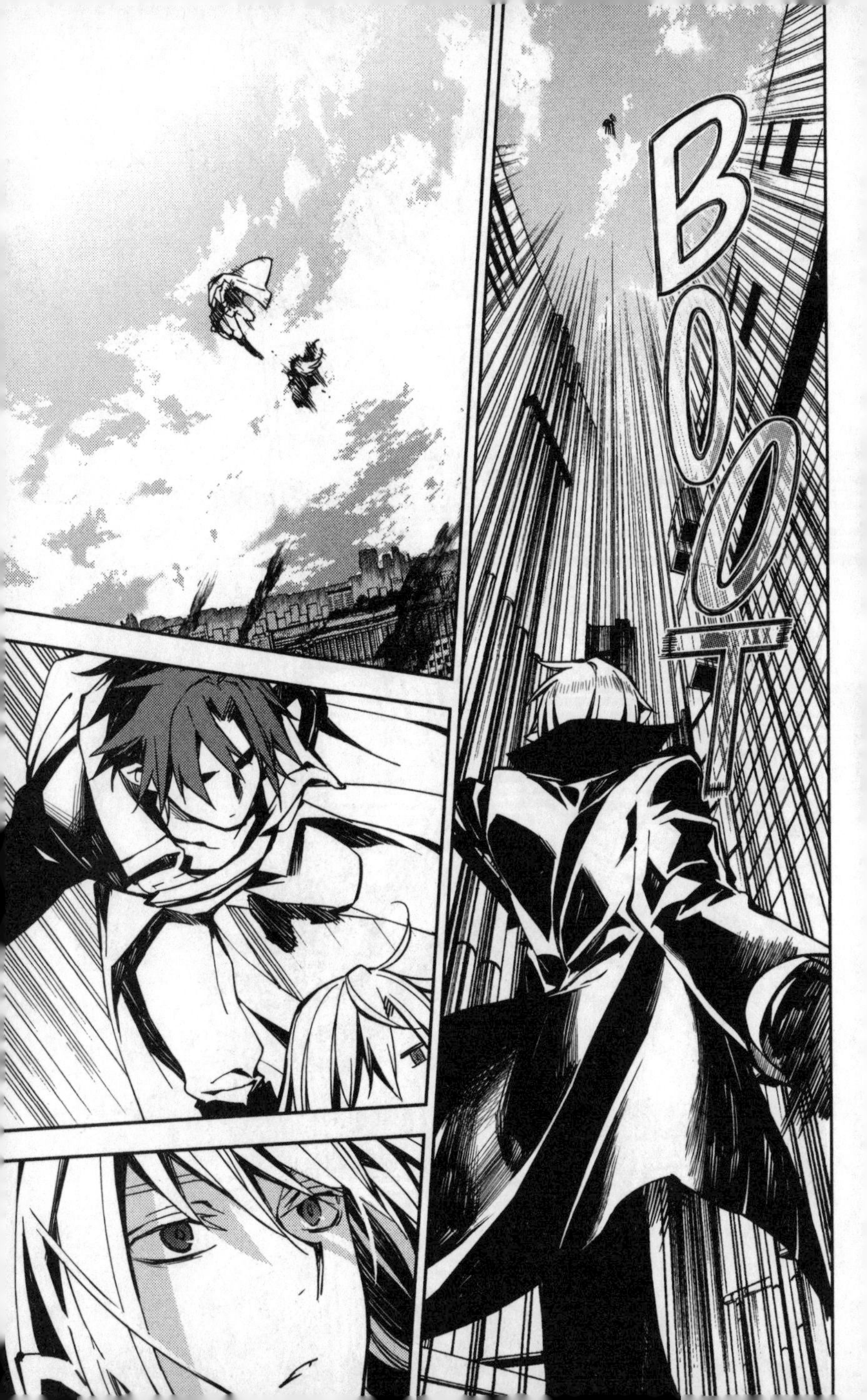
BOOOT

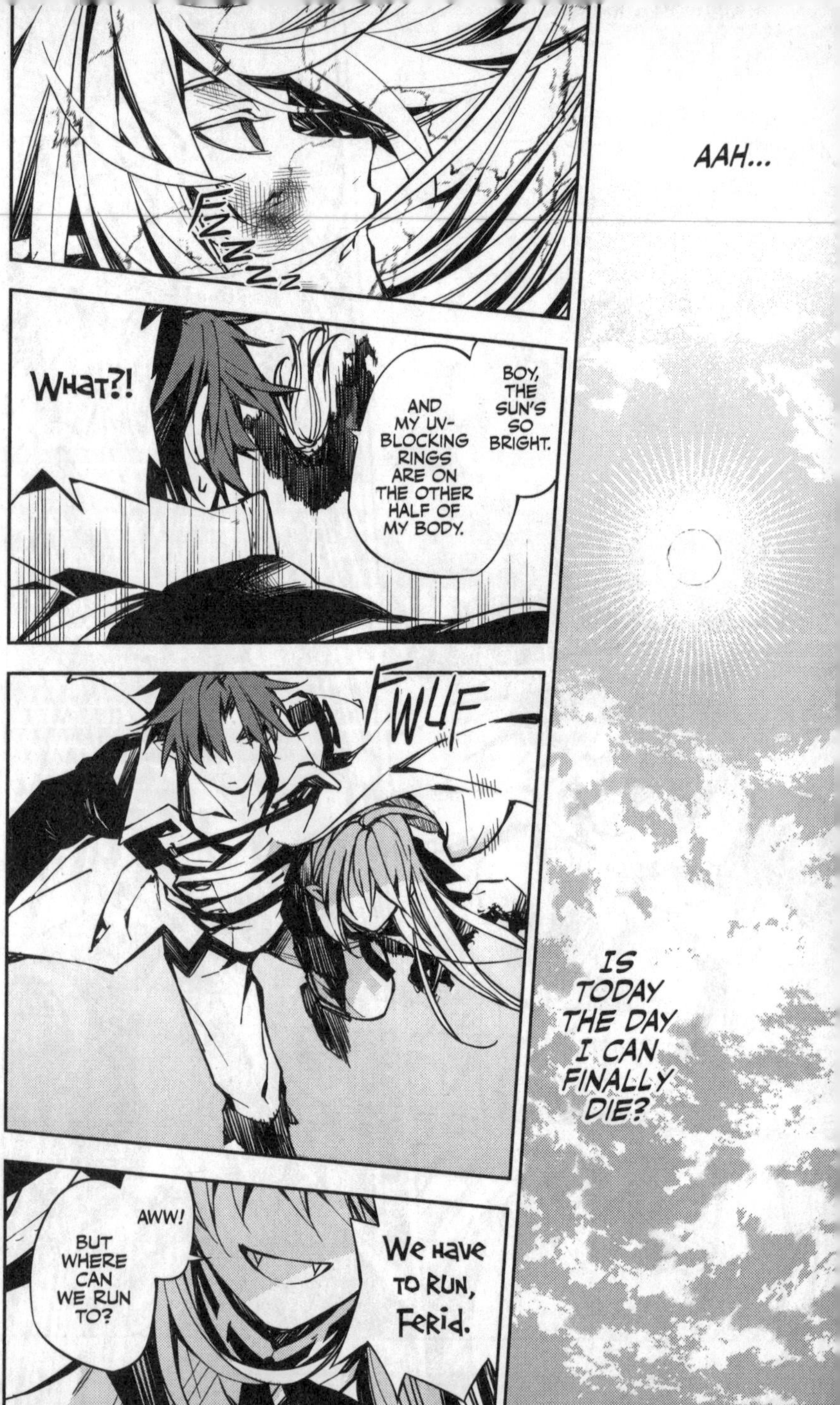

AAH...
IS TODAY THE DAY I CAN FINALLY DIE?
FZZZZZ
BOY, THE SUN'S SO BRIGHT.
AND MY UV-BLOCKING RINGS ARE ON THE OTHER HALF OF MY BODY.
WHAT?!
FWUF
We have to run, Ferid.
AWW!
BUT WHERE CAN WE RUN TO?

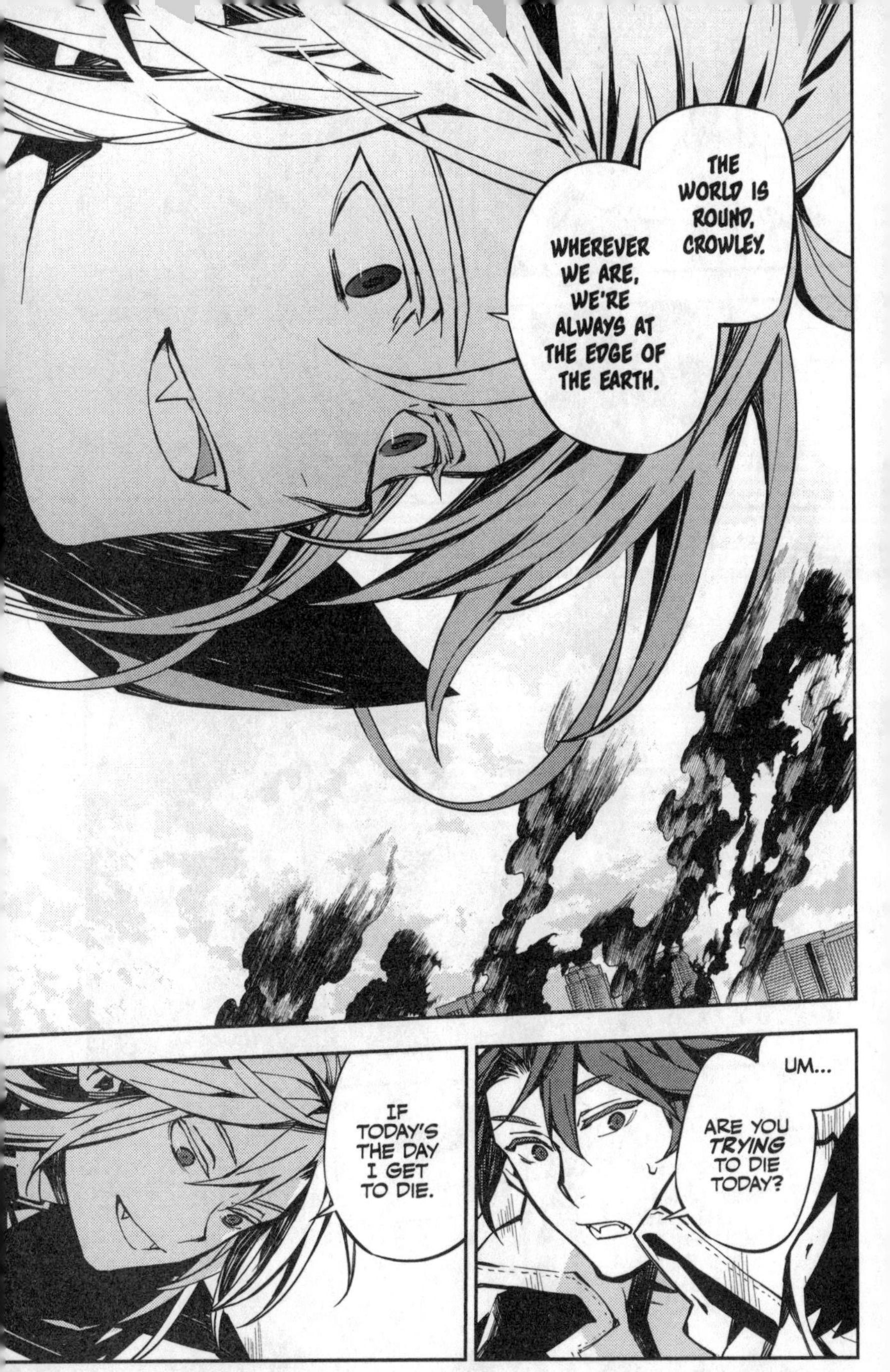

THE WORLD IS ROUND, CROWLEY.
WHEREVER WE ARE, WE'RE ALWAYS AT THE EDGE OF THE EARTH.
UM...
ARE YOU *TRYING* TO DIE TODAY?
IF TODAY'S THE DAY I GET TO DIE.

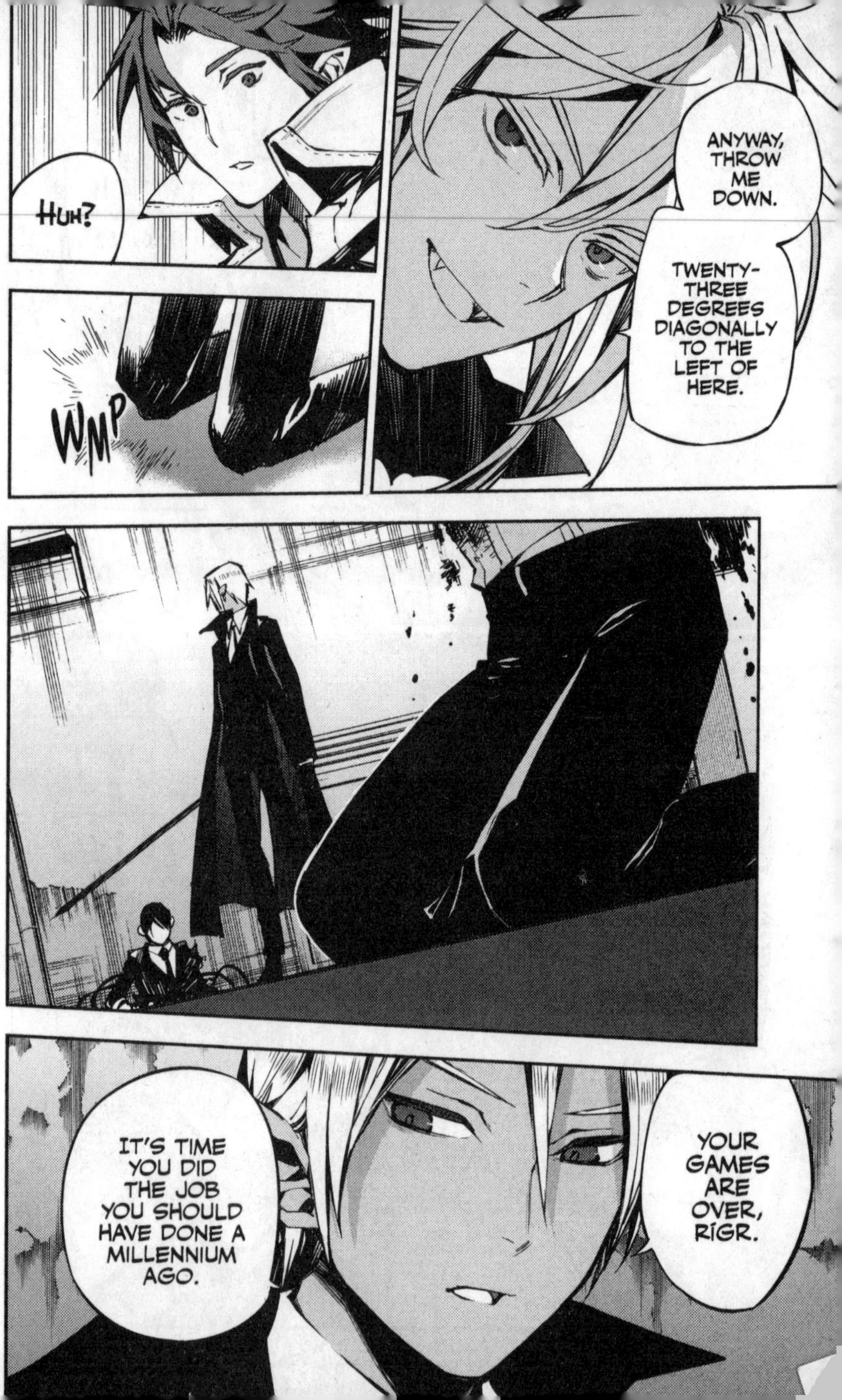
ANYWAY, THROW ME DOWN.
TWENTY-THREE DEGREES DIAGONALLY TO THE LEFT OF HERE.
HUH?
WMP
YOUR GAMES ARE OVER, RIGR.
IT'S TIME YOU DID THE JOB YOU SHOULD HAVE DONE A MILLENNIUM AGO.

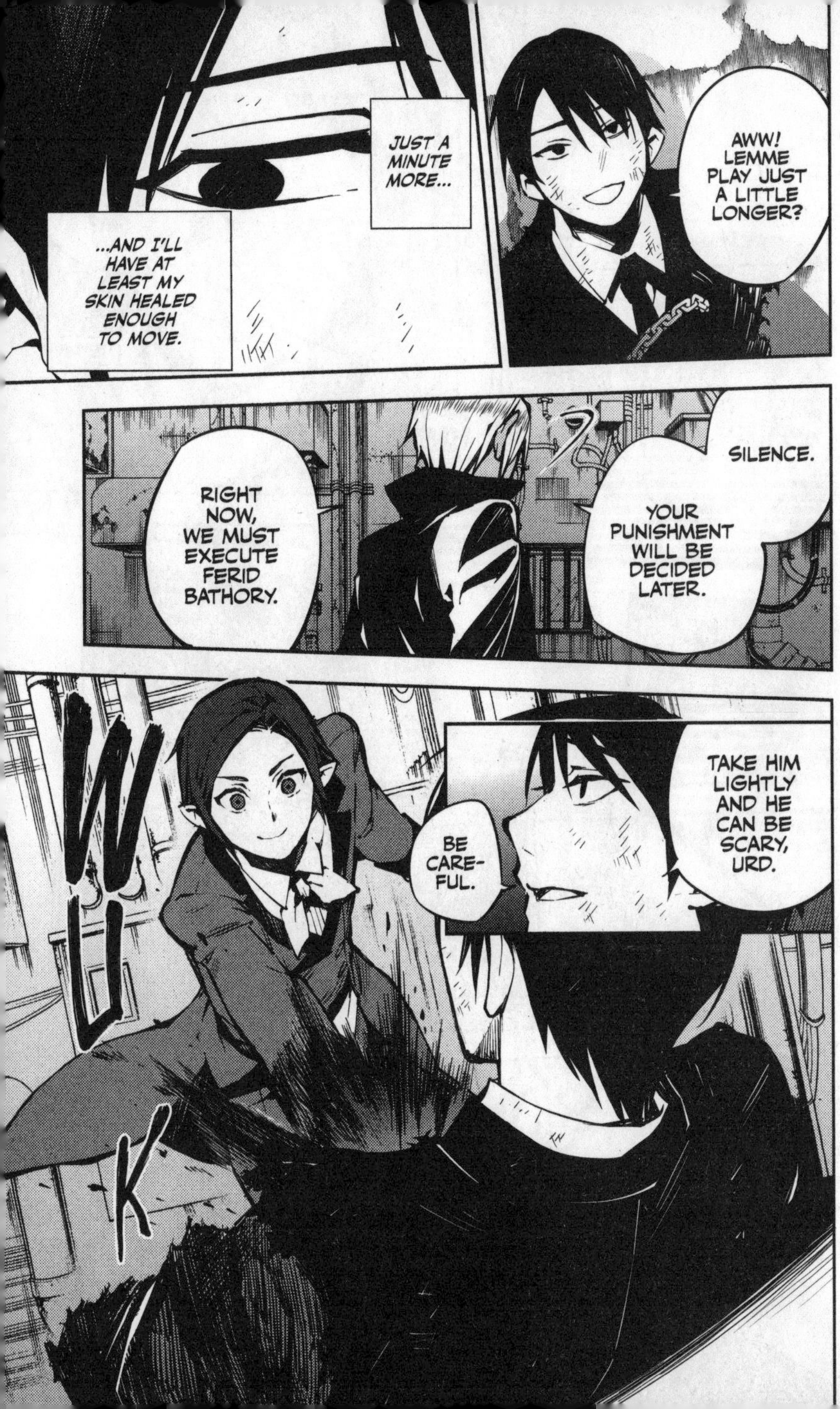
AWW! LEMME PLAY JUST A LITTLE LONGER?
JUST A MINUTE MORE...
...AND I'LL HAVE AT LEAST MY SKIN HEALED ENOUGH TO MOVE.
SILENCE.
YOUR PUNISHMENT WILL BE DECIDED LATER.
RIGHT NOW, WE MUST EXECUTE FERID BATHORY.
TAKE HIM LIGHTLY AND HE CAN BE SCARY, URD.
BE CARE-FUL.
WLK

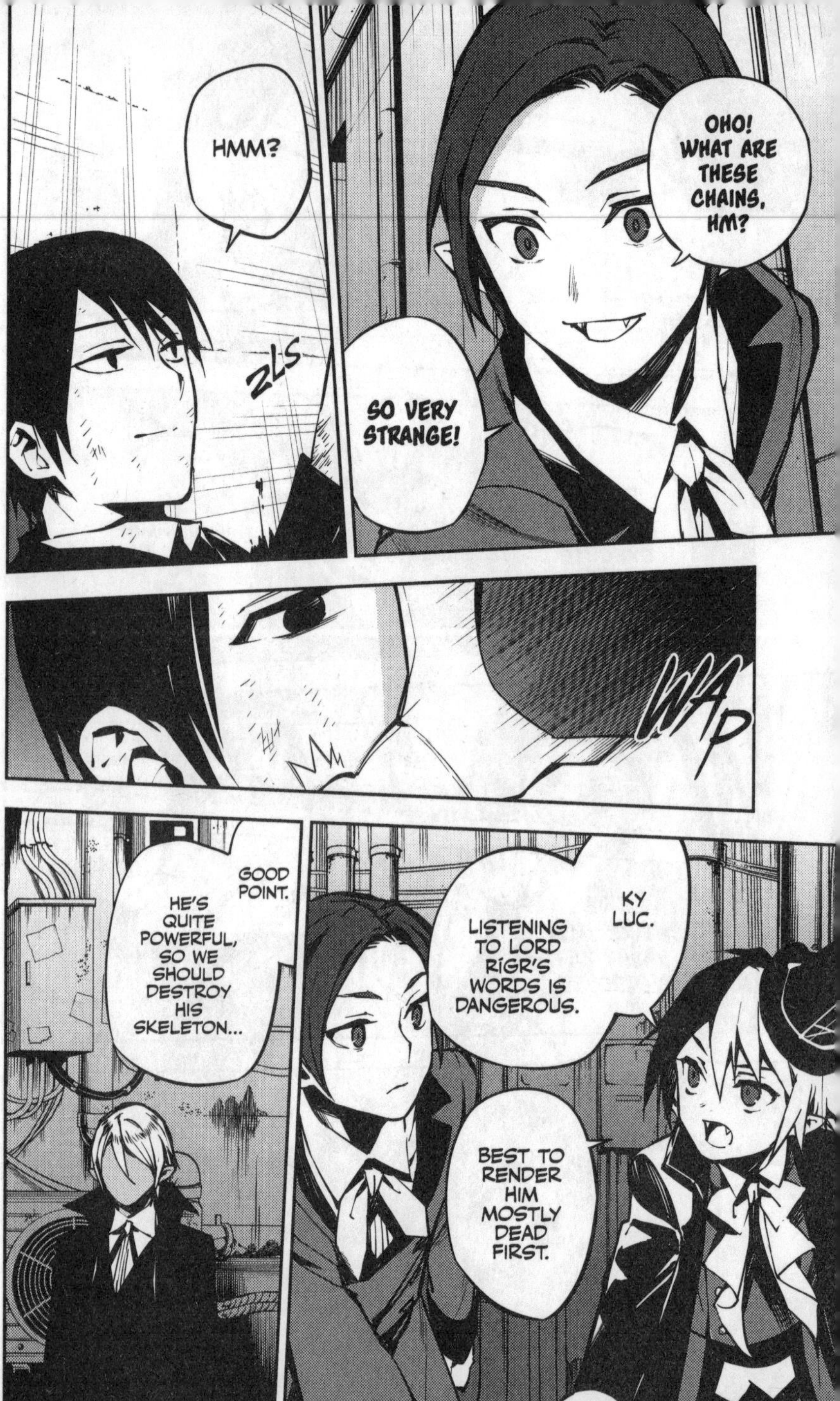
OHO! WHAT ARE THESE CHAINS, HM?
SO VERY STRANGE!
HMM?
ZLS
WAP
KY LUC.
LISTENING TO LORD RÍGR'S WORDS IS DANGEROUS.
BEST TO RENDER HIM MOSTLY DEAD FIRST.
GOOD POINT.
HE'S QUITE POWERFUL, SO WE SHOULD DESTROY HIS SKELETON...

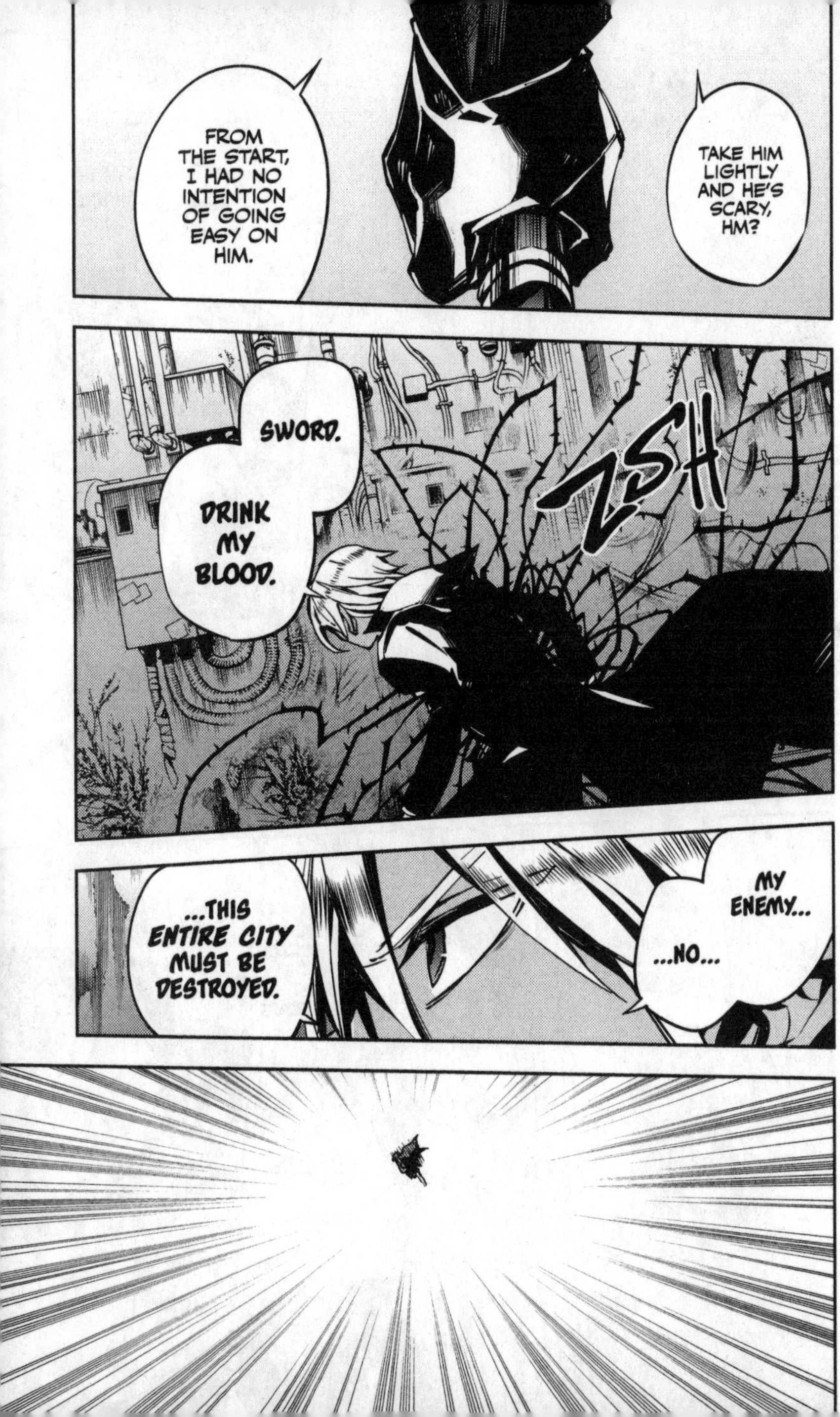
TAKE HIM LIGHTLY AND HE'S SCARY, HM?
FROM THE START, I HAD NO INTENTION OF GOING EASY ON HIM.
ZSH
SWORD.
DRINK MY BLOOD.
MY ENEMY...
...NO...
...THIS ENTIRE CITY MUST BE DESTROYED.

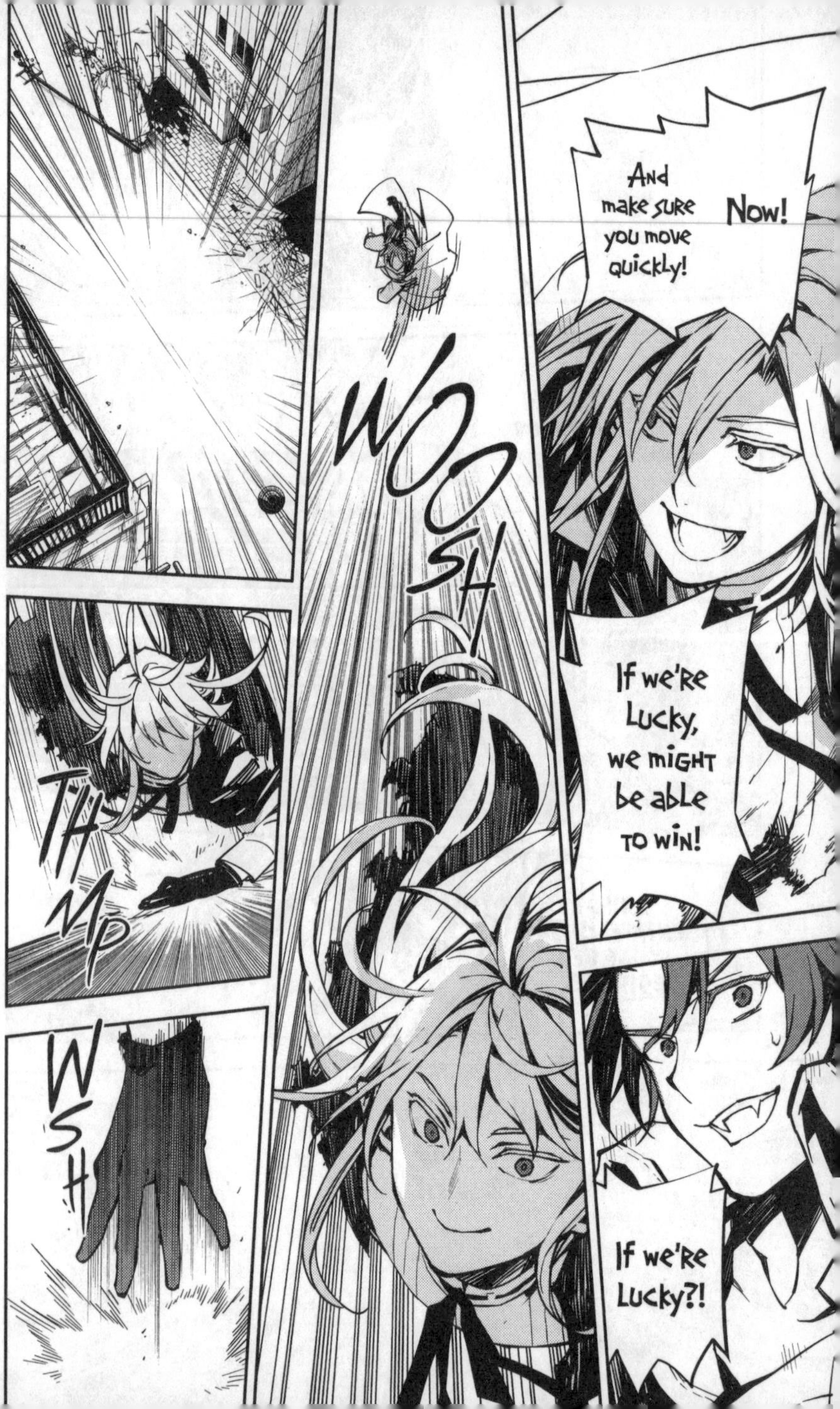
Now!
And make sure you move quickly!
If we're lucky, we might be able to win!
If we're lucky?!
WOOSH
THMP
WSH

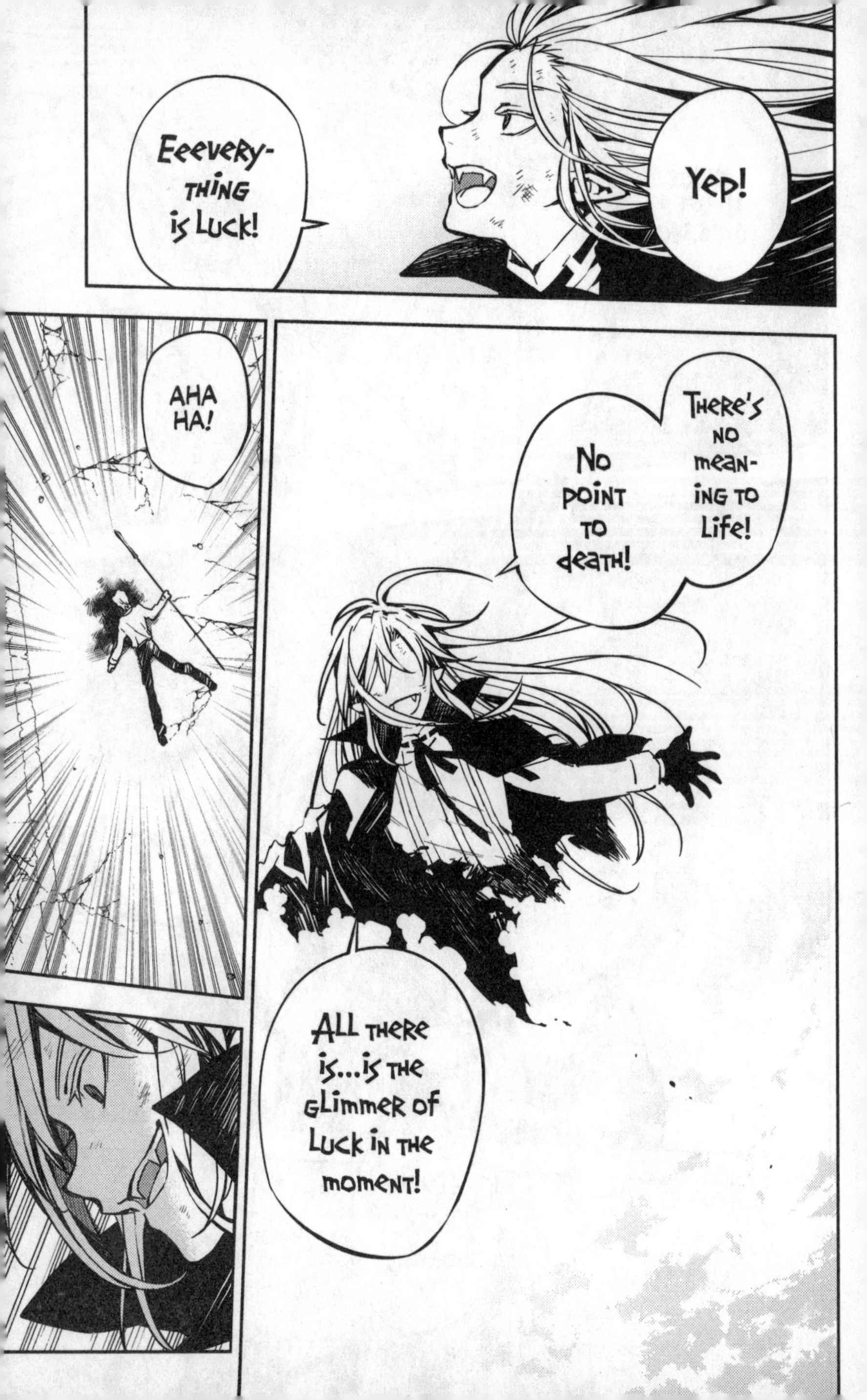
Yep!
Eeevery-thing is Luck!
There's no mean-ing to Life!
No point to death!
All there is...is the glimmer of Luck in the moment!
AHA HA!

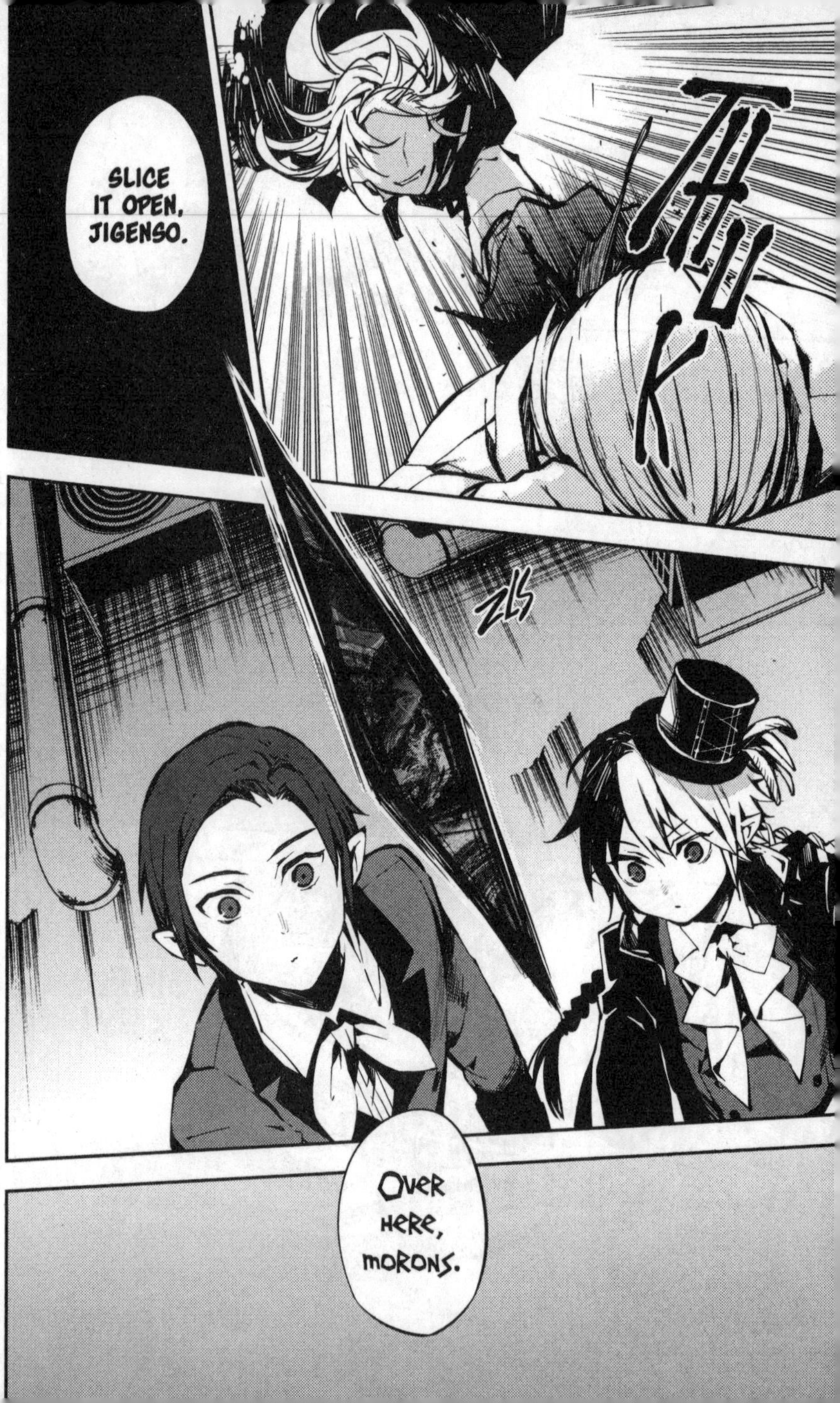
THUK
SLICE IT OPEN, JIGENSO.
ZLS
Over here, morons.

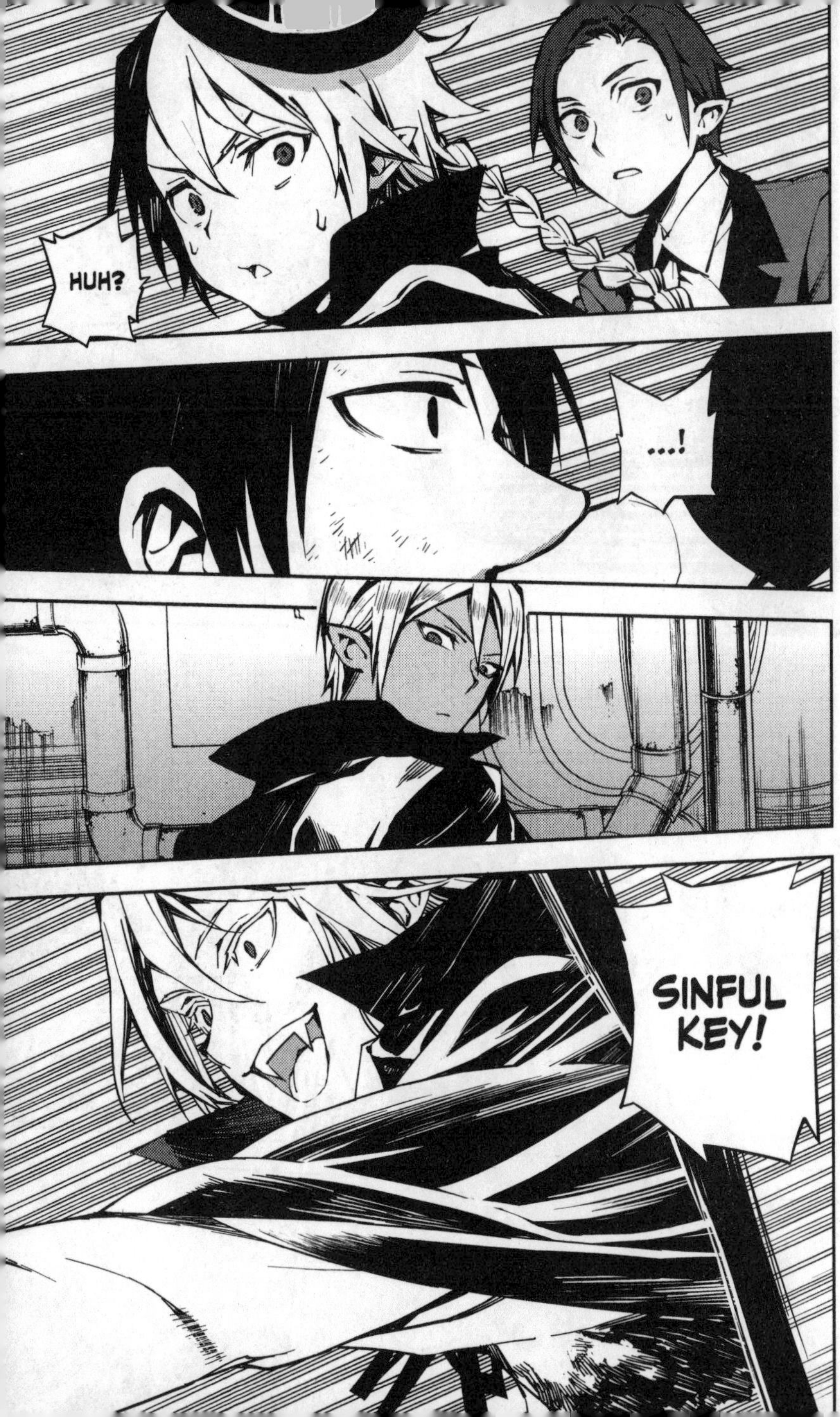
HUH?
...!
SINFUL KEY!

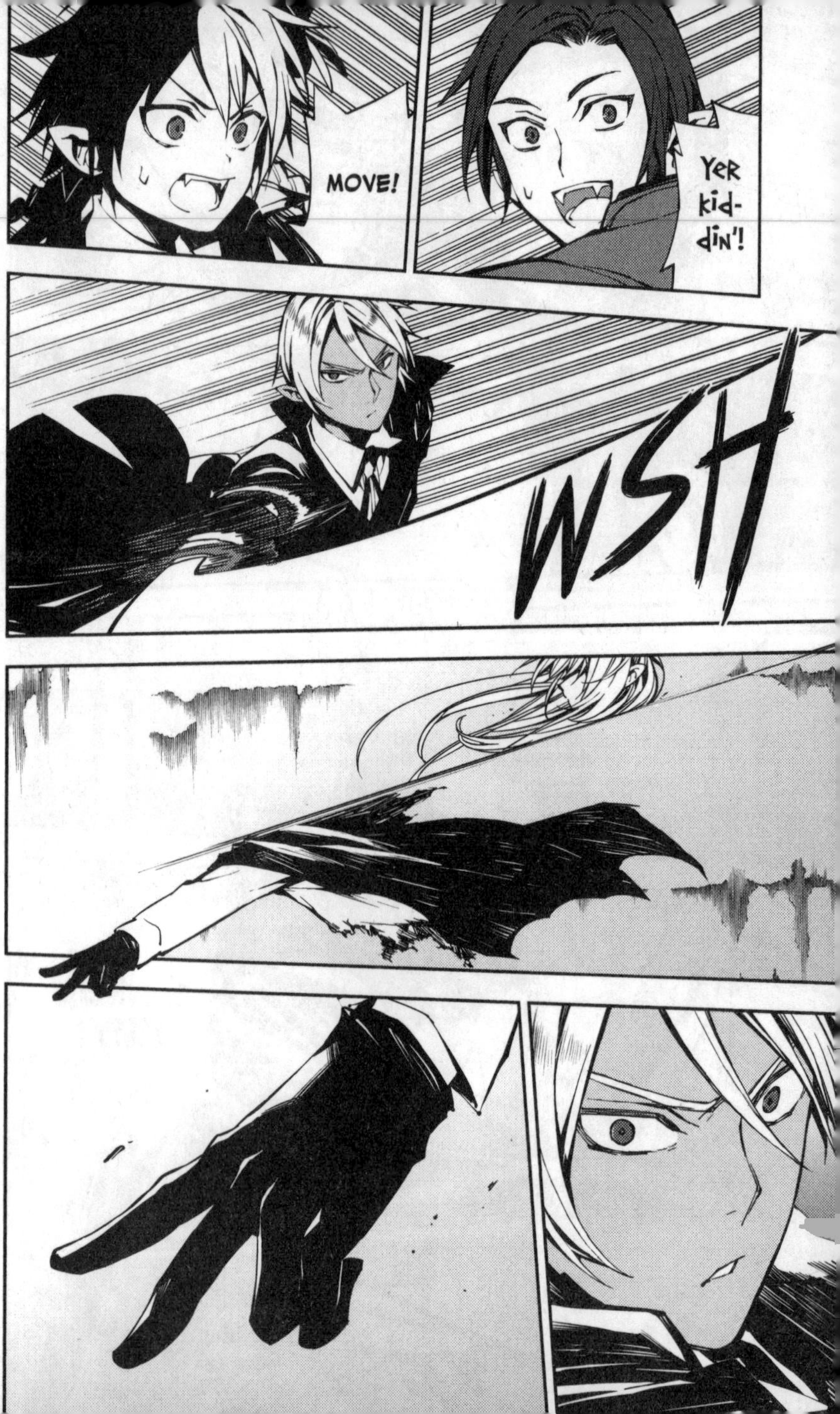
Yer kid-din'!
MOVE!
WSH

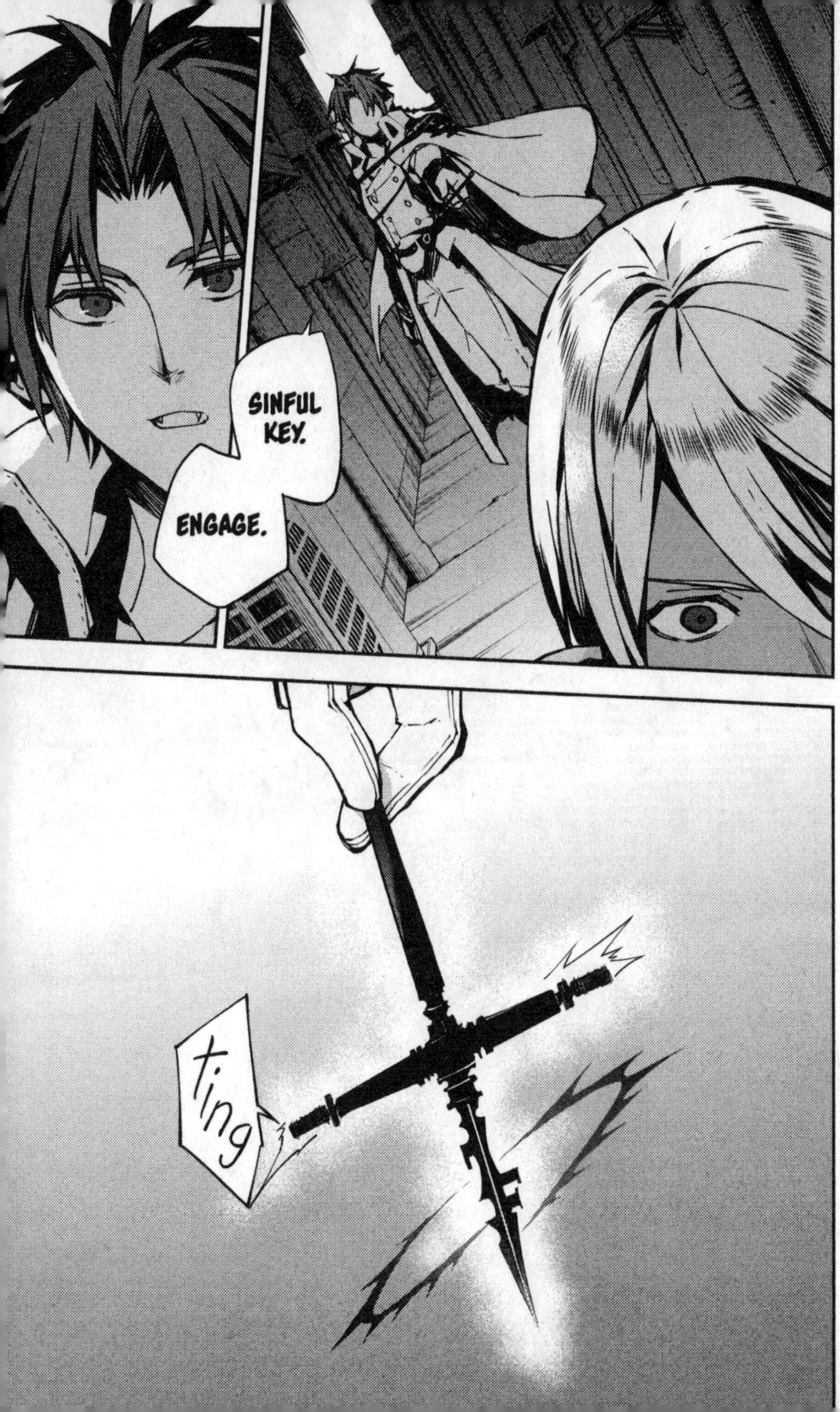
SINFUL KEY.
ENGAGE.
ting

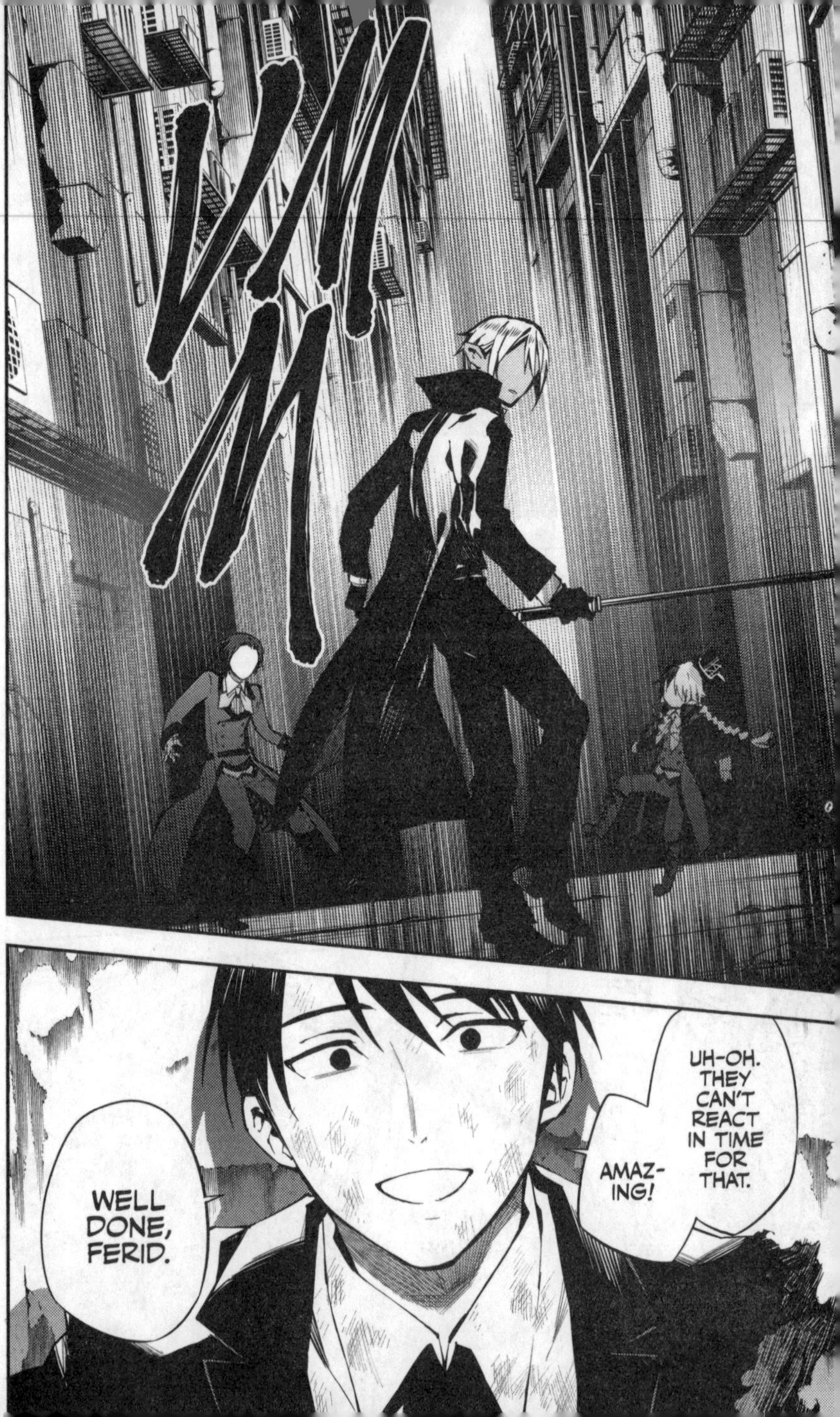
UH-OH. THEY CAN'T REACT IN TIME FOR THAT.
AMAZ-ING!
WELL DONE, FERID.

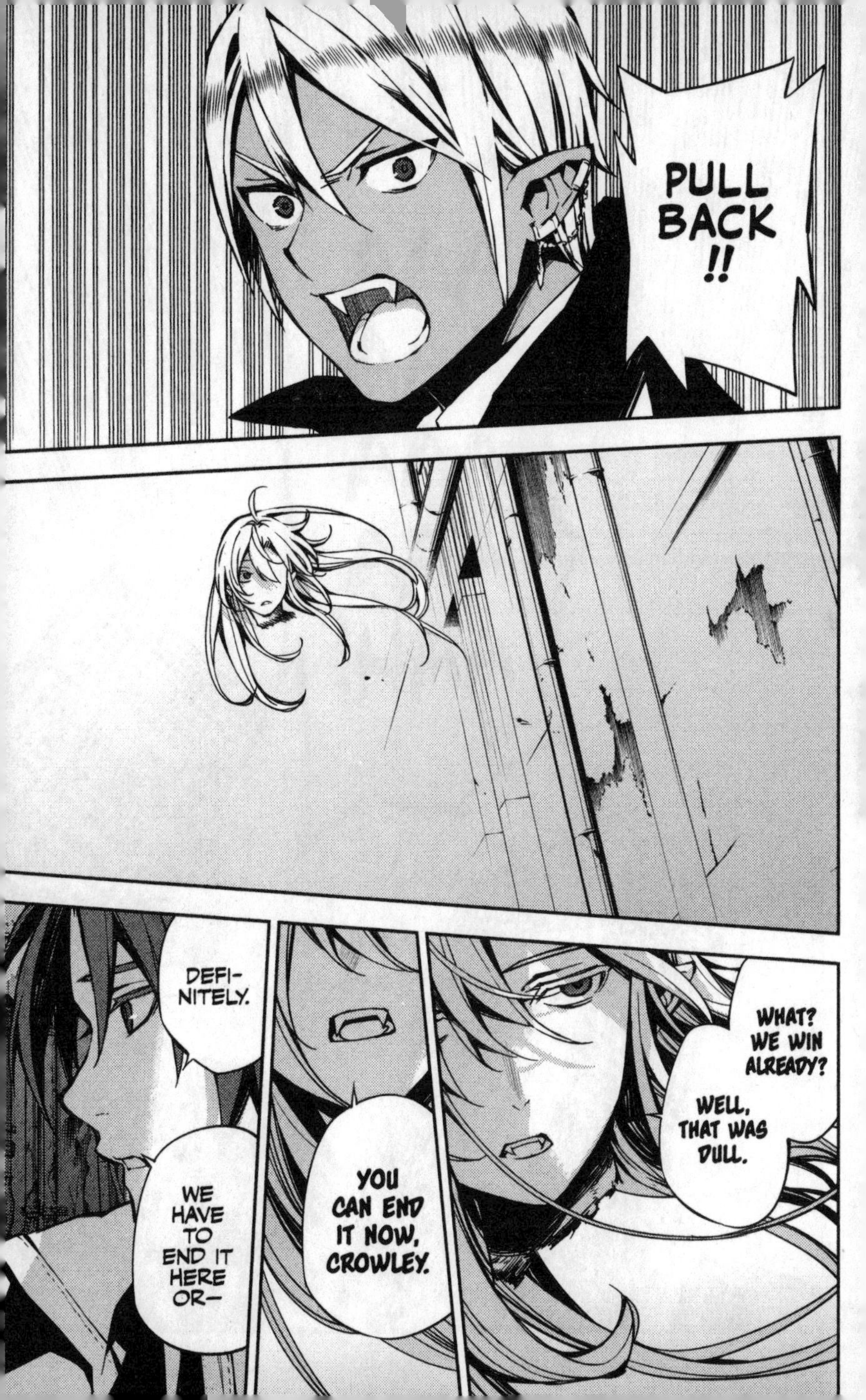
PULL BACK!!
WHAT? WE WIN ALREADY?
WELL, THAT WAS DULL.
YOU CAN END IT NOW, CROWLEY.
DEFI-NITELY.
WE HAVE TO END IT HERE OR—

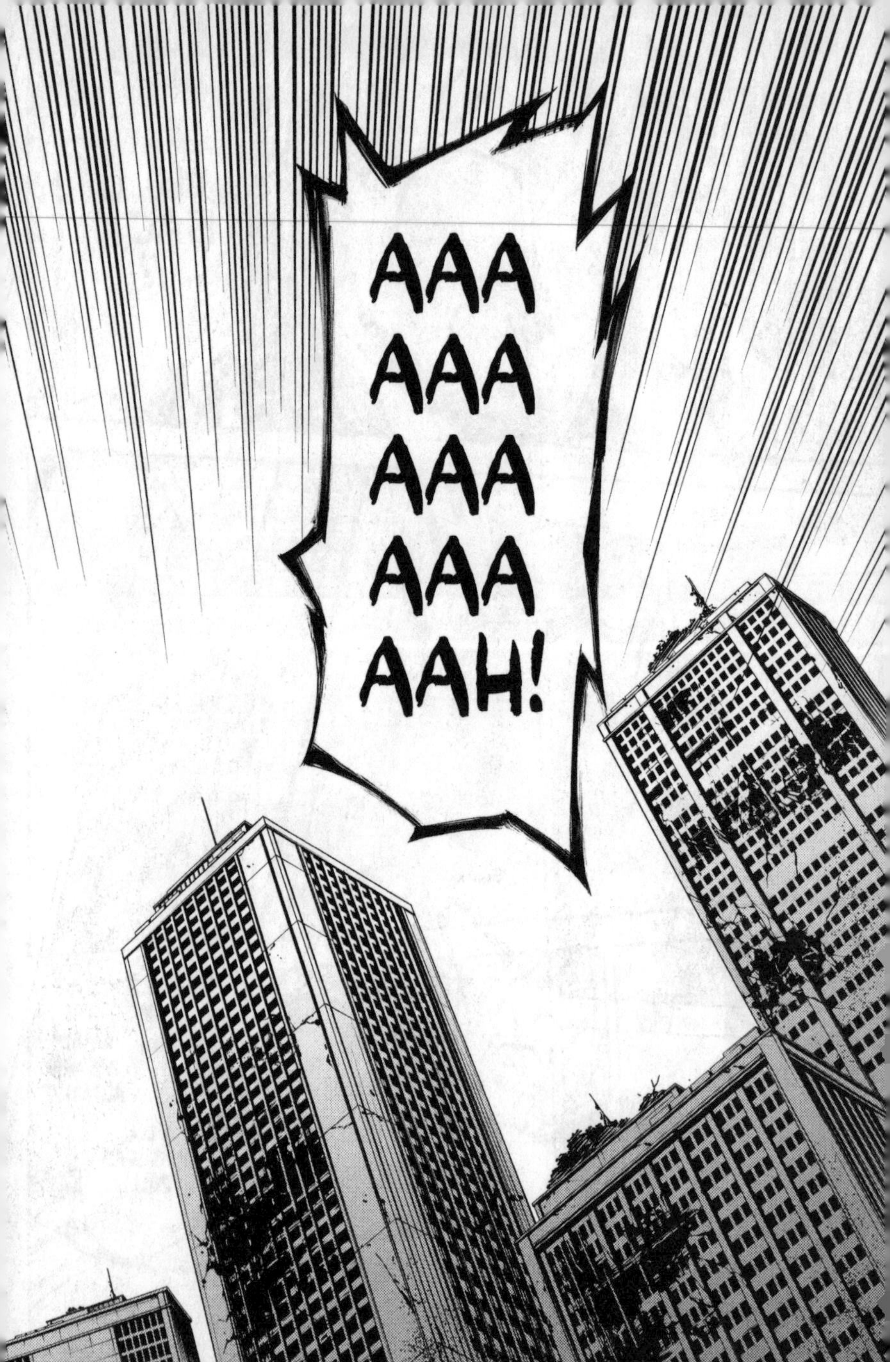
AAAAAAAAAAAAAAH!

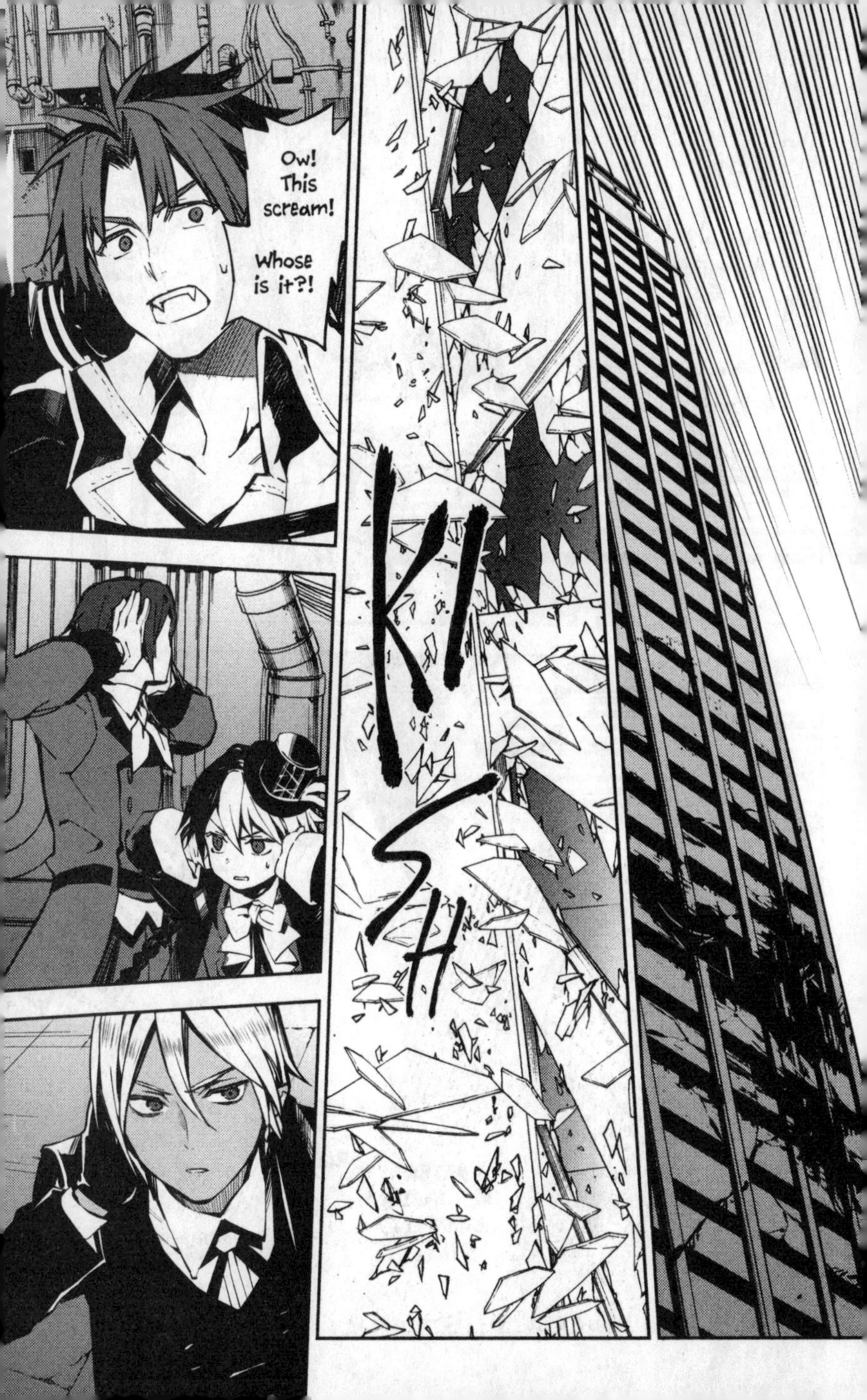
KISH
Ow! This scream!
Whose is it?!

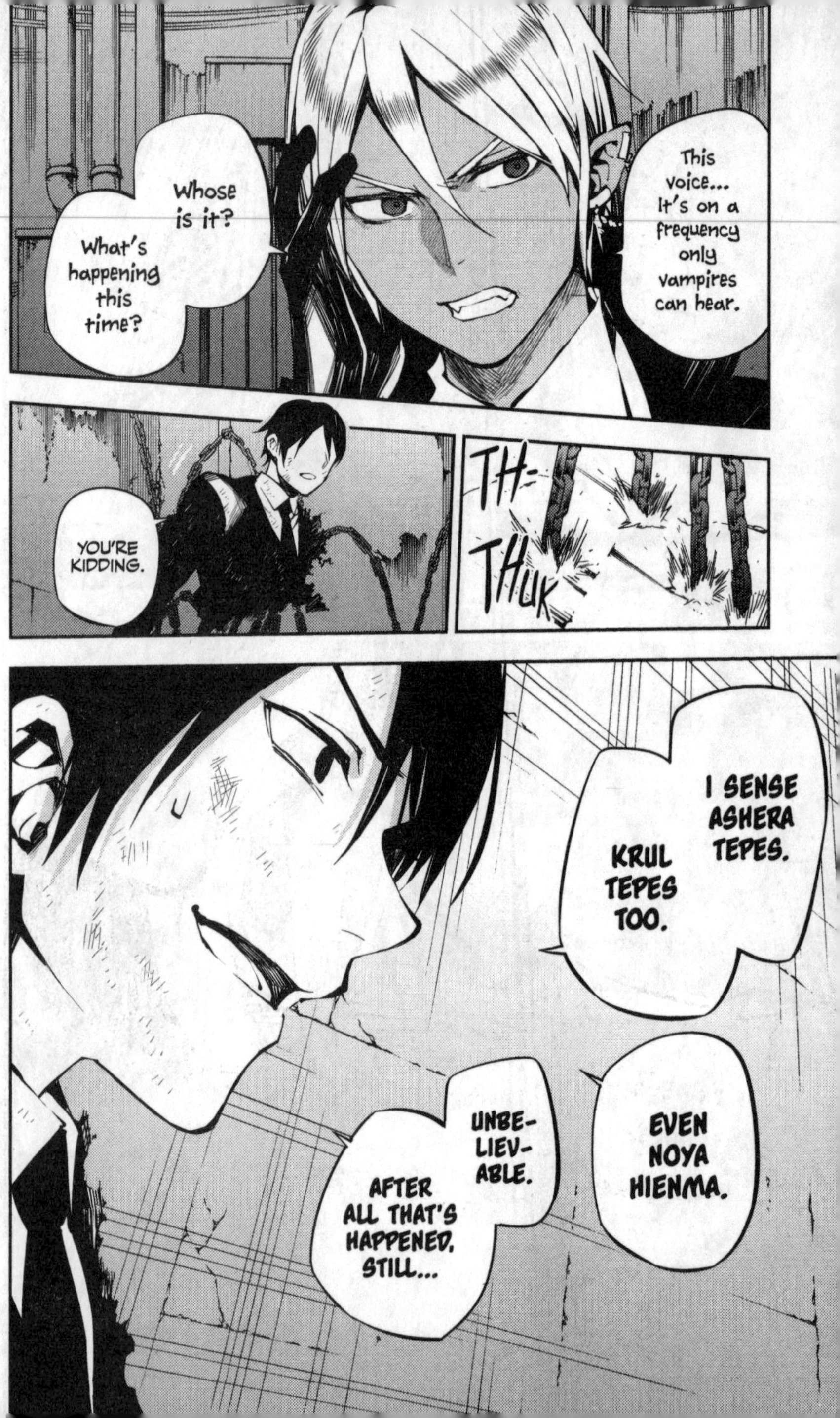
This voice... It's on a frequency only vampires can hear.
Whose is it?
What's happening this time?
TH-THUK
YOU'RE KIDDING.
I SENSE ASHERA TEPES.
KRUL TEPES TOO.
EVEN NOYA HIENMA.
UNBELIEVABLE.
AFTER ALL THAT'S HAPPENED, STILL...

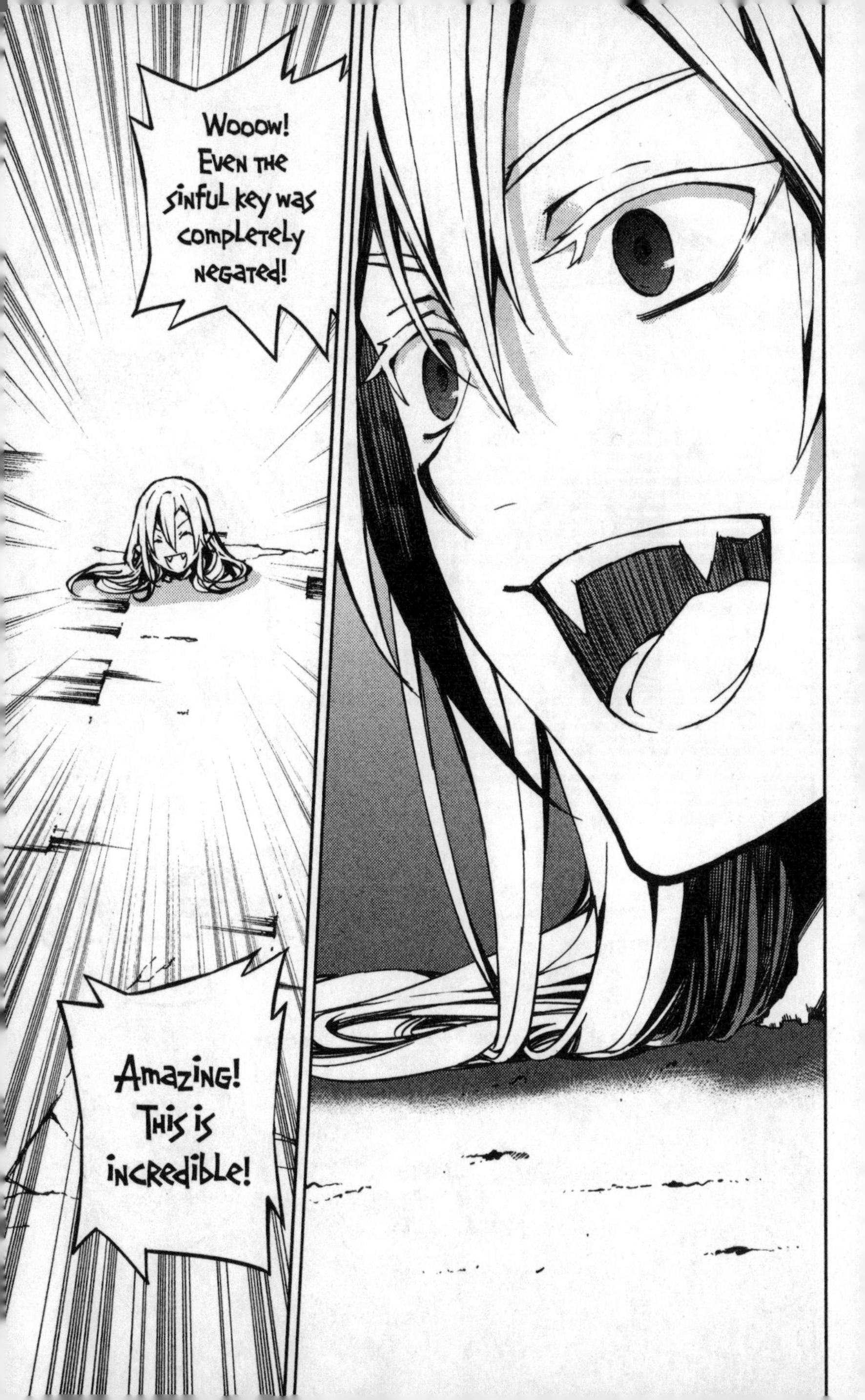
Wooow! Even the sinful key was completely negated!
Amazing! This is incredible!

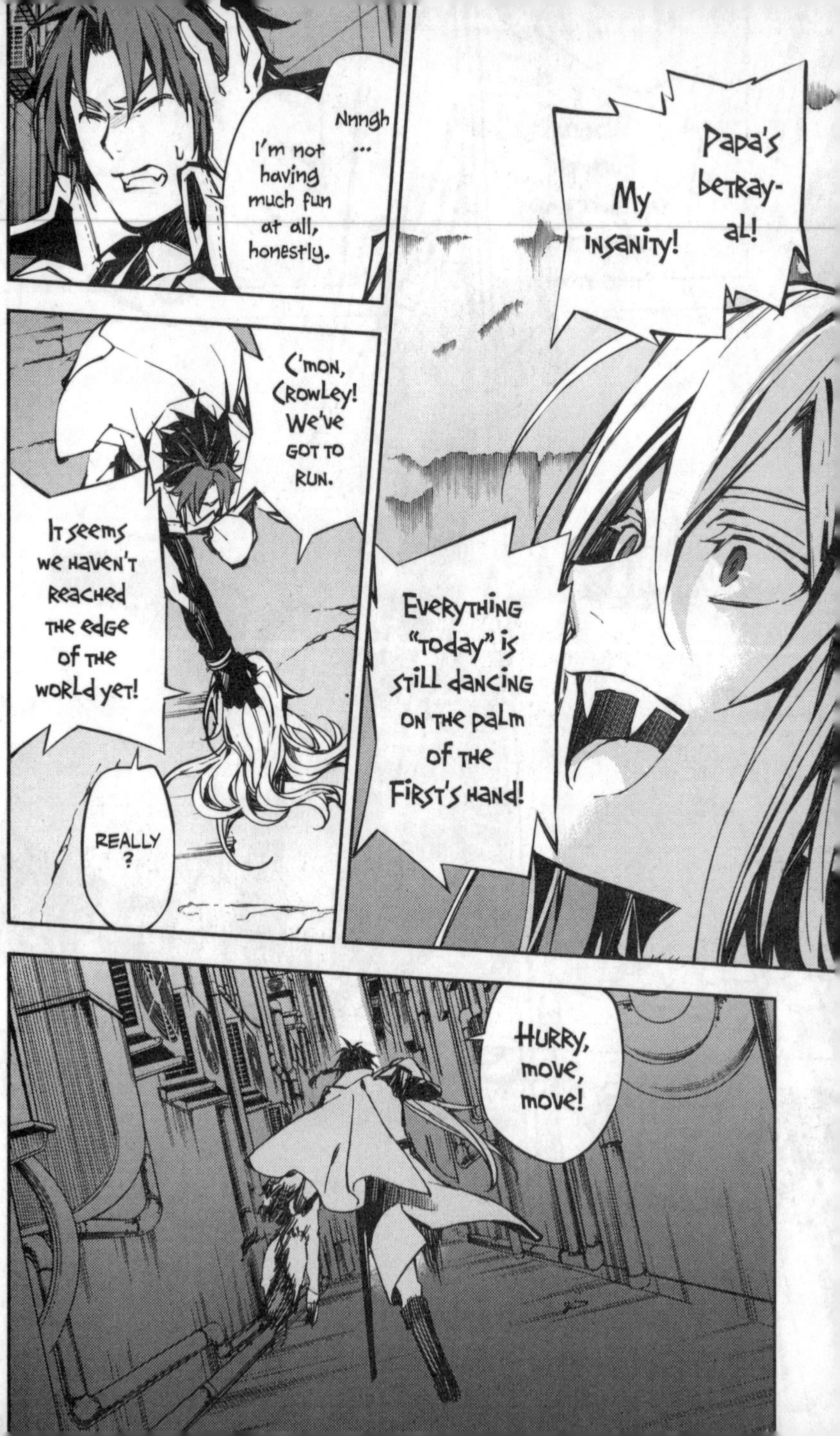
Papa's betray-al!
My insanity!
Everything "today" is still dancing on the palm of the First's hand!
Nnngh ...
I'm not having much fun at all, honestly.
C'mon, Crowley! We've got to run.
It seems we haven't reached the edge of the world yet!
REALLY ?
Hurry, move, move!

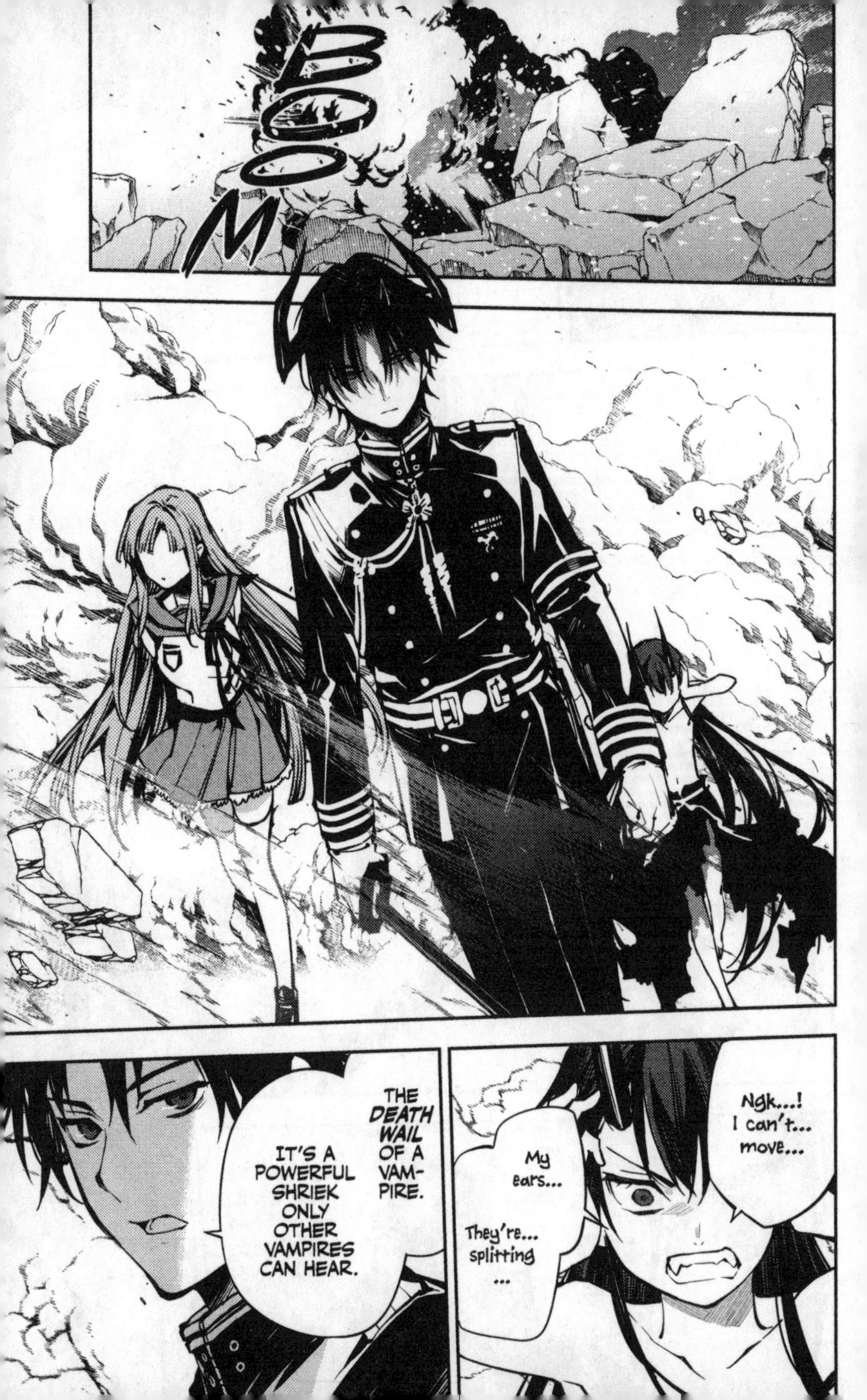
BOOM
THE DEATH WAIL OF A VAMPIRE.
IT'S A POWERFUL SHRIEK ONLY OTHER VAMPIRES CAN HEAR.
Ngk...! I can't... move...
My ears...
They're... splitting ...

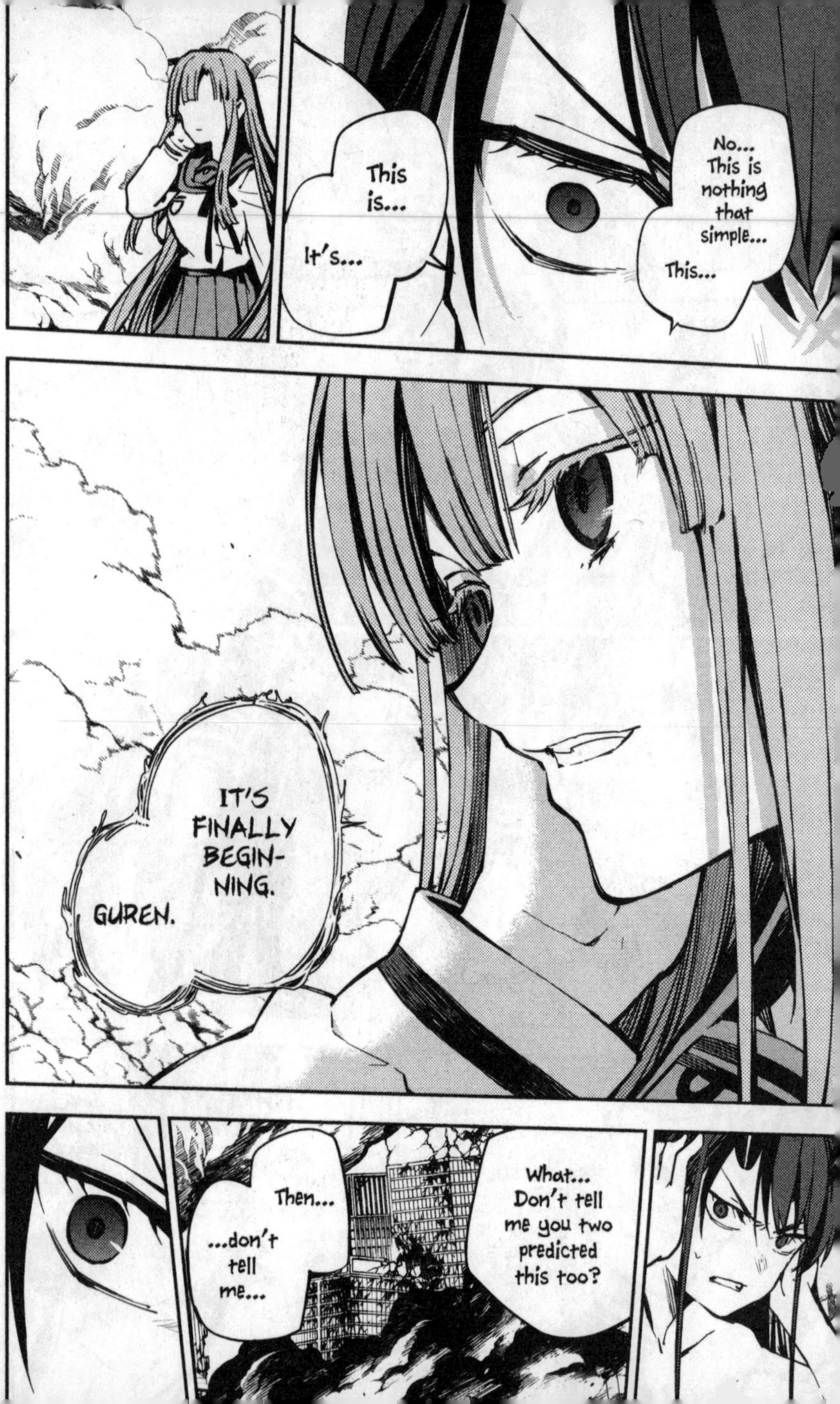
This is...
It's...
No... This is nothing that simple...
This...
IT'S FINALLY BEGIN-NING.
GUREN.
What... Don't tell me you two predicted this too?
Then...
...don't tell me...

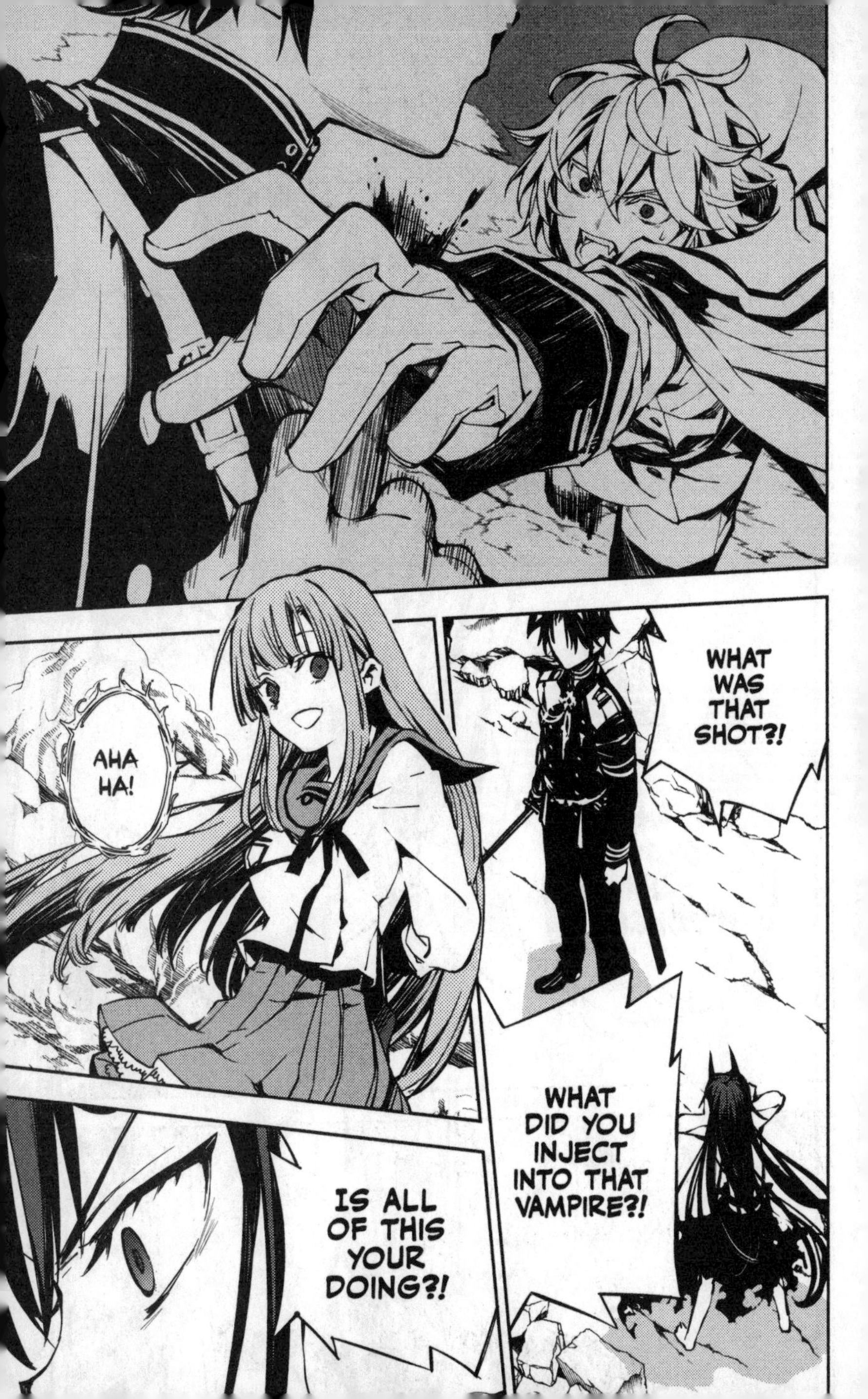
WHAT WAS THAT SHOT?!
AHA HA!
WHAT DID YOU INJECT INTO THAT VAMPIRE?!
IS ALL OF THIS YOUR DOING?!

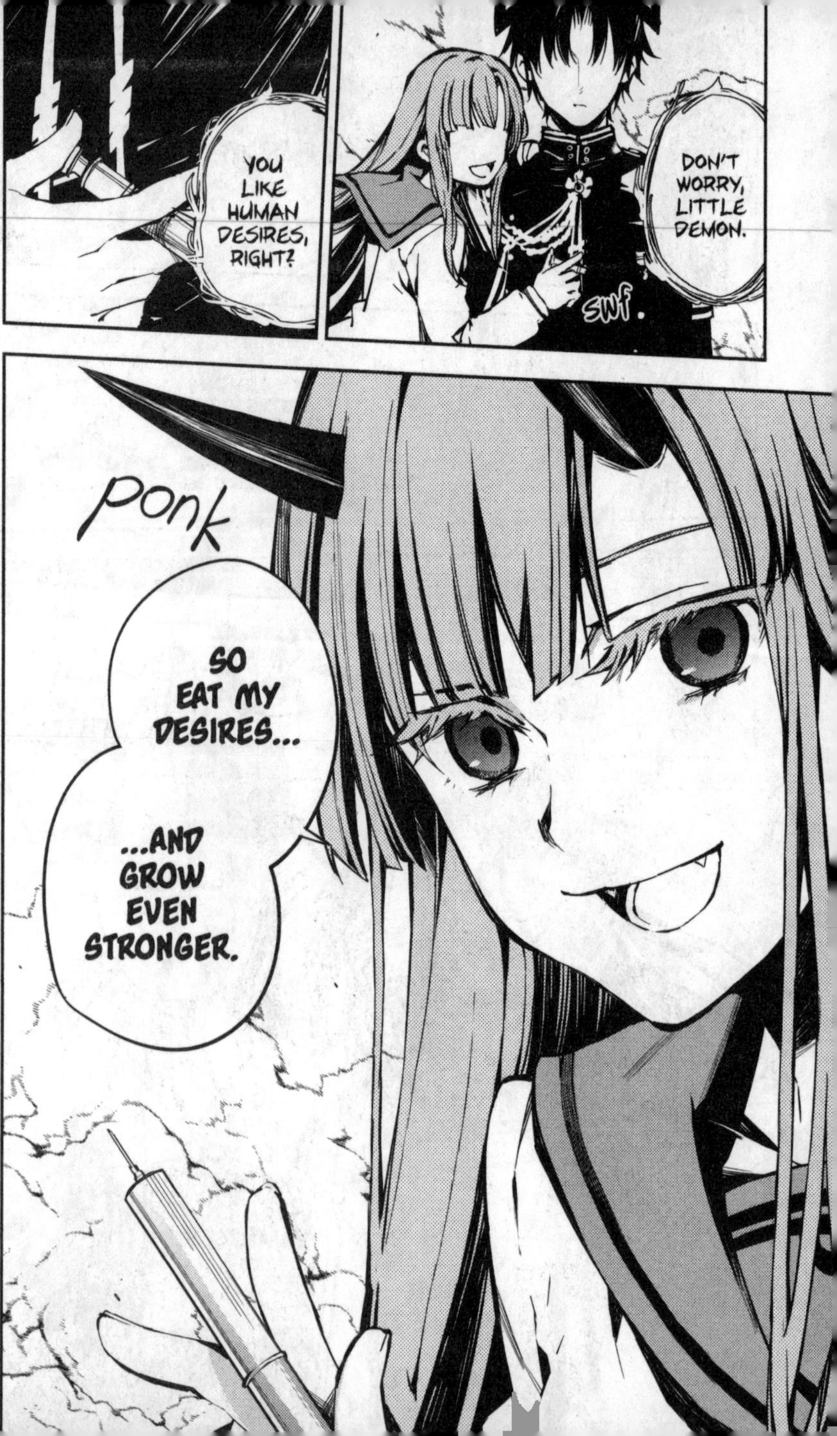
DON'T WORRY, LITTLE DEMON.
swf
YOU LIKE HUMAN DESIRES, RIGHT?
ponk
SO EAT MY DESIRES...
...AND GROW EVEN STRONGER.

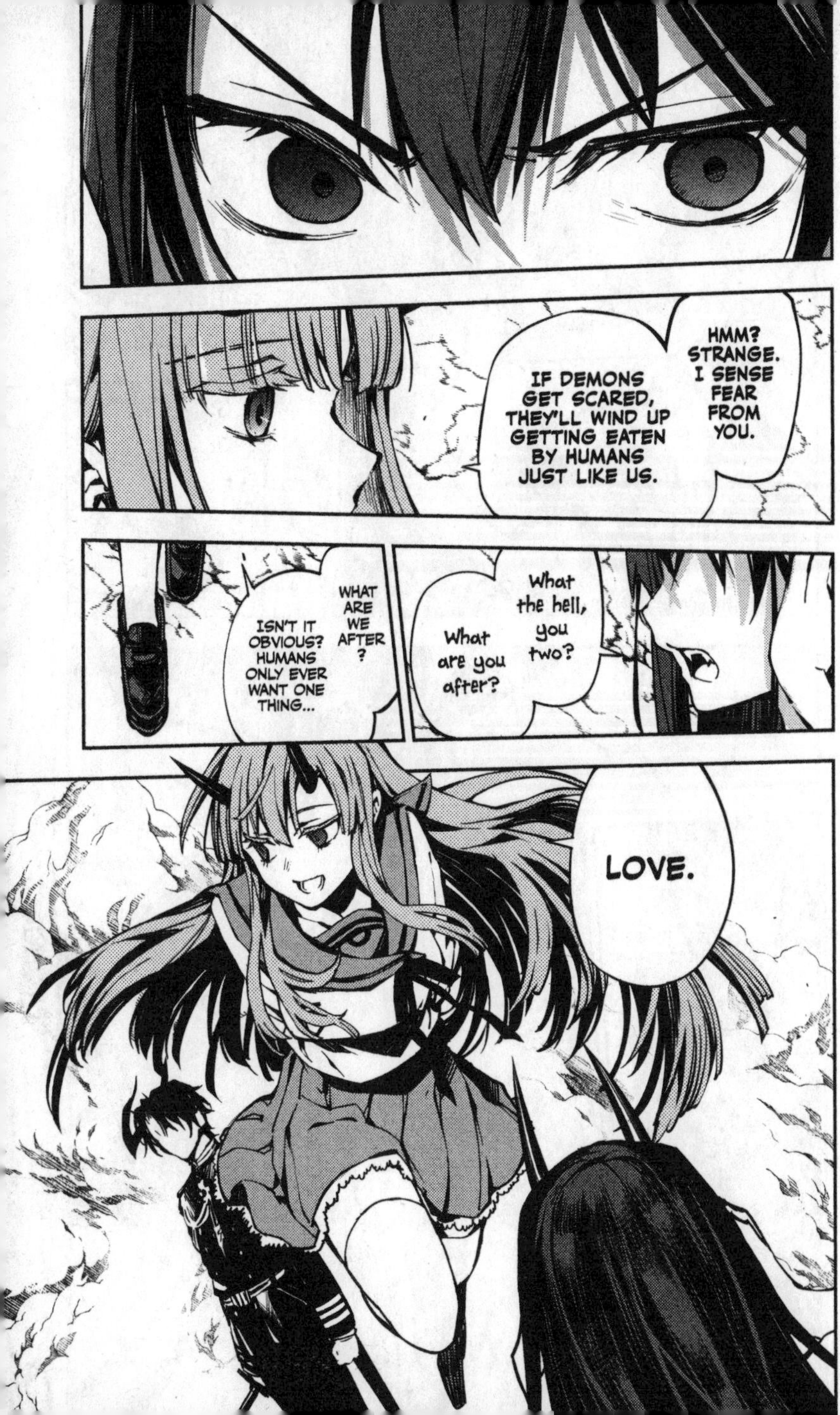
HMM? STRANGE. I SENSE FEAR FROM YOU.
IF DEMONS GET SCARED, THEY'LL WIND UP GETTING EATEN BY HUMANS JUST LIKE US.
What the hell, you two?
What are you after?
WHAT ARE WE AFTER?
ISN'T IT OBVIOUS? HUMANS ONLY EVER WANT ONE THING...
LOVE.

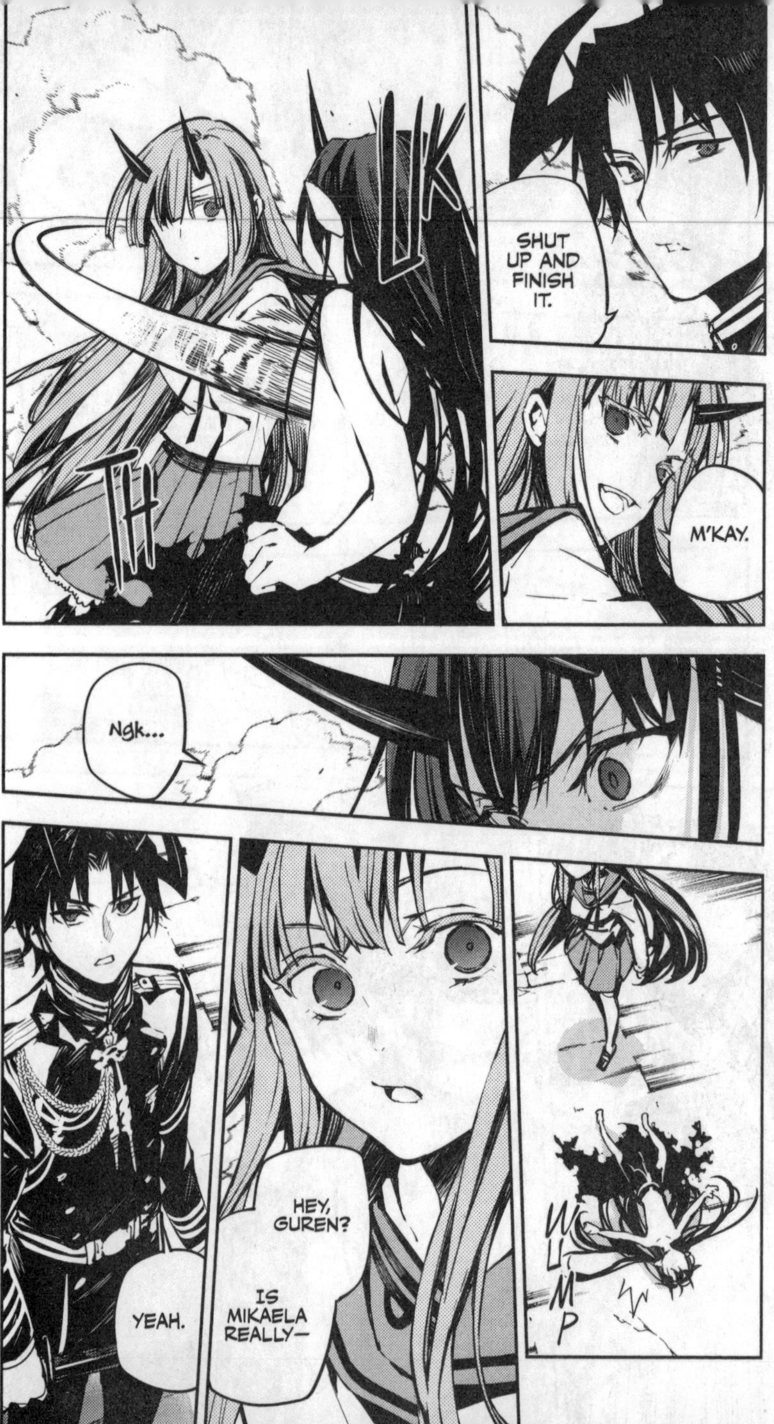
SHUT UP AND FINISH IT.
M'KAY.
UK
TH
Ngk...
WUMP
HEY, GUREN?
IS MIKAELA REALLY—
YEAH.

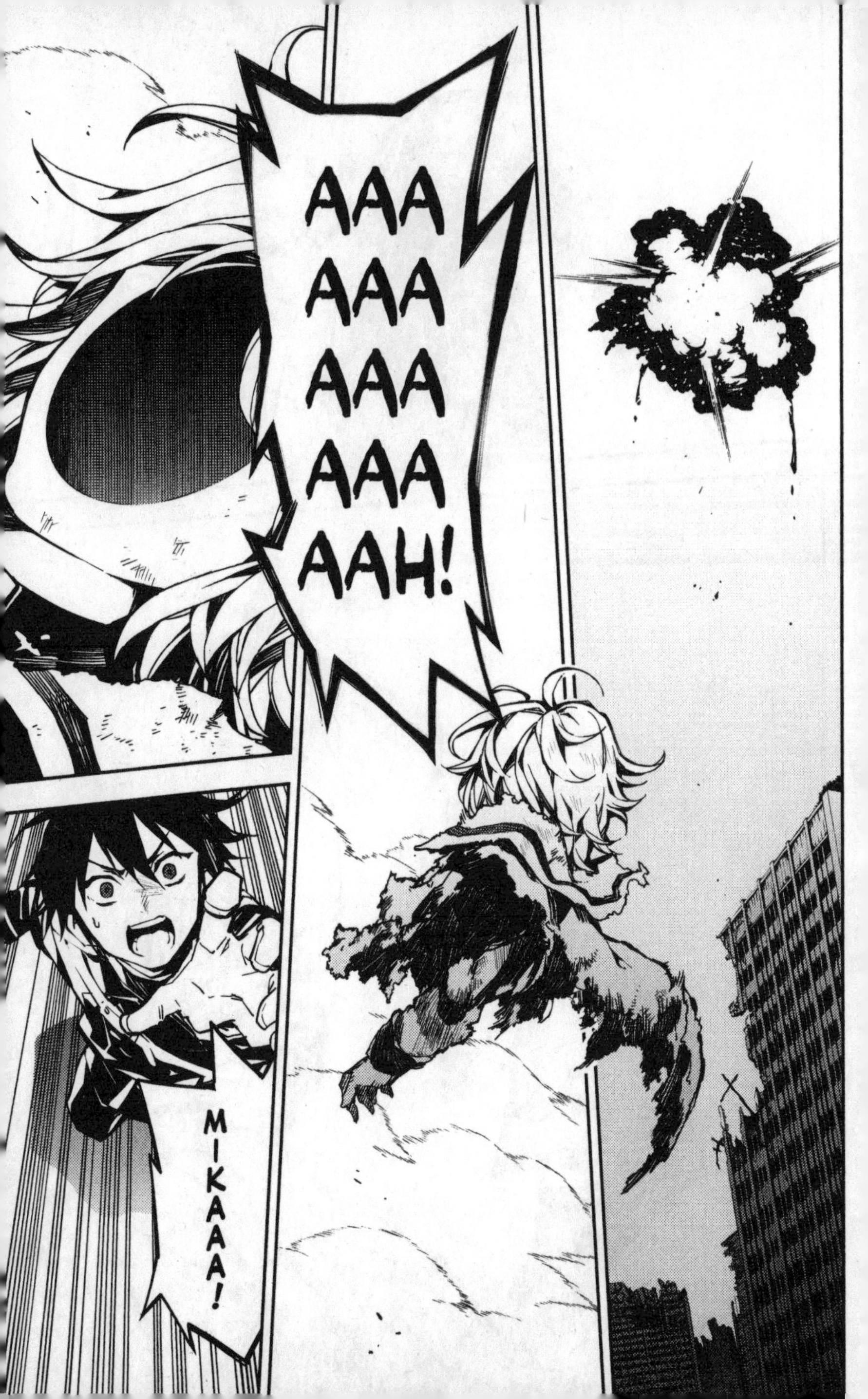
AAA AAA AAA AAA AAH!
MIKAAAA!

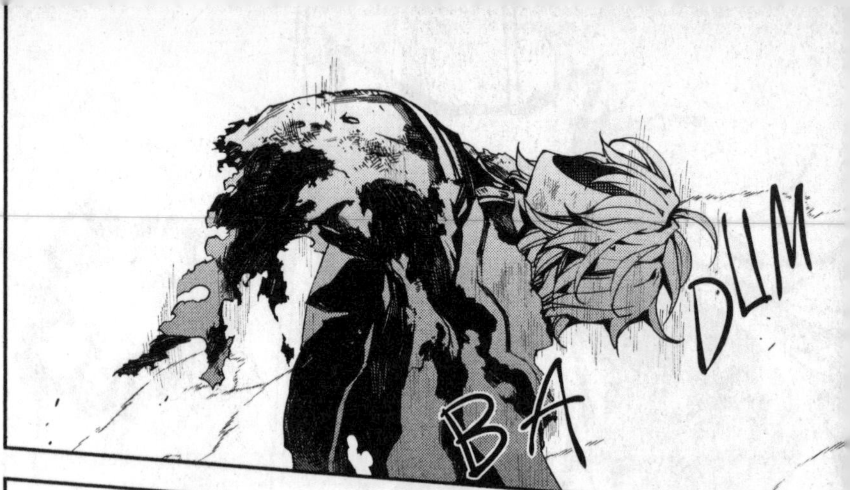
BA DUM
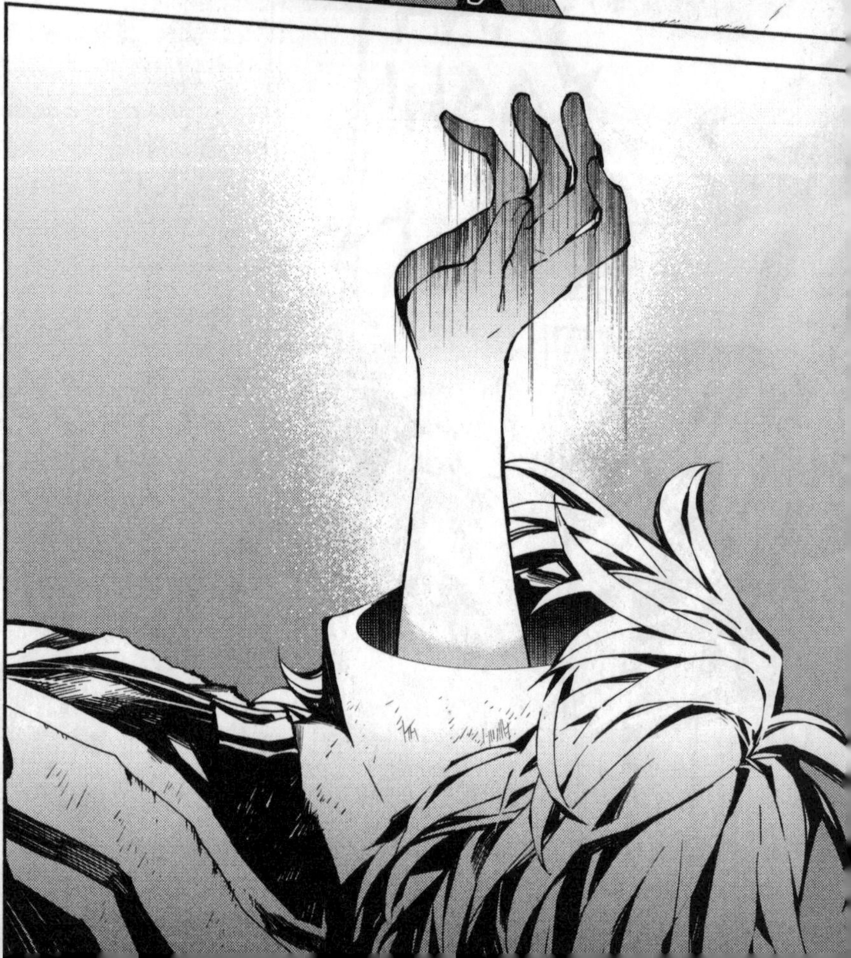

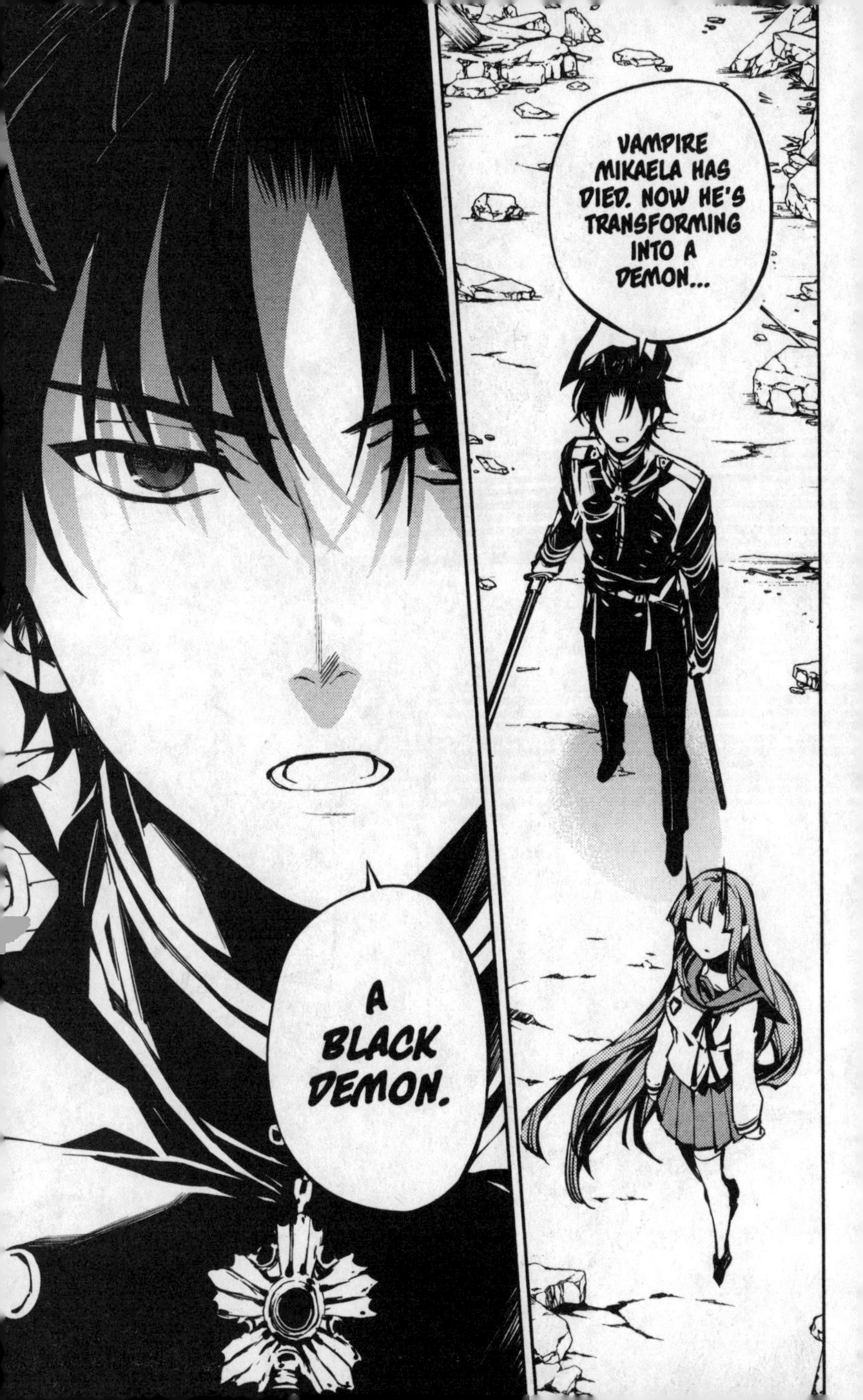
VAMPIRE MIKAELA HAS DIED. NOW HE'S TRANSFORMING INTO A DEMON...
A BLACK DEMON.

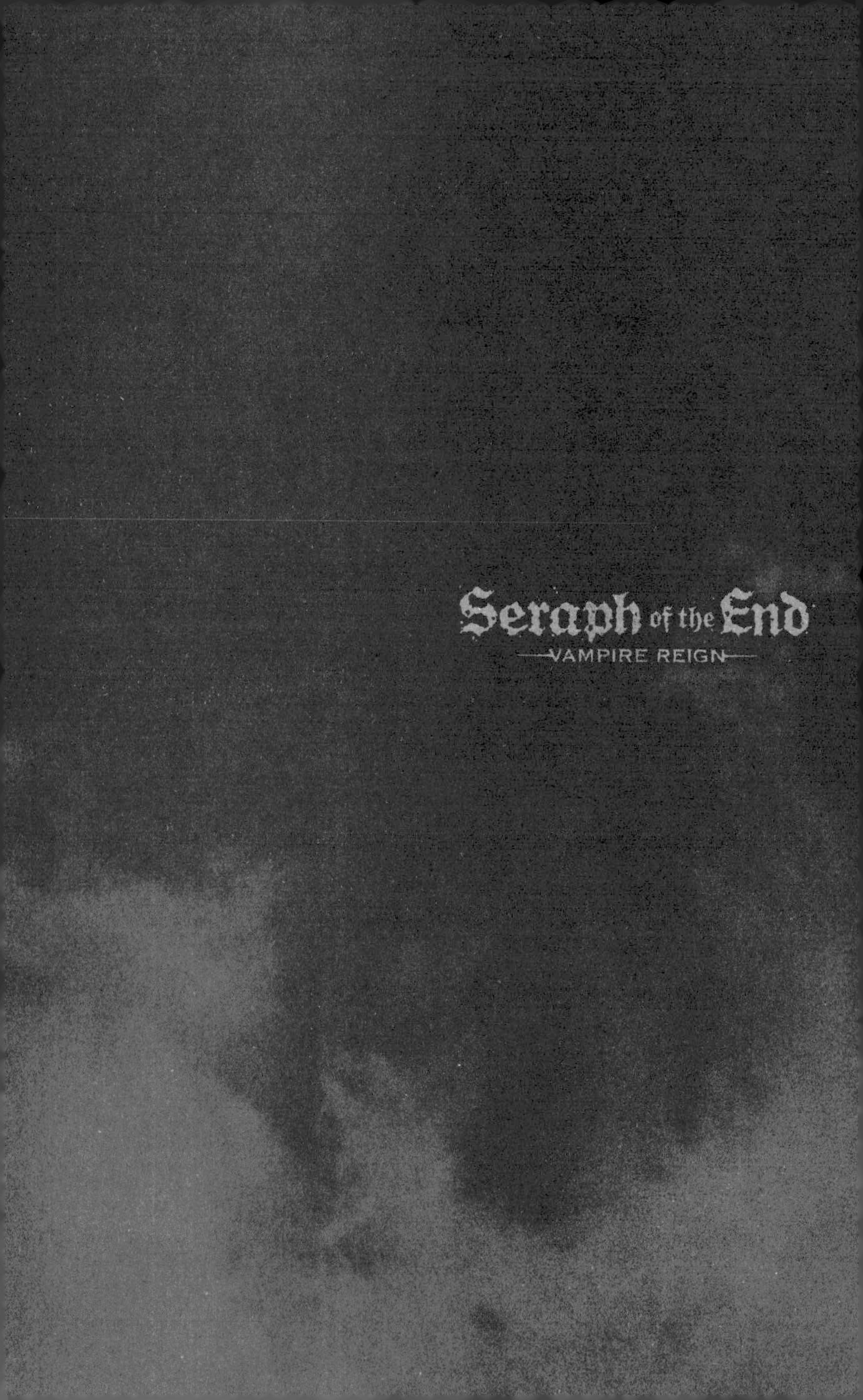
Seraph of the End
VAMPIRE REIGN

Chapter 93
Desire Within Desire

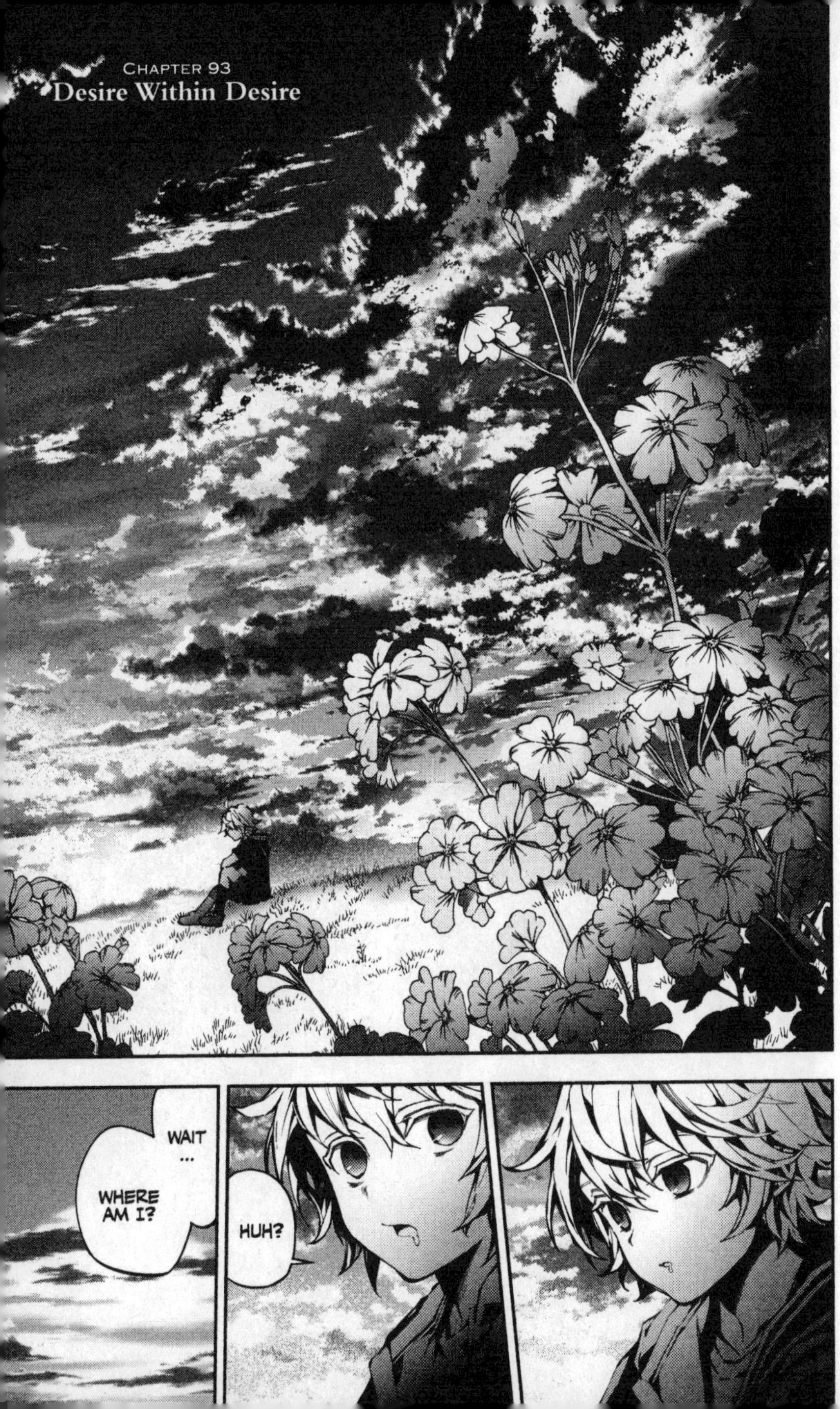
HUH?
WAIT ... WHERE AM I?

CHAPTER 93
Desire Within Desire

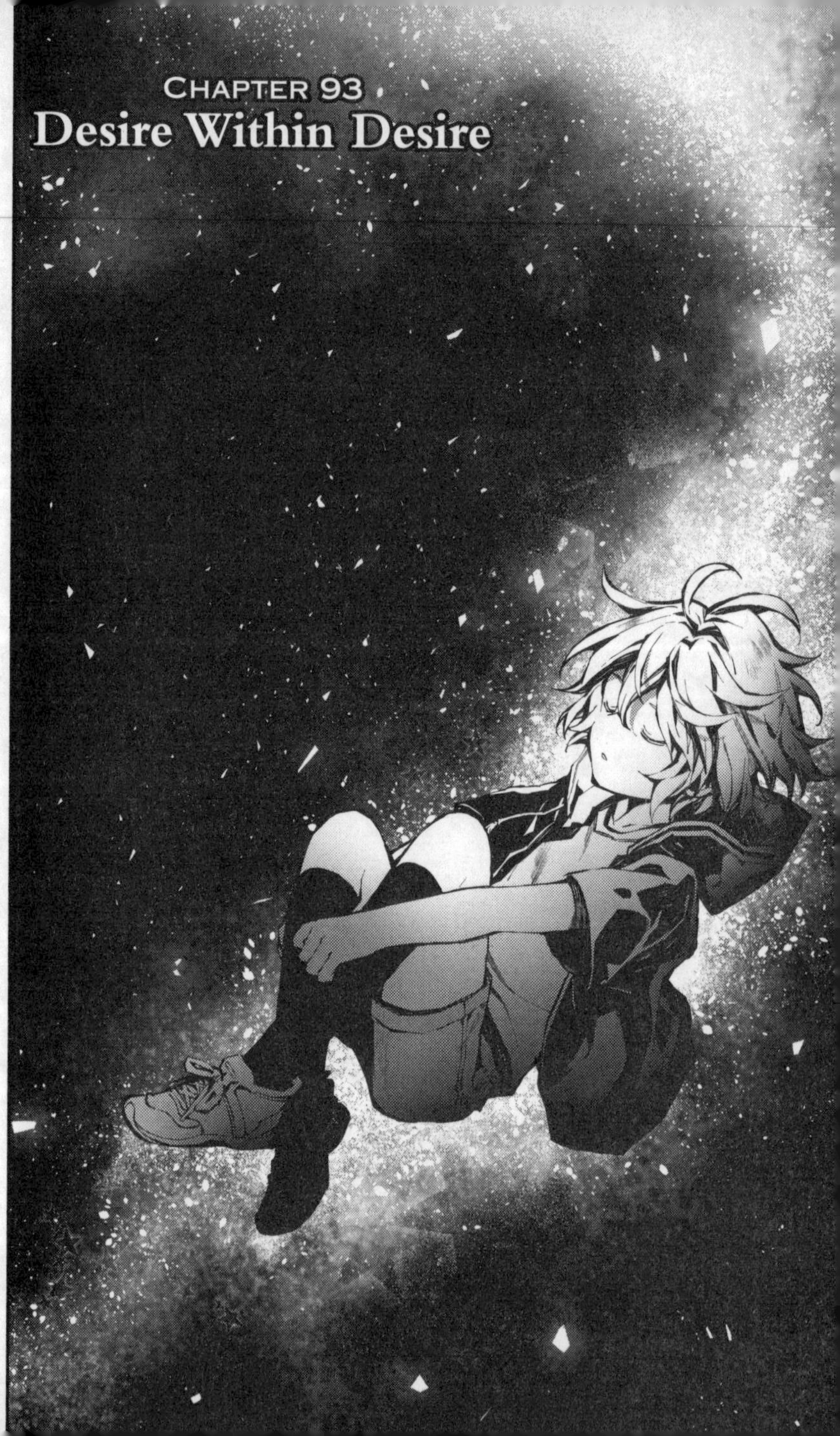

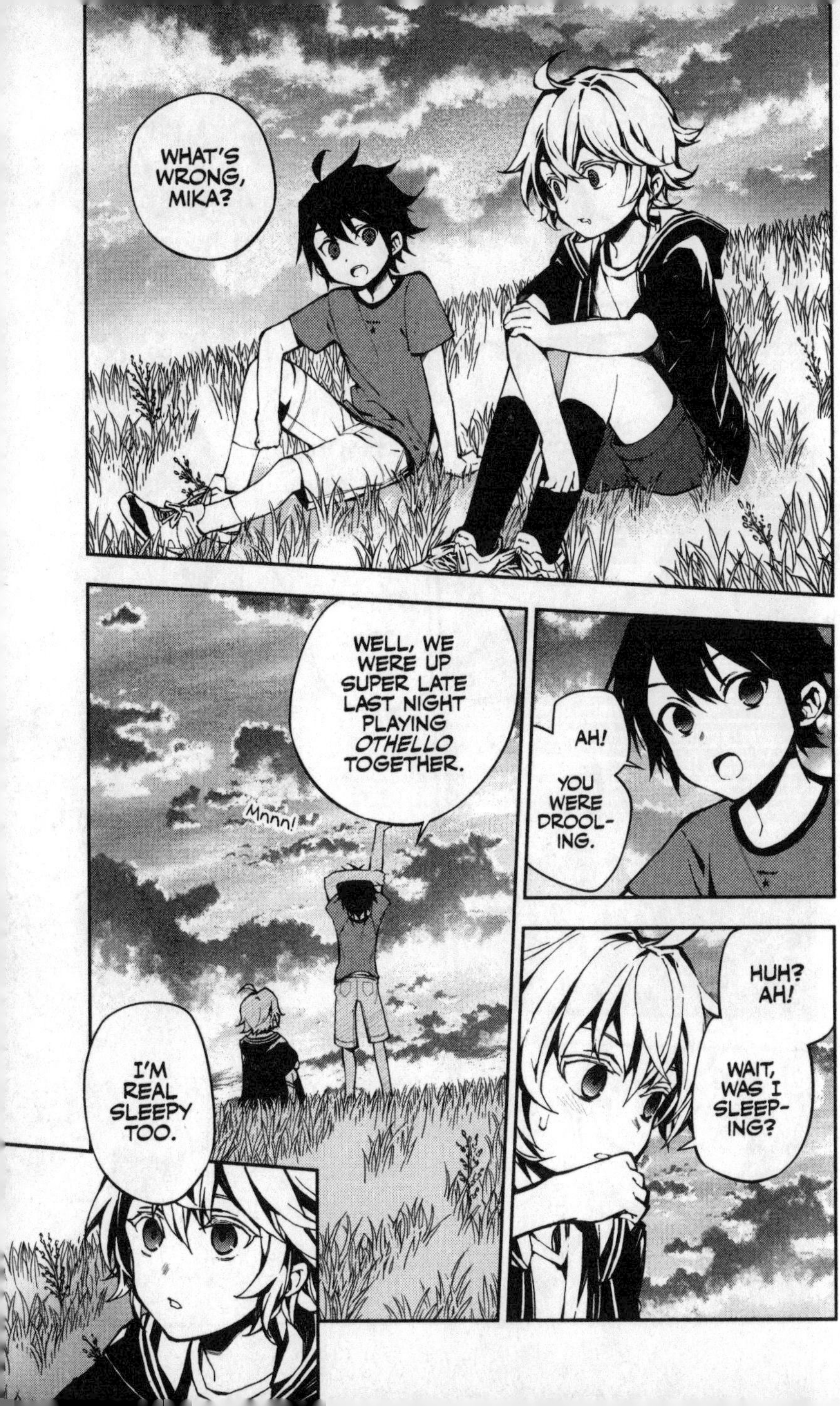
WHAT'S WRONG, MIKA?
AH!
YOU WERE DROOL-ING.
HUH? AH!
WAIT, WAS I SLEEP-ING?
WELL, WE WERE UP SUPER LATE LAST NIGHT PLAYING *OTHELLO* TOGETHER.
Mnnn!
I'M REAL SLEEPY TOO.

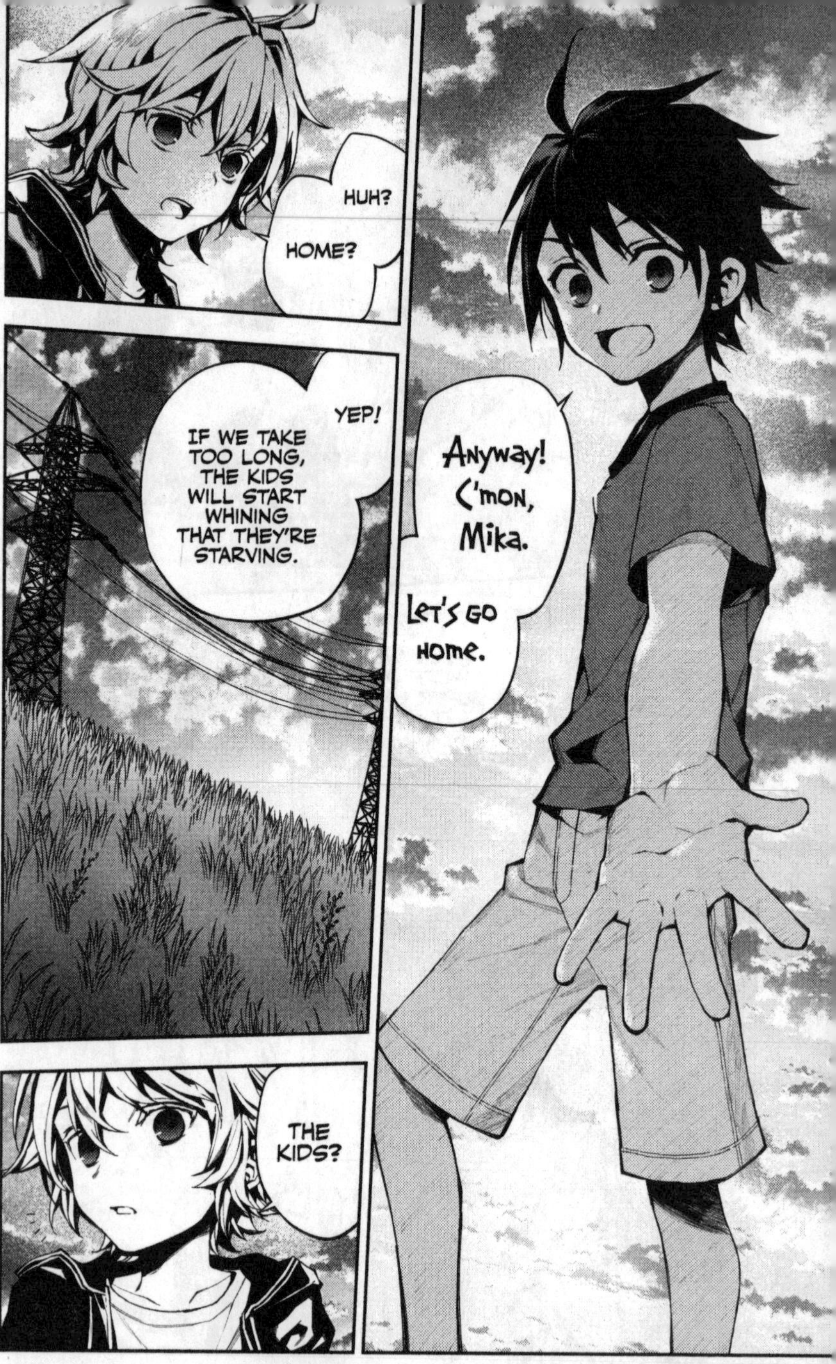
Anyway! C'mon, Mika.
Let's go home.
HUH?
HOME?
YEP!
IF WE TAKE TOO LONG, THE KIDS WILL START WHINING THAT THEY'RE STARVING.
THE KIDS?

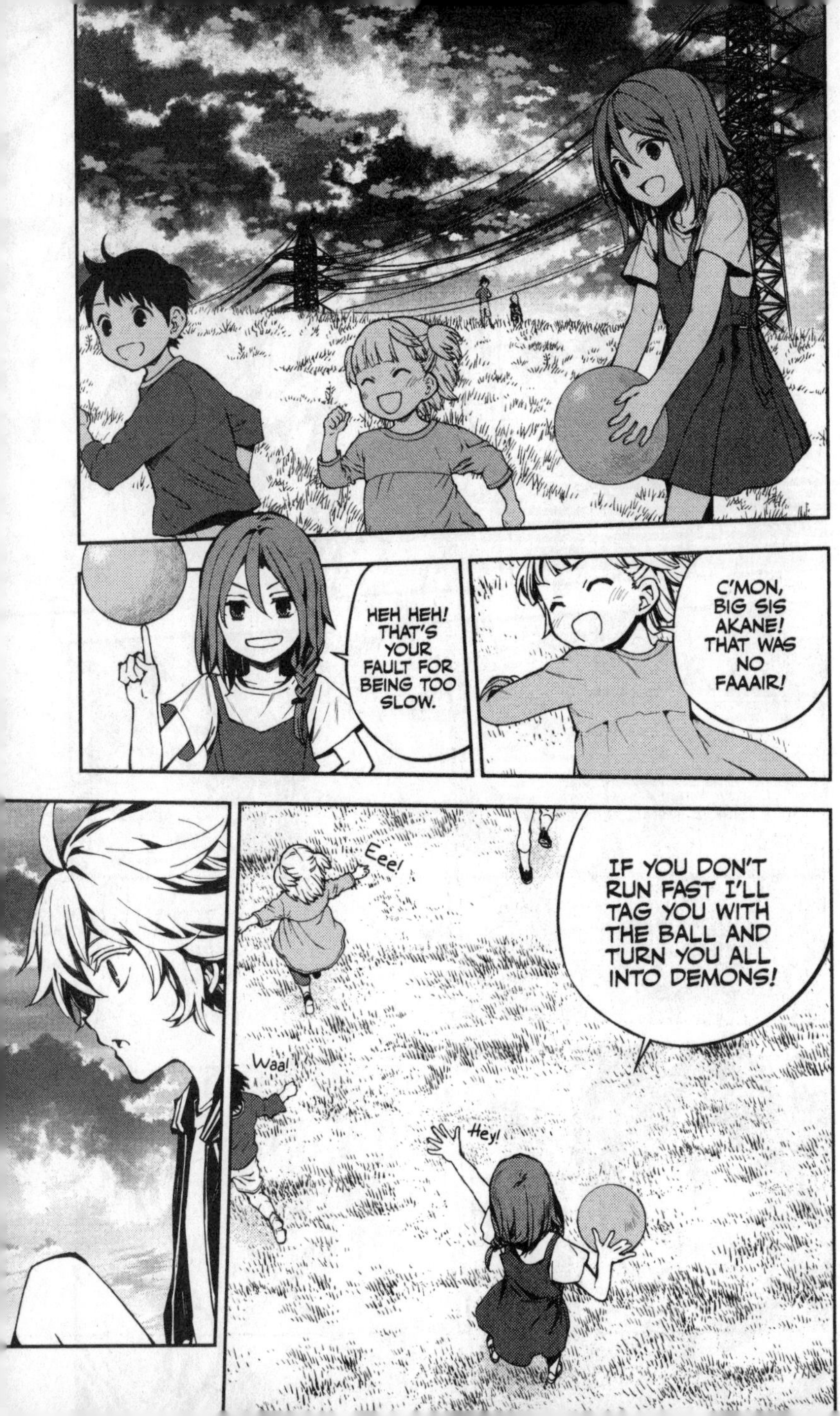
C'MON, BIG SIS AKANE! THAT WAS NO FAAAIR!
HEH HEH! THAT'S YOUR FAULT FOR BEING TOO SLOW.
IF YOU DON'T RUN FAST I'LL TAG YOU WITH THE BALL AND TURN YOU ALL INTO DEMONS!
Eee!
Waa!
Hey!

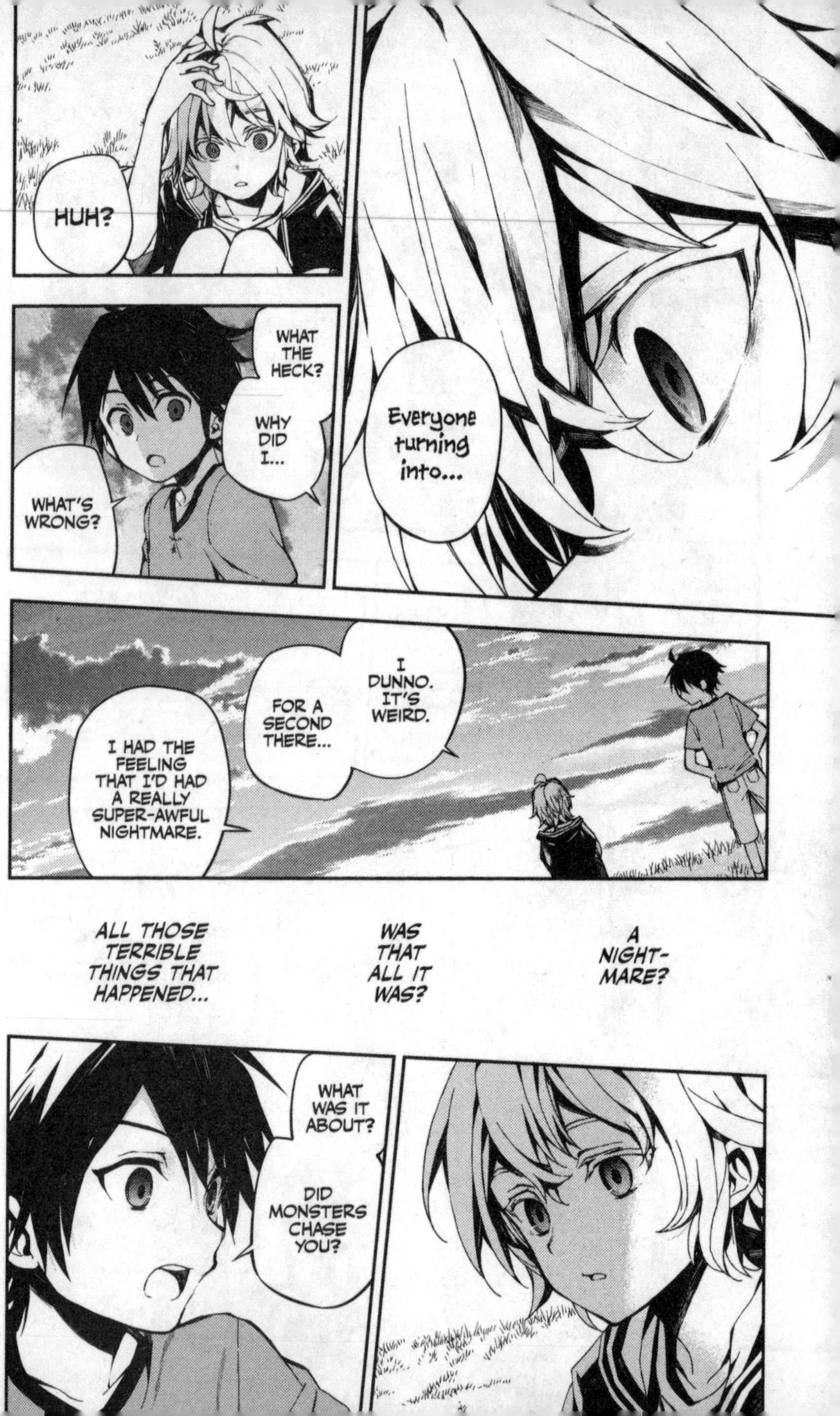
Everyone turning into...
HUH?
WHAT THE HECK?
WHY DID I...
WHAT'S WRONG?
I DUNNO. IT'S WEIRD.
FOR A SECOND THERE...
I HAD THE FEELING THAT I'D HAD A REALLY SUPER-AWFUL NIGHTMARE.
A NIGHT-MARE?
WAS THAT ALL IT WAS?
ALL THOSE TERRIBLE THINGS THAT HAPPENED...
WHAT WAS IT ABOUT?
DID MONSTERS CHASE YOU?

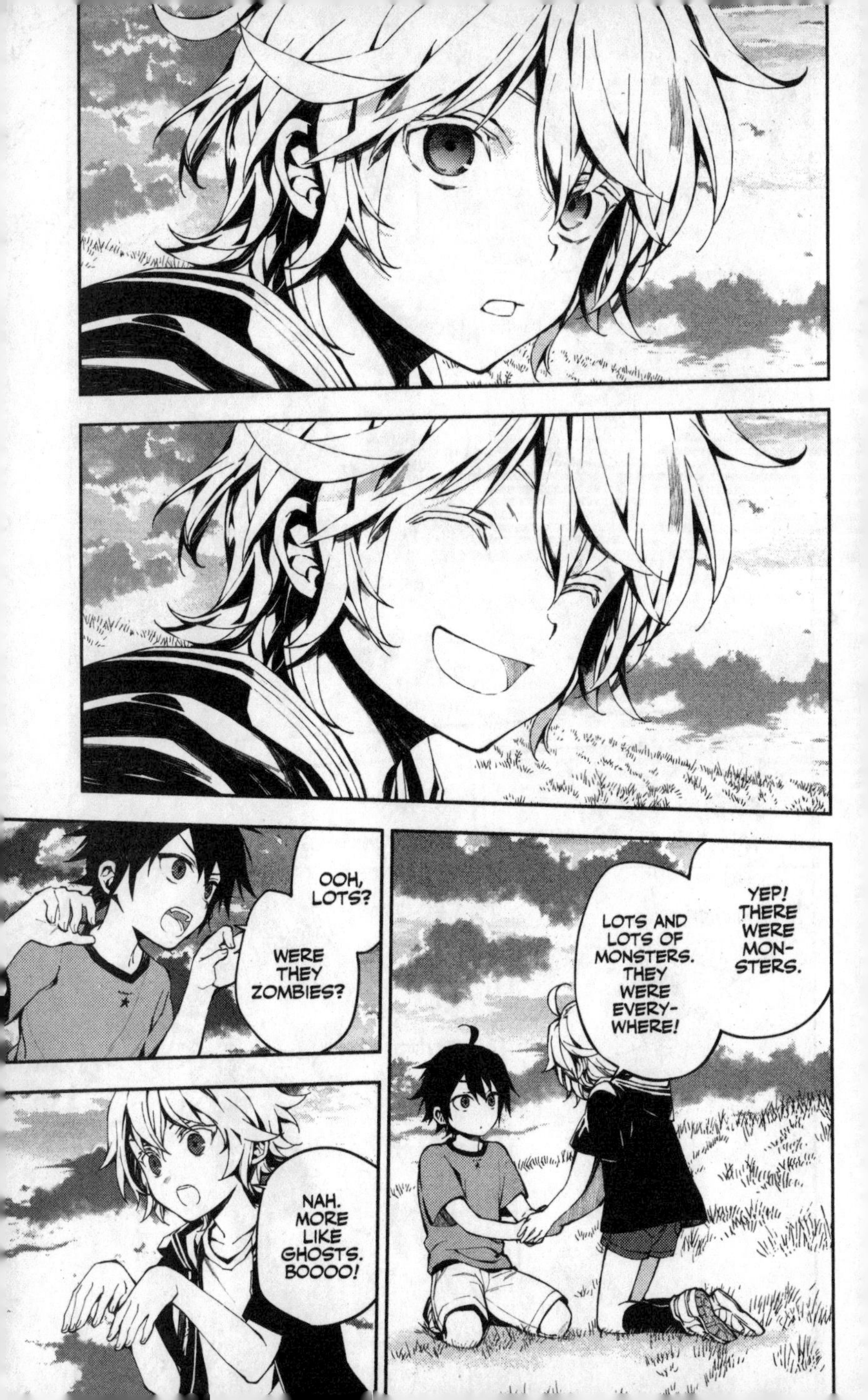
YEP! THERE WERE MONSTERS.
LOTS AND LOTS OF MONSTERS. THEY WERE EVERYWHERE!
OOH, LOTS?
WERE THEY ZOMBIES?
NAH. MORE LIKE GHOSTS. BOOOO!

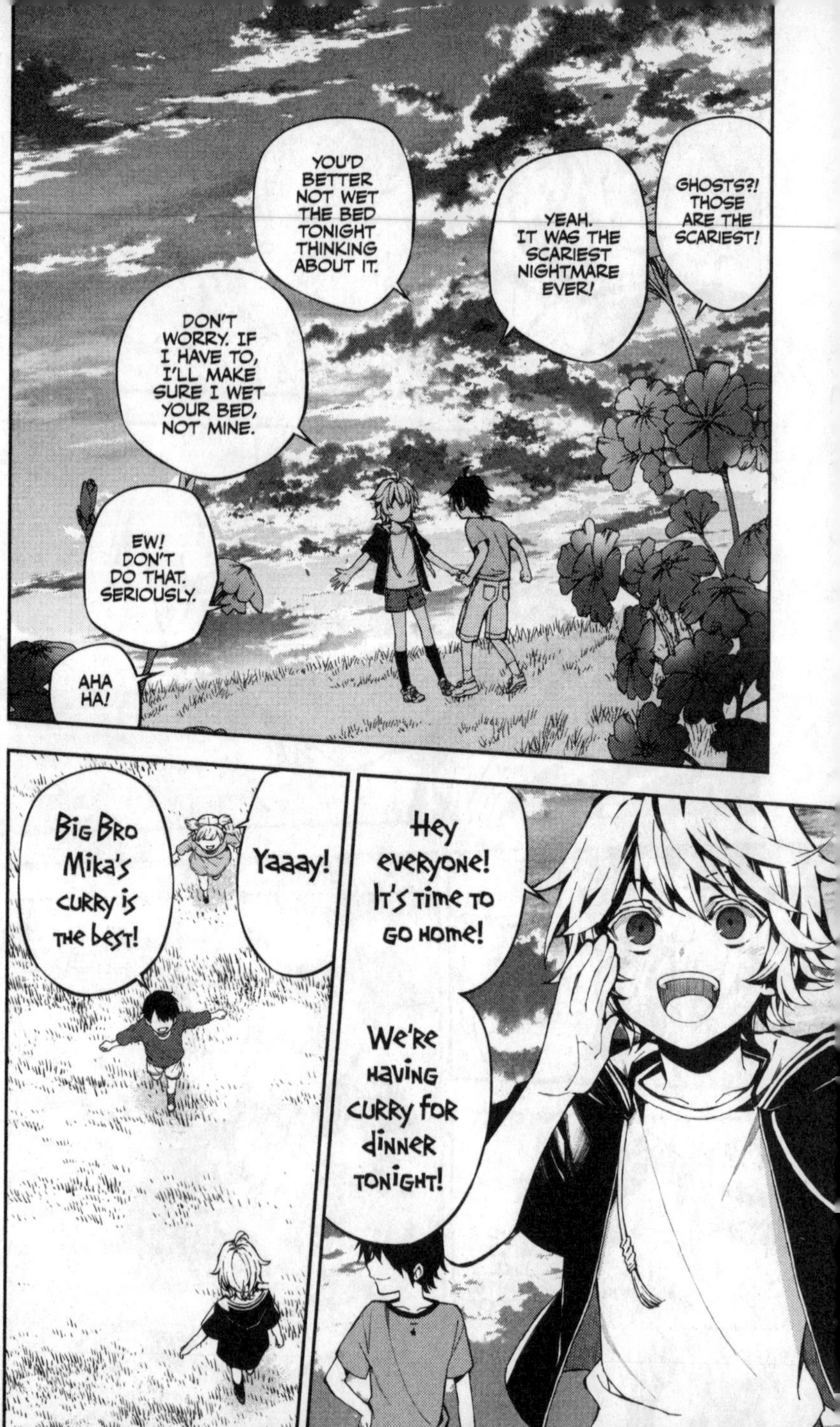
GHOSTS?! THOSE ARE THE SCARIEST!
YEAH. IT WAS THE SCARIEST NIGHTMARE EVER!
YOU'D BETTER NOT WET THE BED TONIGHT THINKING ABOUT IT.
DON'T WORRY. IF I HAVE TO, I'LL MAKE SURE I WET YOUR BED, NOT MINE.
EW! DON'T DO THAT. SERIOUSLY.
AHA HA!
Hey everyone! It's time to go home!
We're having curry for dinner tonight!
Yaaay!
Big Bro Mika's curry is the best!

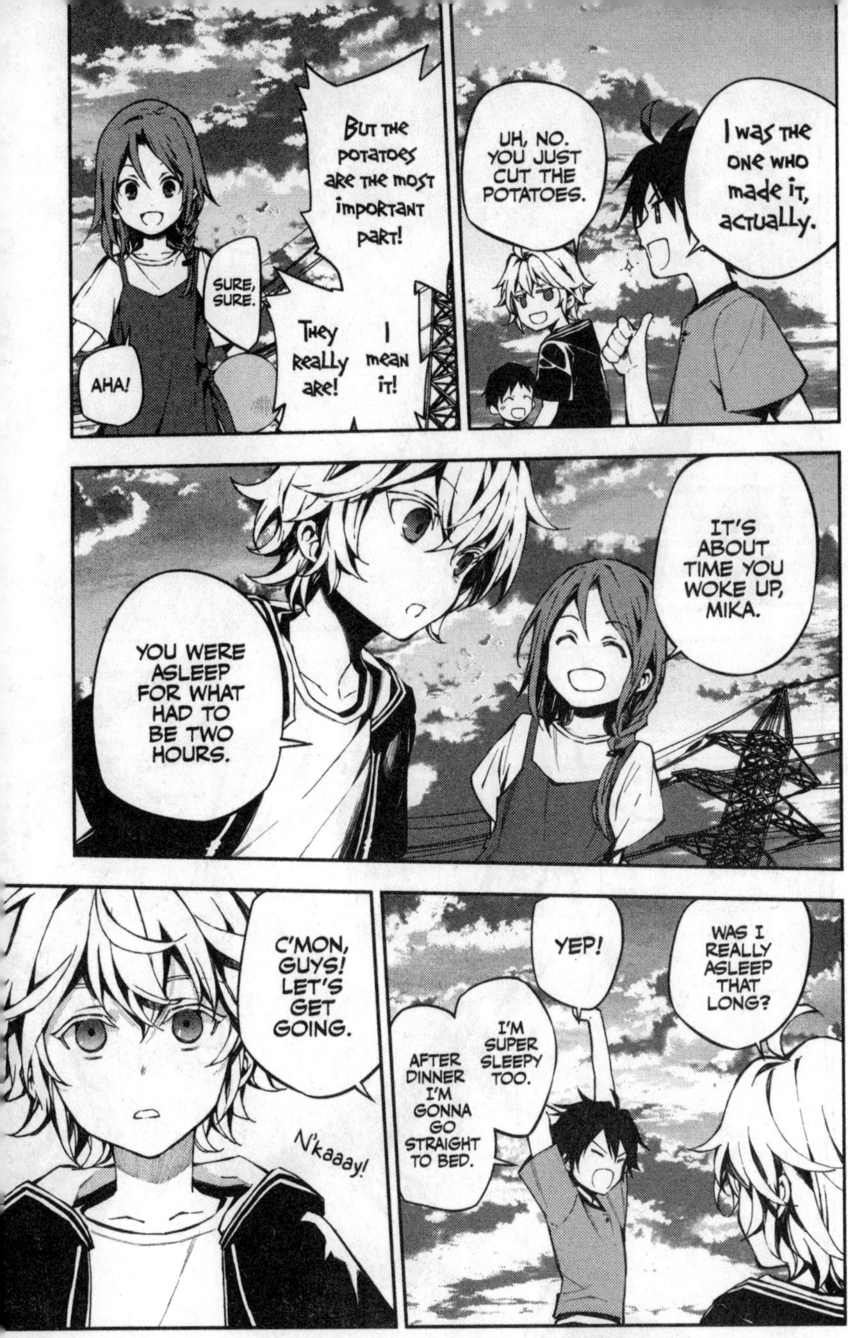
I was the one who made it, actually.
UH, NO. YOU JUST CUT THE POTATOES.
But the potatoes are the most important part!
They really are! I mean it!
SURE, SURE.
AHA!
IT'S ABOUT TIME YOU WOKE UP, MIKA.
YOU WERE ASLEEP FOR WHAT HAD TO BE TWO HOURS.
WAS I REALLY ASLEEP THAT LONG?
YEP!
I'M SUPER SLEEPY TOO.
AFTER DINNER I'M GONNA GO STRAIGHT TO BED.
C'MON, GUYS! LET'S GET GOING.
N'kaaay!

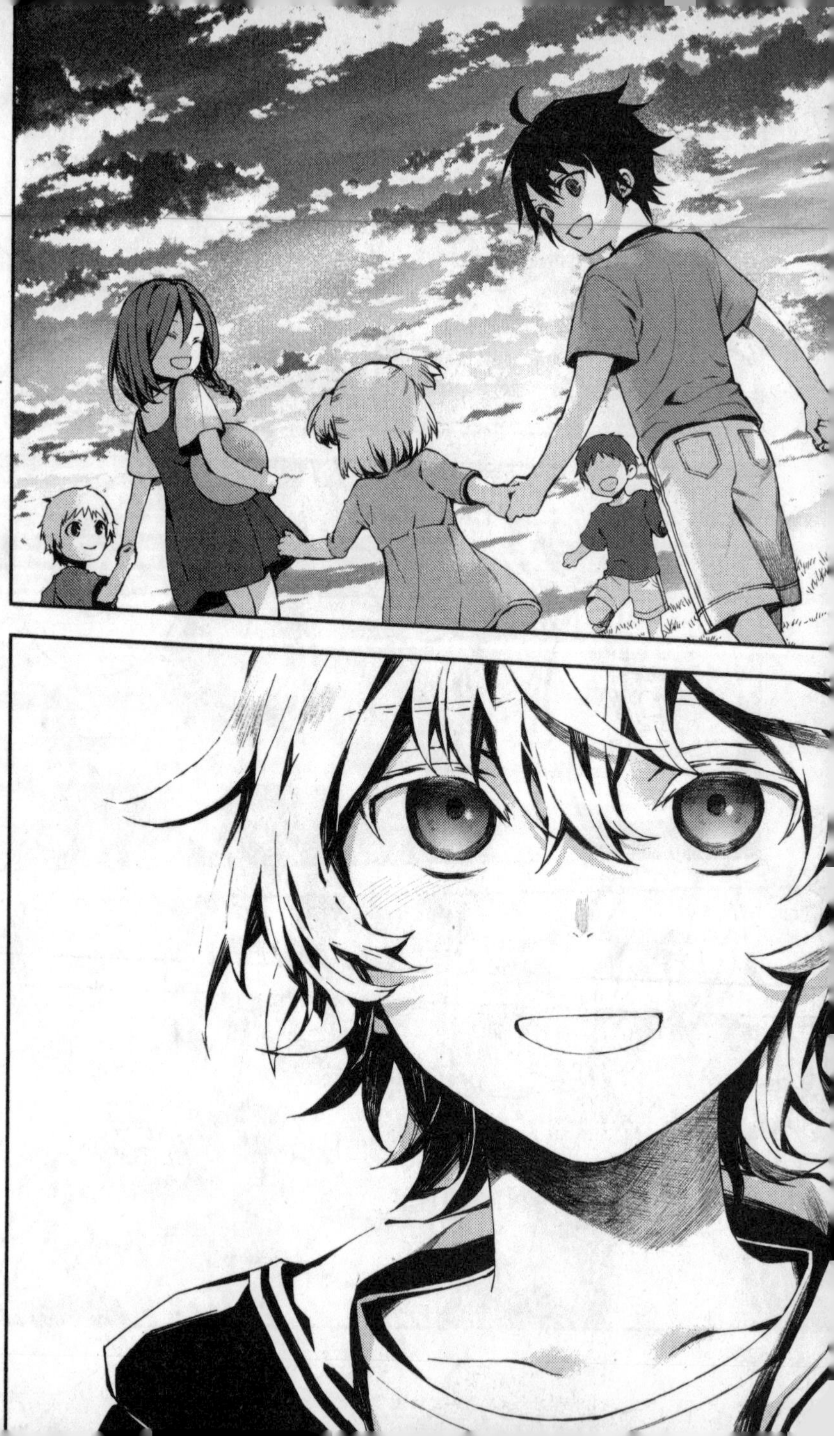

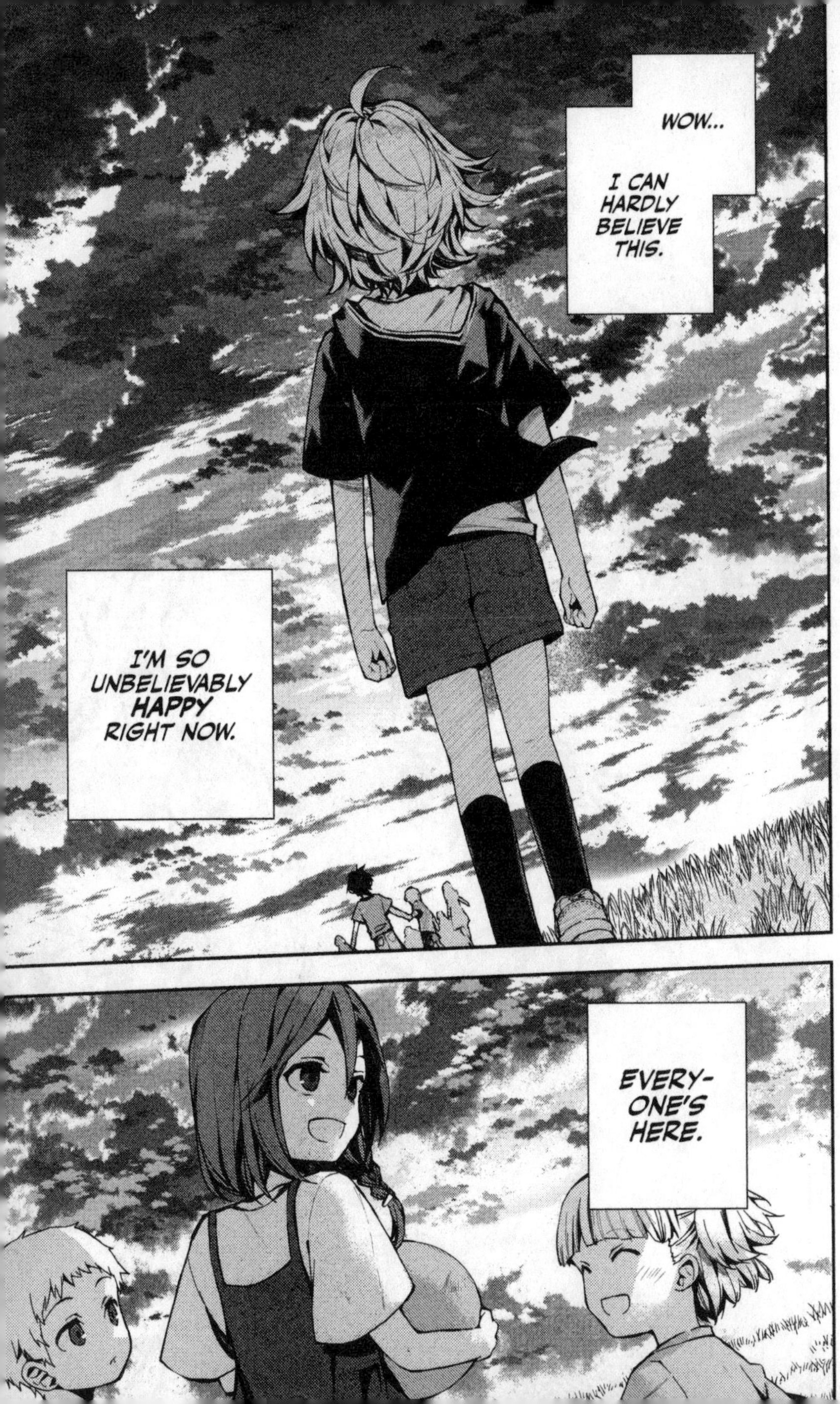
WOW...
I CAN HARDLY BELIEVE THIS.
I'M SO UNBELIEVABLY **HAPPY** RIGHT NOW.
EVERY-ONE'S HERE.

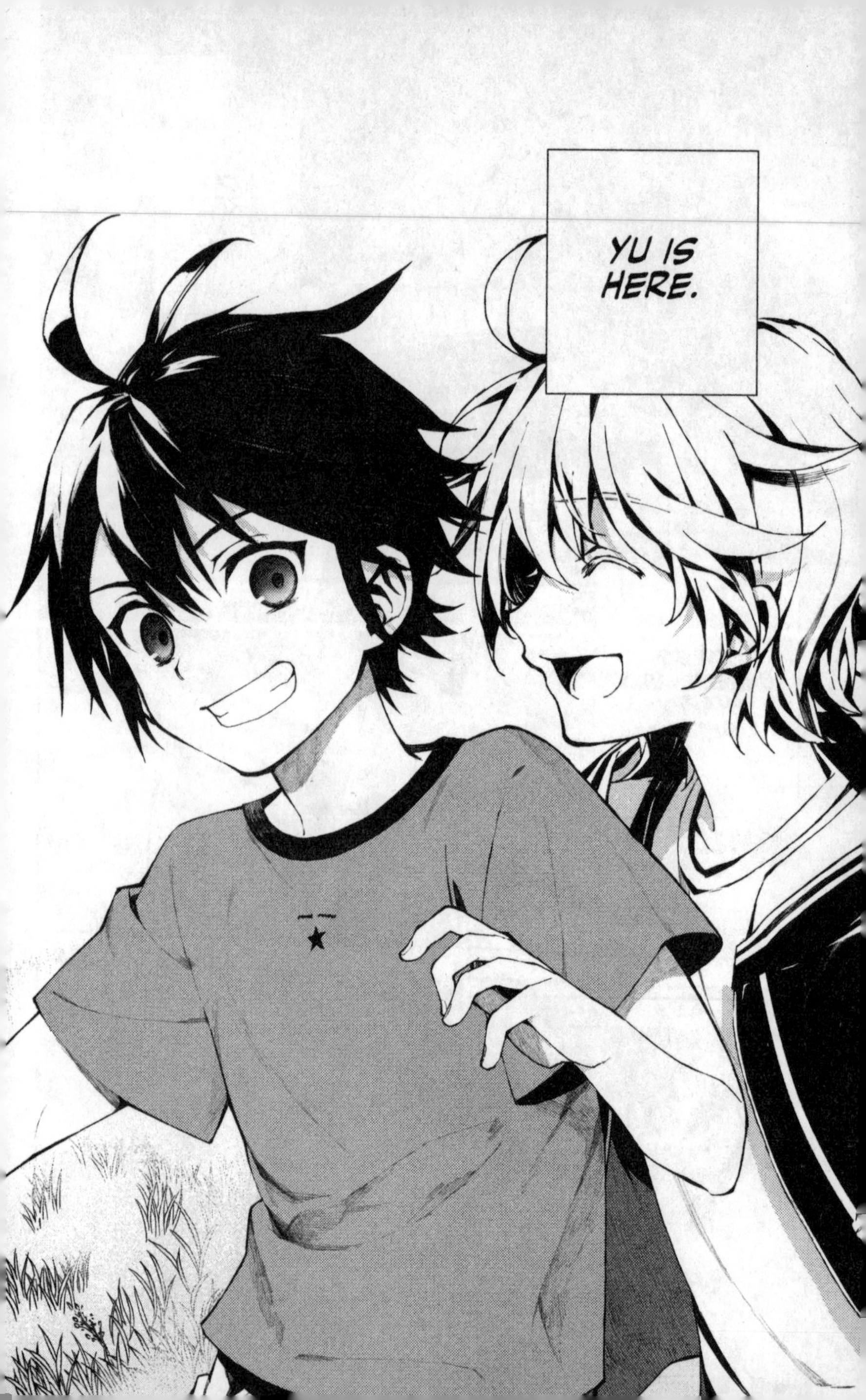
YU IS HERE.

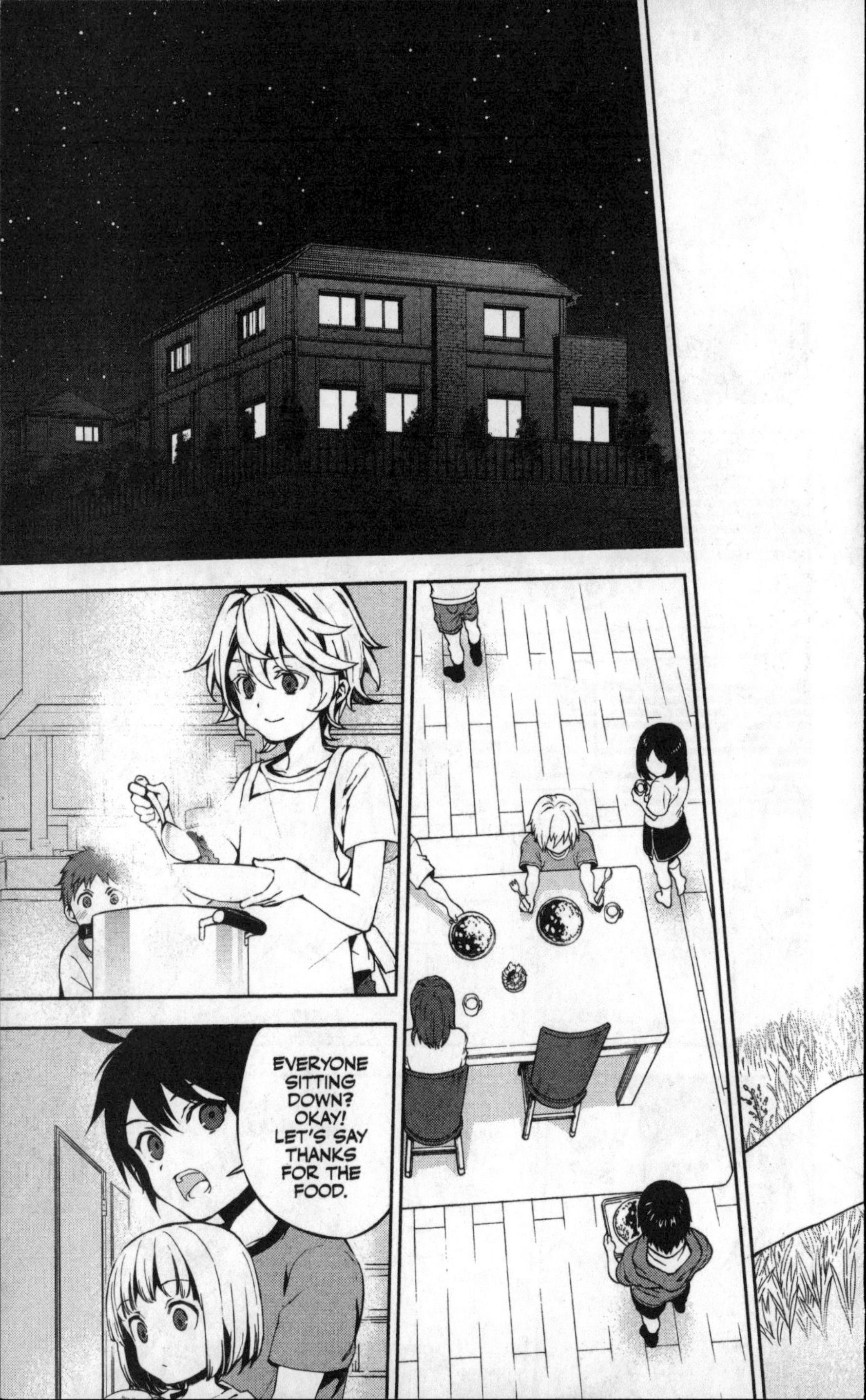
EVERYONE SITTING DOWN? OKAY! LET'S SAY THANKS FOR THE FOOD.

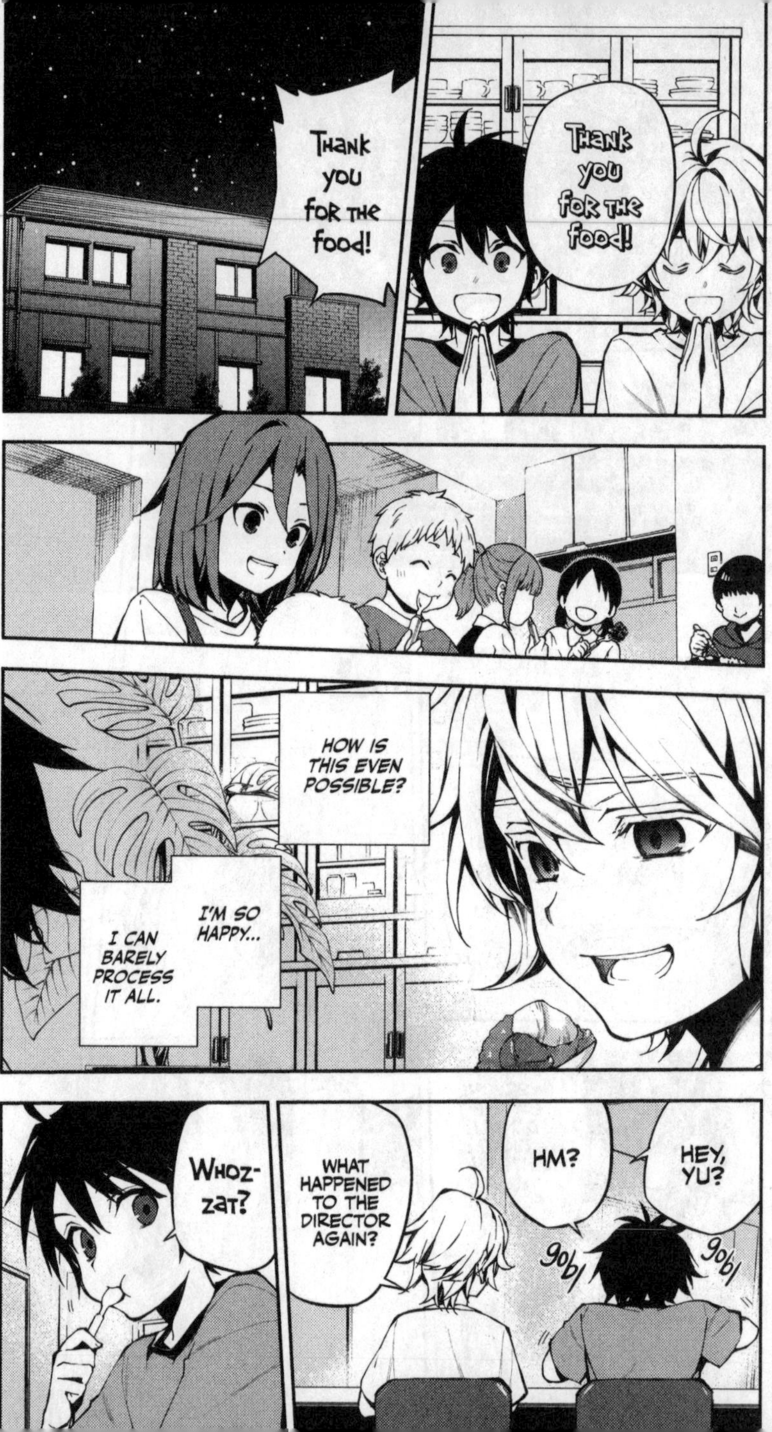
Thank you for the food!
Thank you for the food!
HOW IS THIS EVEN POSSIBLE?
I'M SO HAPPY...
I CAN BARELY PROCESS IT ALL.
HEY, YU?
gob!
HM?
gob!
WHAT HAPPENED TO THE DIRECTOR AGAIN?
Whoz-zat?

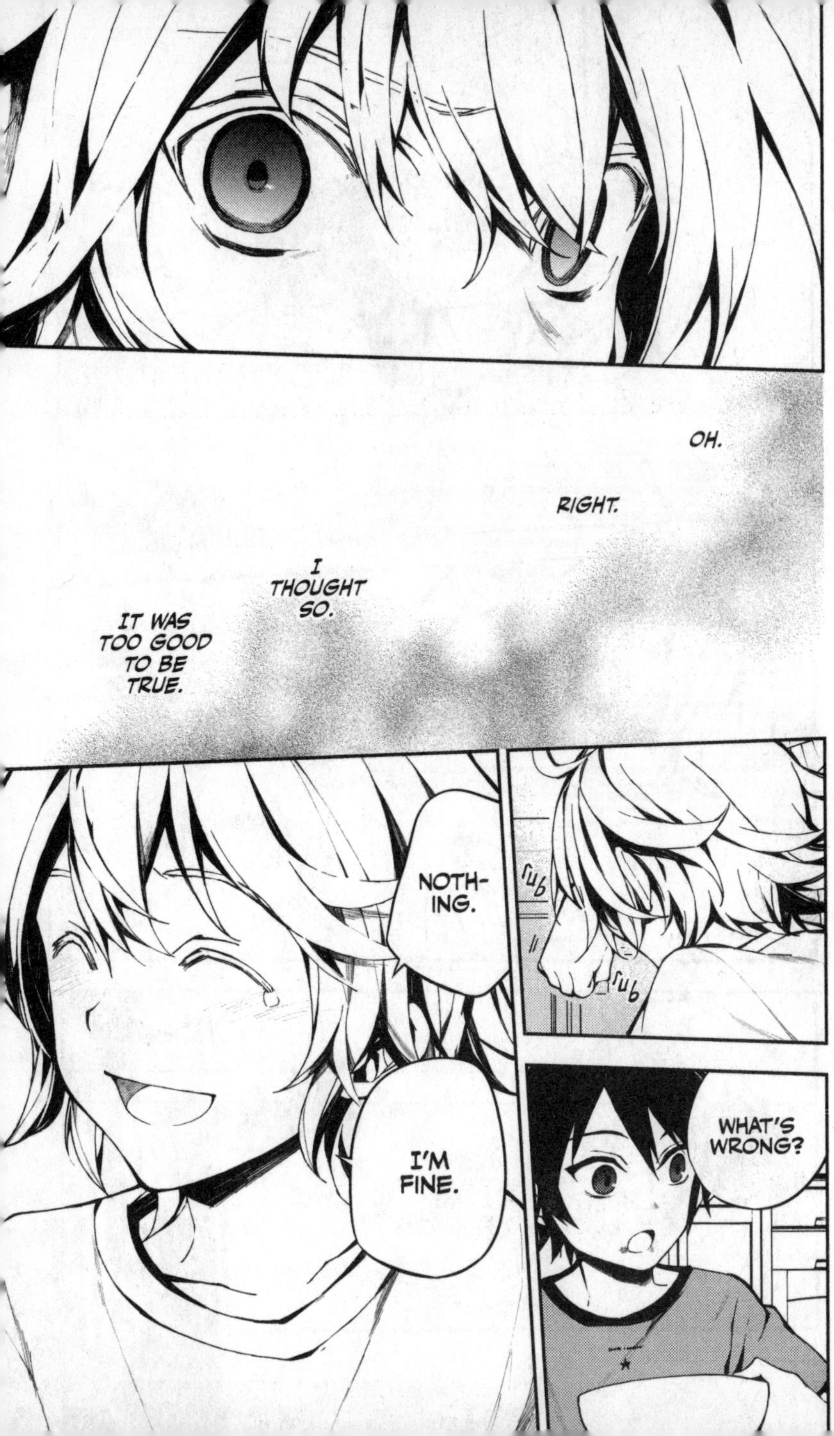
OH.
RIGHT.
I THOUGHT SO.
IT WAS TOO GOOD TO BE TRUE.
rub
rub
WHAT'S WRONG?
NOTH-ING.
I'M FINE.

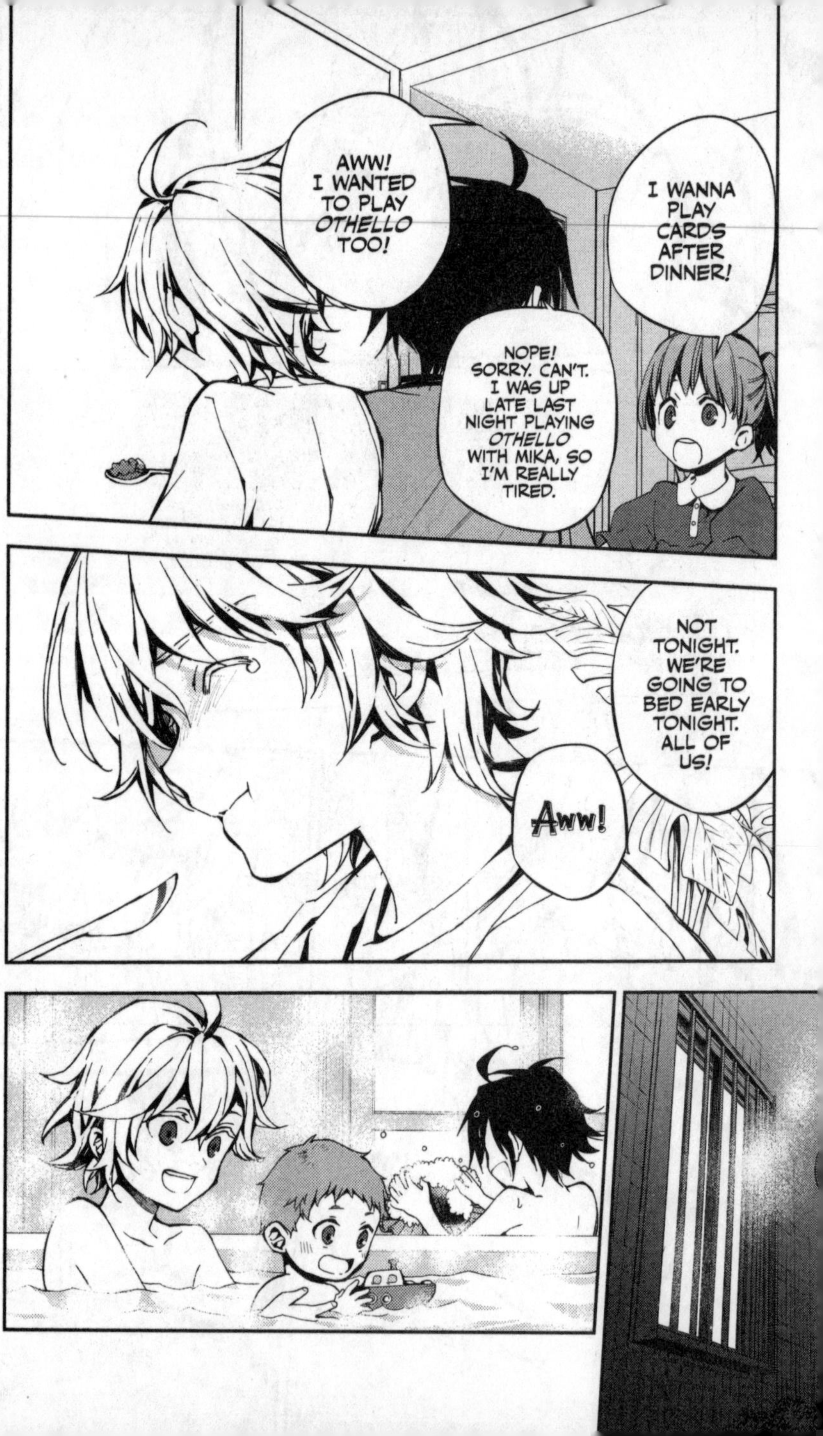
I WANNA PLAY CARDS AFTER DINNER!
AWW! I WANTED TO PLAY *OTHELLO* TOO!
NOPE! SORRY. CAN'T. I WAS UP LATE LAST NIGHT PLAYING *OTHELLO* WITH MIKA, SO I'M REALLY TIRED.
NOT TONIGHT. WE'RE GOING TO BED EARLY TONIGHT. ALL OF US!
AWW!

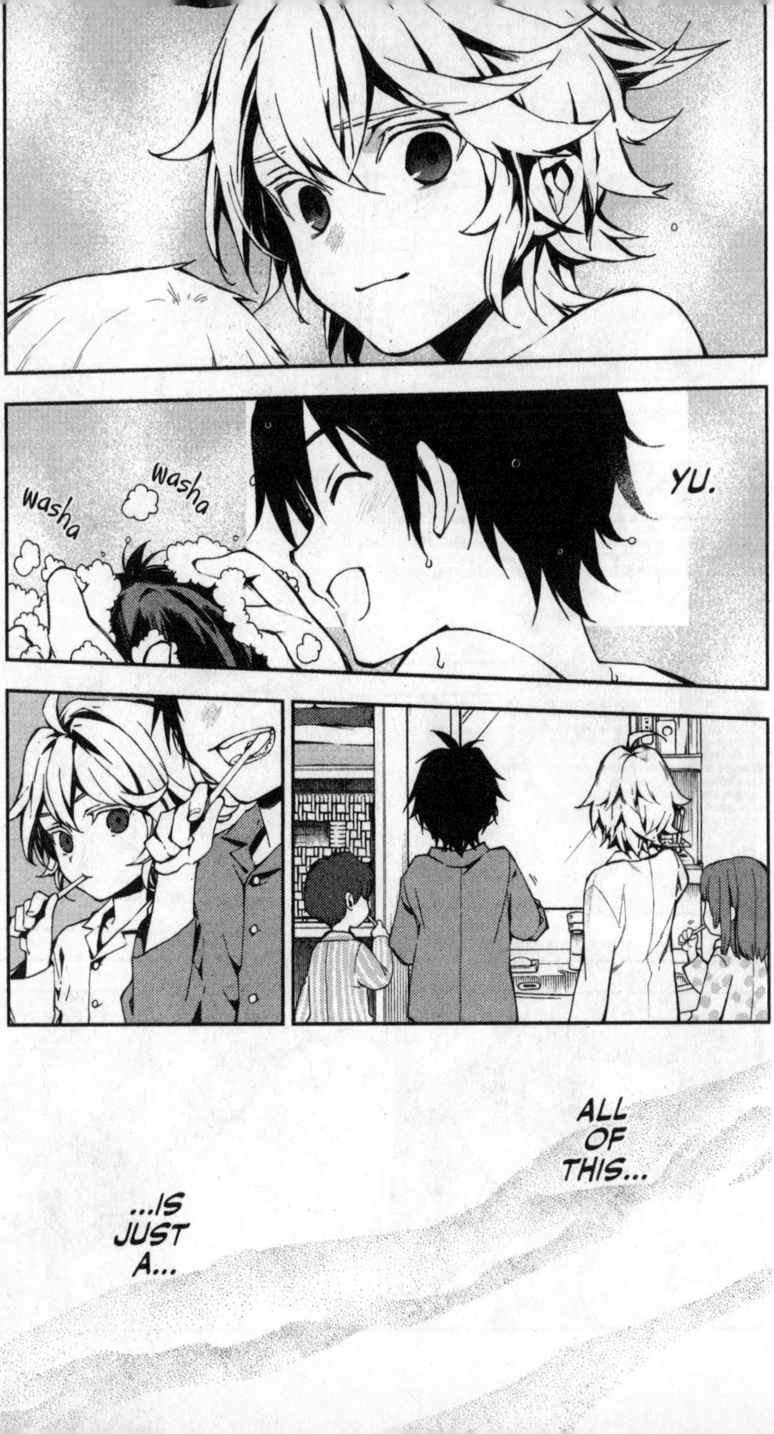
YU.
washa
washa
ALL OF THIS...
...IS JUST A...

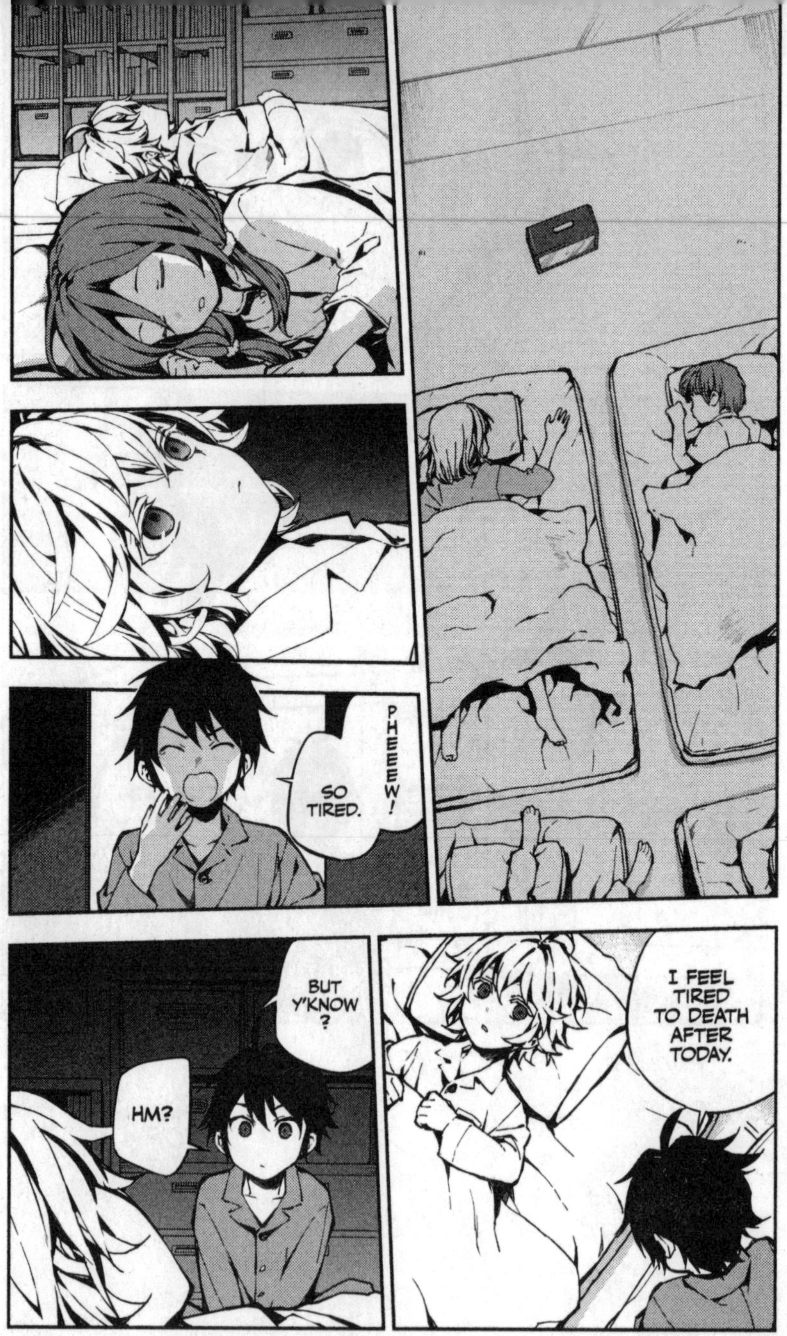
PHEEEW!
SO TIRED.
I FEEL TIRED TO DEATH AFTER TODAY.
BUT Y'KNOW?
HM?

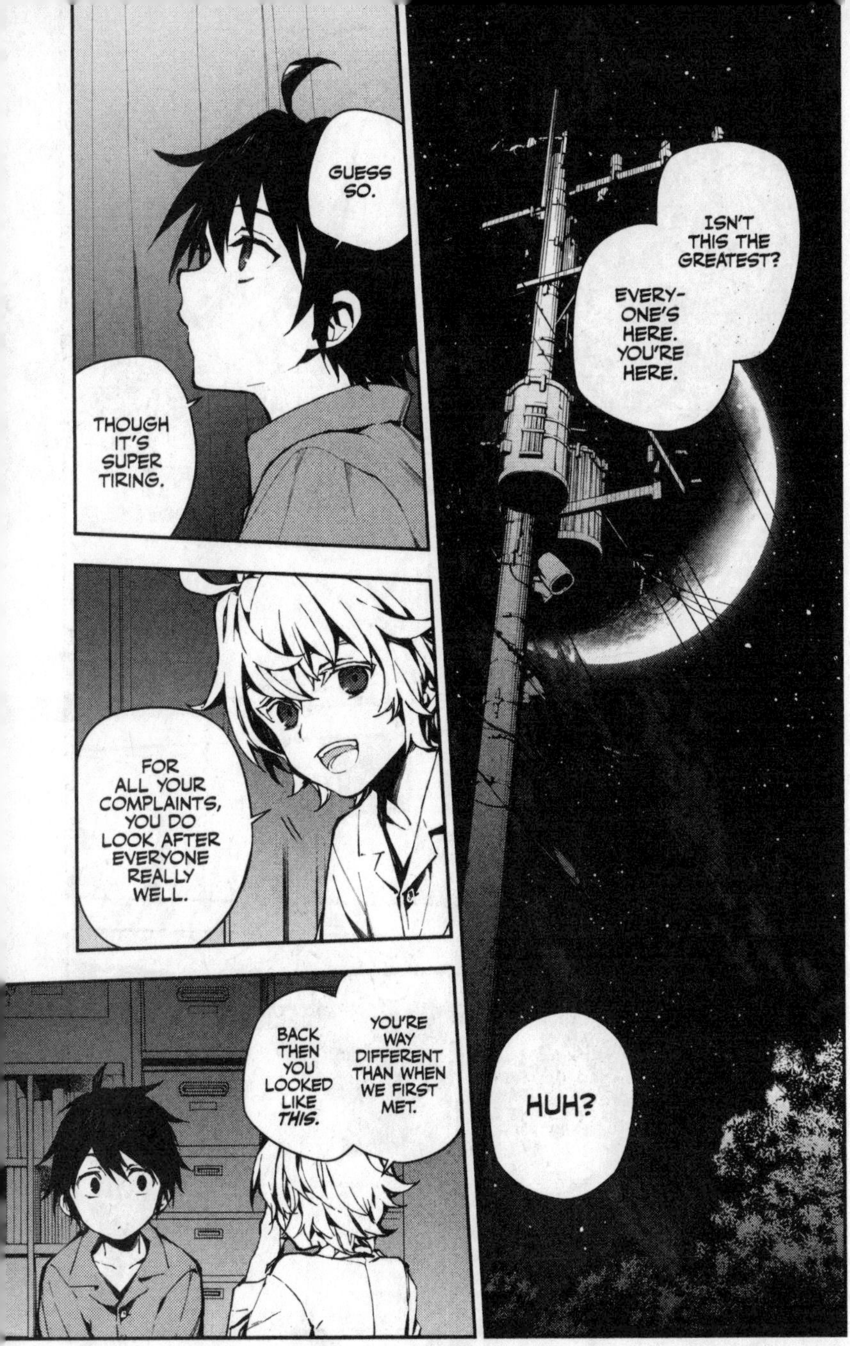
ISN'T THIS THE GREATEST?
EVERYONE'S HERE. YOU'RE HERE.
GUESS SO.
THOUGH IT'S SUPER TIRING.
FOR ALL YOUR COMPLAINTS, YOU DO LOOK AFTER EVERYONE REALLY WELL.
YOU'RE WAY DIFFERENT THAN WHEN WE FIRST MET.
BACK THEN YOU LOOKED LIKE *THIS.*
HUH?

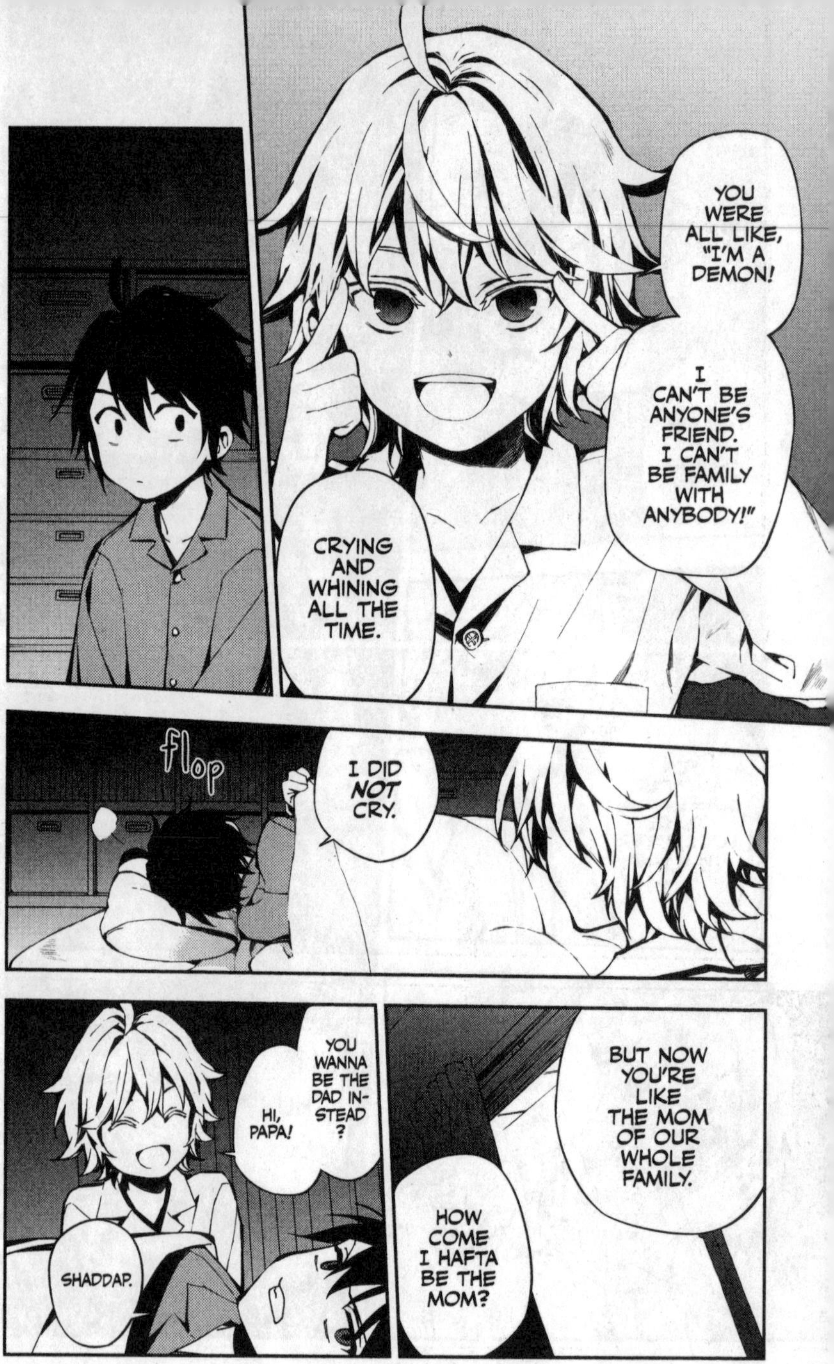
YOU WERE ALL LIKE, "I'M A DEMON!
I CAN'T BE ANYONE'S FRIEND. I CAN'T BE FAMILY WITH ANYBODY!"
CRYING AND WHINING ALL THE TIME.
I DID *NOT* CRY.
flop
BUT NOW YOU'RE LIKE THE MOM OF OUR WHOLE FAMILY.
HOW COME I HAFTA BE THE MOM?
YOU WANNA BE THE DAD IN-STEAD?
HI, PAPA!
SHADDAP.

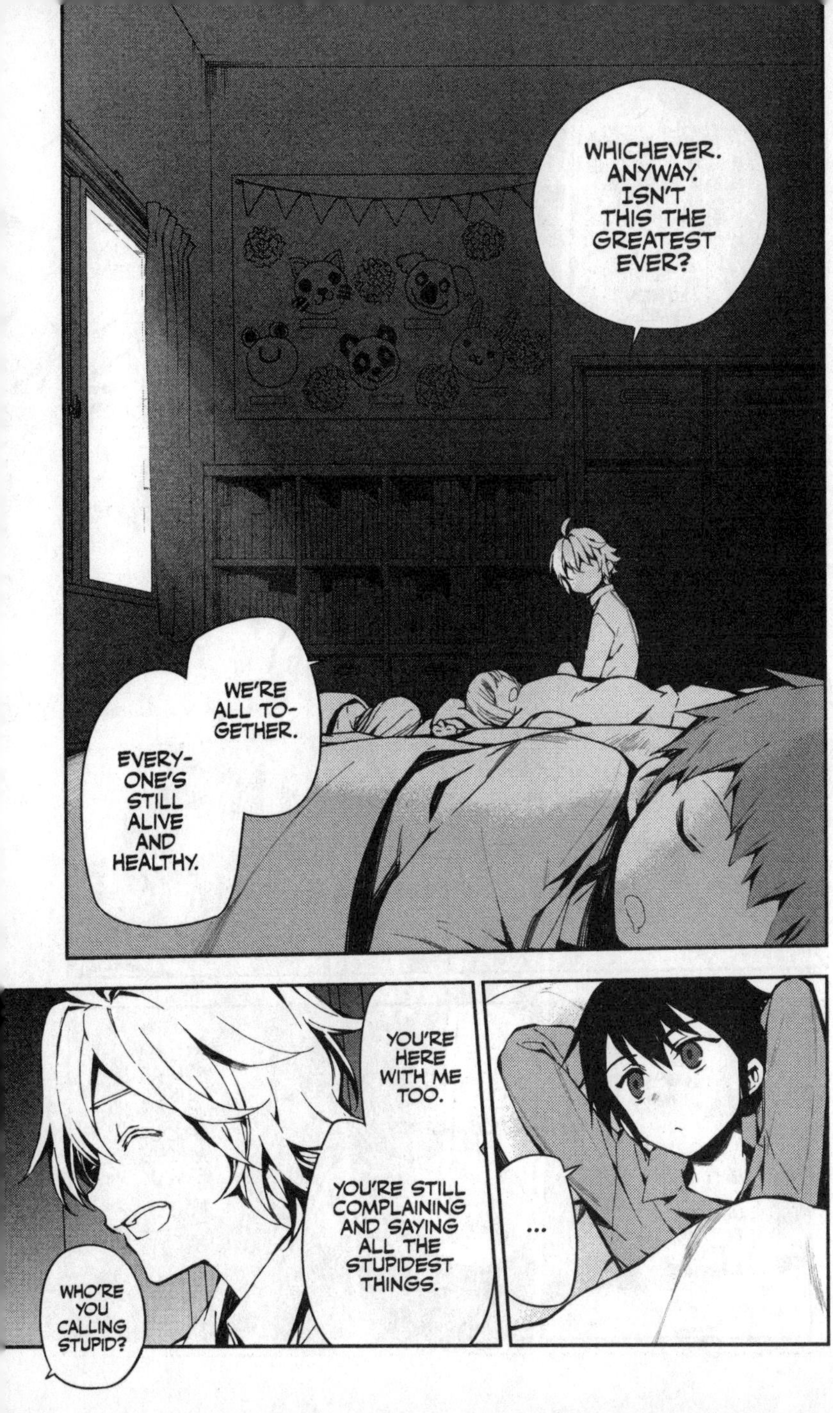
WHICHEVER. ANYWAY. ISN'T THIS THE GREATEST EVER?
WE'RE ALL TO-GETHER.
EVERY-ONE'S STILL ALIVE AND HEALTHY.
...
YOU'RE HERE WITH ME TOO.
YOU'RE STILL COMPLAINING AND SAYING ALL THE STUPIDEST THINGS.
WHO'RE YOU CALLING STUPID?

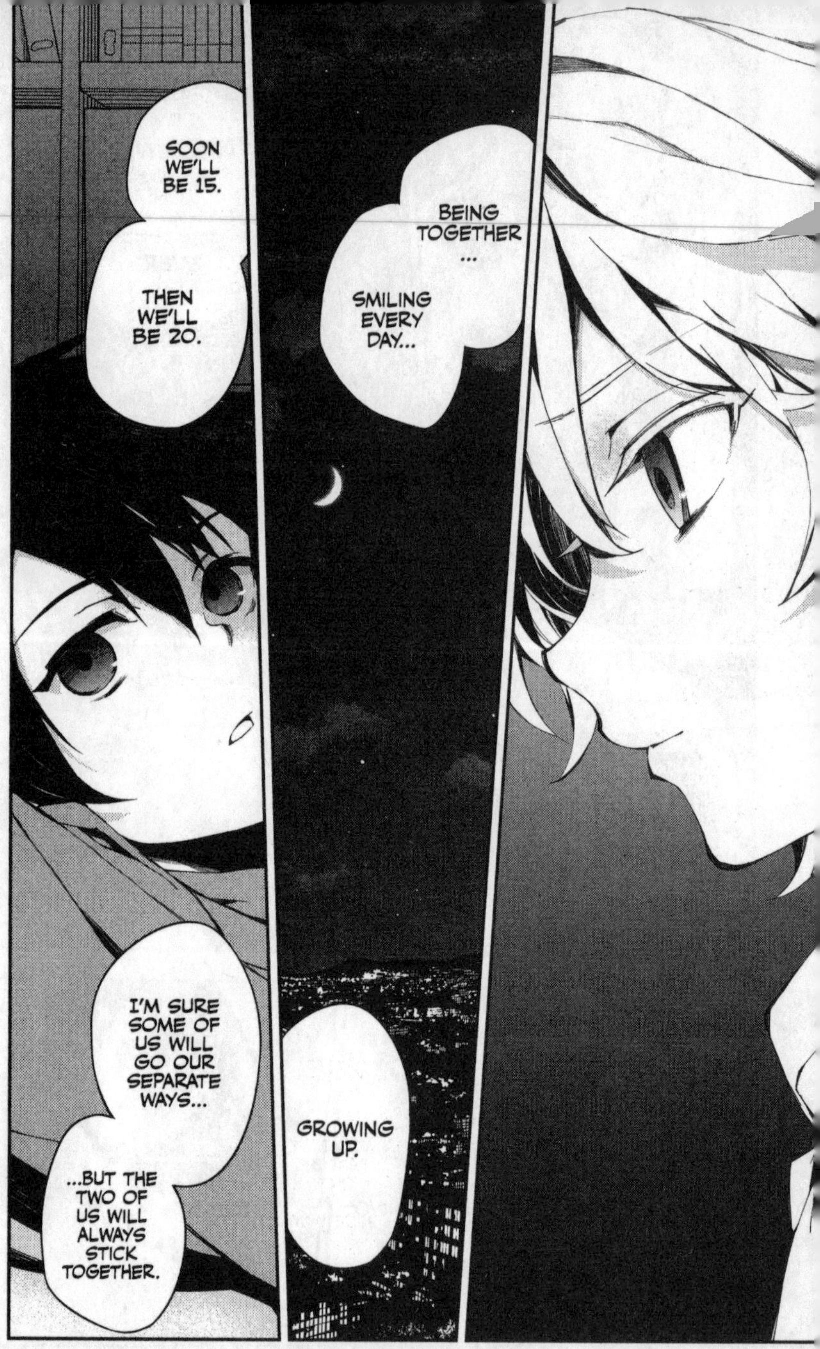
BEING TOGETHER ...
SMILING EVERY DAY...
GROWING UP.
SOON WE'LL BE 15.
THEN WE'LL BE 20.
I'M SURE SOME OF US WILL GO OUR SEPARATE WAYS...
...BUT THE TWO OF US WILL ALWAYS STICK TOGETHER.

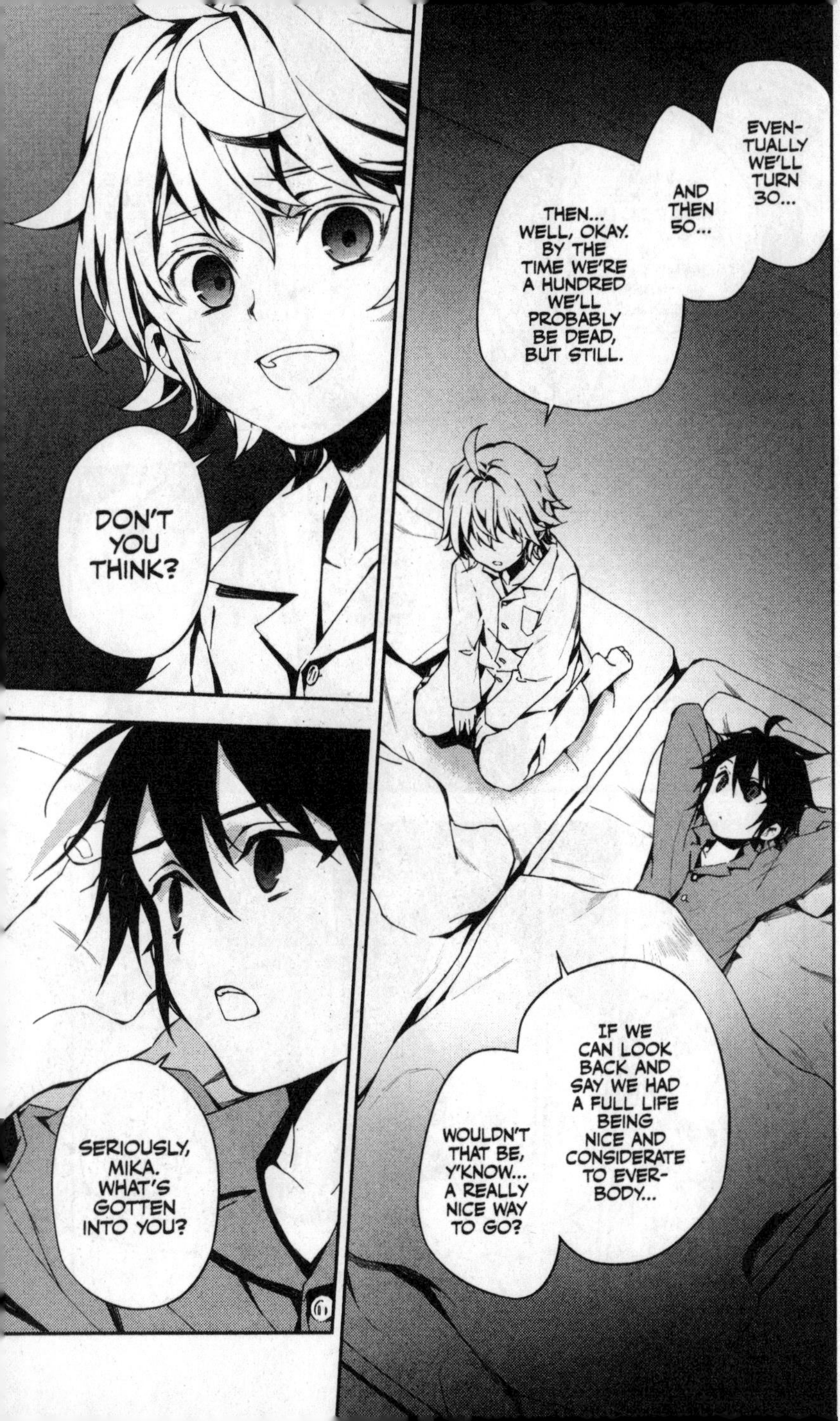
EVEN-TUALLY WE'LL TURN 30...
AND THEN 50...
THEN... WELL, OKAY. BY THE TIME WE'RE A HUNDRED WE'LL PROBABLY BE DEAD, BUT STILL.
IF WE CAN LOOK BACK AND SAY WE HAD A FULL LIFE BEING NICE AND CONSIDERATE TO EVER-BODY...
WOULDN'T THAT BE, Y'KNOW... A REALLY NICE WAY TO GO?
DON'T YOU THINK?
SERIOUSLY, MIKA. WHAT'S GOTTEN INTO YOU?

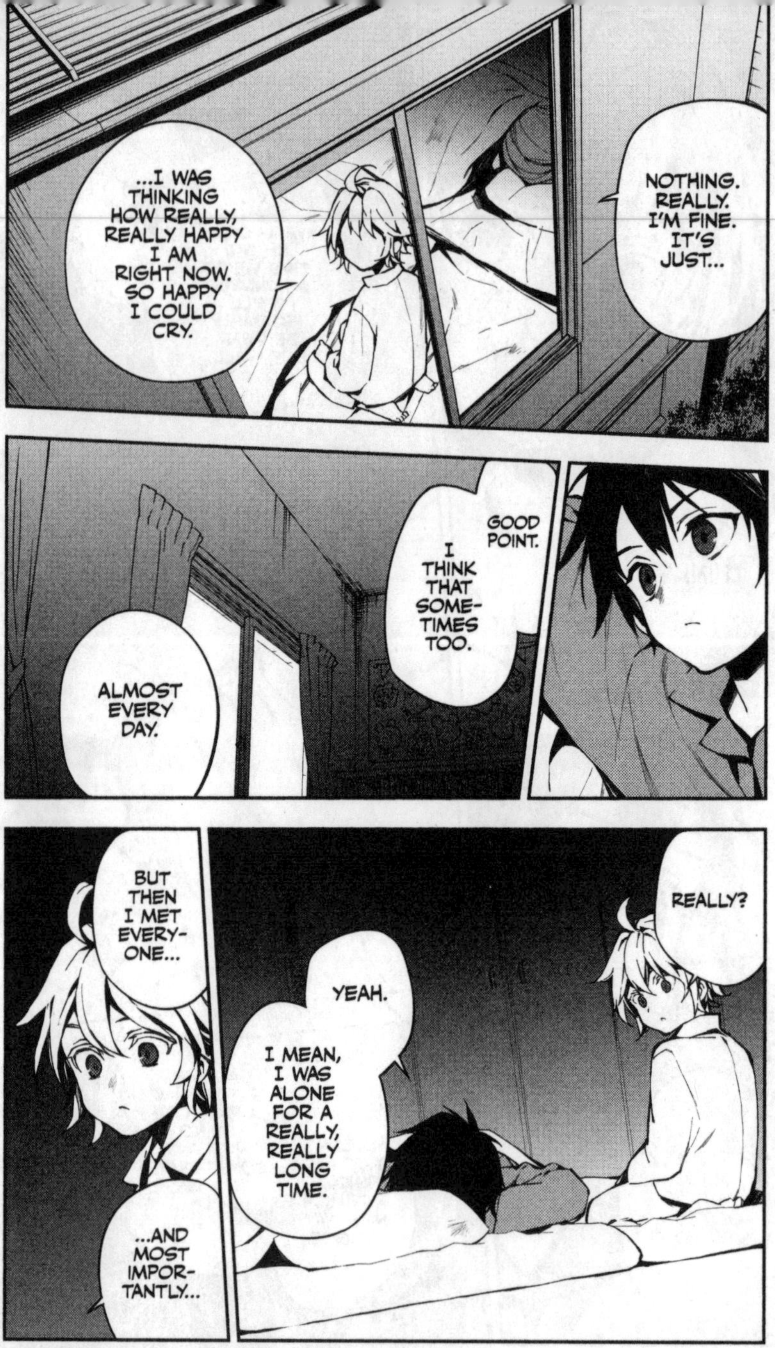
NOTHING. REALLY. I'M FINE. IT'S JUST...
...I WAS THINKING HOW REALLY, REALLY HAPPY I AM RIGHT NOW. SO HAPPY I COULD CRY.
GOOD POINT.
I THINK THAT SOME-TIMES TOO.
ALMOST EVERY DAY.
REALLY?
YEAH.
I MEAN, I WAS ALONE FOR A REALLY, REALLY LONG TIME.
BUT THEN I MET EVERY-ONE...
...AND MOST IMPOR-TANTLY...

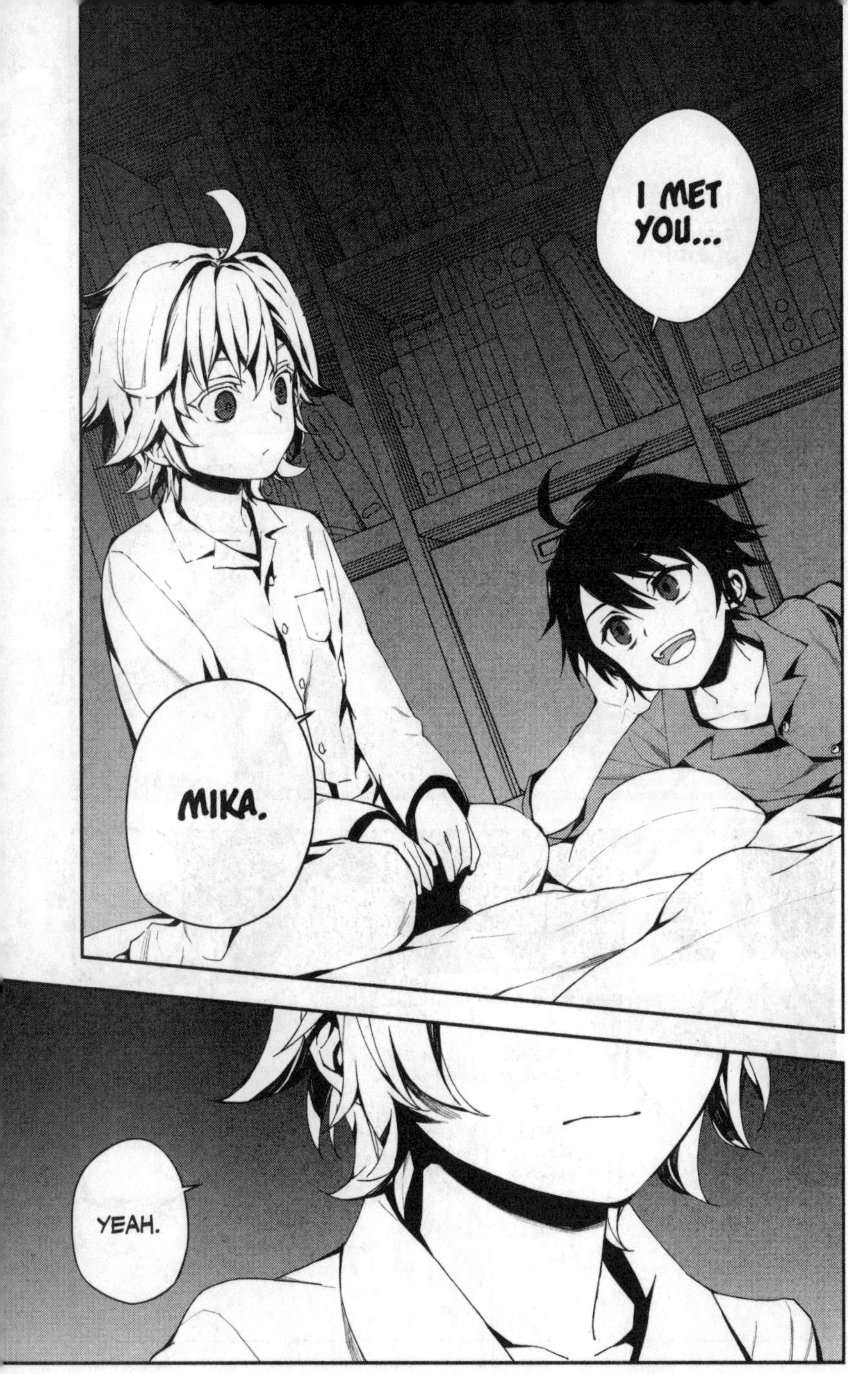
I MET YOU...
MIKA.
YEAH.

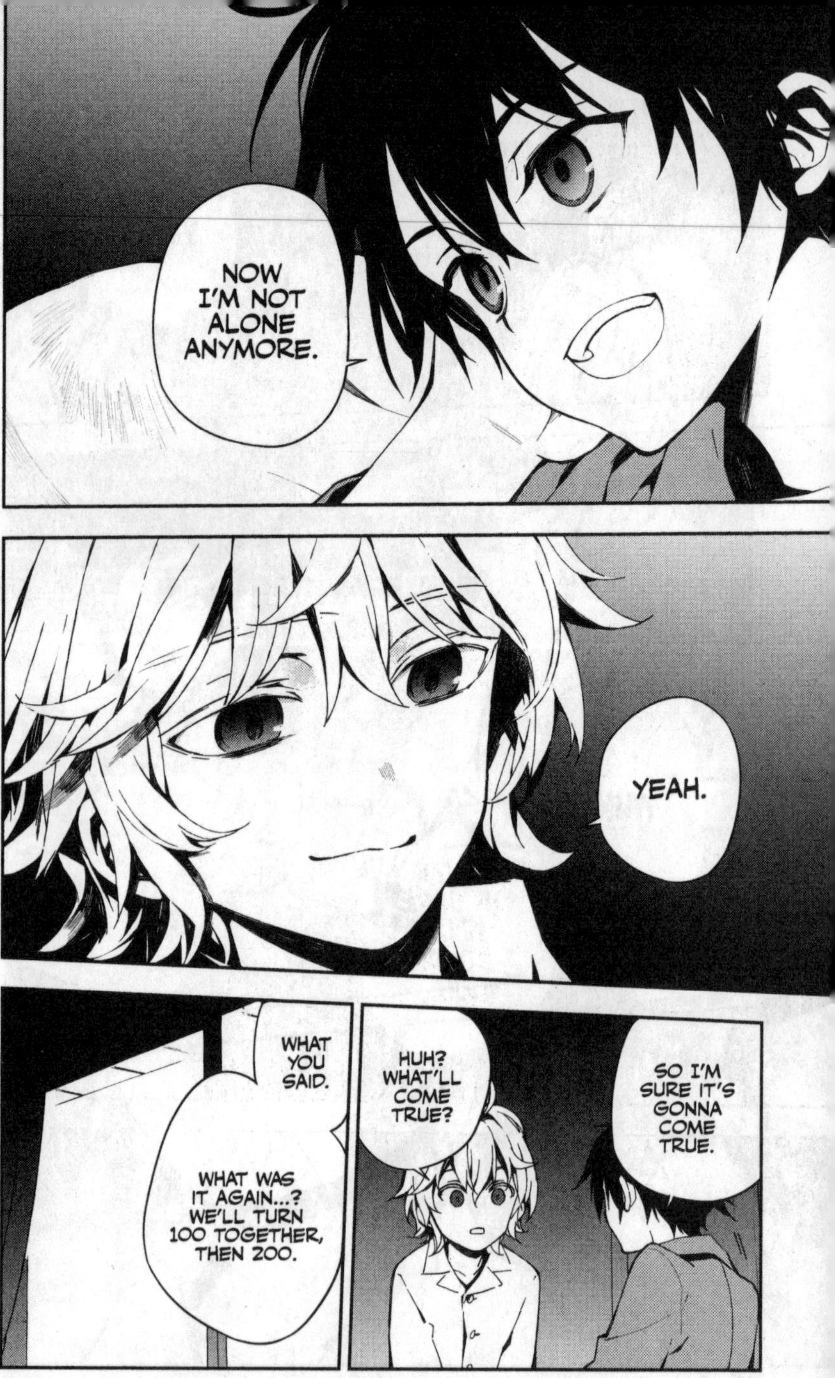
NOW I'M NOT ALONE ANYMORE.
YEAH.
SO I'M SURE IT'S GONNA COME TRUE.
HUH? WHAT'LL COME TRUE?
WHAT YOU SAID.
WHAT WAS IT AGAIN...? WE'LL TURN 100 TOGETHER, THEN 200.

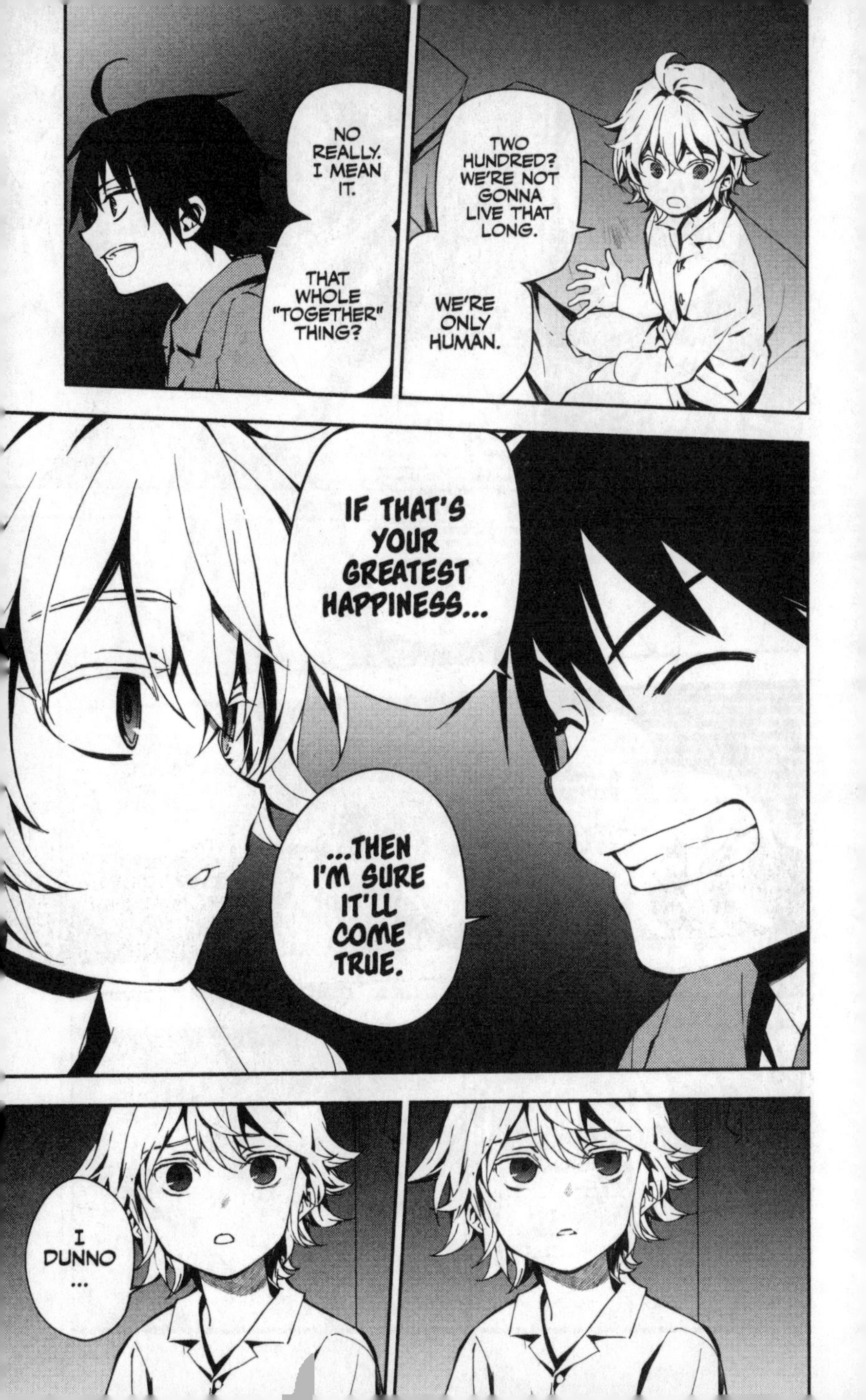
TWO HUNDRED? WE'RE NOT GONNA LIVE THAT LONG.
WE'RE ONLY HUMAN.
NO REALLY. I MEAN IT.
THAT WHOLE "TOGETHER" THING?
IF THAT'S YOUR GREATEST HAPPINESS...
...THEN I'M SURE IT'LL COME TRUE.
I DUNNO ...

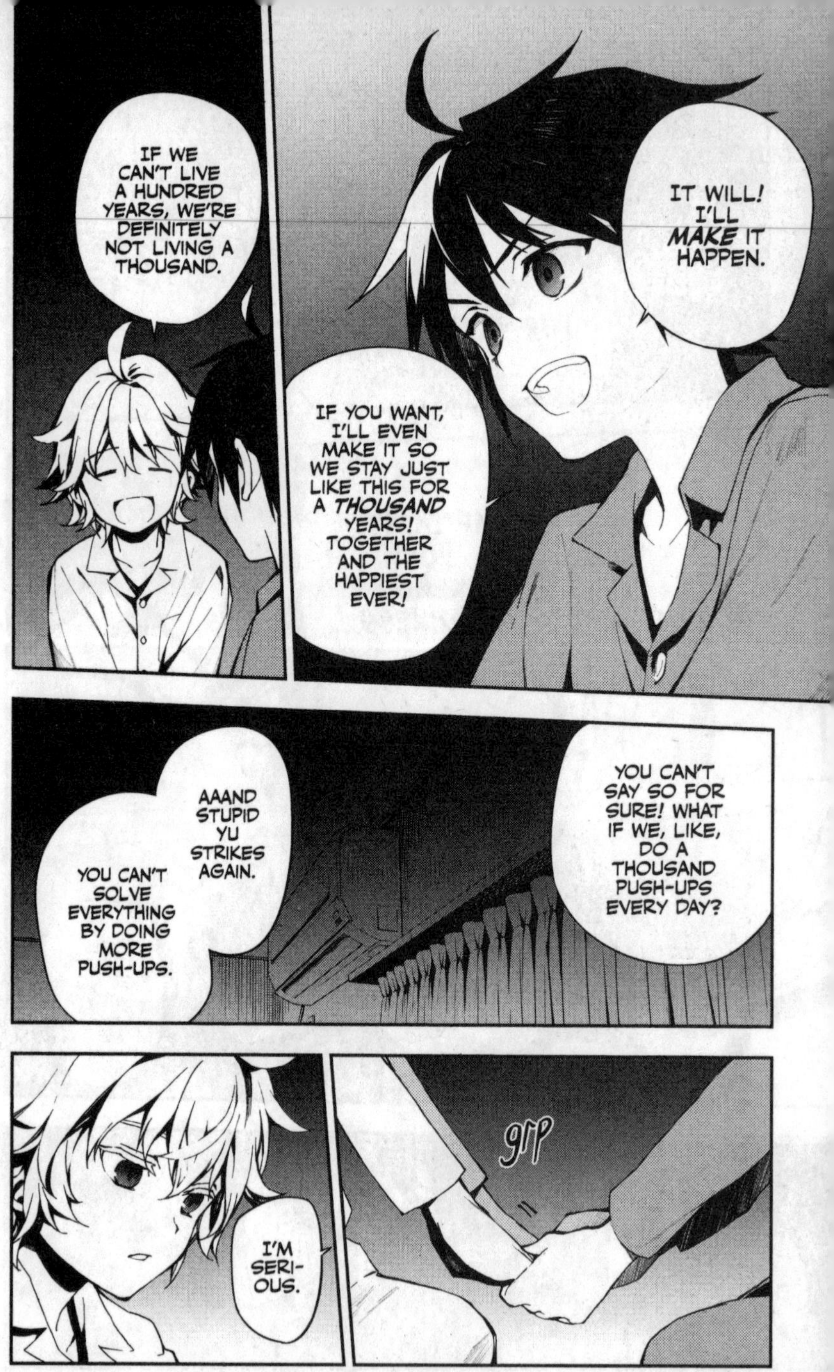
IT WILL! I'LL *MAKE* IT HAPPEN.
IF YOU WANT, I'LL EVEN MAKE IT SO WE STAY JUST LIKE THIS FOR A *THOUSAND* YEARS! TOGETHER AND THE HAPPIEST EVER!
IF WE CAN'T LIVE A HUNDRED YEARS, WE'RE DEFINITELY NOT LIVING A THOUSAND.
YOU CAN'T SAY SO FOR SURE! WHAT IF WE, LIKE, DO A THOUSAND PUSH-UPS EVERY DAY?
AAAND STUPID YU STRIKES AGAIN.
YOU CAN'T SOLVE EVERYTHING BY DOING MORE PUSH-UPS.
grip
I'M SERI-OUS.

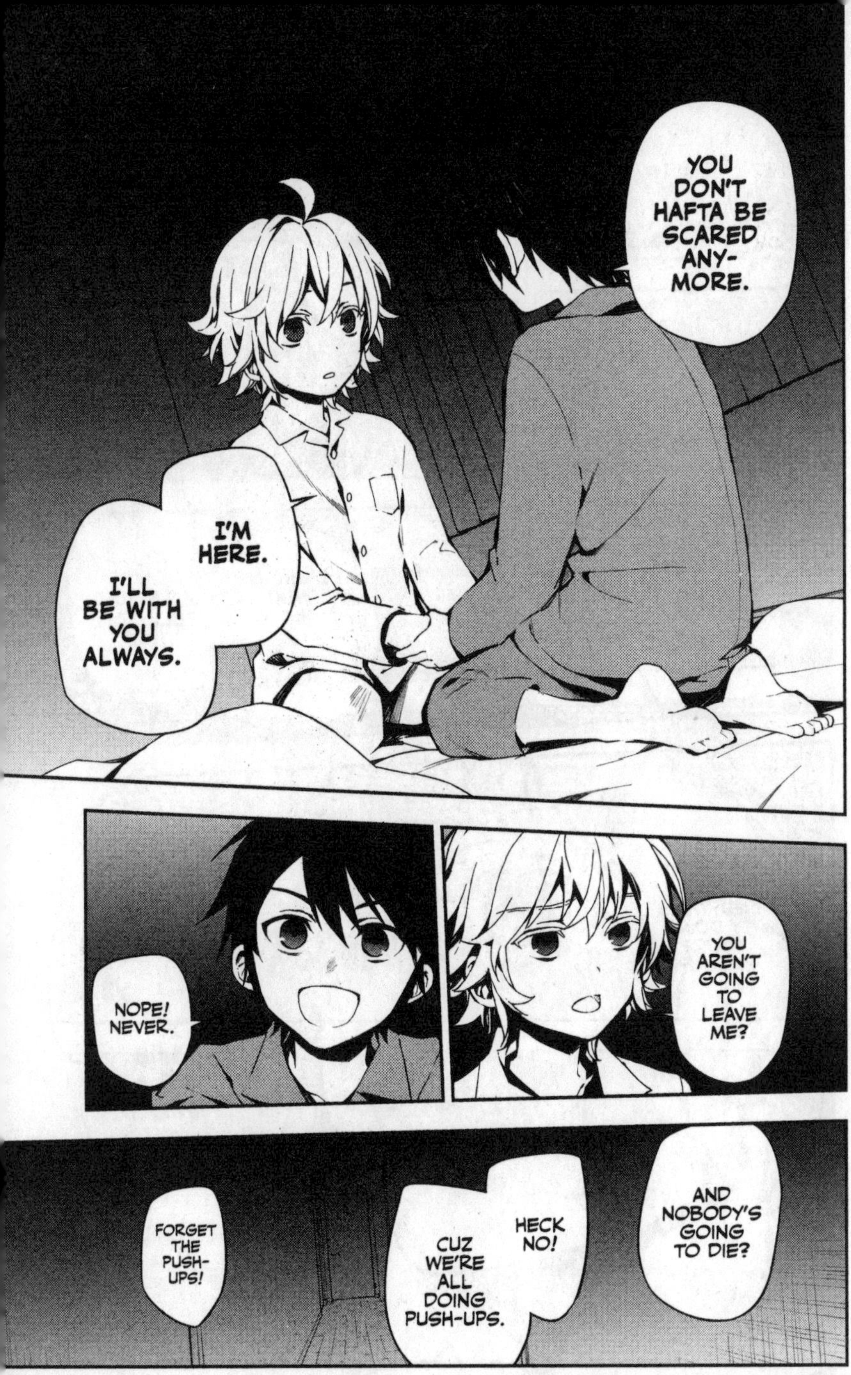
YOU DON'T HAFTA BE SCARED ANY-MORE.
I'M HERE.
I'LL BE WITH YOU ALWAYS.
YOU AREN'T GOING TO LEAVE ME?
NOPE! NEVER.
AND NOBODY'S GOING TO DIE?
HECK NO!
CUZ WE'RE ALL DOING PUSH-UPS.
FORGET THE PUSH-UPS!

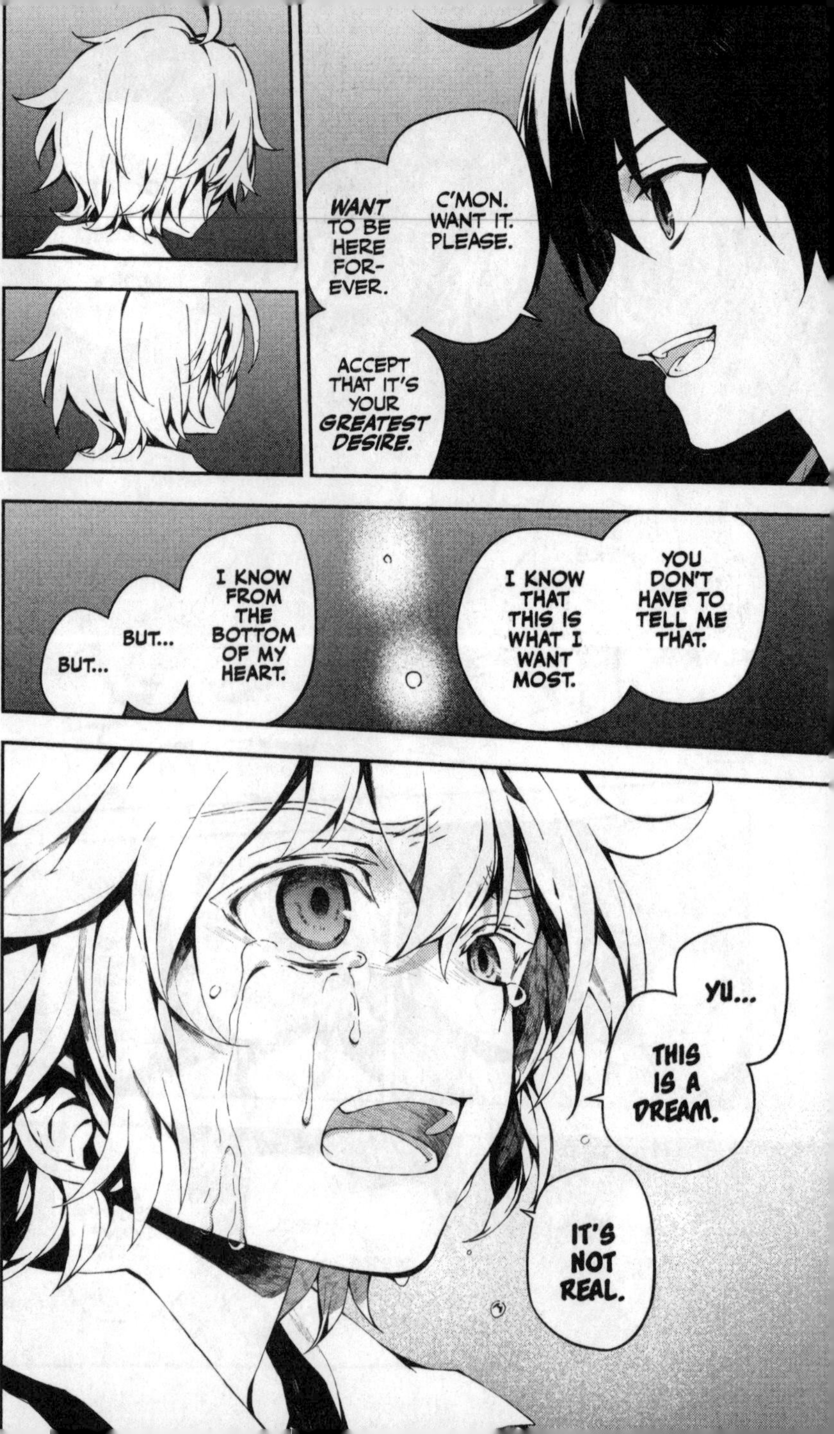
C'MON. WANT IT. PLEASE.
WANT TO BE HERE FOREVER.
ACCEPT THAT IT'S YOUR *GREATEST DESIRE.*
YOU DON'T HAVE TO TELL ME THAT.
I KNOW THAT THIS IS WHAT I WANT MOST.
I KNOW FROM THE BOTTOM OF MY HEART.
BUT...
BUT...
YU...
THIS IS A DREAM.
IT'S NOT REAL.

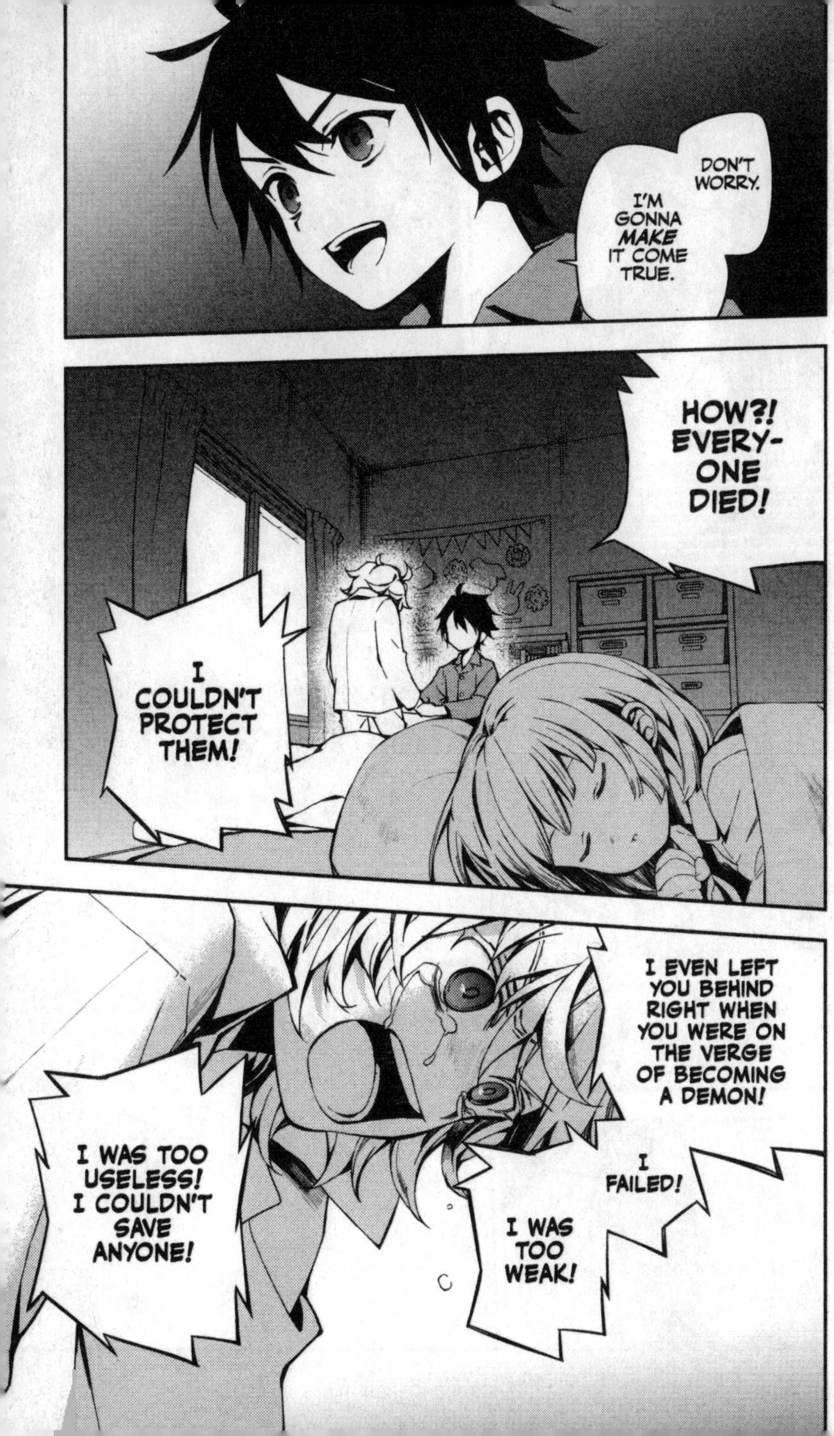
DON'T WORRY.
I'M GONNA *MAKE* IT COME TRUE.
HOW?! EVERY-ONE DIED!
I COULDN'T PROTECT THEM!
I EVEN LEFT YOU BEHIND RIGHT WHEN YOU WERE ON THE VERGE OF BECOMING A DEMON!
I FAILED!
I WAS TOO WEAK!
I WAS TOO USELESS! I COULDN'T SAVE ANYONE!

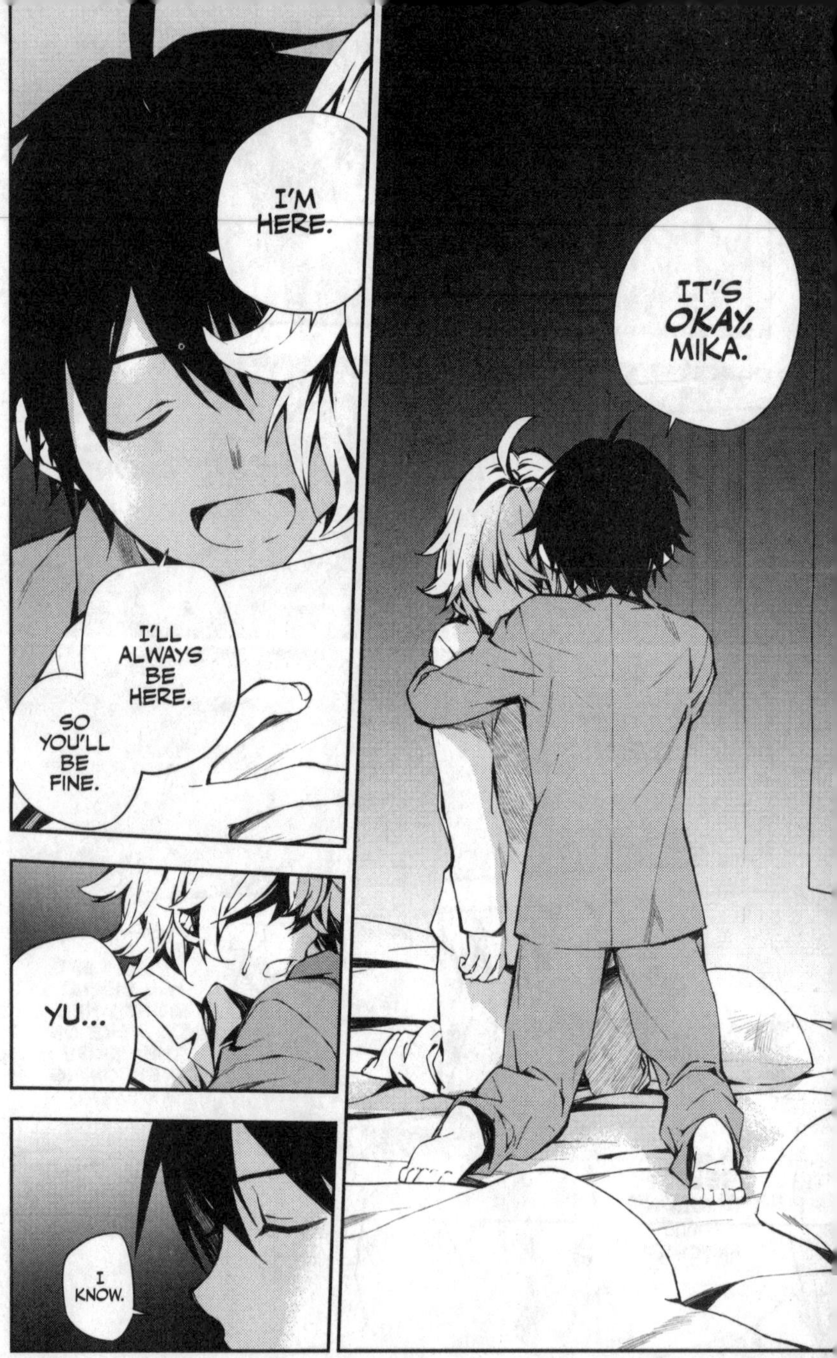
IT'S OKAY, MIKA.
I'M HERE.
I'LL ALWAYS BE HERE.
SO YOU'LL BE FINE.
YU...
I KNOW.

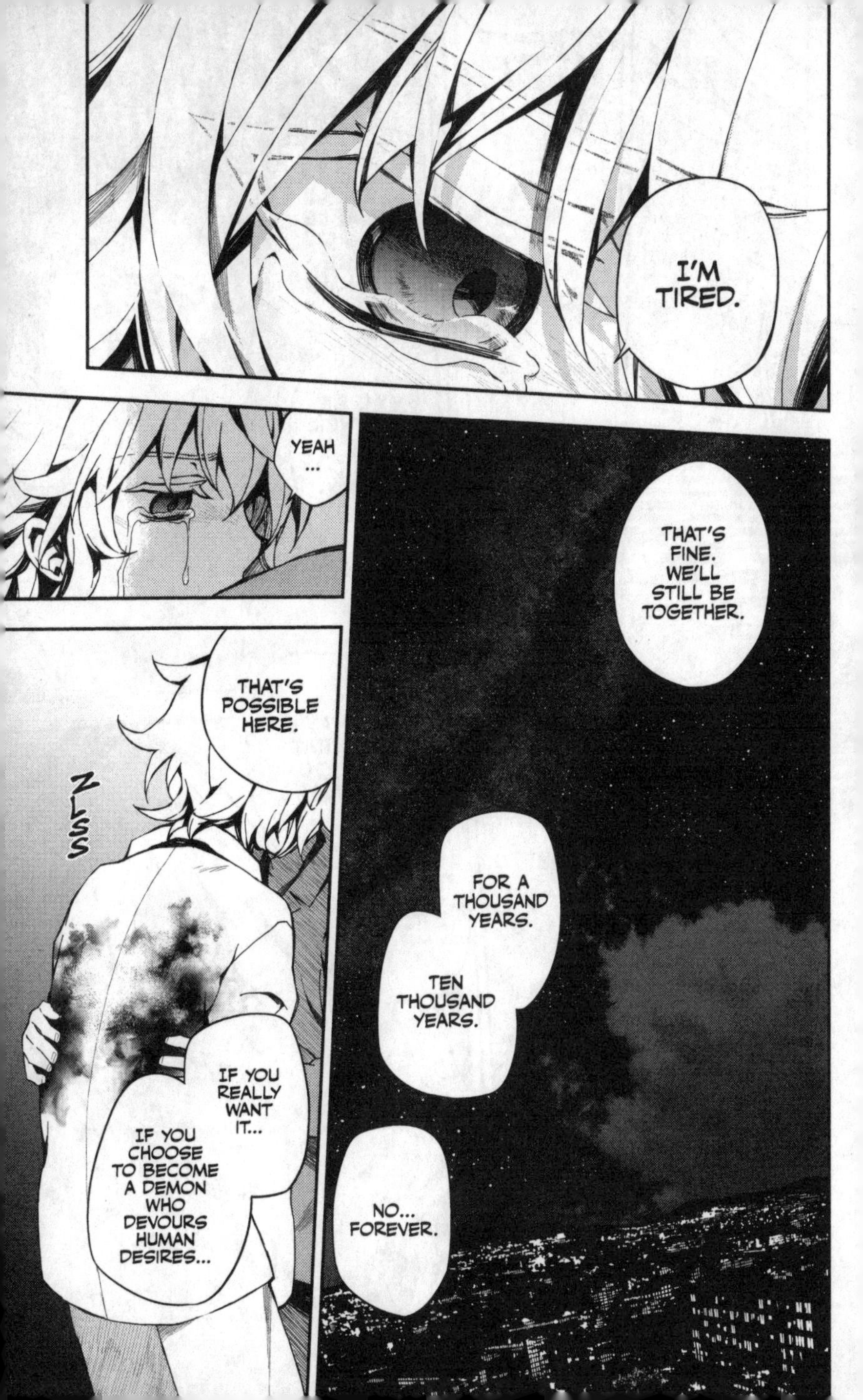
I'M TIRED.
THAT'S FINE. WE'LL STILL BE TOGETHER.
FOR A THOUSAND YEARS.
TEN THOUSAND YEARS.
NO... FOREVER.
YEAH ...
THAT'S POSSIBLE HERE.
ZLSS
IF YOU REALLY WANT IT...
IF YOU CHOOSE TO BECOME A DEMON WHO DEVOURS HUMAN DESIRES...

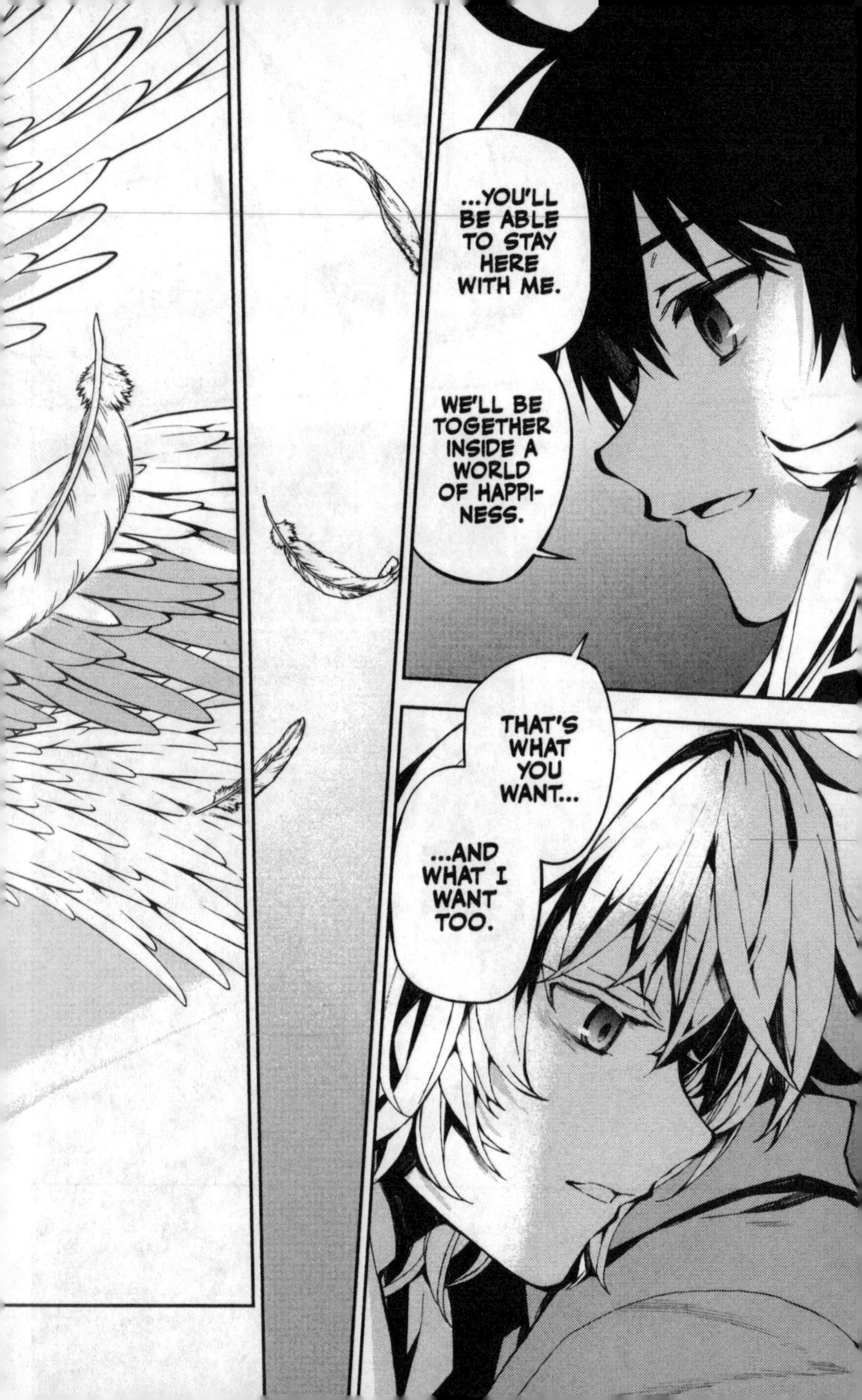
...YOU'LL BE ABLE TO STAY HERE WITH ME.
WE'LL BE TOGETHER INSIDE A WORLD OF HAPPI-NESS.
THAT'S WHAT YOU WANT...
...AND WHAT I WANT TOO.

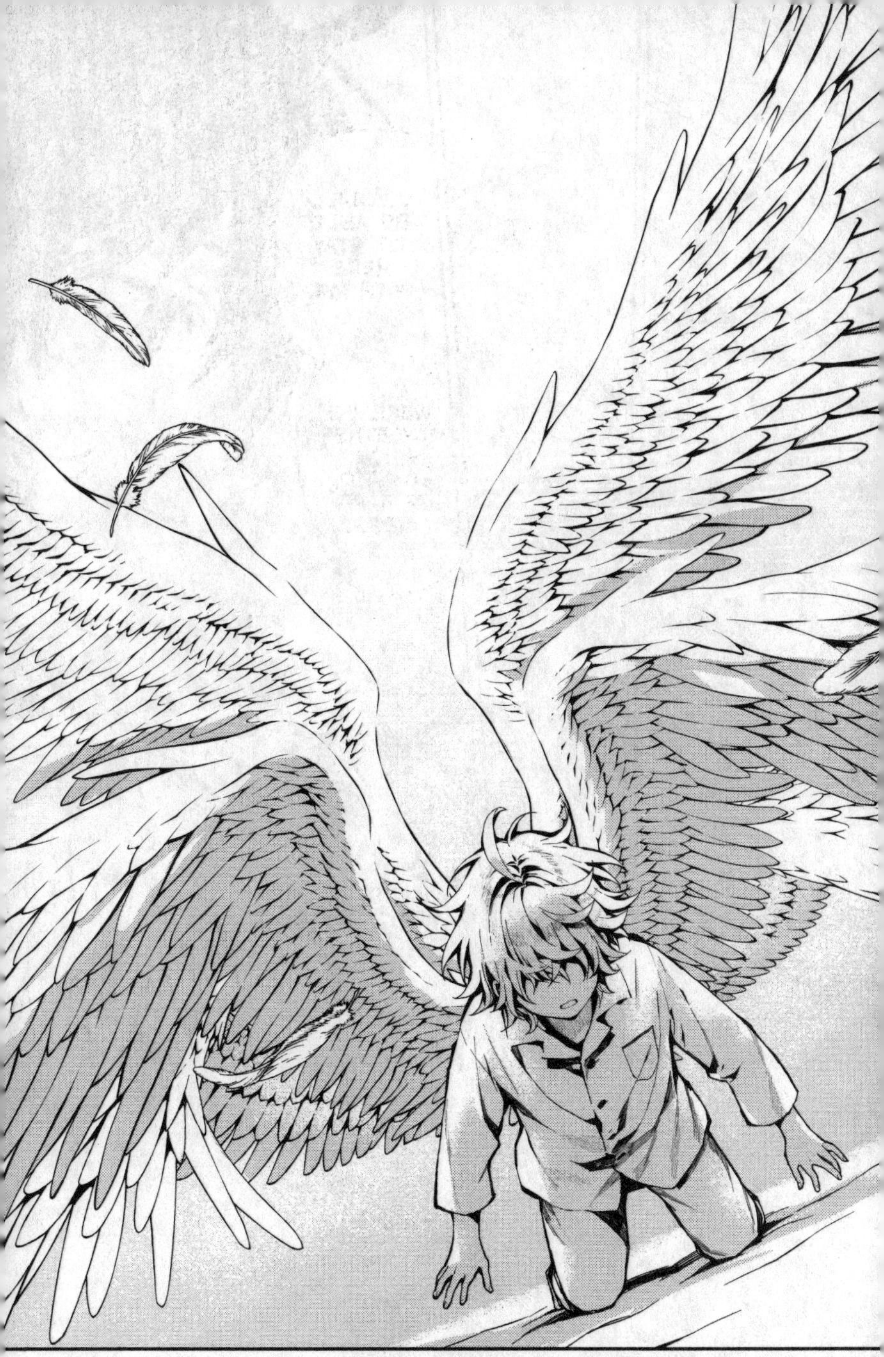

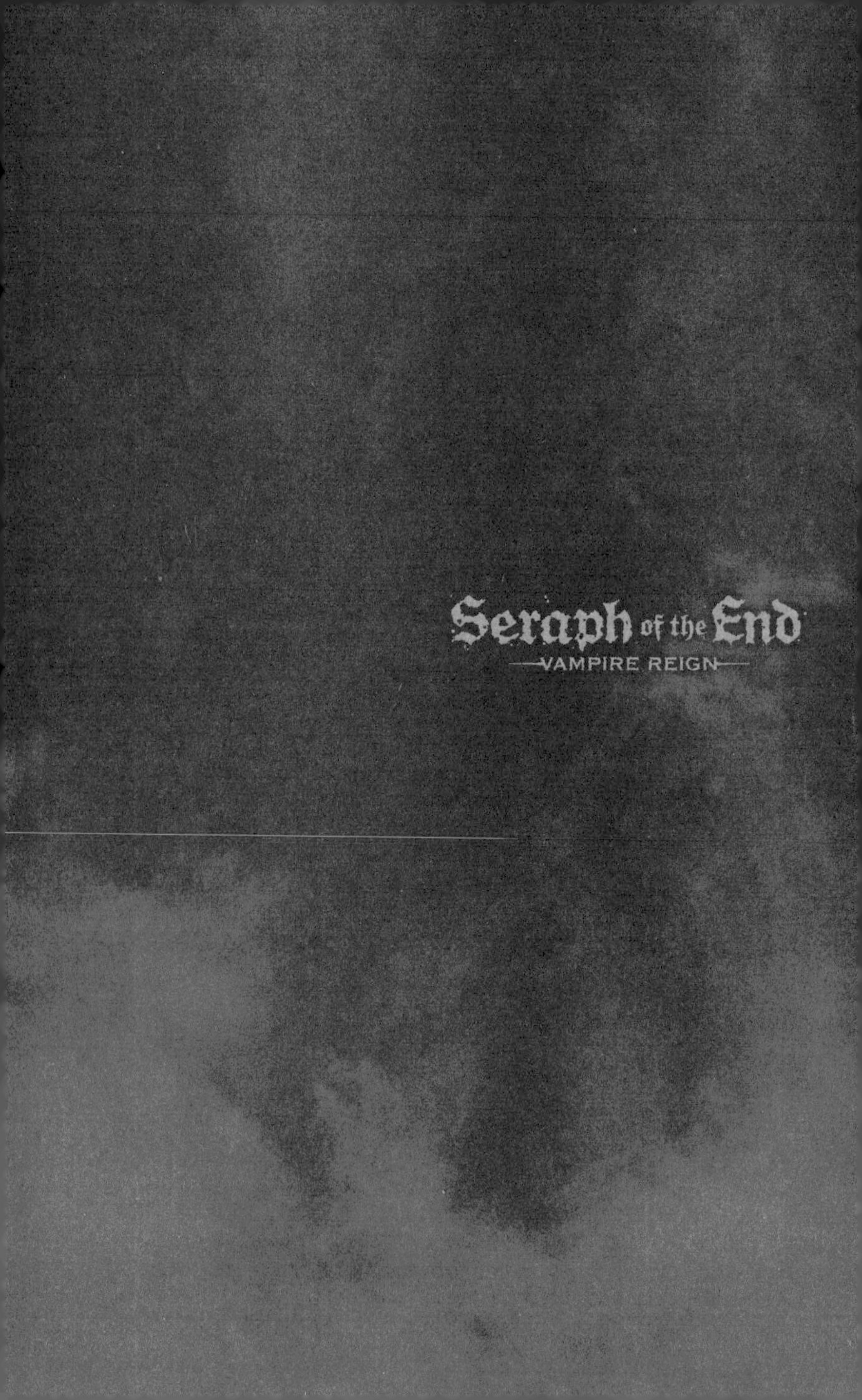
Seraph of the End
VAMPIRE REIGN

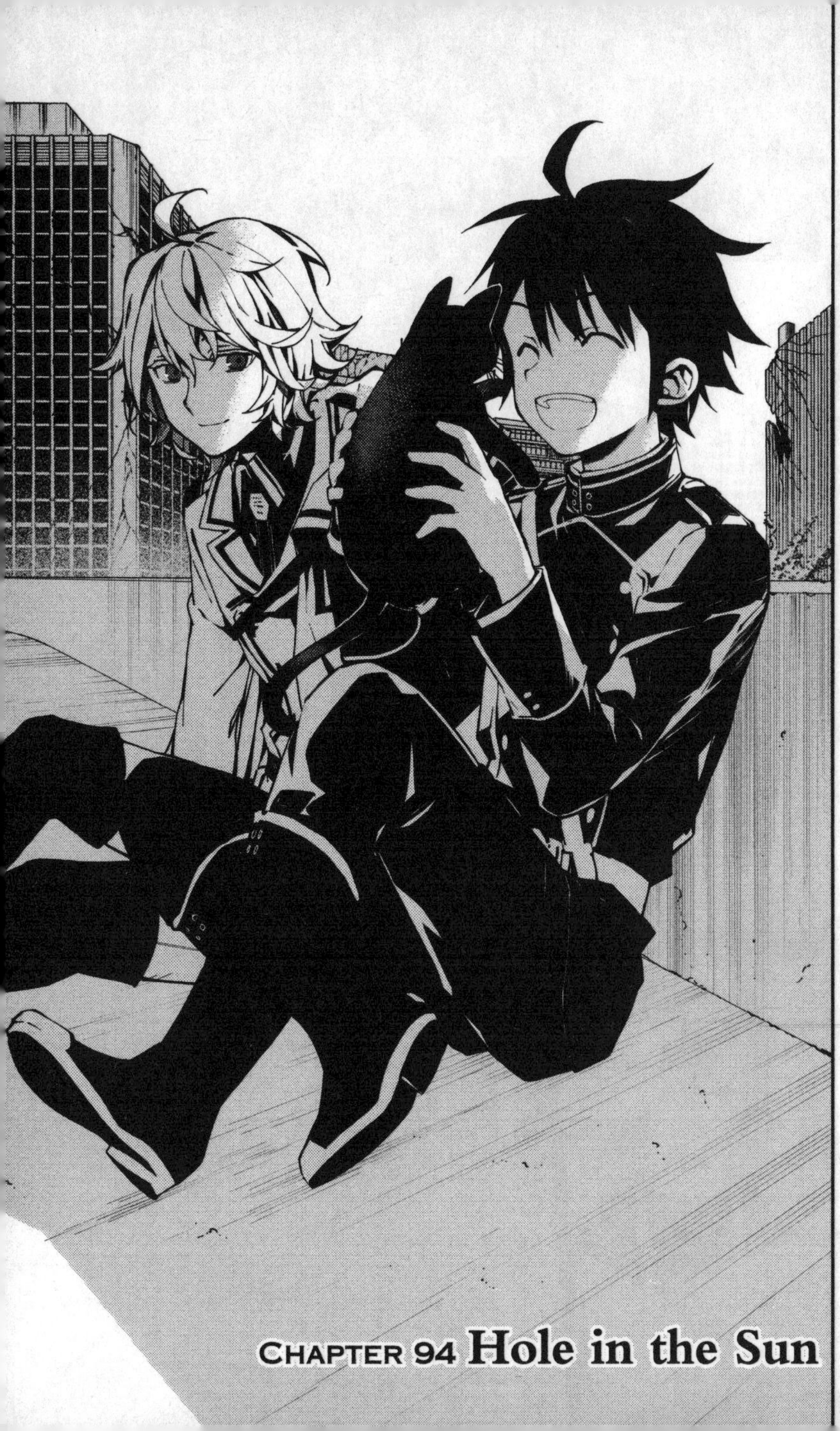

CHAPTER 94 Hole in the Sun

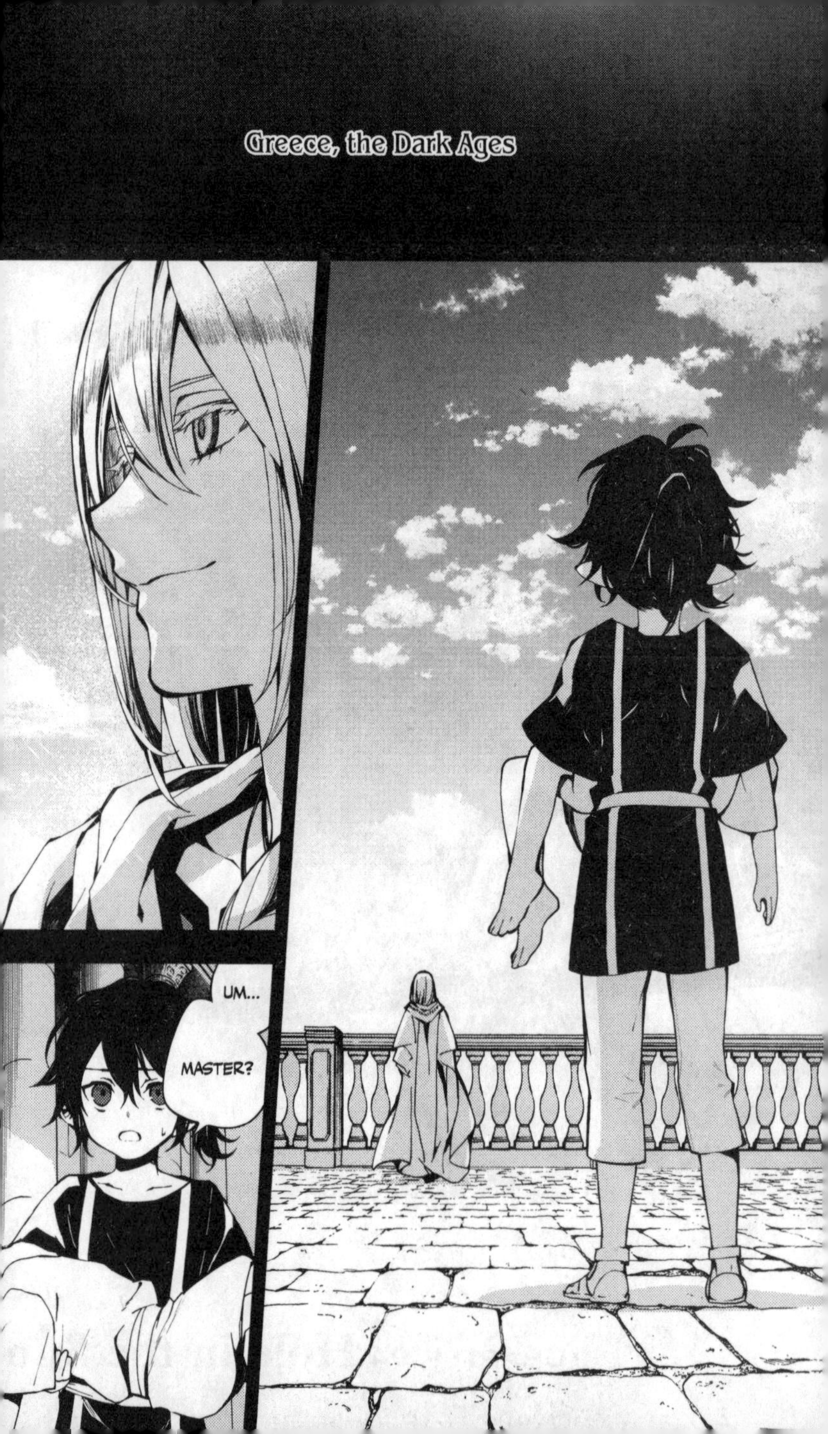
Greece, the Dark Ages
UM...
MASTER?

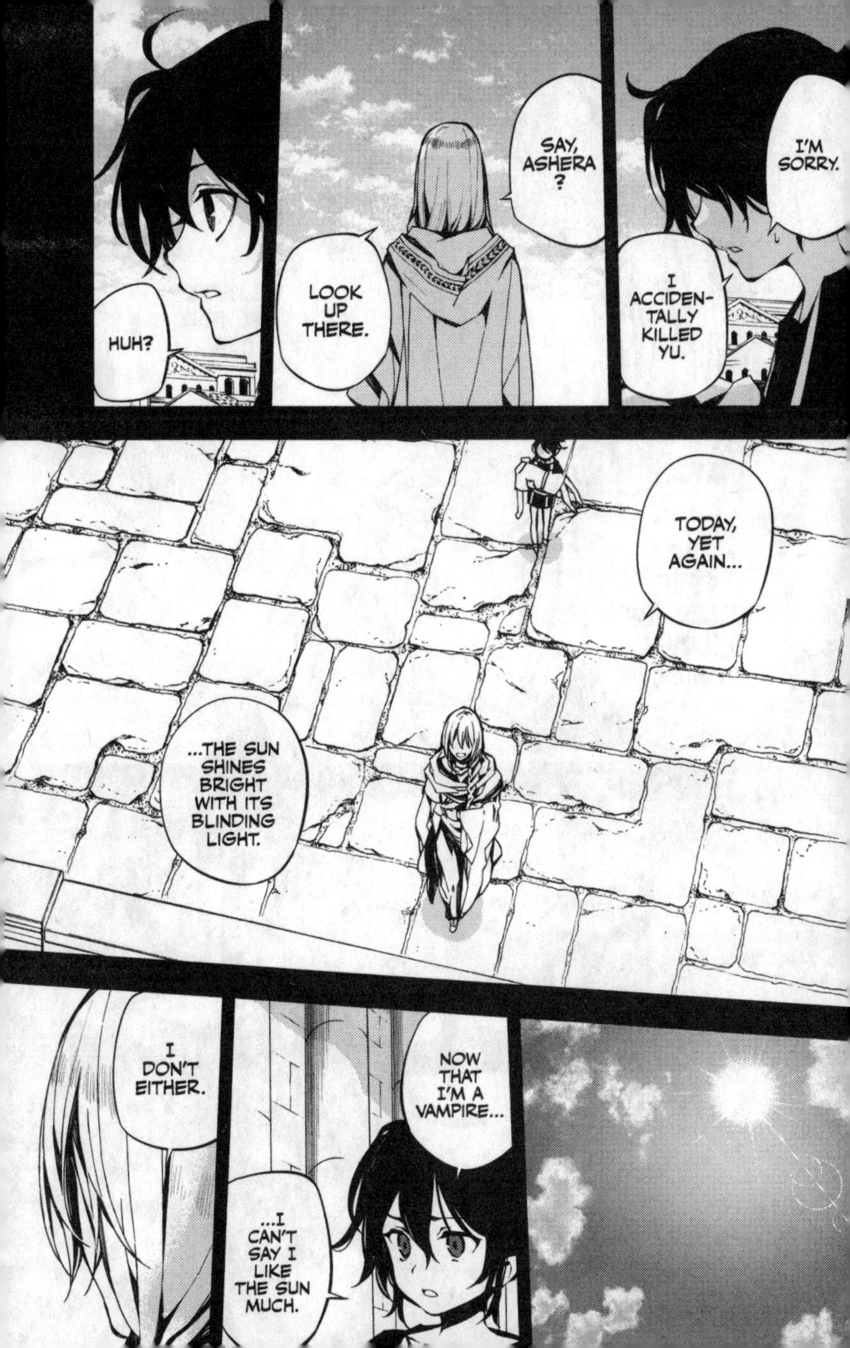
I'M SORRY.
I ACCIDEN-TALLY KILLED YU.
SAY, ASHERA?
LOOK UP THERE.
HUH?
TODAY, YET AGAIN...
...THE SUN SHINES BRIGHT WITH ITS BLINDING LIGHT.
NOW THAT I'M A VAMPIRE...
...I CAN'T SAY I LIKE THE SUN MUCH.
I DON'T EITHER.

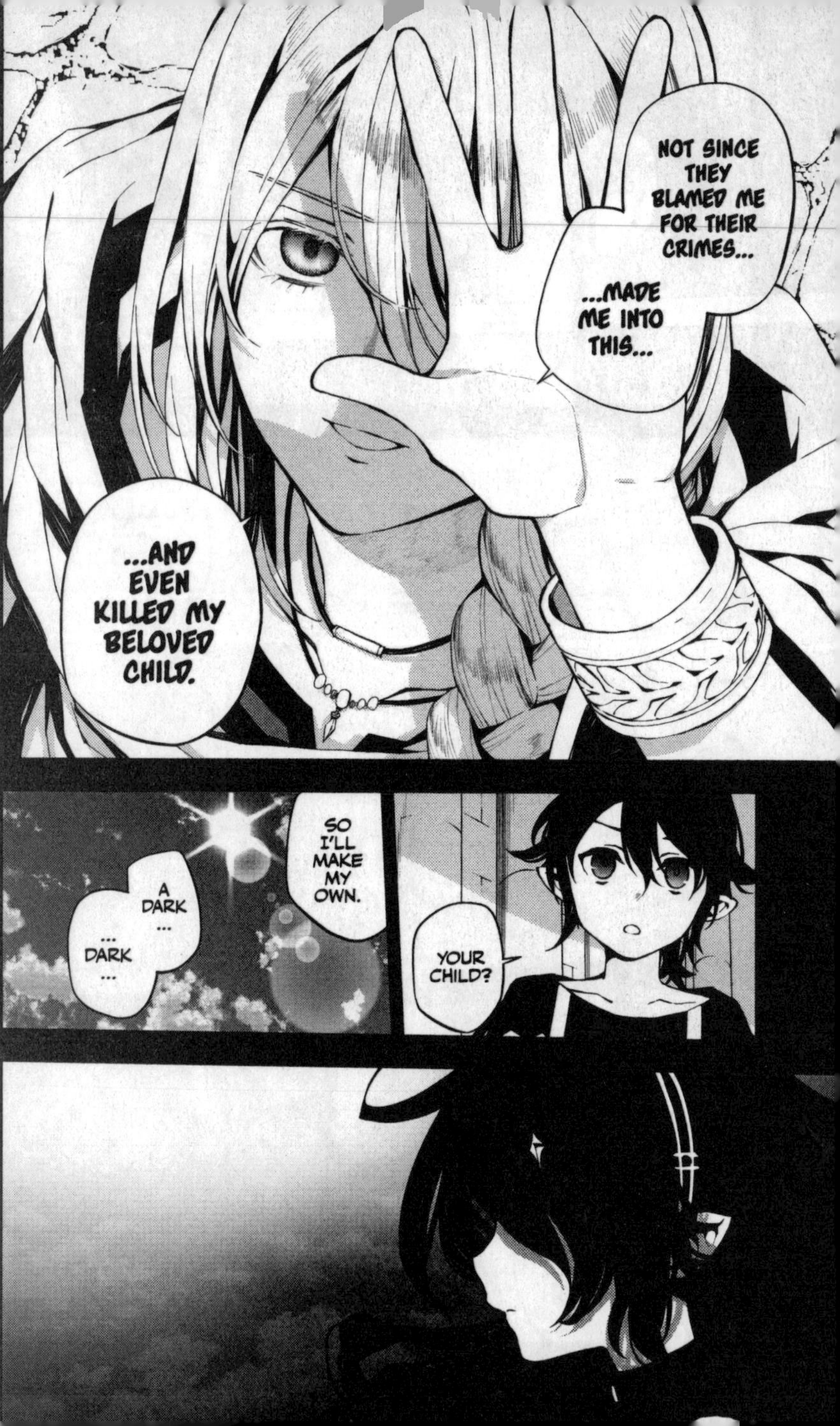
NOT SINCE THEY BLAMED ME FOR THEIR CRIMES...
...MADE ME INTO THIS...
...AND EVEN KILLED MY BELOVED CHILD.
YOUR CHILD?
SO I'LL MAKE MY OWN.
A DARK ...
... DARK ...

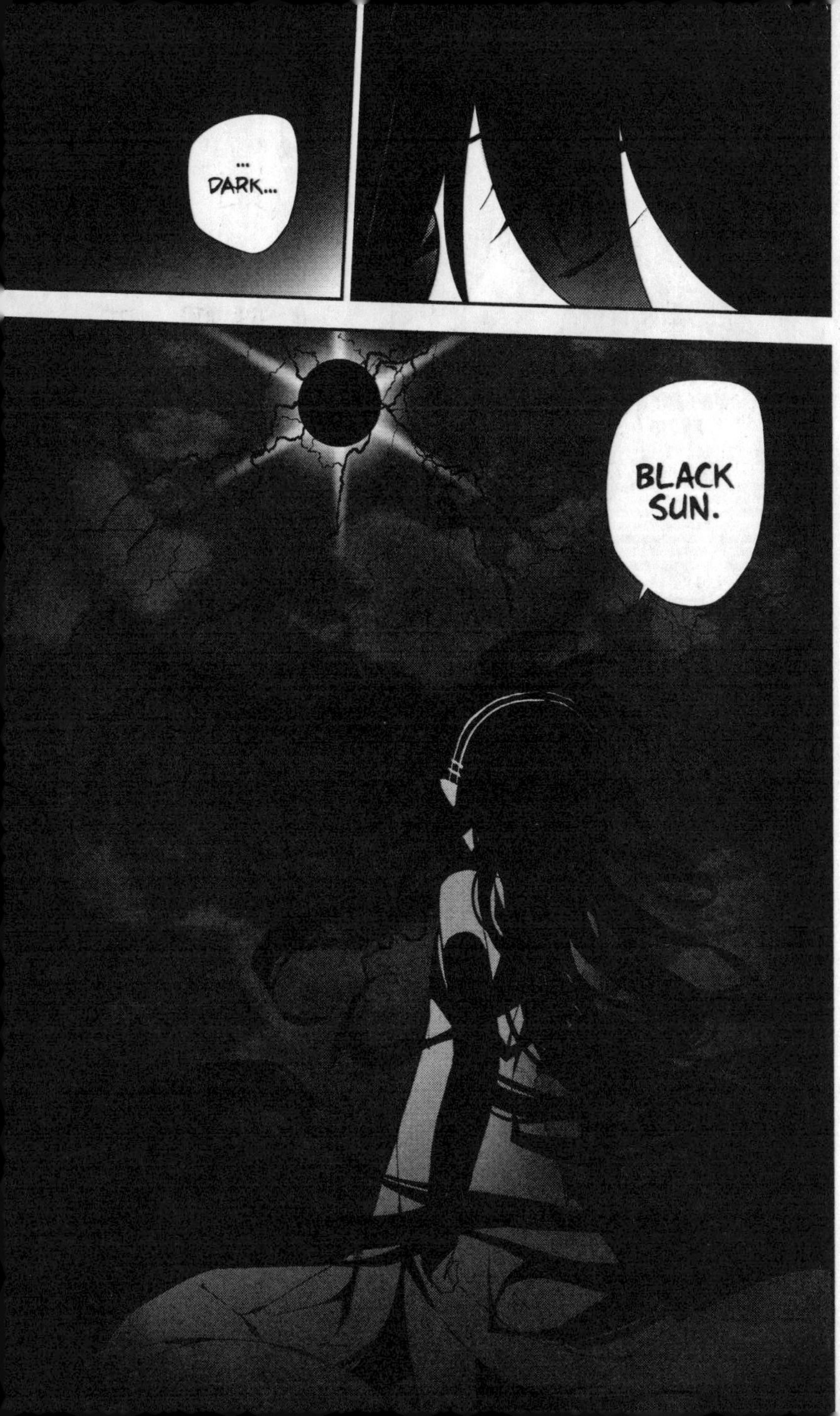
... DARK...
BLACK SUN.

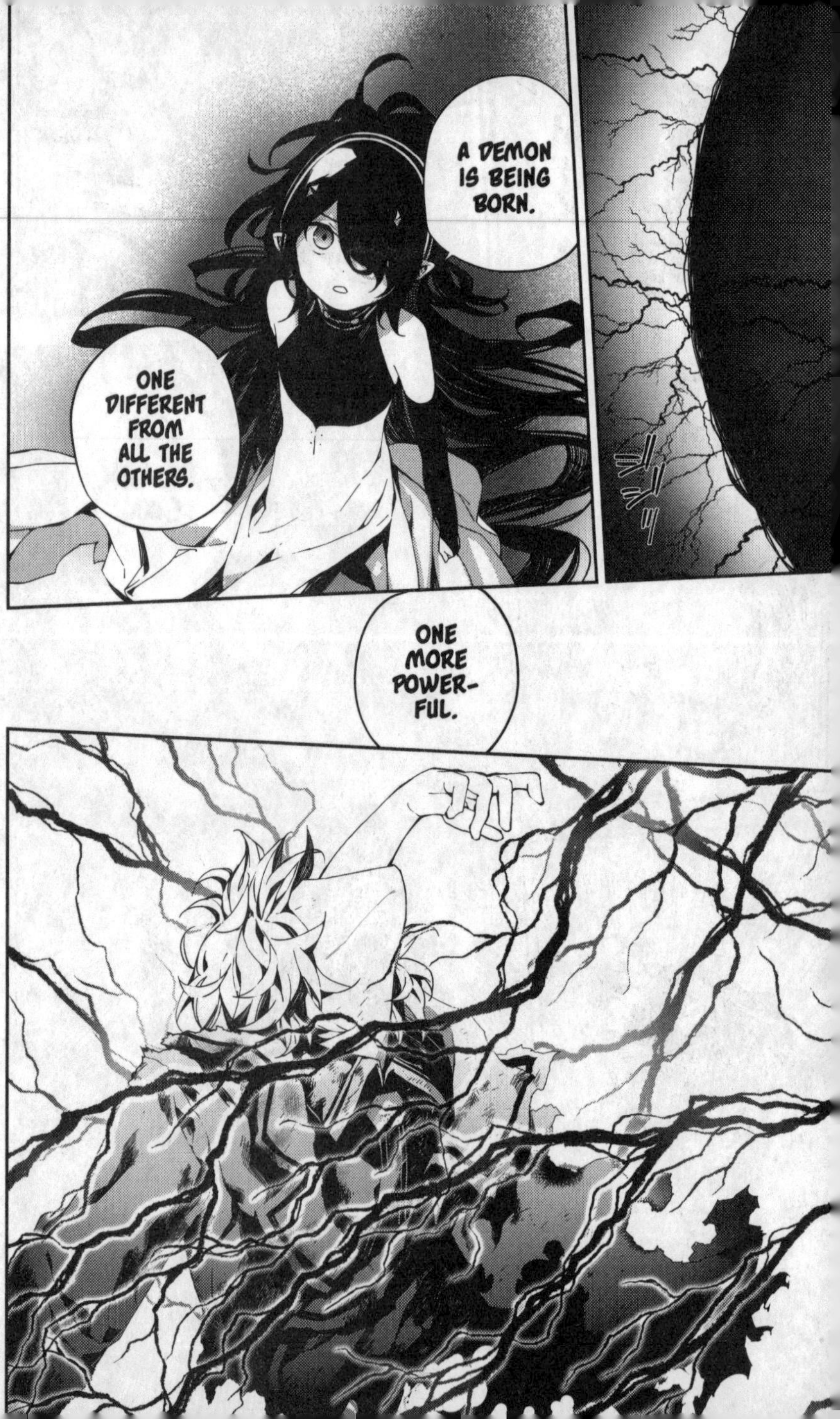
ジジジッ
A DEMON IS BEING BORN.
ONE DIFFERENT FROM ALL THE OTHERS.
ONE MORE POWER-FUL.

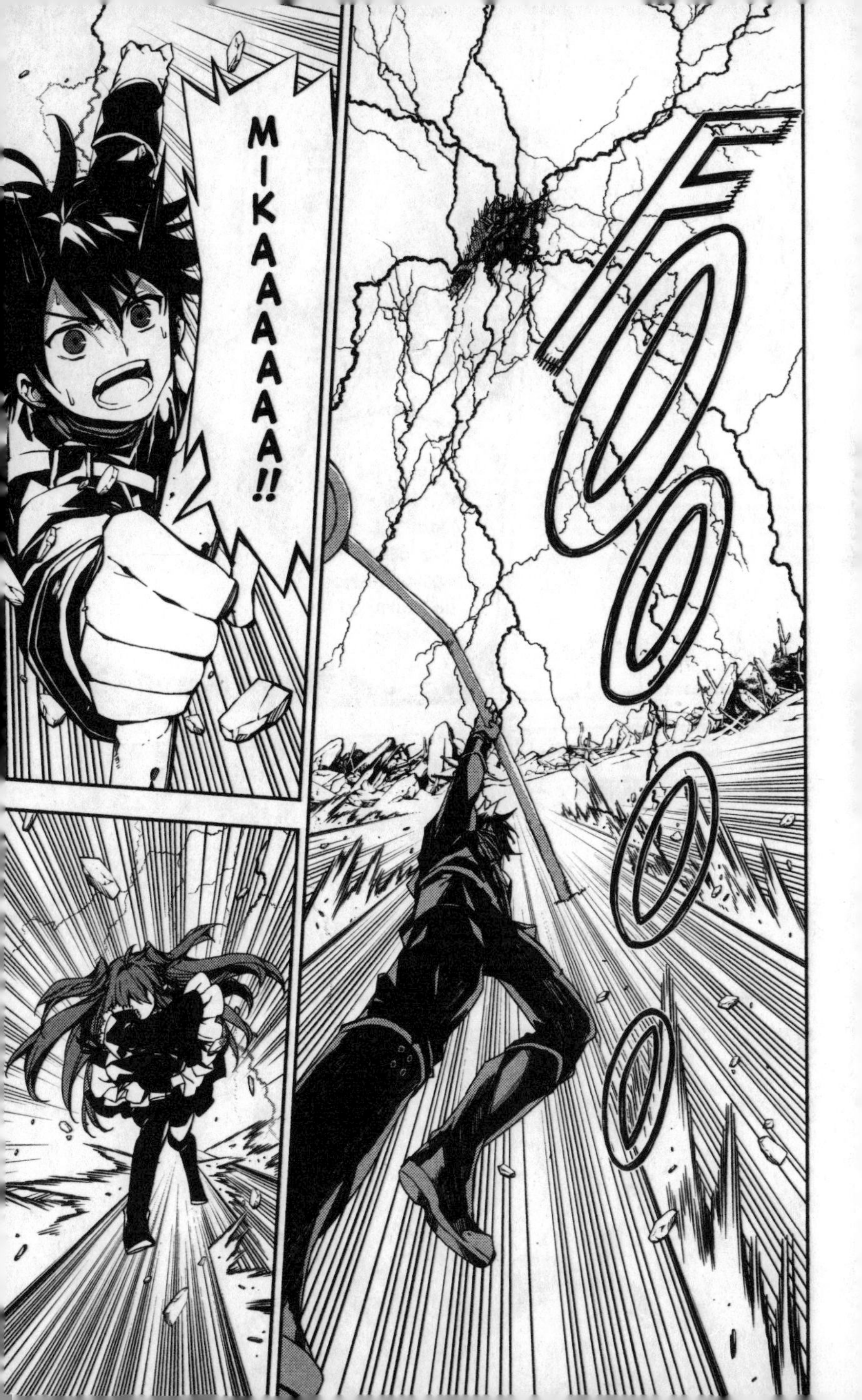
FOOOO
MIKAAAAAA!!

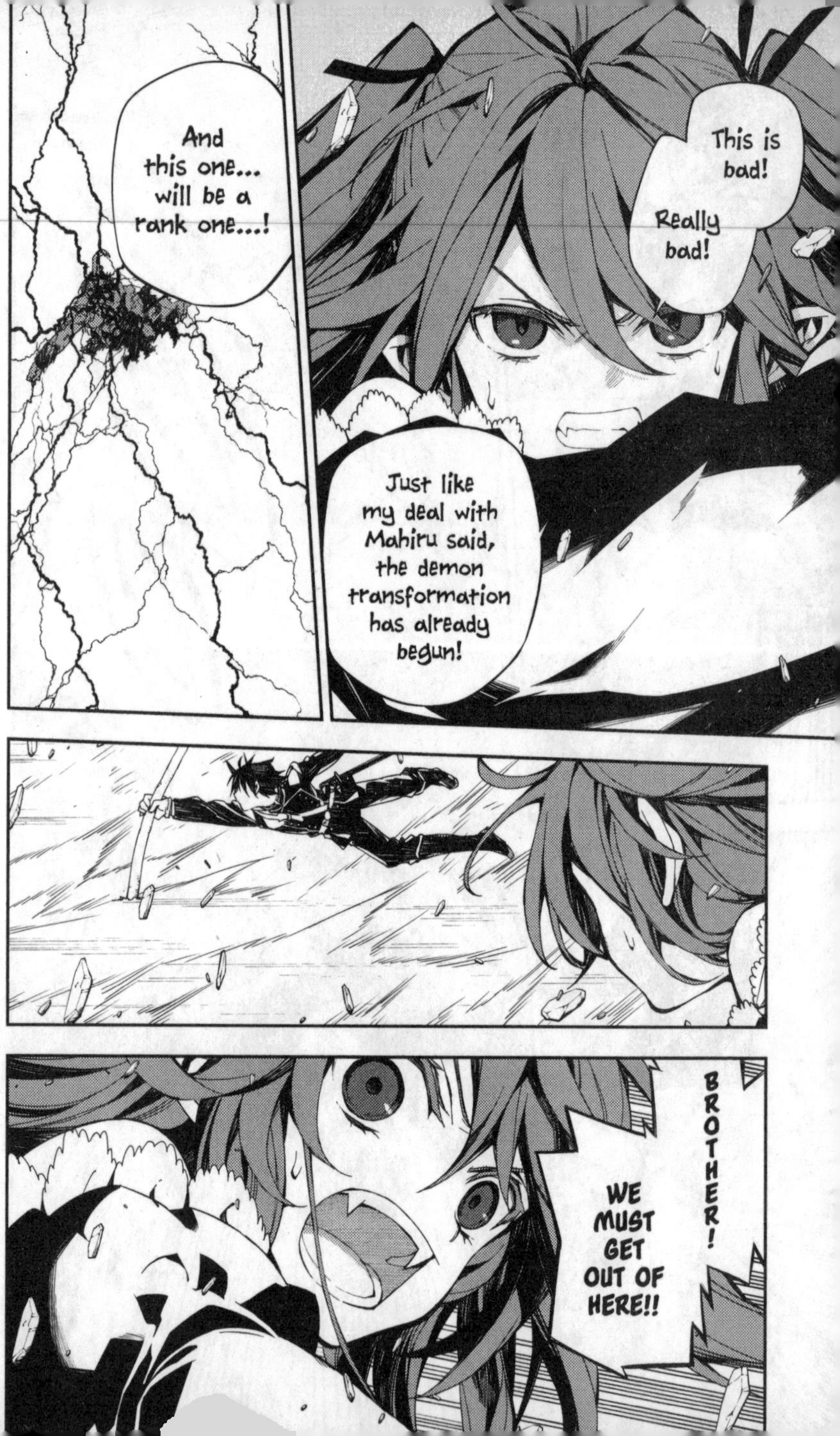
This is bad!
Really bad!
Just like my deal with Mahiru said, the demon transformation has already begun!
And this one... will be a rank one...!
BROTHER!
WE MUST GET OUT OF HERE!!

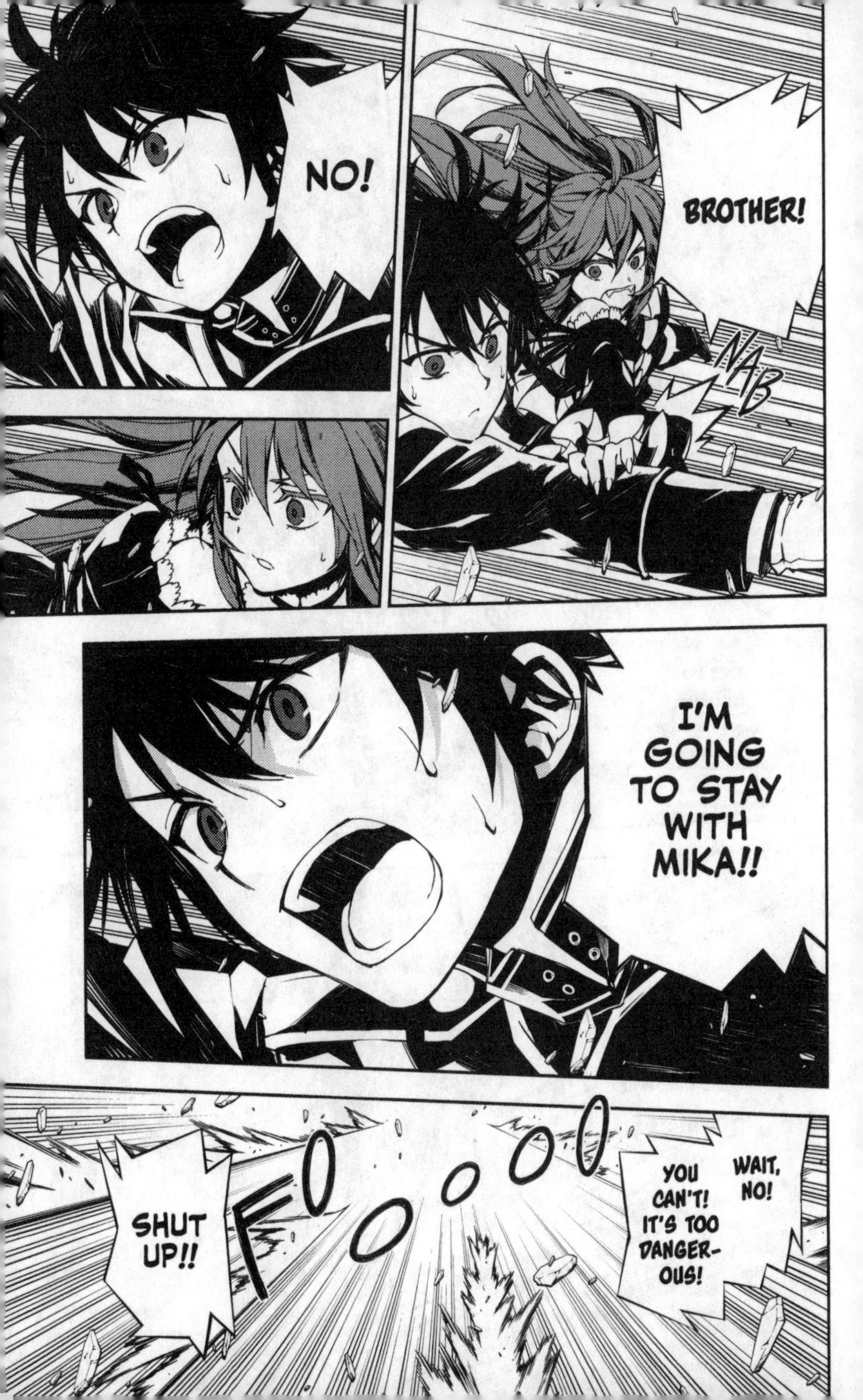
BROTHER!
NAB
NO!
I'M GOING TO STAY WITH MIKA!!
WAIT, NO!
YOU CAN'T! IT'S TOO DANGER-OUS!
FOOOOOOOO
SHUT UP!!

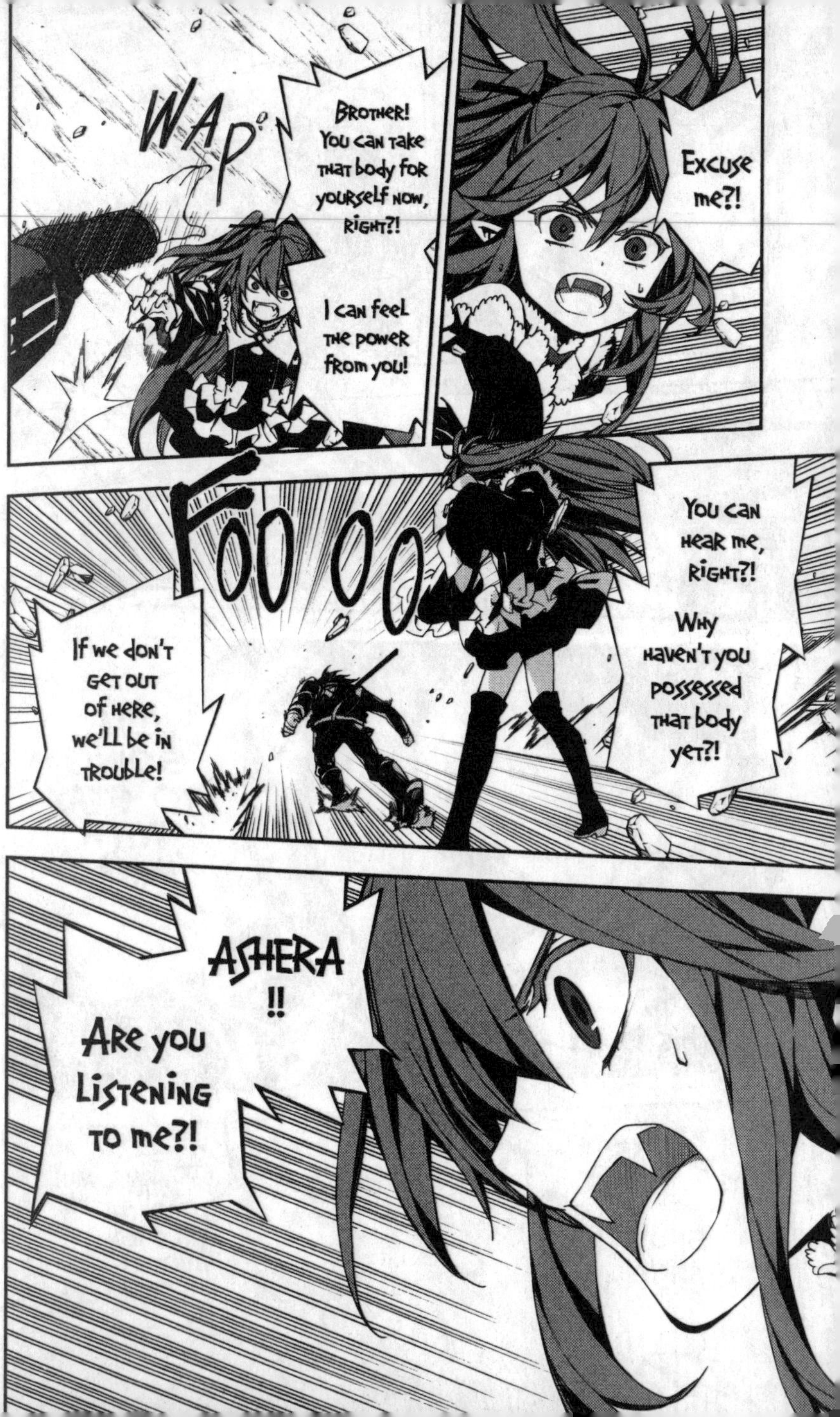
Excuse me?!
WAP
Brother! You can take that body for yourself now, right?!
I can feel the power from you!
You can hear me, right?!
Why haven't you possessed that body yet?!
FOOOOO
If we don't get out of here, we'll be in trouble!
ASHERA!!
Are you listening to me?!

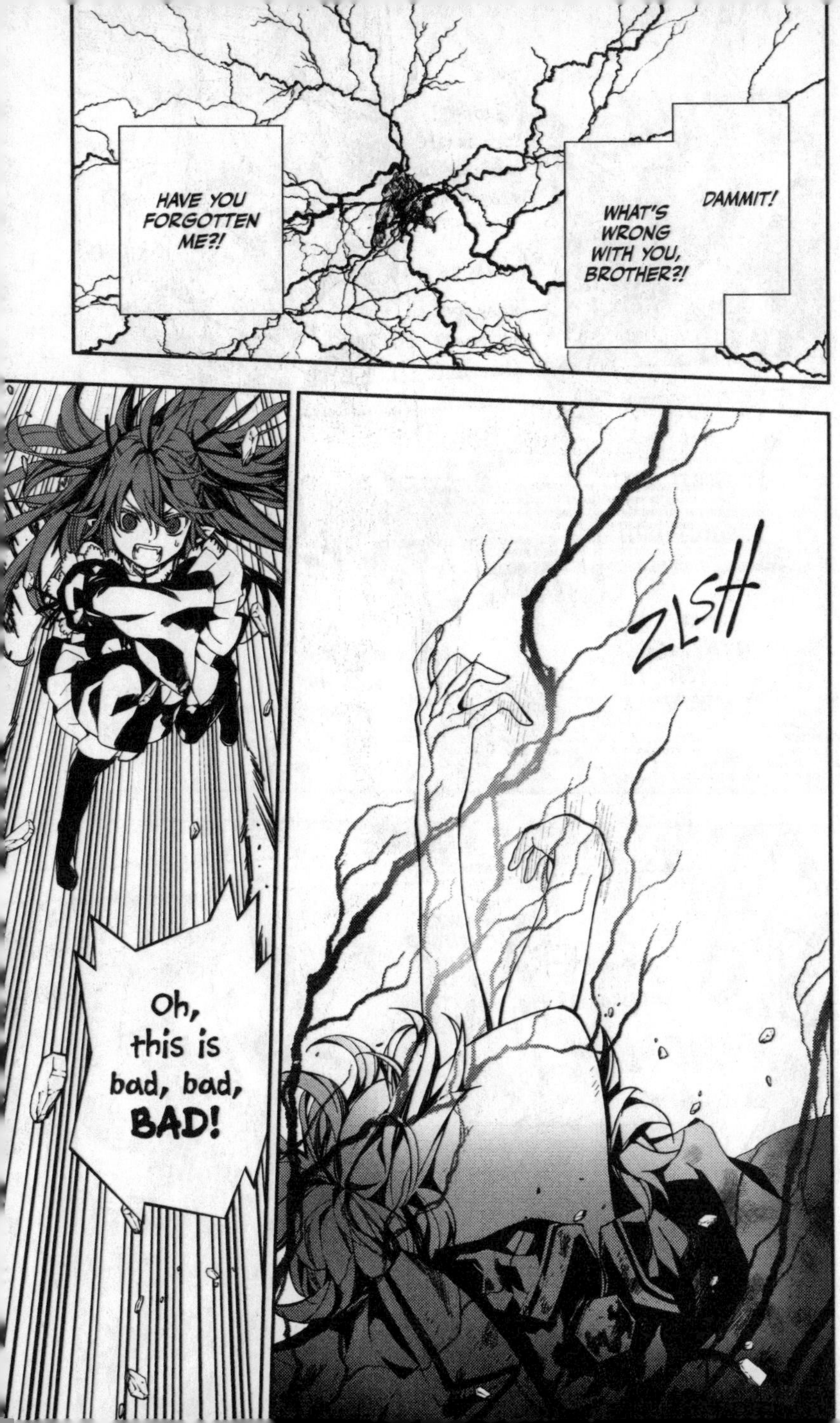
DAMMIT!
WHAT'S WRONG WITH YOU, BROTHER?!
HAVE YOU FORGOTTEN ME?!
ZISH
Oh, this is bad, bad, BAD!

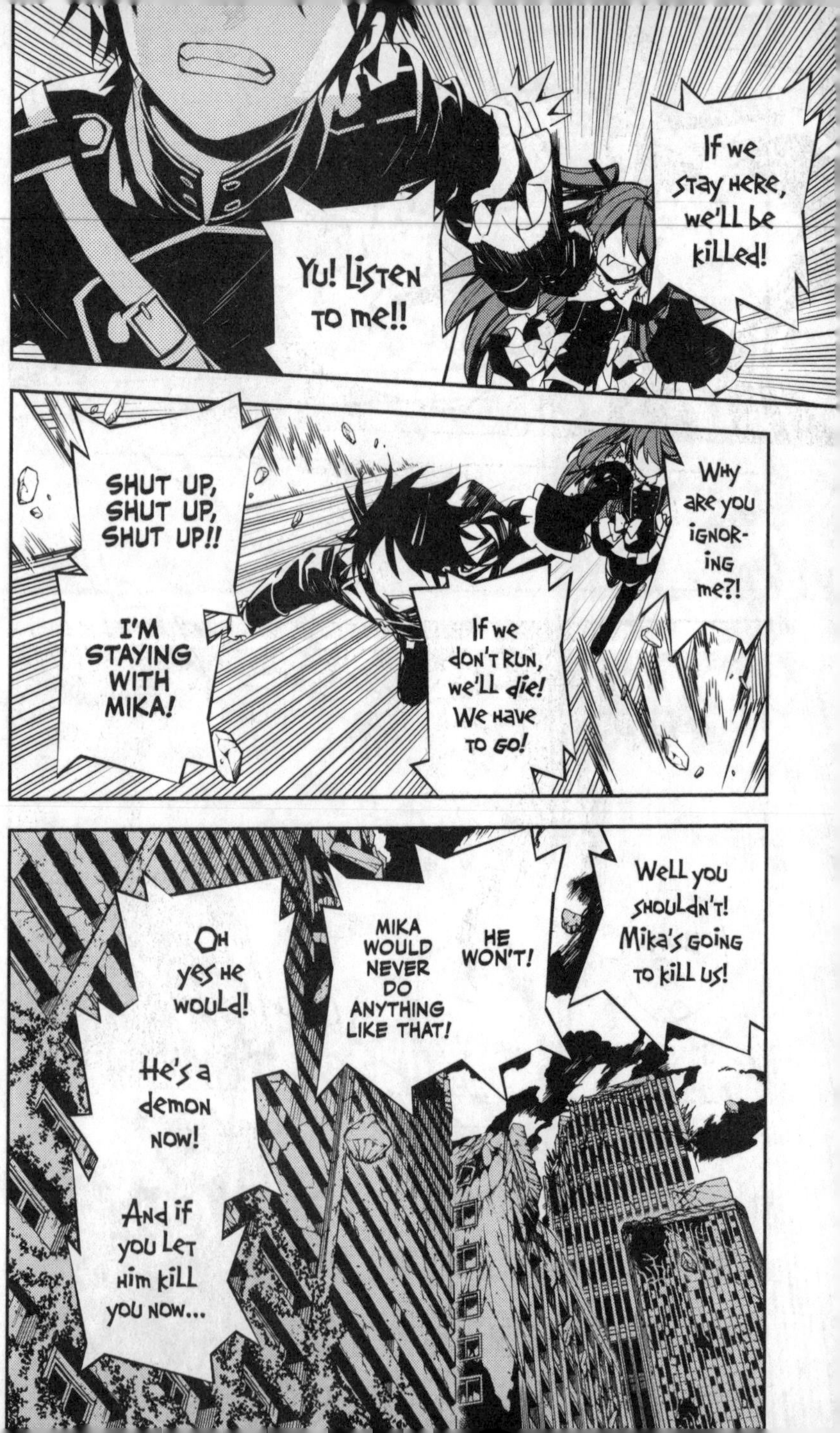
If we stay here, we'll be killed!
Yu! Listen to me!!
Why are you ignor-ing me?!
If we don't run, we'll die! We have to go!
SHUT UP, SHUT UP, SHUT UP!!
I'M STAYING WITH MIKA!
Well you shouldn't! Mika's going to kill us!
HE WON'T!
MIKA WOULD NEVER DO ANYTHING LIKE THAT!
Oh yes he would!
He's a demon now!
And if you let him kill you now...

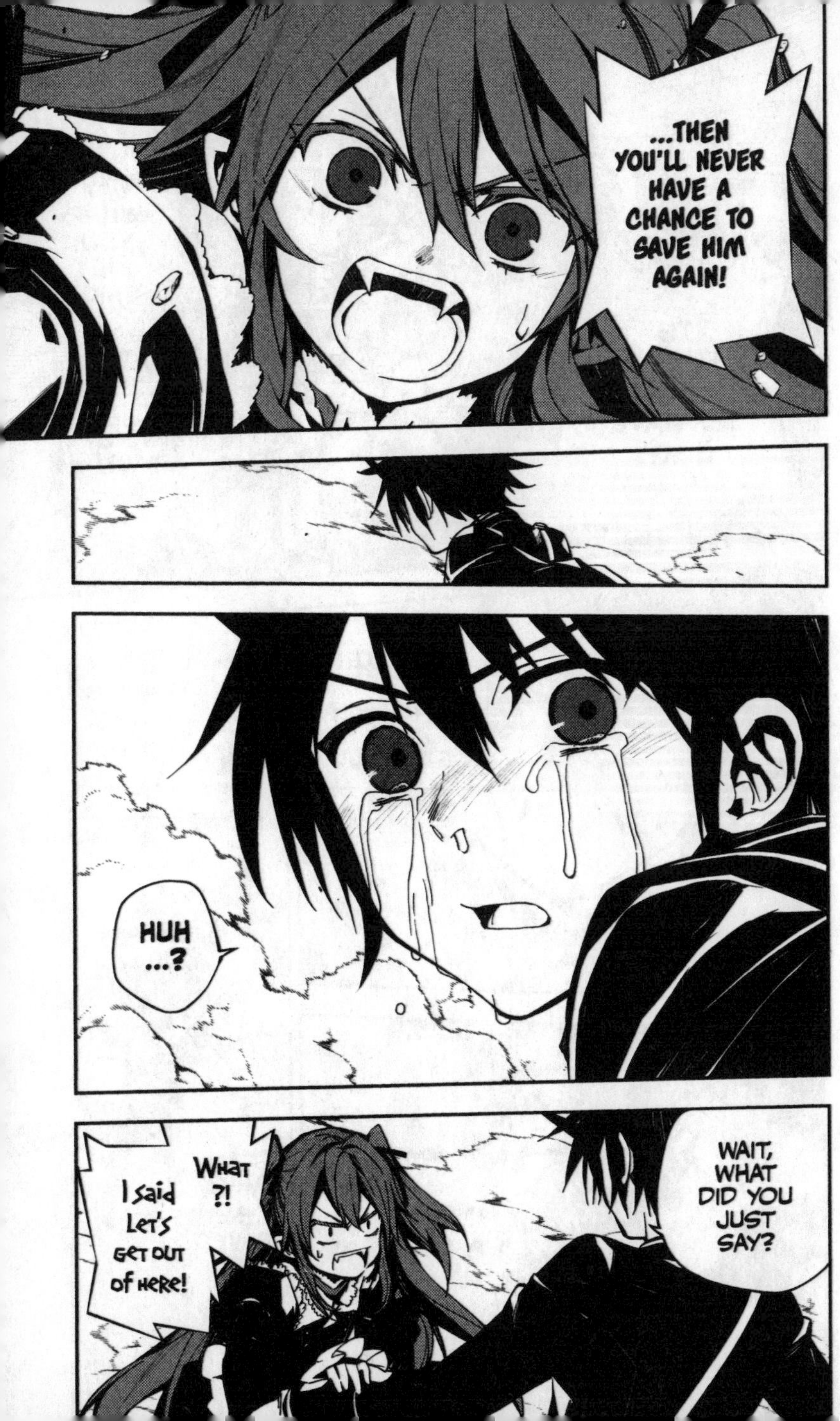
...THEN YOU'LL NEVER HAVE A CHANCE TO SAVE HIM AGAIN!
HUH ...?
WAIT, WHAT DID YOU JUST SAY?
WHAT ?!
I said let's get out of here!

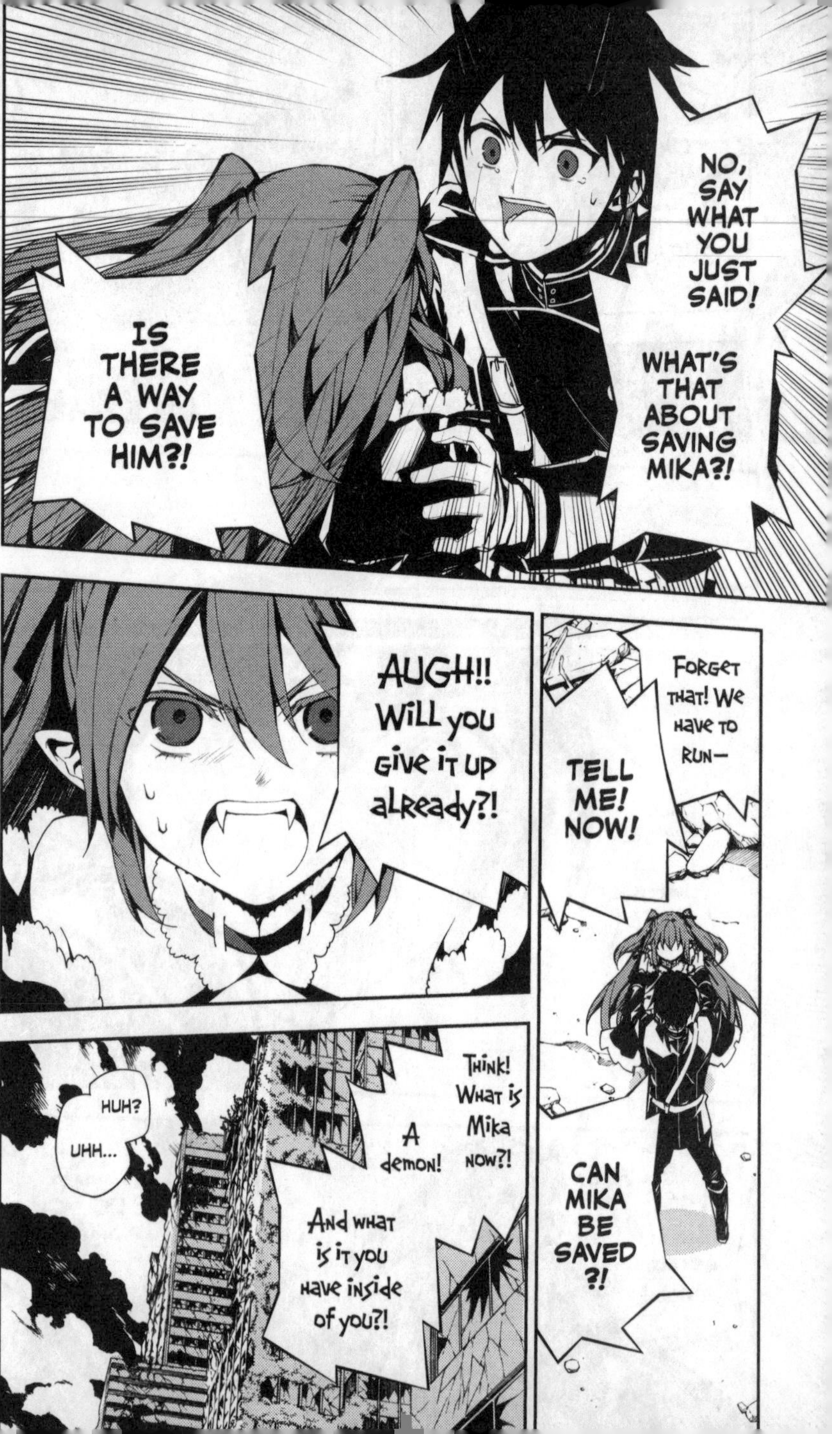
NO, SAY WHAT YOU JUST SAID!
WHAT'S THAT ABOUT SAVING MIKA?!
IS THERE A WAY TO SAVE HIM?!
Forget that! We have to run—
TELL ME! NOW!
CAN MIKA BE SAVED?!
AUGH!! Will you give it up already?!
Think! What is Mika now?!
A demon!
And what is it you have inside of you?!
HUH?
UHH...

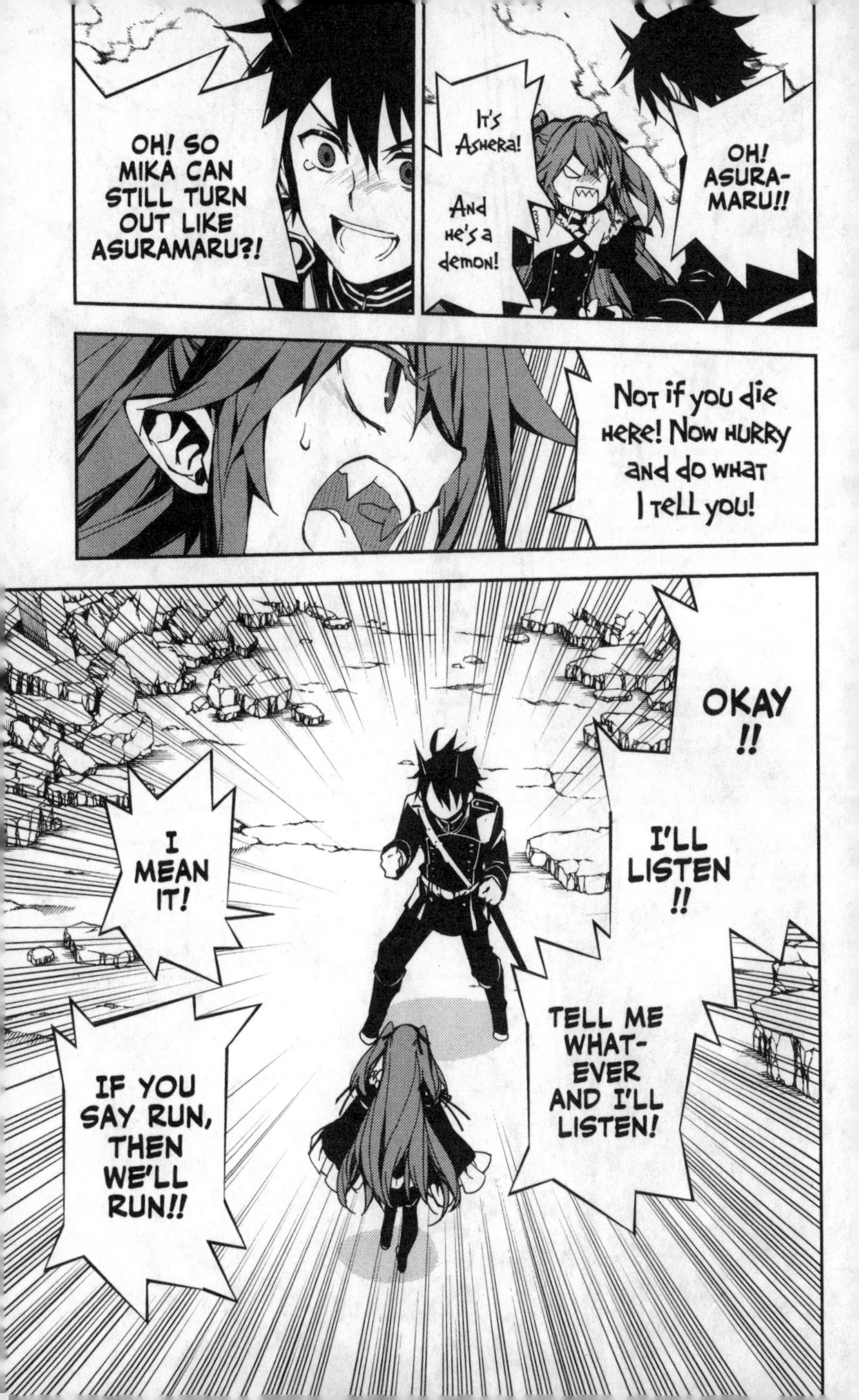
OH! ASURA-MARU!!
It's Ashera!
And he's a demon!
OH! SO MIKA CAN STILL TURN OUT LIKE ASURAMARU?!
Not if you die here! Now hurry and do what I tell you!
OKAY!!
I'LL LISTEN!!
I MEAN IT!
TELL ME WHAT-EVER AND I'LL LISTEN!
IF YOU SAY RUN, THEN WE'LL RUN!!

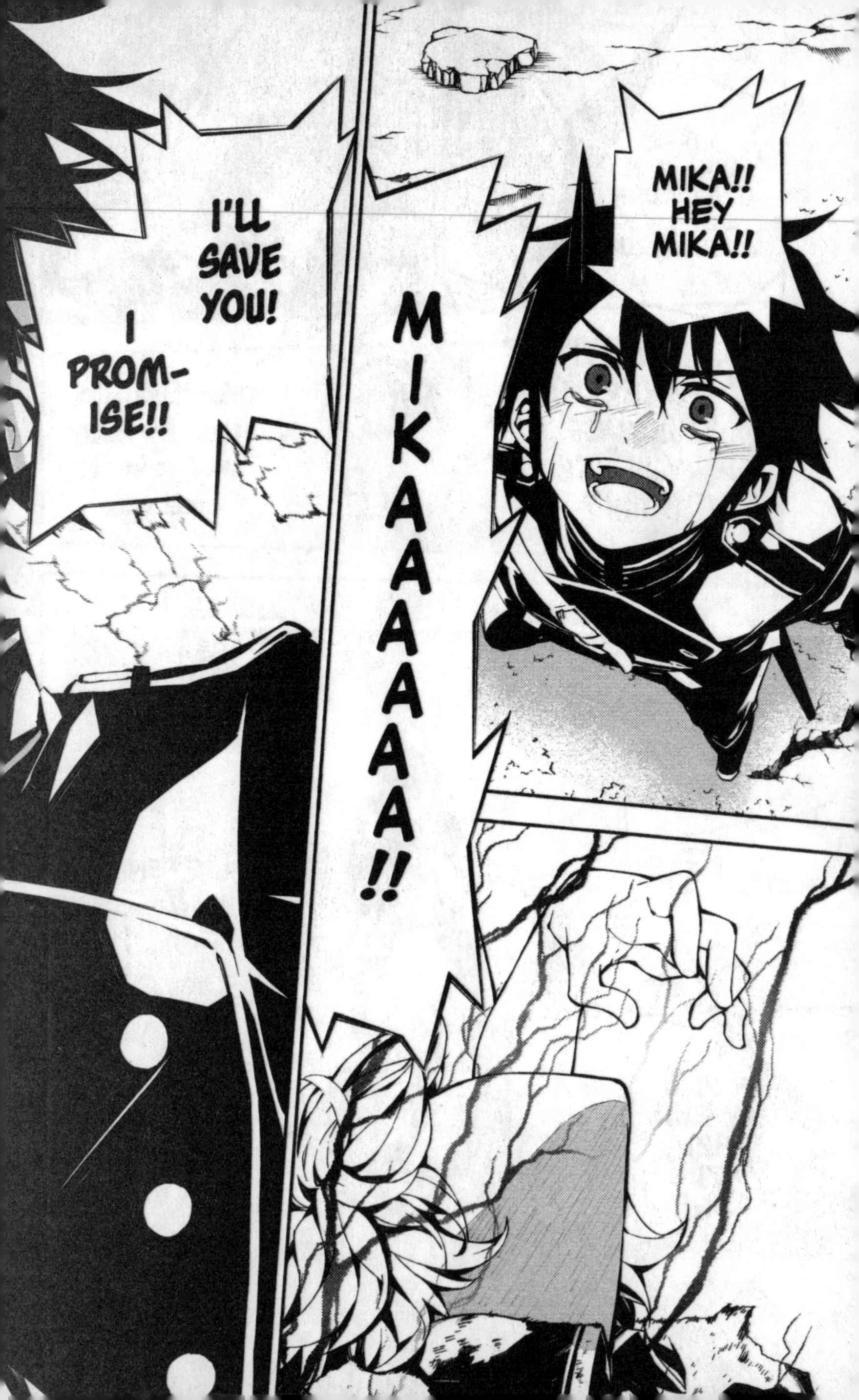
MIKA!! HEY MIKA!!
MIKAAAAAAA!!
I'LL SAVE YOU!
I PROMISE!!

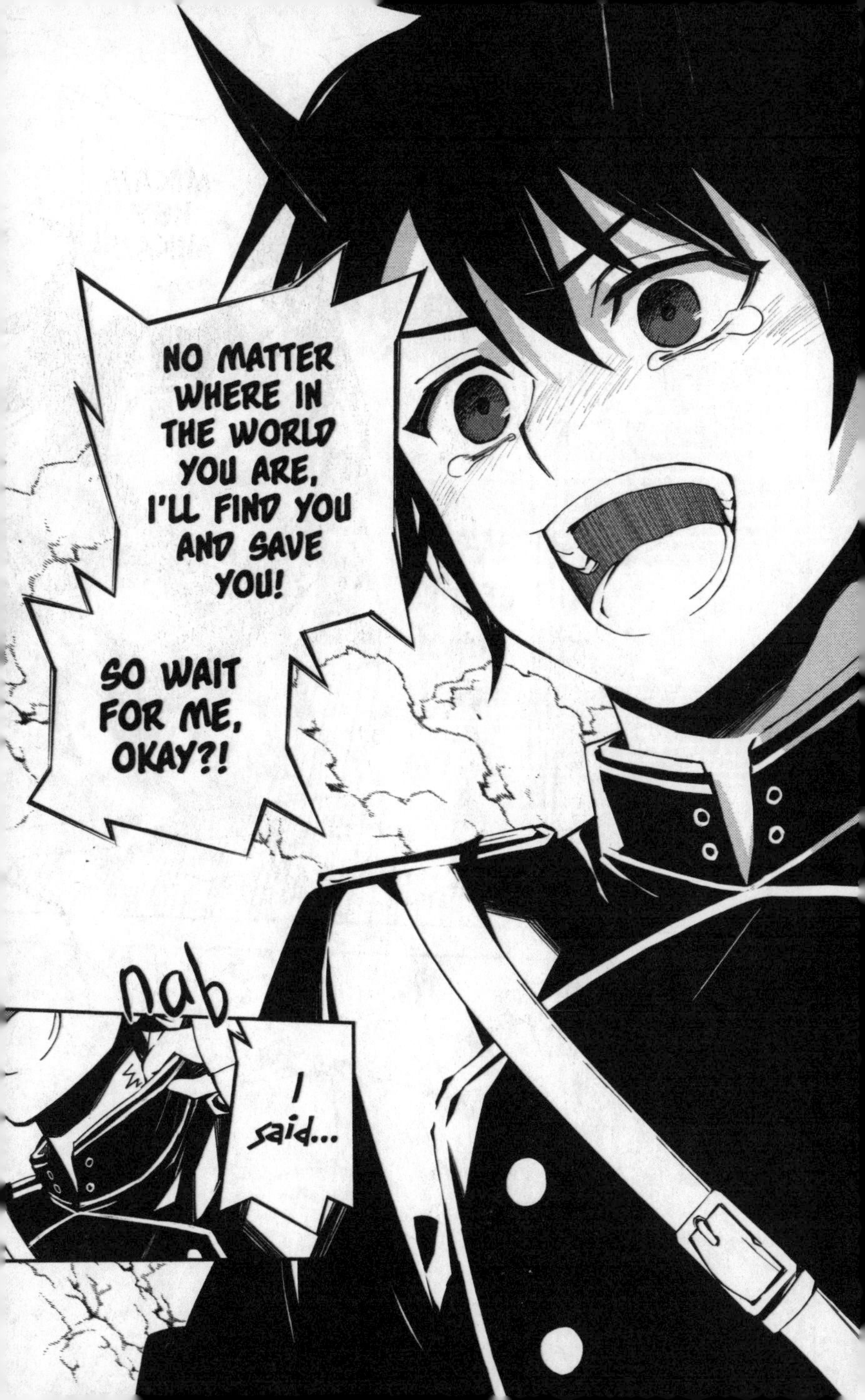
NO MATTER WHERE IN THE WORLD YOU ARE, I'LL FIND YOU AND SAVE YOU!
SO WAIT FOR ME, OKAY?!
nab
I said...

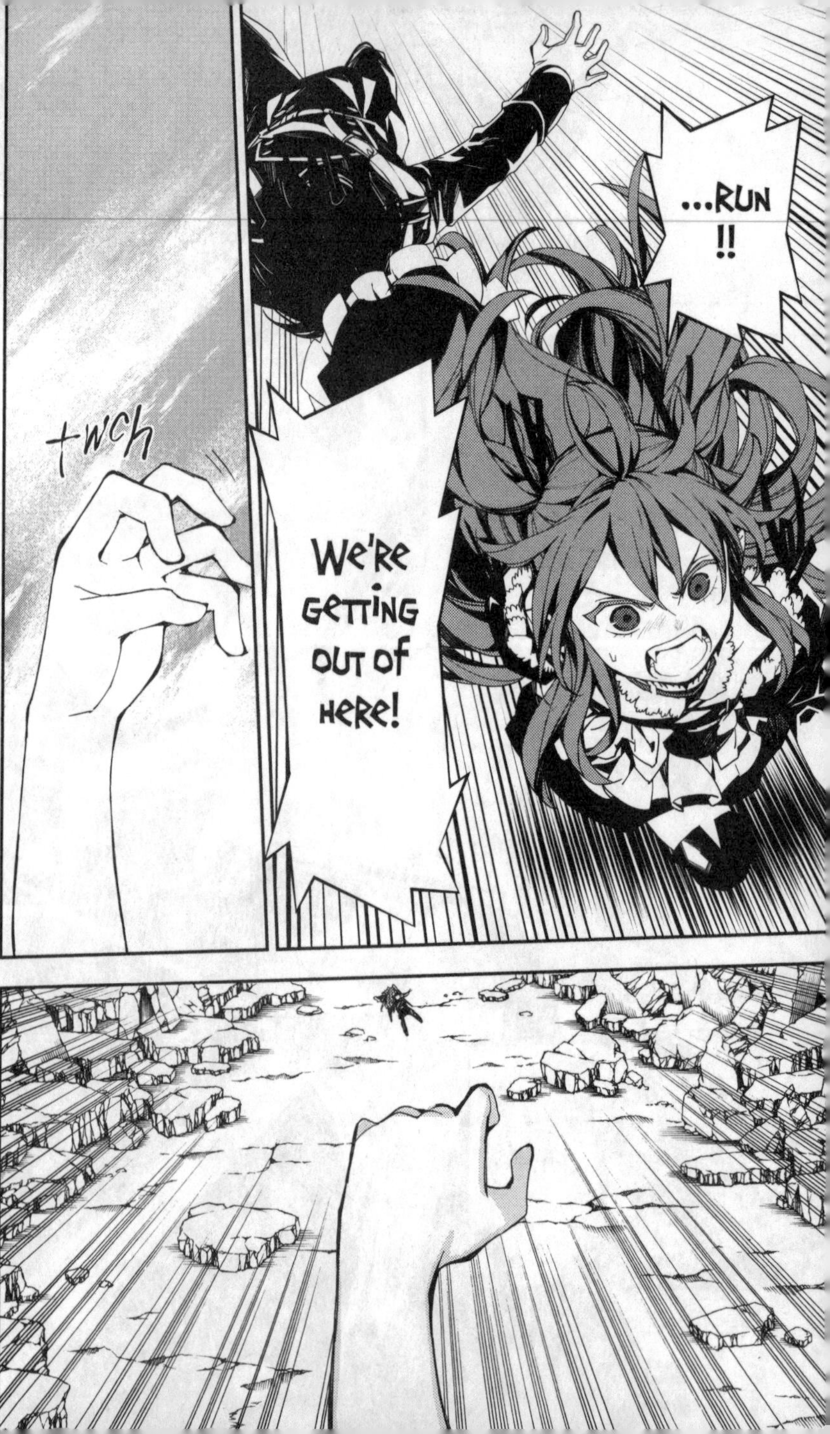
...RUN !!
We're getting out of here!
twch

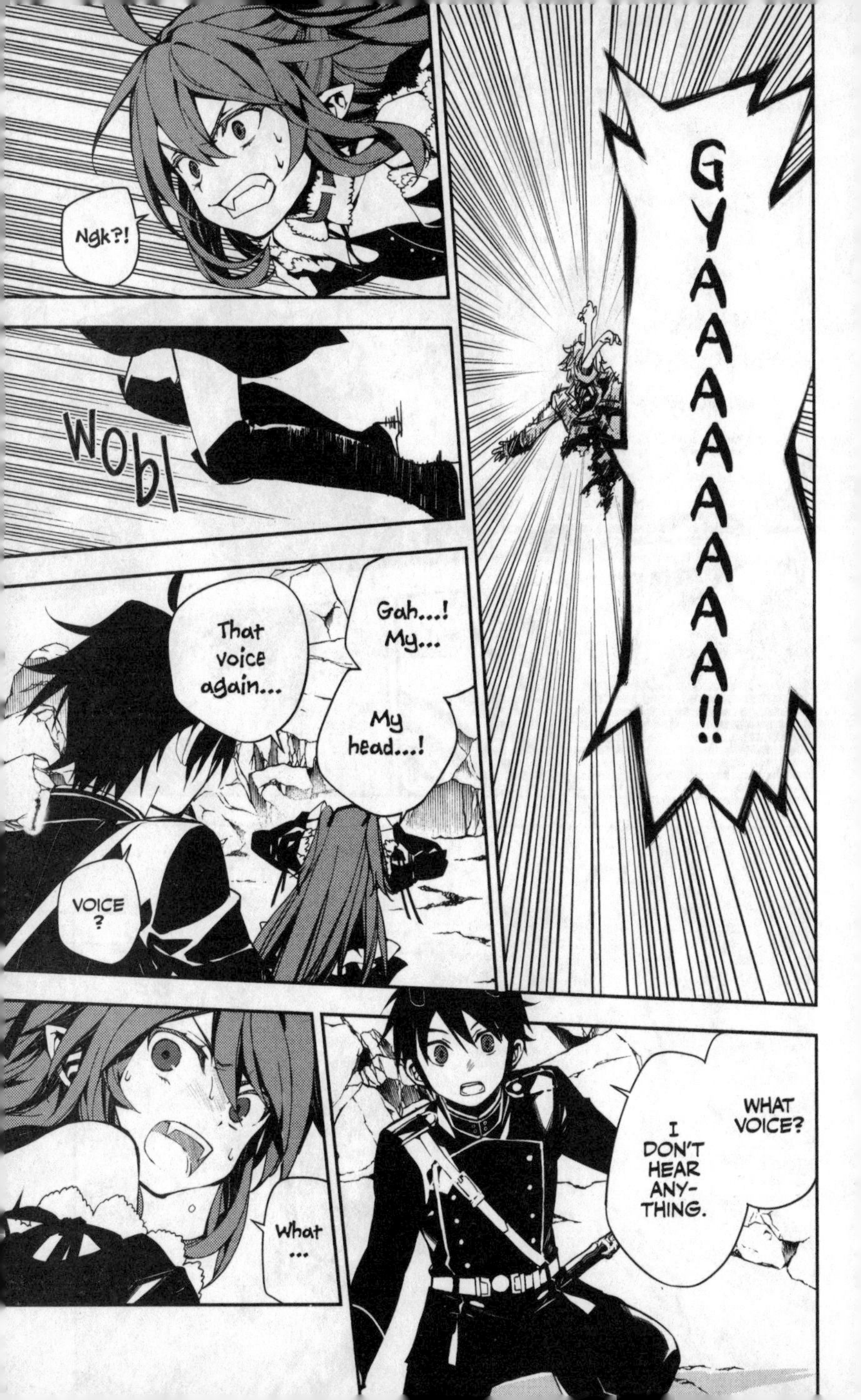
GYAAAAAAAA!!
Ngk?!
WObl
Gah...! My...
My head...!
That voice again...
VOICE?
WHAT VOICE?
I DON'T HEAR ANY-THING.
What ...

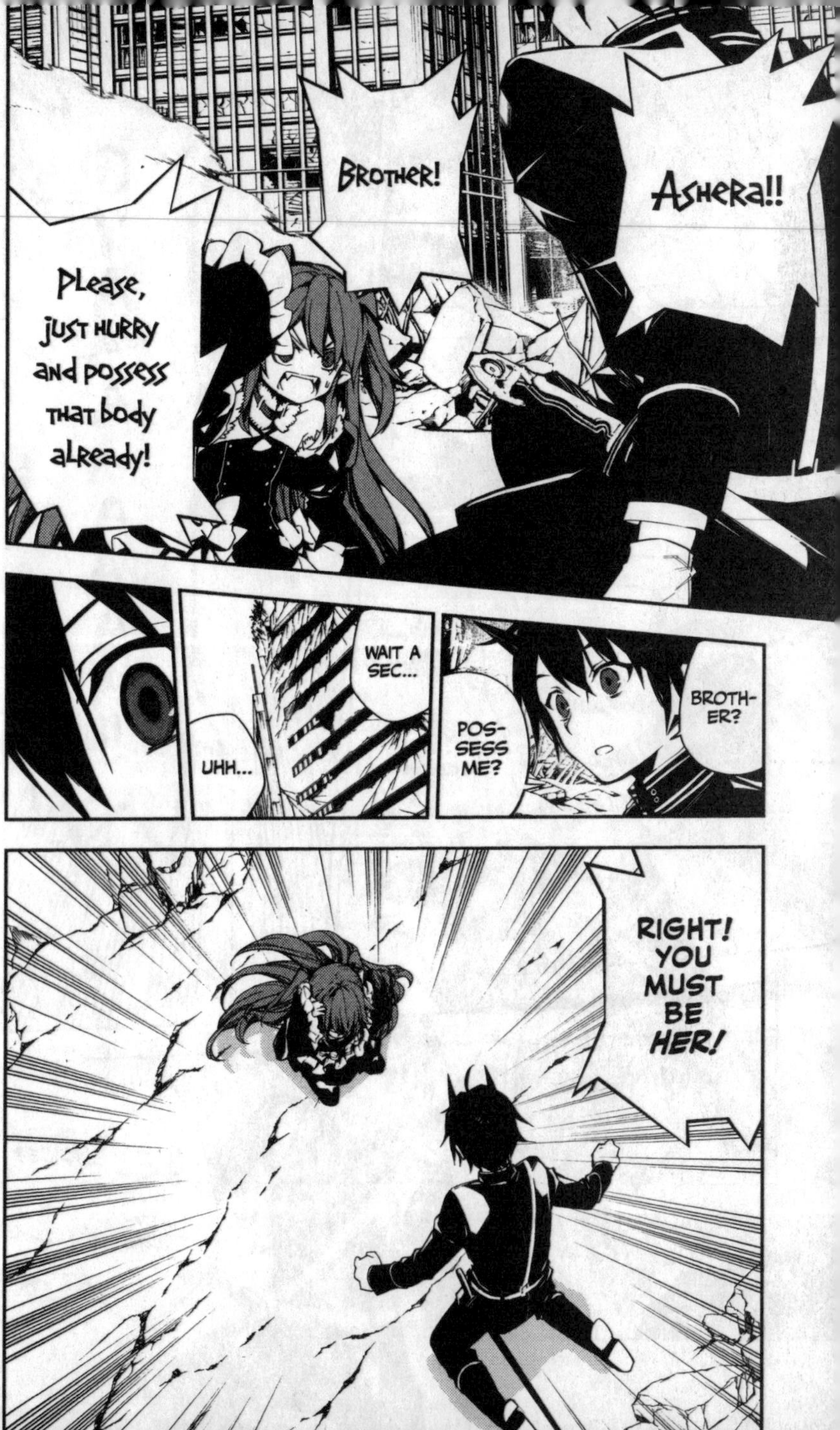
Ashera!!
Brother!
Please, just hurry and possess that body already!
BROTHER?
POSSESS ME?
WAIT A SEC...
UHH...
RIGHT! YOU MUST BE HER!

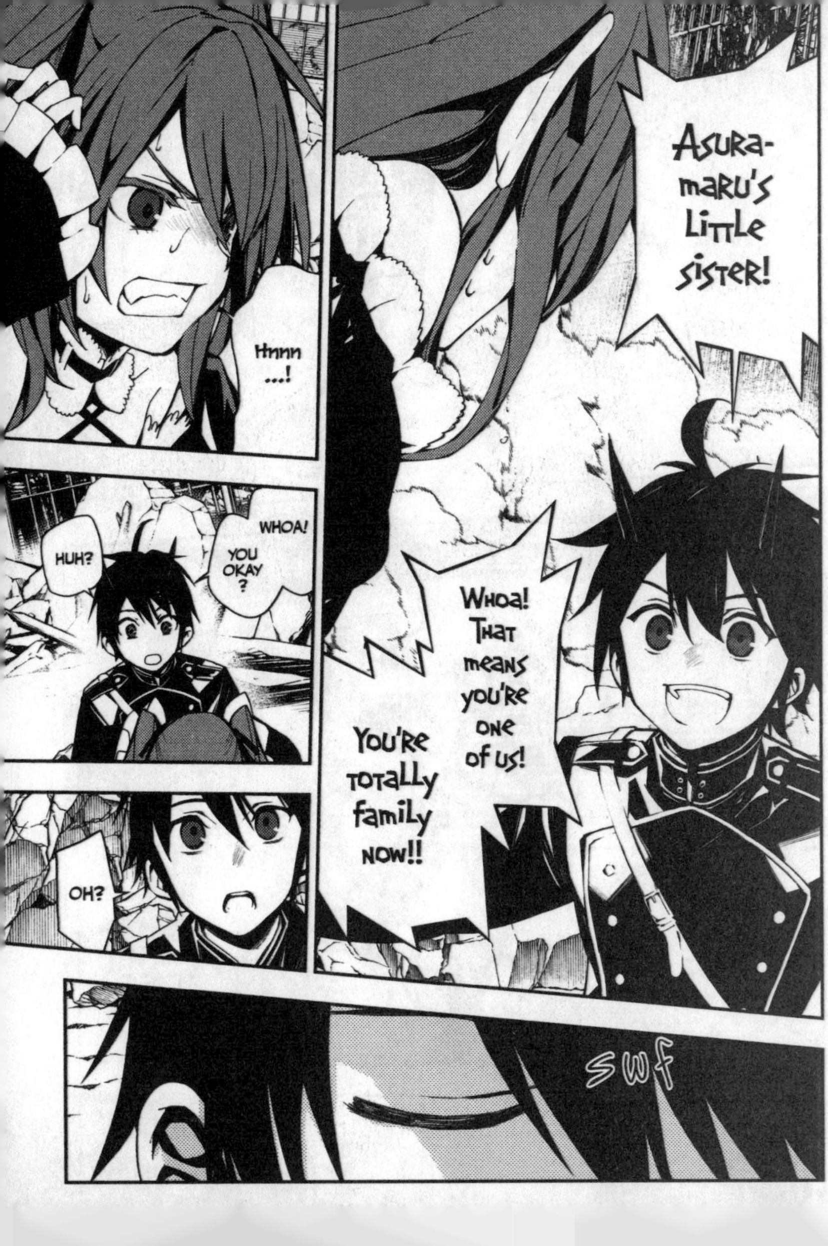
Asura-maru's Little sister!
Whoa! That means you're one of us!
You're totally family now!!
Hnnn ...!
WHOA!
YOU OKAY?
HUH?
OH?
swf

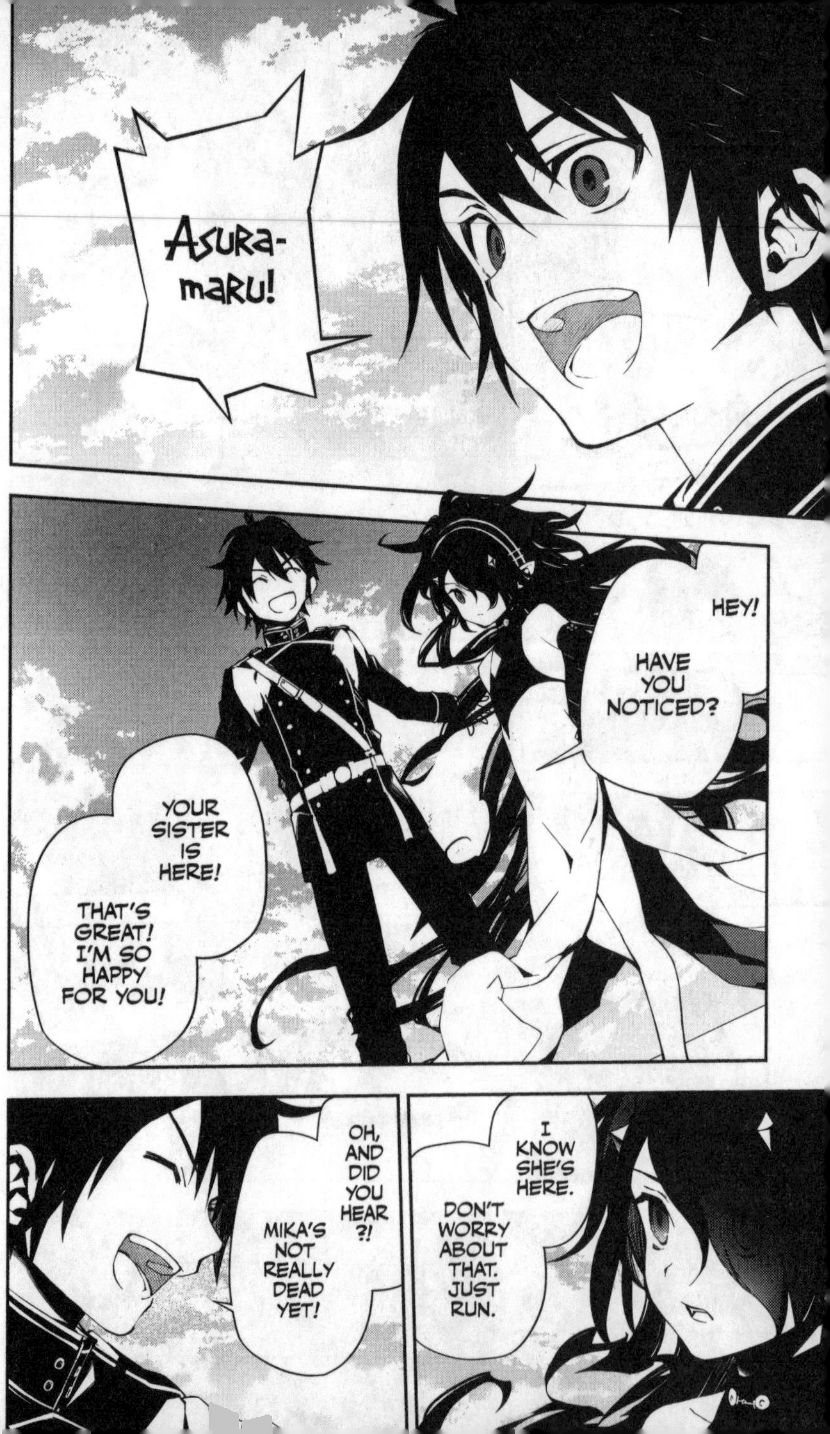
Asura-maru!
HEY!
HAVE YOU NOTICED?
YOUR SISTER IS HERE!
THAT'S GREAT! I'M SO HAPPY FOR YOU!
I KNOW SHE'S HERE.
DON'T WORRY ABOUT THAT. JUST RUN.
OH, AND DID YOU HEAR?!
MIKA'S NOT REALLY DEAD YET!

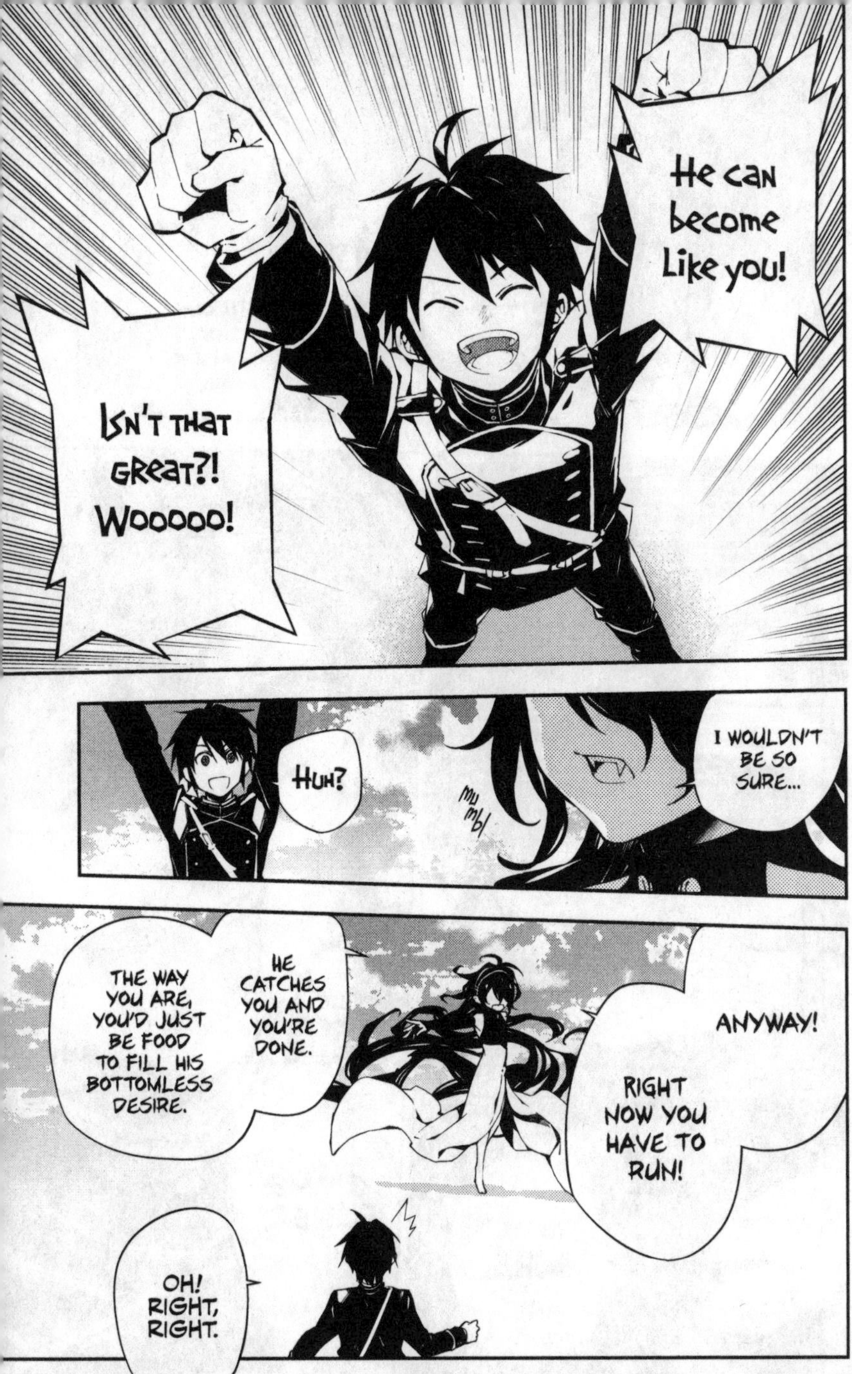
He can become Like you!
Isn't that great?! Woooo!
I WOULDN'T BE SO SURE...
mumbl
HUH?
ANYWAY! RIGHT NOW YOU HAVE TO RUN!
HE CATCHES YOU AND YOU'RE DONE.
THE WAY YOU ARE, YOU'D JUST BE FOOD TO FILL HIS BOTTOMLESS DESIRE.
OH! RIGHT, RIGHT.

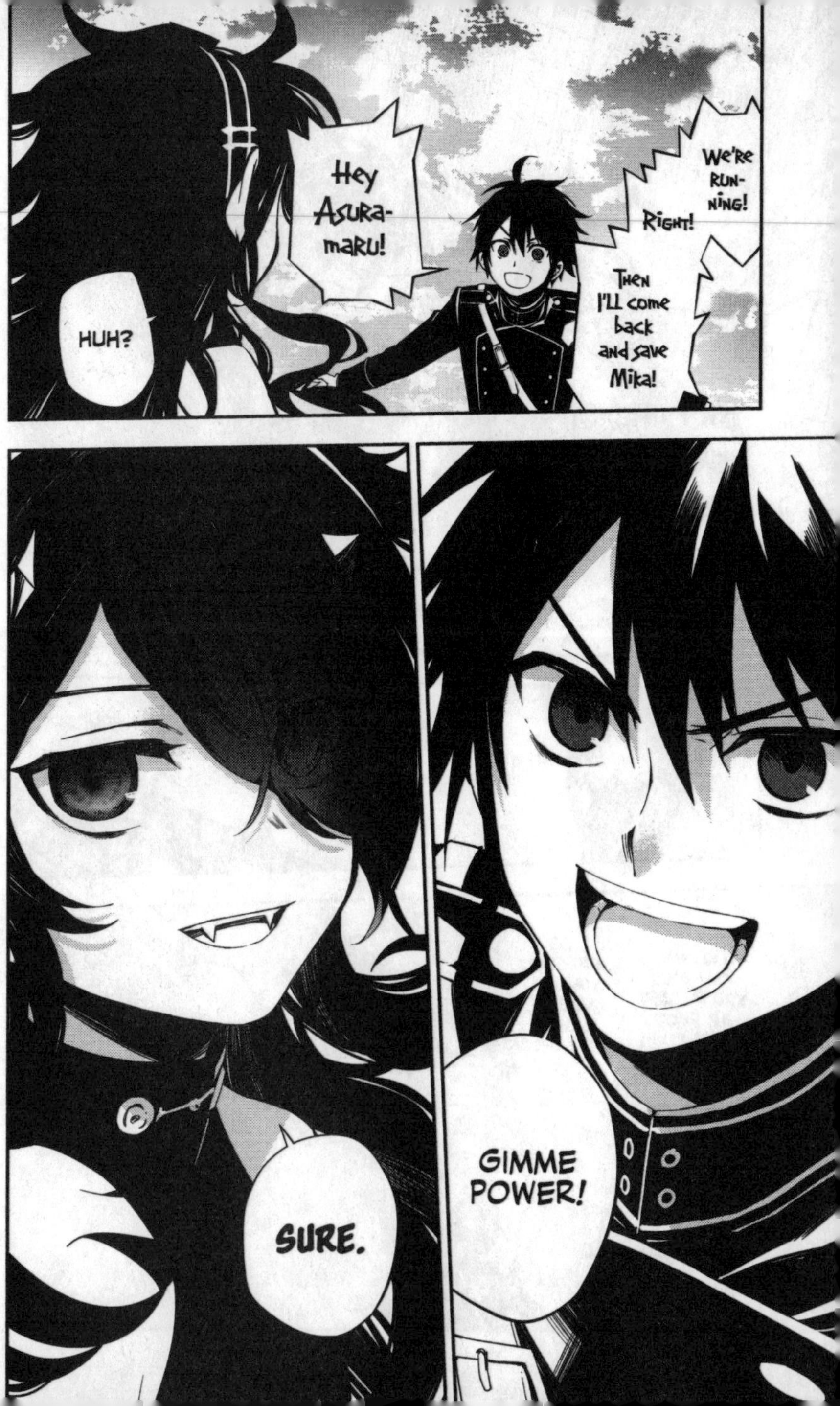
We're RUN-NING!
RIGHT!
Then I'll come back and save Mika!
Hey Asura-maru!
HUH?
GIMME POWER!
SURE.

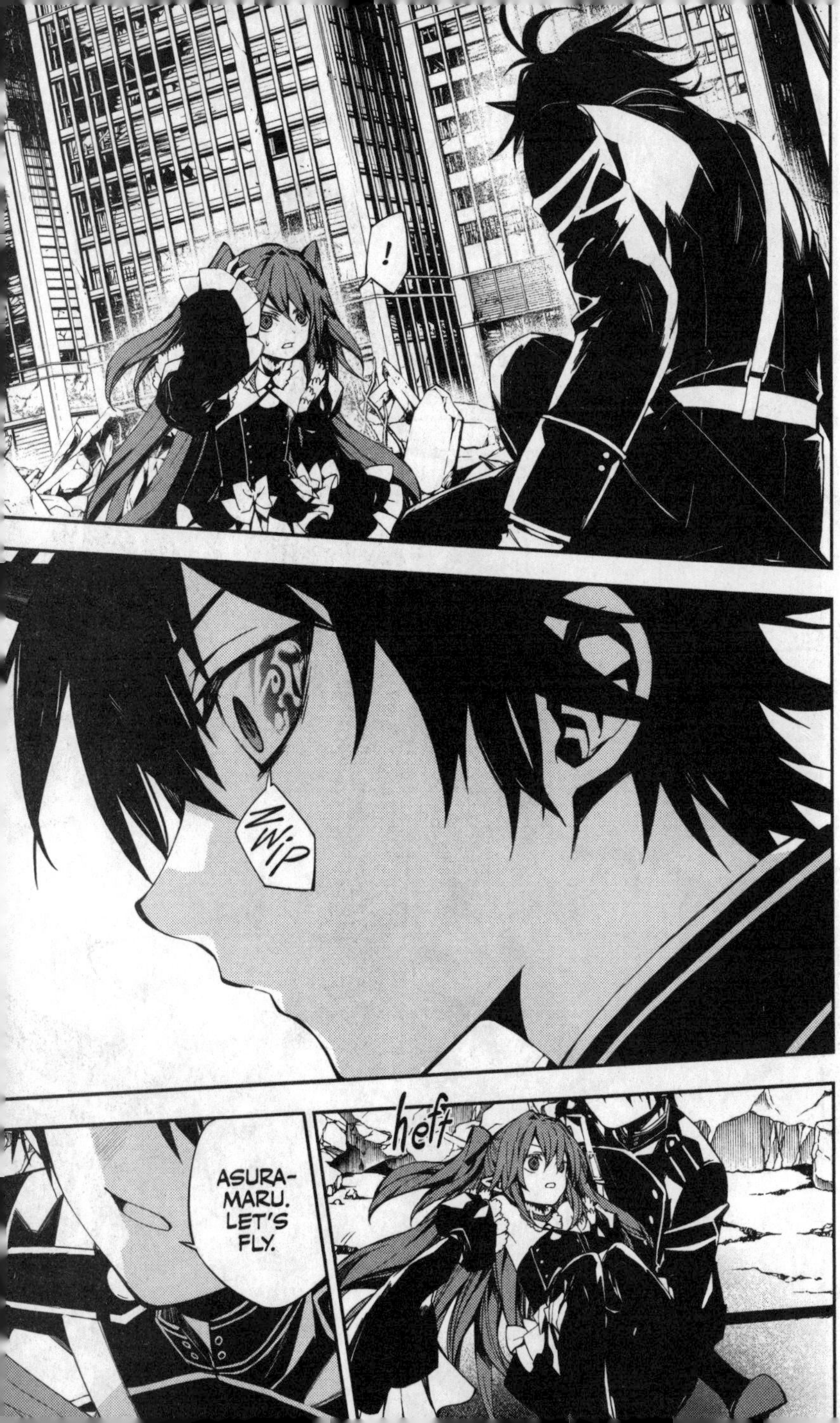
!
WHIP
heft
ASURA-MARU. LET'S FLY.

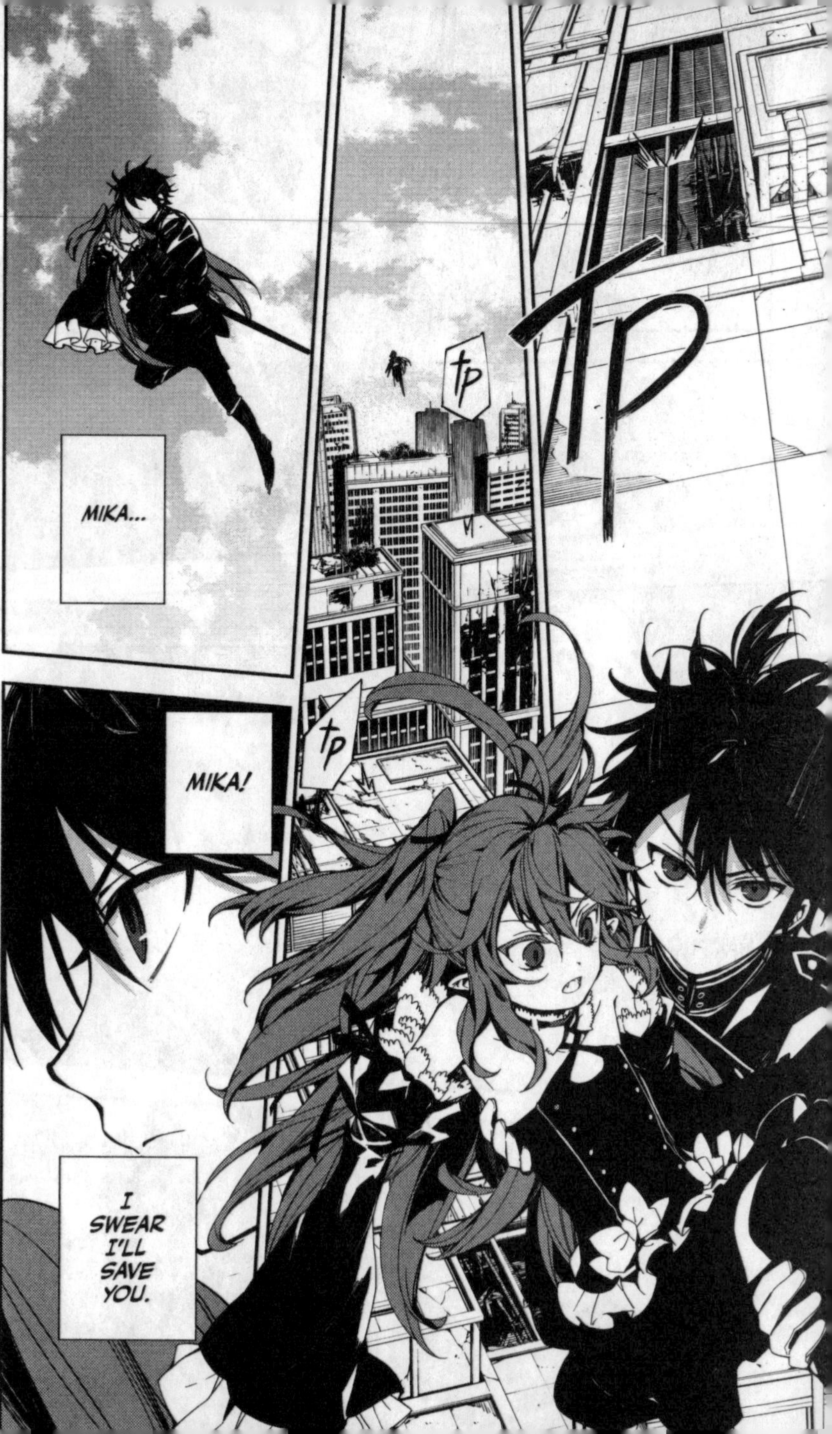
TP
tp
tp
MIKA...
MIKA!
I SWEAR I'LL SAVE YOU.

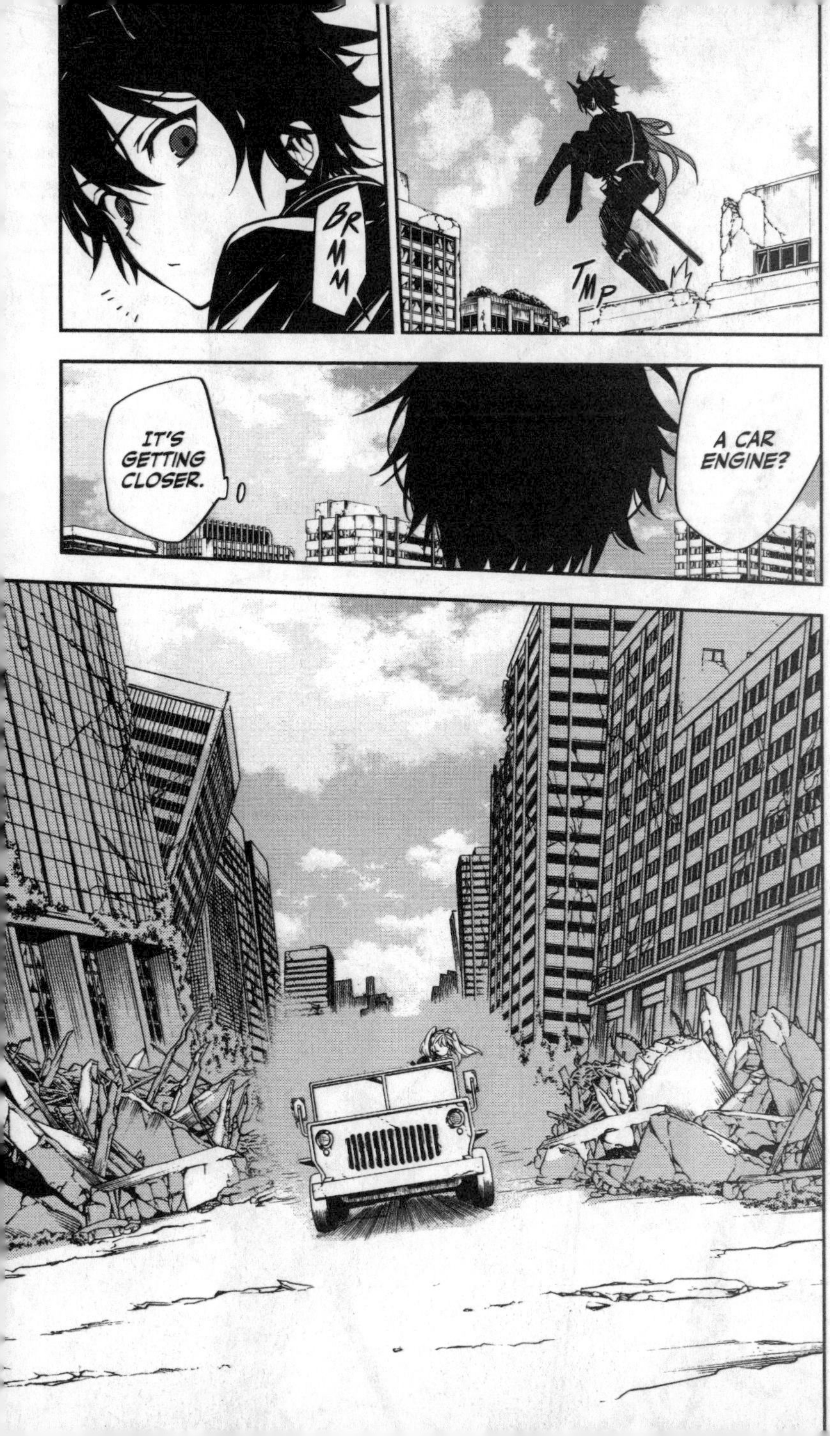
TMP
BRMMM
A CAR ENGINE?
IT'S GETTING CLOSER.

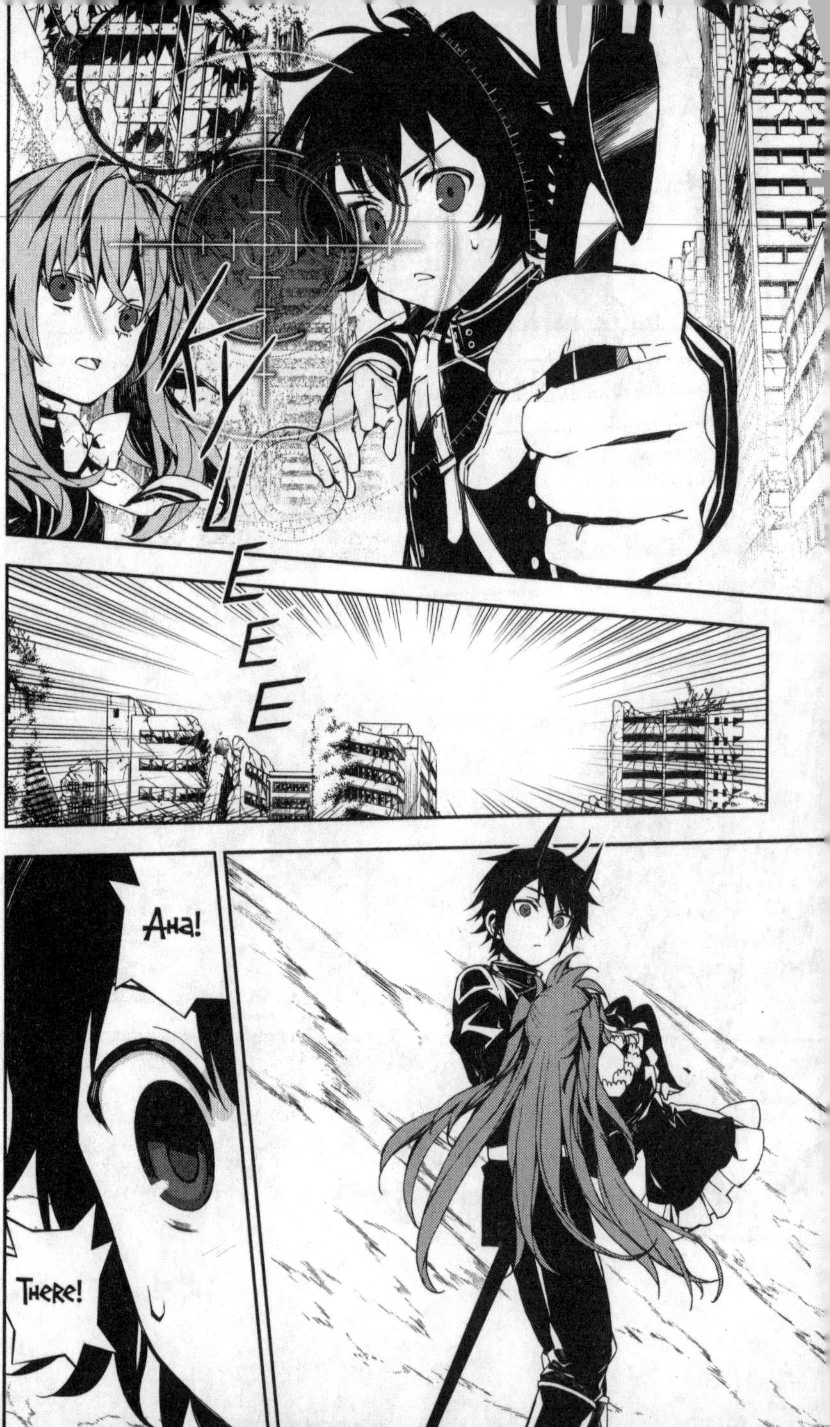
KYIIEEEE
Aha!
There!

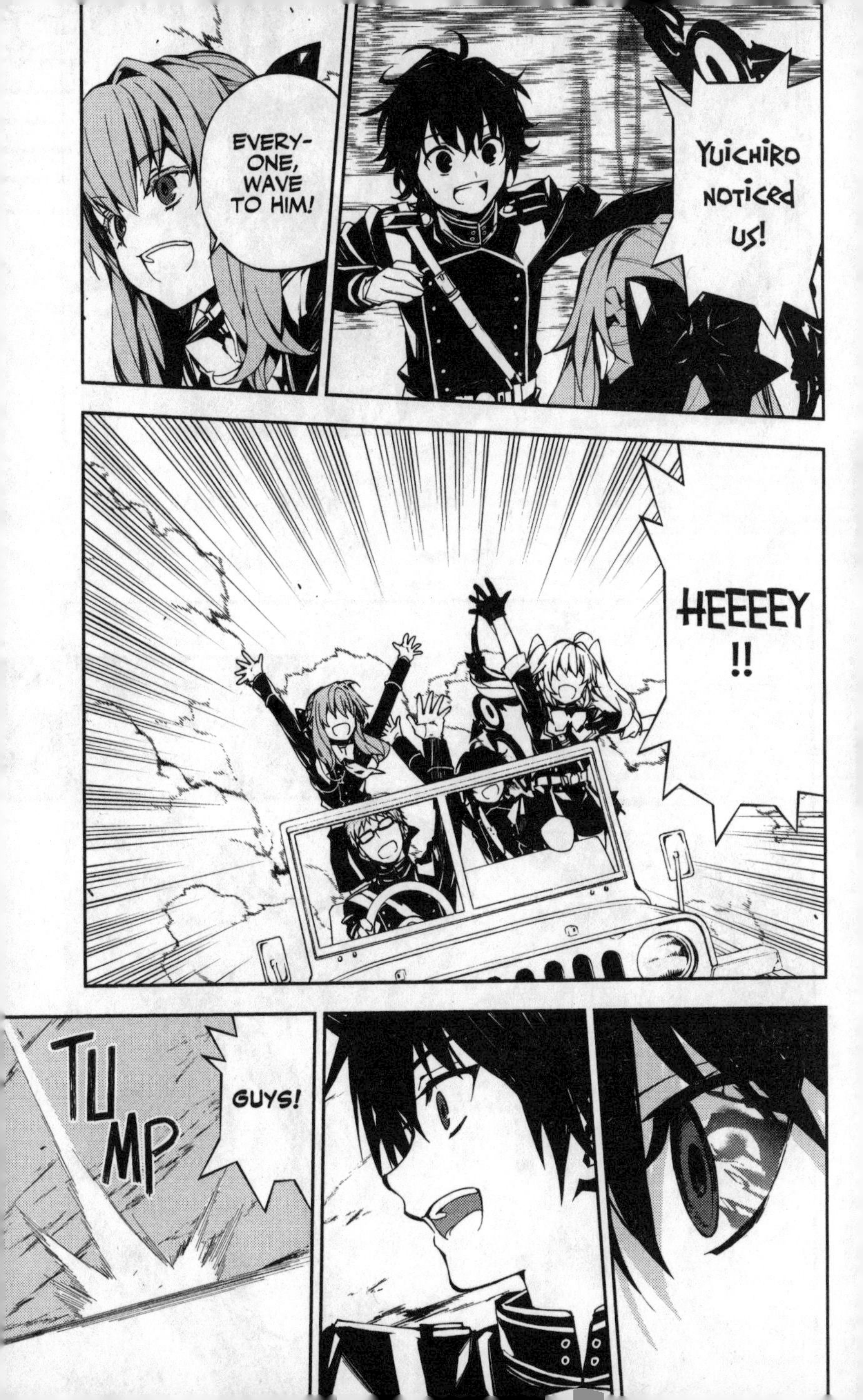
YUICHIRO NOTICED US!
EVERY-ONE, WAVE TO HIM!
HEEEEY !!
GUYS!
TUMP

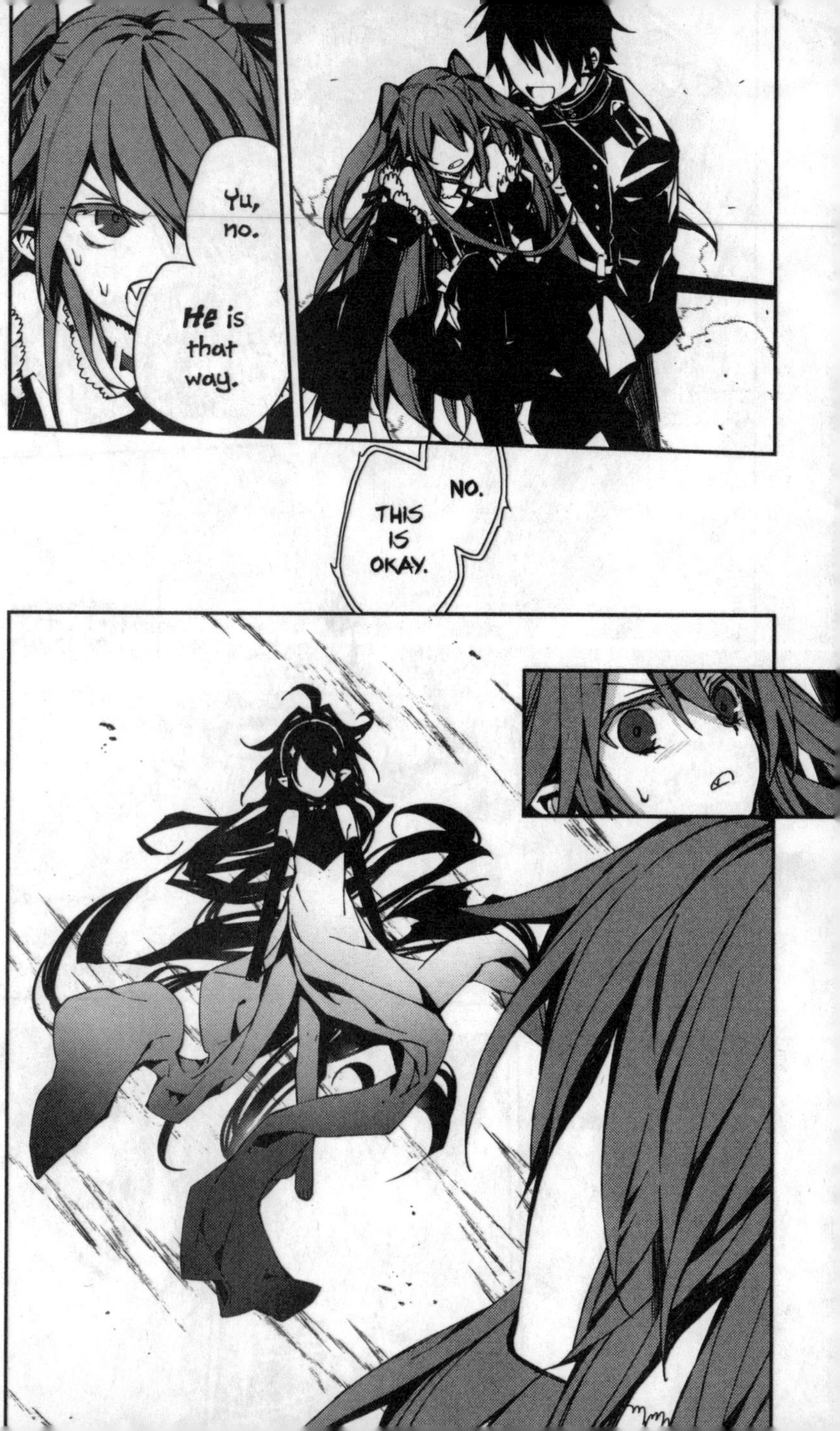
Yu, no.
He is that way.
NO.
THIS IS OKAY.

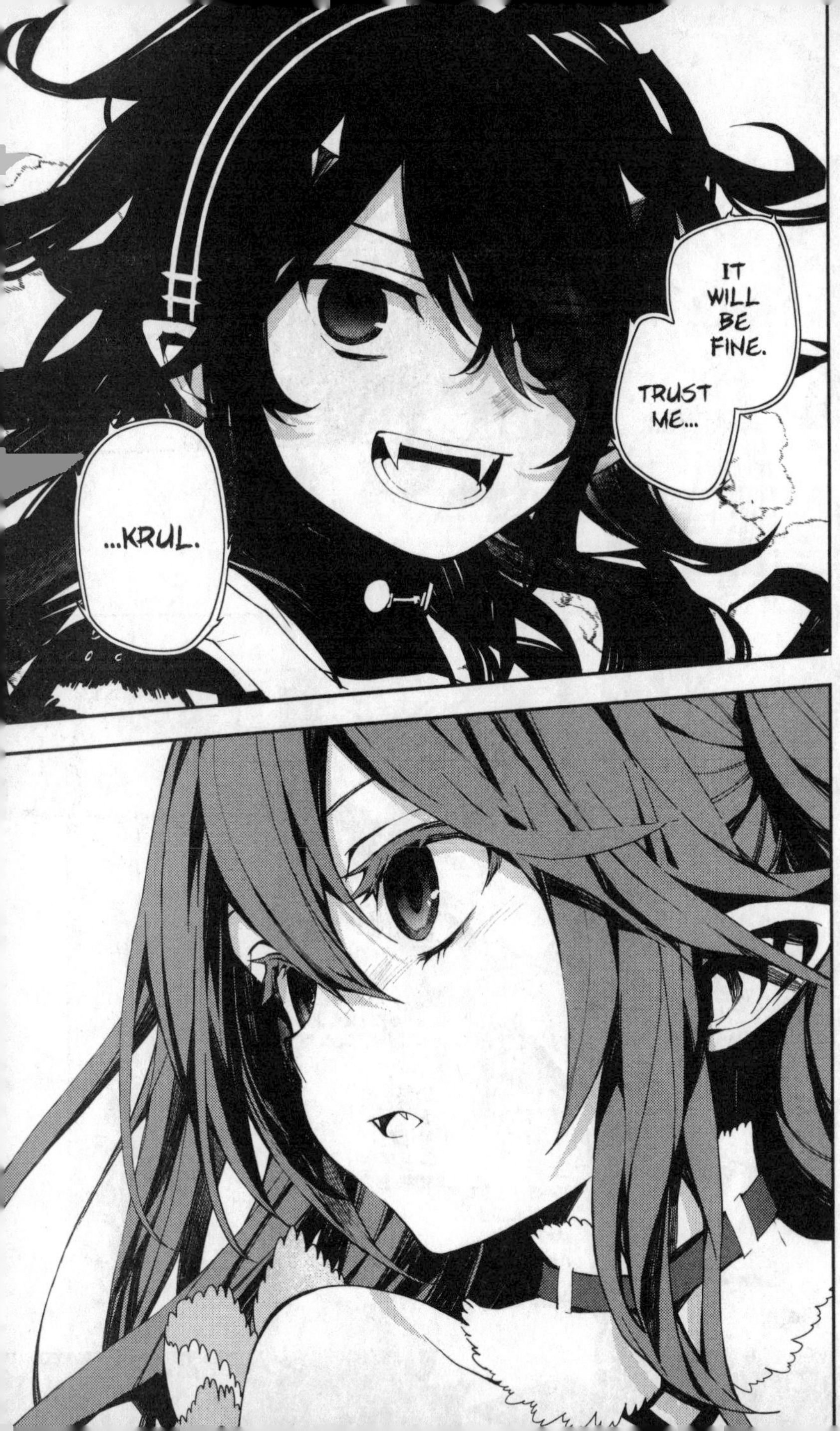
IT WILL BE FINE.
TRUST ME...
...KRUL.

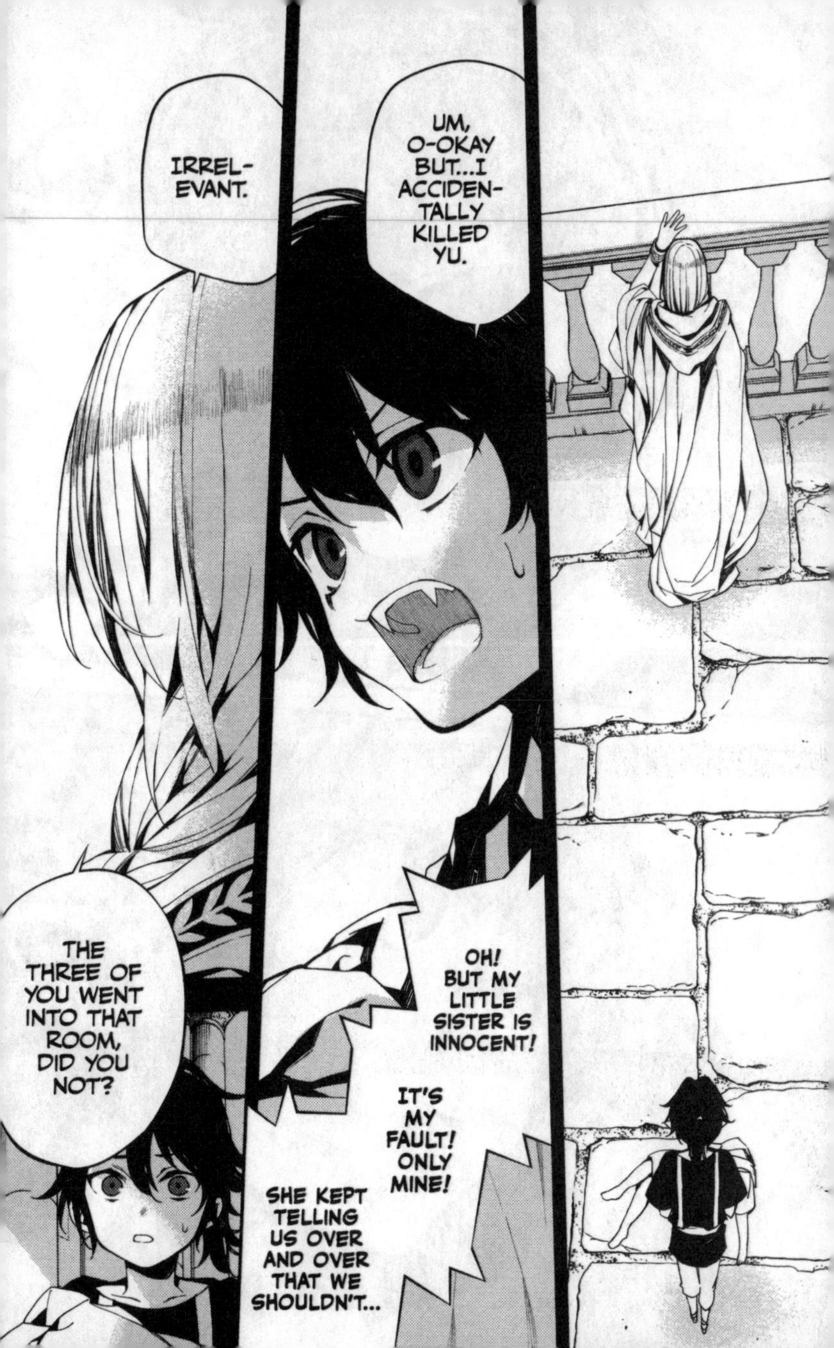
UM, O-OKAY BUT...I ACCIDEN-TALLY KILLED YU.
OH! BUT MY LITTLE SISTER IS INNOCENT!
IT'S MY FAULT! ONLY MINE!
SHE KEPT TELLING US OVER AND OVER THAT WE SHOULDN'T...
IRREL-EVANT.
THE THREE OF YOU WENT INTO THAT ROOM, DID YOU NOT?

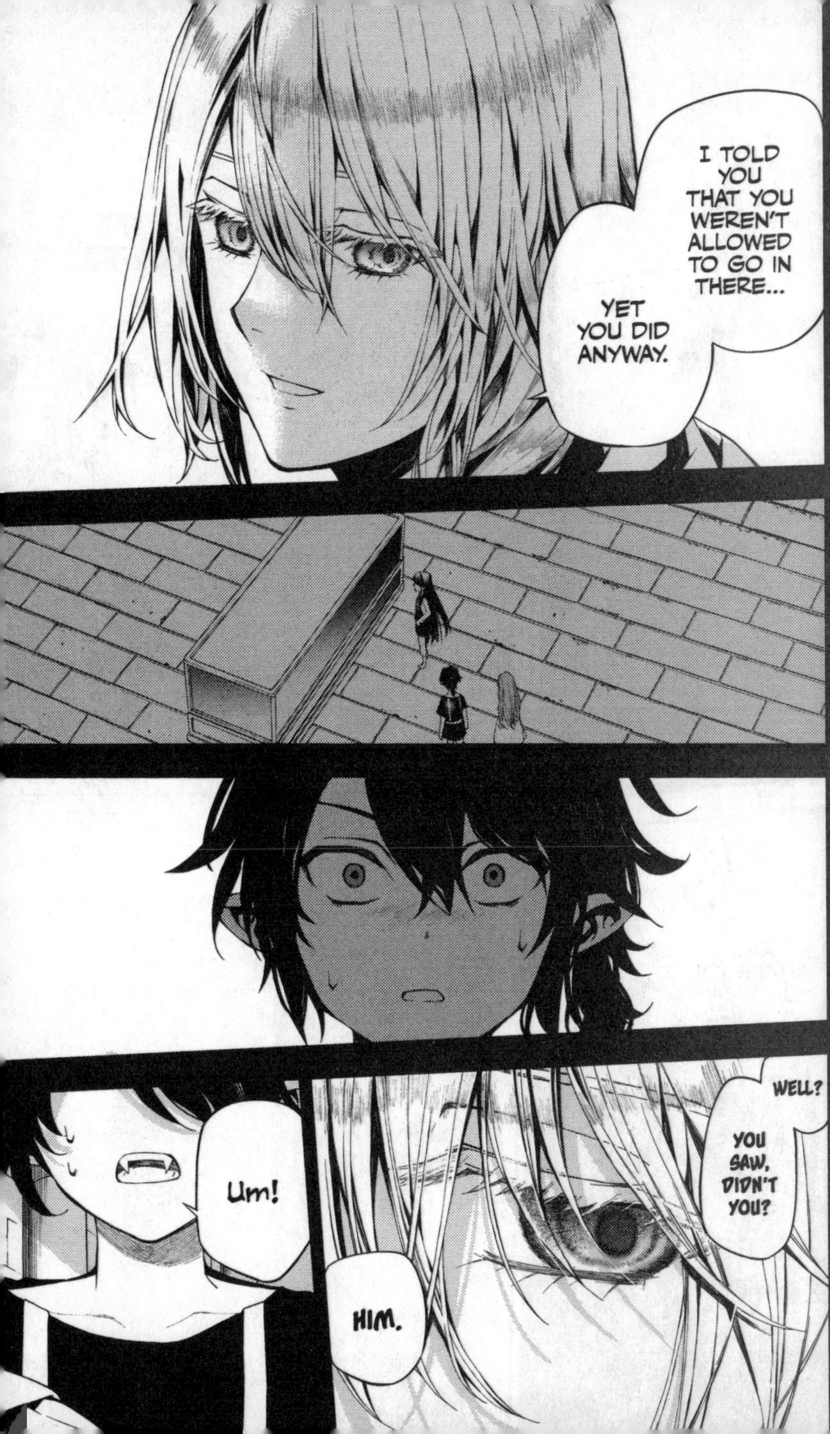
I TOLD YOU THAT YOU WEREN'T ALLOWED TO GO IN THERE...
YET YOU DID ANYWAY.
WELL?
YOU SAW, DIDN'T YOU?
HIM.
Um!

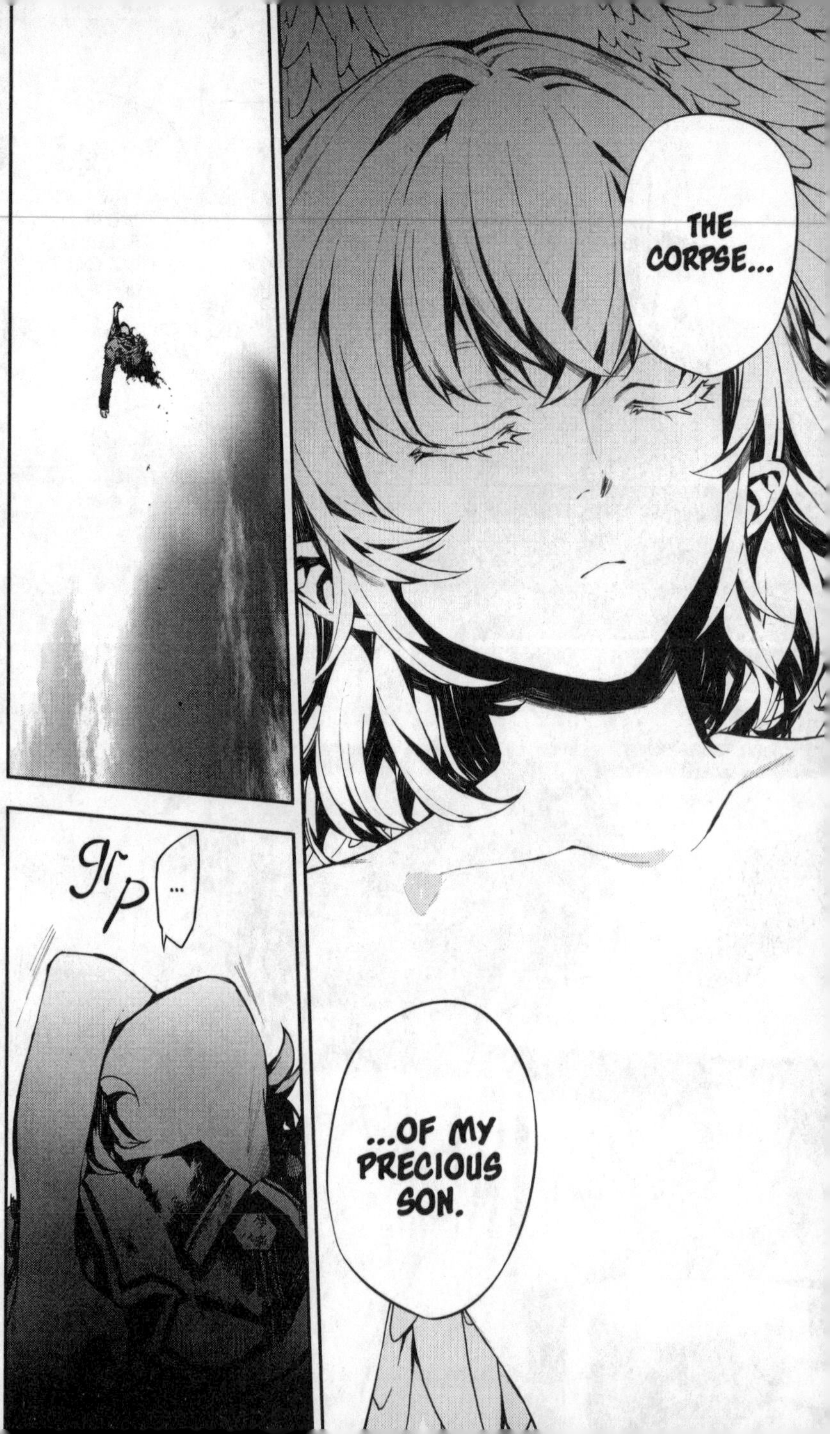
THE CORPSE...
...OF MY PRECIOUS SON.
GRIP
...

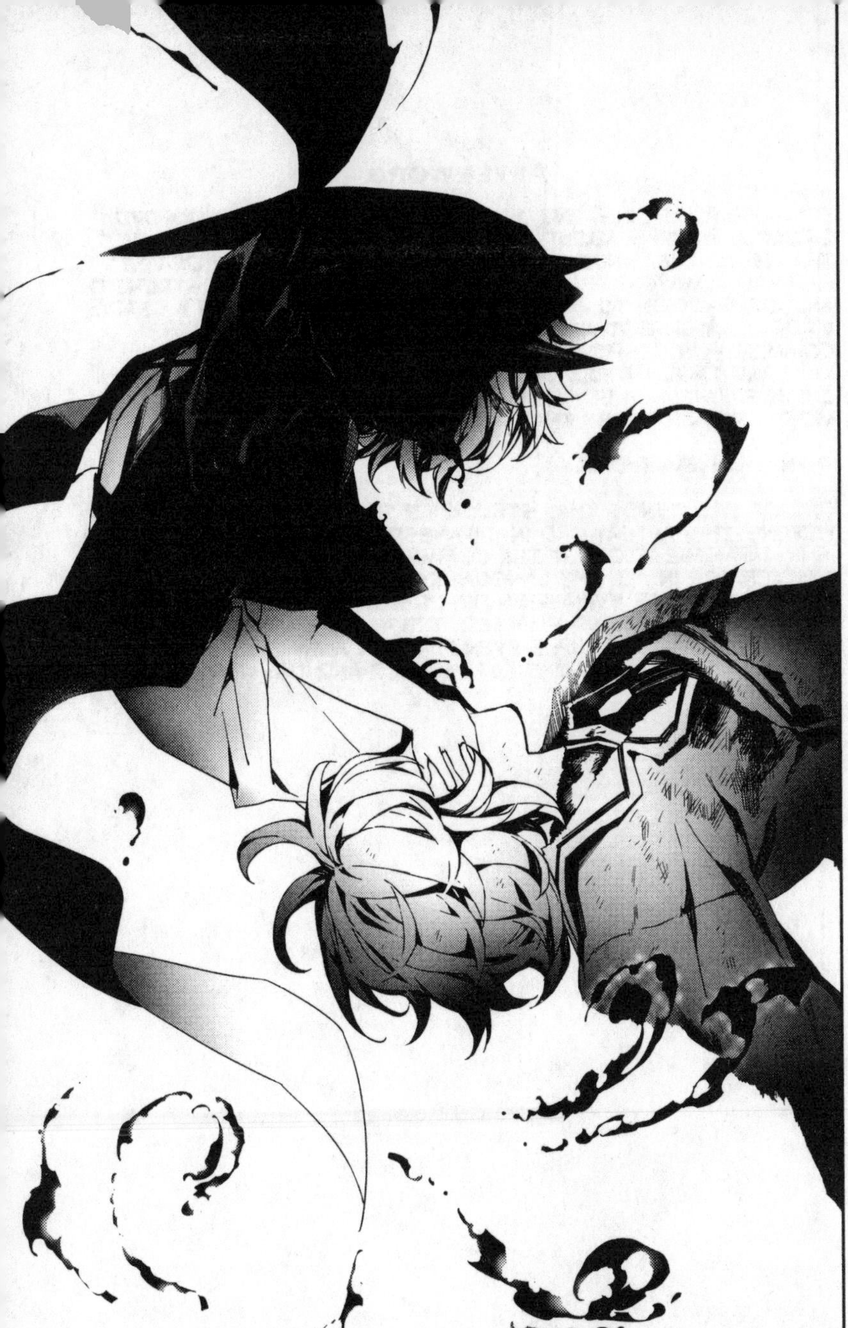

Seraph of the End: Vampire Reign 22 / END

AFTERWORD

HOW ARE YOU DOING, EVERYONE? IN MY PREVIOUS AFTERWORD, I RECALL WRITING ABOUT HOW THE WORLD WAS IN A TIGHT SPOT THANKS TO THE PANDEMIC AND HOW I BELIEVE *SERAPH OF THE END* HAD ALWAYS BEEN ABOUT HOW HUMANITY HAS THE STRENGTH AND COMPASSION TO OVERCOME OBSTACLES JUST LIKE A DEADLY VIRUS. I LATER GOT A LOT OF FAN LETTERS AND TWITTER COMMENTS IN RESPONSE TO IT. EVERY ONE OF THEM WAS KIND AND THOUGHTFUL, MENTIONING HOW MY AFTERWORD HAD CHEERED THEM UP. BUT REALLY, I WAS THE ONE WHO WAS THE MOST CHEERED UP BY THAT AFTERWORD.

THANK YOU, EVERYONE.

ONE OF THE THINGS THAT STRUCK ME THE MOST IS THAT I AM WRITING THIS AFTERWORD IN JAPANESE. THE MANGA I'M CREATING IS IN JAPANESE TOO. BUT THE COMMENTS I'VE RECEIVED ON TWITTER ARE IN ALL THE LANGUAGES OF THE WORLD, MANY OF WHICH I'VE NEVER EVEN SEEN BEFORE. THE WORLD REALLY IS GETTING SMALLER AND SMALLER. THESE DAYS, WE CAN CONNECT EVEN FASTER WITH PEOPLE EVEN FARTHER AWAY THAN WE EVER HAVE BEFORE, BOTH IN THE REAL WORLD AND THE WORLD OF THE INTERNET.

OF COURSE, THAT'S WHY THE VIRUS SPREAD EVEN FARTHER AND FASTER THAN MANY HAD BEFORE, BUT I LIKE TO THINK IT HELPS HUMAN SYMPATHY AND HUMAN FRIENDSHIPS SPREAD EVEN FASTER. RECENTLY, I'VE STARTED TO THINK HELPING THAT SPREAD ALONG COULD BE PART OF THE JOB OF ENTERTAINMENT.

THE MORE PEOPLE THERE ARE IN THE WORLD, THE MORE VIOLENCE AND DISCRIMINATION THERE WILL BE. THERE'S A MOUNTAIN OF THINGS WE HAVE TO DO—DIFFICULT THINGS—TO GET RID OF IT ALL, BUT I LIKE TO THINK THAT ENTERTAINMENT HAS BROUGHT PEOPLE TOGETHER FASTER THAN THE REAL WORLD HAS SO FAR.

AH WELL. I GUESS WHAT I'M TRYING TO SAY HERE IS THAT WE'RE ALL HERE, LIVING IN THIS WORLD TOGETHER, SO WE MIGHT AS WELL ALL BE FRIENDS.

THANK YOU, EVERYONE, FOR EVERYTHING. THANK YOU FOR YOUR KIND FAN LETTERS AND ALL YOUR COMMENTS ON TWITTER.

ALSO, *SERAPH OF THE END* HAS BEEN ON A SCHEDULE OF TWO VOLUMES RELEASED PER YEAR FOR A WHILE NOW, BUT STARTING WITH THIS VOLUME WE'RE PLANNING ON GETTING BACK UP TO THREE VOLUMES PER YEAR!

I HOPE YOU WILL ALL KEEP CHEERING US ON!

—TAKAYA KAGAMI

A brilliant sketch of Yuichiro by the author!

TAKAYA KAGAMI is a prolific light novelist whose works include the action and fantasy series *The Legend of the Legendary Heroes*, which has been adapted into manga, anime and a video game. His previous series, *A Dark Rabbit Has Seven Lives*, also spawned a manga and anime series.

❝ If you're wearing a mask in the summer, do you still need to put sunscreen on your face? I'm consumed with curiosity. Not that I regularly wear sunscreen. ❞

YAMATO YAMAMOTO, born 1983, is an artist and illustrator whose works include the *Kure-nai* manga and the light novels *Kure-nai*, *9S -Nine S-* and *Denpa Teki na Kanojo*. Both *Denpa Teki na Kanojo* and *Kure-nai* have been adapted into anime.

❝ This is volume 22. Big changes are in store for Mika. Yuichiro is going to cry a lot... I hope you're looking forward to it! ❞

DAISUKE FURUYA previously assisted Yamato Yamamoto with storyboards for *Kure-nai*.

Seraph of the End
—VAMPIRE REIGN—

VOLUME 22
SHONEN JUMP MANGA EDITION

STORY BY TAKAYA KAGAMI
ART BY YAMATO YAMAMOTO
STORYBOARDS BY DAISUKE FURUYA

TRANSLATION Adrienne Beck
TOUCH-UP ART & LETTERING Sabrina Heep
DESIGN Shawn Carrico
EDITOR Marlene First

Printed in Canada

Published by VIZ Media, LLC
P.O. Box 77010
San Francisco, CA 94107

10 9 8 7 6 5 4 3 2 1
First printing, October 2021

VIZ MEDIA
viz.com
SHONEN JUMP

RATED T+ OLDER TEEN ratings.viz.com

PARENTAL ADVISORY
SERAPH OF THE END is rated T+ for Older Teen and is recommended for ages 16 and up. This volume contains violence and some adult themes.

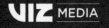

Twin ☆ Star Exorcists
ONMYOJI

STORY AND ART BY Yoshiaki Sukeno

The action-packed romantic comedy from the creator of *Good Luck Girl!*

Rokuro dreams of becoming *anything* but an exorcist!
Then mysterious Benio turns up. The pair are dubbed the
"Twin Star Exorcists" and learn they are fated to marry...

Can Rokuro escape both fates?

YOU'RE READING THE
WRONG WAY!

SERAPH OF THE END
reads from right to left, starting in the upper-right corner. Japanese is read from right to left, meaning that action, sound effects, and word-balloon order are completely reversed from English order.

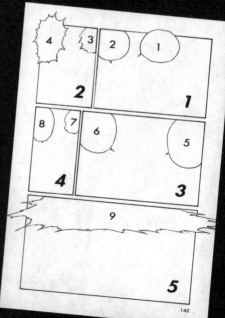